Dealing Fairly with Developing Country Debt

Library of Congress Cataloging-in-Publication Data

Dealing fairly with developing country debt / edited by Christian
Barry, Lydia Tomitova, Barry Herman.
   p. cm.
   Includes index.
   ISBN 978-1-4051-8034-4
   1. Debts, Public–Developing countries. 2. Debt relief–Developing
countries. I. Barry, Christian. II. Tomitova, Lydia. III. Herman,
Barry.

   HJ8899.D382 2007
   336.3'6091724–dc22

2007045718

Blackwell Publishing, Inc.
350 Main Street
Malden, MA 02148 USA

Blackwell Publishing, Ltd.
9600 Garsington Road
Oxford OX4 2DQ
United Kingdom

CARNEGIE COUNCIL
The Voice
for Ethics in
International
Policy

The Carnegie Council for Ethics in International Affairs is the leading voice promoting
ethical leadership on issues of war, peace, religion in politics, and global social justice.
The Council convenes agenda-setting forums and creates educational resources for
a worldwide audience of teachers and students, journalists, international affairs
professionals, and concerned citizens.

The Carnegie Council is independent and nonpartisan. We encourage and give a
voice to a variety of ethical approaches to the most challenging moral issues in world
politics. The Council promotes innovative thinking and intellectual integrity, and
gives practical guidance featuring specific examples of ethical principles in action.

Cover photo courtesy of Ann Pettifor.

FOREWORD

Governing is hard work. Budgeting, taxing, and borrowing are among the hardest aspects of governing to carry out effectively, efficiently, and fairly. My experiences in the United States Senate and as Governor of the State of Nebraska have made this crystal clear to me. It can only be more difficult to carry out these economic and financial sides of governing in developing countries that do not have the size, strength, and resources of the United States. Small, less-diversified economies, depending on a limited range of exports, vulnerable to the changing moods of international investors and even of official development agencies—it is no wonder that at one time or another the governments of so many developing countries slipped into sovereign debt crises, suspended payments to their foreign creditors and suffered the consequences. Even if not surprising, is this fair? And are the terms on which developing countries can seek relief from their debt burdens fair?

There is every reason to suspect the poor pay most heavily in a government debt crisis. Indeed, the movement to cancel the debts of poor countries in crisis has been led by activists from churches and other civil society organizations in developing and developed countries mainly on the grounds of injustice to the poor. And they have succeeded in convincing the creditor governments to cancel a substantial amount of debt. Banks and bondholders have also had to absorb losses on loans to developing country governments, if not out of moral obligation, then out of realizing that the economic pain of repaying them was beyond what a polity could support. But what are their moral obligations? Some people argue creditors should be held responsible for knowing that the funds will be used for "odious" purposes, and if so, the debts should be cancelled. Others find that view impractical, if not extreme. These are not simple questions.

Poor-country debt is a continuing story. Multiple crises in Latin America, Africa, Asia, and parts of Europe in the early 1980s were resolved for middle-income countries by the early 1990s, only to see many of them plunged back into crisis by the end of the decade. The lowest-income countries never emerged from their crises. Today, this second crisis cycle seems to be ending, as a lot of debt of middle-income and poor countries has been written off and economic growth has returned in most of them. But few think the debt problem is solved for the long run. Should we not be better prepared ahead of time for the next set of crises?

Because so many questions like these arise when people talk about sovereign debt, I was very happy when our Graduate Program in International Affairs at The New School teamed up with the Carnegie Council for Ethics in International Affairs to ask where justice lay in dealing with debt crises. I was happy to personally welcome the experts they brought together from different walks of life to The New School as they began their work. I am indebted to Joel H. Rosenthal, President of the Carnegie Council, for cooperation on the project, and to Michael Cohen, Director of the International Affairs Program, for encouraging the initiative. Both of our institutions are indebted to the Ford Foundation for supporting the project.

This book is the result. In it you will find authors who step back from ordinary policy discussions to try to articulate general principles that could help assess practices of lending to sovereigns, borrowing by them, and dealing with insolvency crises when they occur. Some of the authors engage with existing international policy on sovereign debt, and a number of specific proposals are put on the table as well. In all, the book can be read as a call to think more deeply about the problem, and then to construct stronger and more equitable international policies on incurring and discharging sovereign debt in developing countries. This undertaking is timely and worthwhile.

Bob Kerrey
President, The New School

Contents

Part I: The Matter of Fairness in Developing Country Debt
Excessive Indebtedness as an Ethical Problem
The Editors 1

The Players and the Game of Sovereign Debt
Barry Herman 9

Part II: Identifying Responsibility for Sovereign Debt
Fairness in Sovereign Debt
Christian Barry and Lydia Tomitova 41

International Debt: The Constructive Implications of Some
Moral Mathematics
Sanjay G. Reddy 81

Should They Honor the Promises of Their Parents' Leaders?
Axel Gosseries 99

Risks of Lending and Liability of Lenders
Kunibert Raffer 127

National Responsibility and the Just Distribution of Debt Relief
Alexander W. Cappelen, Rune Jansen Hagen, and Bertil Tungodden 151

Part III: Perspectives from Theology
Judeo-Christian Tradition on Debt: Political, Not Just Ethical
Ton Veerkamp 167

Making the Case for Jubilee: The Catholic Church and the Poor-Country
Debt Movement
Elizabeth A. Donnelly 189

Argentina, the Church, and the Debt
Thomas J. Trebat 219

Part IV: International Policy Reforms
Achieving Democracy
Thomas Pogge 249

The Due Diligence Model: A New Approach to the Problem of Odious Debts
Jonathan Shafter 275

Reviving Troubled Economies
Jack Boorman 297

The Constructive Role of Private Creditors
Arturo C. Porzecanski 307

Resolving International Debt Crises Fairly
Ann Pettifor 321

Contributors 331

Index 335

Excessive Indebtedness as an Ethical Problem
The Editors

The mere existence of sovereign debt, even in very large amounts, is not in itself a matter of ethical concern. Indeed, the ability of national governments to enter into loan contracts can serve a very important role in the sound management of national affairs. Governments can even out their spending over revenue cycles through short-term borrowing during months of revenue shortfall and repayment of the debt in surplus months. Similarly, taking out short-term loans in foreign currency allows them to smooth international transactions over time and thus helps to limit short-term volatility in the currency exchange rate. Governments can also maintain public spending without having to raise taxes during periods of economic recession by taking out medium-term loans, and repaying them in the next boom period. Finally, governments can borrow for investment in longer-term projects, such as improvements in infrastructure, education, and health care, without imposing the burden of financing them solely on present taxpayers. Since improvements in a country's highways or ports, schools, and hospital care, for example, benefit future taxpayers, long-term borrowing allows the government to share the present costs of such projects with future taxpayers through interest and principal repayments. Governments, just like enterprises and households, would pass up far too many opportunities for promoting valuable objectives if they did not borrow at all. In short, it is very hard to imagine, in the modern world at least, how countries could govern themselves well without their national government enjoying some rights (though not necessarily rights of unlimited scope) to borrow in the name of their present and future citizens.

And yet, many developing countries—indeed, exclusively developing countries—repeatedly find themselves in debt crises. Debt becomes a matter of quite serious ethical concern when such governments, like many enterprises and households, find that their debt has grown beyond what they can reasonably manage, especially (but not only) when this leads people to suffer severe shortfalls in their standard of living. The recent Argentine experience illustrates the dimensions a debt crisis can take even in a so-called middle-income country. In Argentina, where life expectancy at birth is 75 years and approximately 97 percent of the population is literate, almost half the population was pushed below the poverty line by the trough of the economic crisis in 2002, the year following the country's debt default and collapse of its fixed exchange rate system.[1] Thus, when high debt levels force countries into financial crisis, their economies no longer provide the jobs and incomes to sustain an adequate standard of living. Excessive sovereign debt also severely limits the capacities of governments to provide basic social services, and diverts resources and energy from the pursuit of short and long-term strategies that further their peoples' well-being. These effects are particularly acute in the poorest countries. For example, Tanzania was reported to be spending nine times more on debt service than on basic health before its major debt cancellations.[2] In 1991, while President Fujimori of Peru more than doubled the country's monthly debt repayment to $150 million, Peru became the epicenter of a cholera epidemic that spread throughout Latin America. To generate part of the revenue for the debt repayment, the government had instituted policies that raised the costs of basic sanitary products and put them out of reach of the poorest of its people, and did not have an adequate emergency health-care budget to tackle the epidemic when it broke out.[3]

Sovereign debt crises are not isolated occurrences. The International Monetary Fund counts fifty-six countries that had arrears in their foreign debt payments or rescheduled their debt servicing obligations during 1999–2003.[4] Together, these countries accounted for one-fifth of the world's population, or over 1 billion people, but less than 6 percent of the world's gross product. As can be inferred, the debt crisis countries are mostly low-income ones, although middle-income countries have also had to restructure those external debts that they could no longer service, including Argentina, the Dominican Republic, and Iraq in 2005.[5] Moreover, even the populations of poor and middle-income countries that are deemed not to be in crisis often suffer very significant social costs as a result of the extent to which their countries' budgets are devoted to servicing their debts. Brazil is a case in point, where despite reductions in interest rates and greater focus on anti-poverty programs in recent years, the government still expected to devote more federal expenditure in 2006 to interest payments than to social security, health and sanitation, and education added together.[6]

The significant social costs engendered by excessive indebtedness seem particularly problematic because many countries' debt situations have not resulted from the imprudence or recklessness of a government for whose conduct their present and future citizens can reasonably be held to account, but from some combination of other factors, such as the imprudence and recklessness of governments that were not even minimally representative of the interests of their people, the negligence and recklessness of creditors and/or other agents, through sheer bad luck, or due to general features of the international economic order that seem unfair.

Despite the promise made by U.S. Treasury Secretary Nicholas Brady almost two decades ago "to rekindle the hope of the people and leaders of debtor nations that their sacrifices will lead to greater prosperity in the present and the prospect of a future unclouded by the burden of debt,"[7] deterring excessive indebtedness and dealing with it when it nevertheless occurs have thus clearly remained matters of pressing ethical concern.

In recent years there has been growing public recognition of these matters, and increasingly potent popular movements have pressured governments, financial institutions, and the financial community to seek ethical solutions to the debt crisis and the social costs engendered by excessive indebtedness. Some of these movements have led to international policy initiatives, including that for the Heavily Indebted Poor Countries (HIPCs). They have focused political attention on reducing the debt of poor countries to sustainable levels and designing policies to maintain debt at these levels.[8] Still, despite official commitments to significantly raise development assistance and to provide more grants rather than loans, civil society organizations have demanded that governments do better, first, in delivering on the commitments, and second, in raising them so that the poorest countries attain the Millennium Development Goals and other valuable objectives.

Other debt reform proposals have called for new institutional arrangements for restructuring debt that is not payable. One set of proposals would serve a comparable function at the global level of the legal bankruptcy regimes under national law (albeit without the same enforcement authority).[9] Others have proposed mechanisms for distinguishing between debts for which creditors deserve full repayment from those for which creditors either lack claims or have claims that are too weak to recover what they have lent.[10] Still other stakeholders have recommended that new clauses be introduced into bond contracts to enable debts to be restructured more easily and quickly, a proposal that has now been widely adopted.[11]

The merits of most of the aforementioned programs and proposals for dealing with sovereign debt difficulties remain hotly disputed. Such disputes are sometimes purely empirical, with advocates of opposing positions differing only on the best means to achieve shared aims. The intensity of the debate concerning sovereign debt, however, and the heated rhetoric with which it is often conducted, suggest that it may be rooted in deeper disagreements of ethical principle. It is not obvious, however, what disagreements of ethical principle are at stake in this debate. Most participants agree that the current situation is a matter of serious ethical concern and that something must be done to remedy it. However, advocates have seldom articulated *in detail* their underlying justifications for why this situation is unacceptable, and they have thus provided little basis for determining whether their chosen policies would constitute progress. And when the rhetoric in a debate surrounding an important practical dilemma is either heated or evasive (and often both), participants may accuse one another of bad faith or naiveté about the facts of the case.

Thus, some debt relief campaigners have accused creditors and developed country governments of callousness and moral obtuseness in the face of the human costs from high indebtedness. In turn, they have been charged with having failed to appreciate the moral hazard of rewarding irresponsible governments while giving no credit to governments that struggle to keep their budgets in order. In such a charged debate, participants are likely to invoke principles that support their side of the argument without thinking through their argument's broader implications—or perhaps opportunistically ignoring them. These tendencies make it more difficult to identify correctly the true nature of the disagreements, whether empirical or of ethical principle—and hence the evidence and argumentation that could be relevant to resolving them and identifying the institutional and policy reforms that might make the relationships between sovereign debtors and their creditors more acceptable.

Our aim in this volume is thus to generate a more reflective critical debate among diverse stakeholders on the ethical questions raised by problems of sovereign indebtedness; to identify the principles that are relevant for the ethical assessment of proposed solutions to such problems; and to explore the policies and institutional arrangements that such principles would likely demand under present conditions. The chapters that follow include contributions from philosophers, theologians, activist and financial sector scholars, and economists who have made particularly innovative and/or influential interventions in these debates. Some of the contributions seek to explain in detail the type and nature of the disagreements of value that underlie the debate on sovereign debt, and in particular the competing ethical principles that may plausibly be invoked in assessing the conduct of sovereign debtors and their creditors, as well as the institutional arrangements that govern their interactions with each other. Others identify and defend potentially feasible reforms to current policies and institutional arrangements related to sovereign debt contracts.

Nearly all of the essays included in this volume were initially presented at an interdisciplinary conference, "Ethics and Debt," held at The New School in New York in late 2005. To help sharpen the discussion, we asked the contributors to begin to structure their thinking about their essays by considering the following four questions, in the hope that they would provide a principled basis for their responses and at least partially spell out some of the practical implications of their respective views:

1. Into what kinds of contracts should sovereign borrowers and creditors be permitted to enter?
2. Under what circumstances should we deem such contracts to have been entered into legitimately and thus at least prima facie to bind the parties to them?
3. When (if ever) should a contract that has been legitimately entered into by a sovereign borrower no longer be considered to bind it to repay its creditors on the terms stipulated in it?

4. What steps should creditors and others be permitted to take in order to enforce contracts that are considered to bind sovereign debtors?

As a result, each of the essays does indeed engage in detail with aspects of one or more of these questions, and in some cases applies another similarly encompassing framework which the authors have deemed more appropriate to tackling practical dilemmas related to sovereign debt. Given the diversity of positions taken by these authors, we have decided against including a synthesis of the arguments and their implications in this introduction, instead allowing the essays to speak for themselves.[12]

Many people have helped with this project. Above all, we would like to thank the Ford Foundation for providing generous funding for it, and Manuel (Butch) Montes, then at the foundation, for his support and encouragement. The project was also supported by a group of advisors— Frank Fernandez, Jo Marie Griesgraber, Sanjay G. Reddy, Arjun Sengupta, and Joseph E. Stiglitz—who provided invaluable guidance in helping us set the project's direction and its scope. We are especially grateful for the institutional support provided to us by The New School's Graduate Program in International Affairs, and to its director, Michael Cohen, for his substantive contribution to our work. Alys Willman-Navarro and Sabrina Quraishi of The New School provided crucial substantive and organizational support. We are also thankful to the Carnegie Council for Ethics in International Affairs and to all our colleagues there, and especially to Joel H. Rosenthal and Eva Becker for their encouragement and support for the project, to Matt Peterson for his very helpful advice and editorial inputs, and to Madeleine Lynn, Zornitsa Stoyanova-Yerburgh, and Dennis Doyle for creating the Web presence of the project at www.carnegiecouncil.org. We are also very grateful to Terri Teleen of Blackwell Publishing for enthusiastically endorsing and arranging for the publication of this book, as well as to her colleague Jennifer Scarano for skilfully managing its production.

NOTES

[1] More precisely, 45.4 percent of the urban population fell below the poverty line in 2002, roughly double what it was in 1990, and 18.6 percent of the population of the major metropolitan areas was classified as "indigent," compared to 5.2 percent in 1990; poverty line is defined as an income level less than twice the cost of a basic food basket and "indigent" entails income less than

The Editors

the cost of the food basket. See Economic Commission for Latin America and the Caribbean, *Statistical Yearbook for Latin America and the Caribbean, 2005* (Santiago: United Nations, 2006), table 1.6.1.

2 See Oxfam, "Debt Relief for Tanzania: An Opportunity for a Better Future," April 1998; available at www.oxfam.org.uk/what_we_do/issues/debt_aid/papers.htm.

3 For one account, see Noreena Hertz, *The Debt Threat: How Debt Is Destroying the Developing World* (New York: Harper Business, 2004).

4 IMF, *World Economic Outlook*, September 2006, p. 182 and n. 186.

5 See World Bank, *Global Development Finance, 2006*, pp. 73–74.

6 For 2006, the Brazilian government projected spending in the named categories at 18.5 percent of federal expenditures, whereas it projected interest payments at 19.1 percent of expenditures. For social expenditures, see Alcino Ferreira Câmara Neto and Matías Vernengo, "Lula's Social Policies: New Wine in Old Bottles?" Department of Economics, University of Utah, Working Paper 2006-07; available at www.econ.utah.edu/activities/papers/2006_07.pdf. For interest payments data, see IMF, "IMF Executive Board Concludes 2006 Article IV Consultation with Brazil," Public Information Note 06/69, June 19, 2006, at www.imf.org/external/np/sec/pn/2006/pno669.htm.

7 Barbara Rudolph, "Enter the Brady Plan," *Time*, March 20, 1989, p. 54.

8 For the World Bank's description of the HIPC Initiative, see www.worldbank.org/hipc/about/hipcbr/hipcbr.htm.

9 See Kunibert Raffer, "Applying Chapter 9 Insolvency to International Debts: An Economically Efficient Solution with a Human Face," *World Development* 18, no. 2 (1990), pp. 301–13.

10 See Ashfaq Khalfan, Jeff King, and Bryan Thomas, "Advancing the Odious Debt Doctrine" (Montreal: Centre for International Sustainable Development Law, 2003); available at www.cisdl.org/pdf/debtentire.pdf.

11 See Stephen J. Choi and G. Mitu Gulati, "Innovation in Boilerplate Contracts: An Empirical Examination of Sovereign Bonds," *Emory Law Journal* 53 (2004), pp. 929–96.

12 Nevertheless, Christian Barry and Lydia Tomitova explore various aspects of some of the ideas presented in several of the chapters of this volume in "Fairness in Sovereign Debt," this volume, pp. 41–79. Also, Barry Herman has prepared a detailed synthesis of the essays prepared for this project and their possible implications for policy and advocacy. See his "Doing the Right Thing: Dealing with Developing Country Sovereign Debt," *North Carolina Journal of International Law and Commercial Regulation* 32, no. 4 (2007), pp. 773–818.

The Players and the Game of Sovereign Debt

*Barry Herman**

In policy discussions about government debt, especially that of developing countries and particularly in cases when there is a crisis to overcome after a government defaults on its debt, commentators often talk about legal obligations, political necessity, and economic consequences. Implicitly or explicitly, commentators refer to what the "proper," "fair," or "just" actions would be. Typically, what is claimed as fair from the perspective of one group of interests (for example, the holders of defaulted government bonds) is regarded as unfair by another group (for example, the people whose taxes would be raised to pay the bondholders), and vice versa. Ultimately, a compromise is almost always reached between a sovereign debtor in crisis and its creditors. In practice, it is a compromise voluntarily entered into by the parties, under rules of negotiation accepted by all sides, including the understanding that the parties are unequal in negotiating strength. But does the parties' voluntary agreement mean the compromise represents a fair sharing of the burden among the different players?

In fact, sometimes the result is fair and sometimes it is not. That is not a very satisfying conclusion to reach about the predominant method for organizing workouts from debt crises. Other approaches to resolving sovereign debt crises have been conceived, but none has been found generally acceptable. All the reforms introduced thus far in the renegotiation of sovereign debt have aimed to clarify the rules or facilitate reaching a conclusion under them. It is "the only game in town" because all others are deemed inferior by enough of the players to block a change of the game. The dominance of this method may itself be unfair, and if so, how does the world get to an alternative that is fair?

---

* This essay has benefited from comments by Christian Barry, Lydia Tomitova, and Alys Willman-Navarro. All errors are my own fault.

While the operative parts of these questions are policy matters, they beg for assistance from people practiced in the discussion of ethical issues. That assistance follows in the rest of this volume, but first it will be useful to explain in some detail what the sovereign debt game entails, who the major players are, what interests they seek to fulfill, how they interact, and some of the challenges they face.

THE SOVEREIGN DEBTOR

Sovereign indebtedness begins when the national or central government of a state chooses to borrow. The typical borrowings are uncollateralized obligations of the government in domestic or foreign currency, backed only by its "full faith and credit." This debt is recognized as an obligation of the government as a whole, and the executive and legislative arms of the government manage it. The judiciary is responsible for assessing purportedly criminal actions relating to sovereign debt and settling disputes between the government, its creditors, and any financial intermediaries in matters pertaining to government debt issued under domestic law. The courts of a borrowing country are not typically considered (by its creditors) to be the relevant forum for settling disputes involving government debt issued under the laws of other countries, such as bonds issued in New York or London. A borrowing government may be bound by its constitution and accepted practice to abide by the decisions of its own courts. There are no treaties by which governments are required to cede authority to any foreign court in matters of sovereign debt.[1] Only moral suasion, political pressure, or economic threats can make a government honor the decisions of foreign courts.

Types of Government Borrowing

Governments typically borrow for three main purposes: short-term transaction smoothing, medium-term expenditure smoothing, and investment in specific, usually longer-term projects, such as improvements in infrastructure. The first type of borrowing includes loans, usually for up to ninety days, typically as treasury bills or overdrafts from commercial banks, which make it possible for expenditures to follow different cycles than revenues. The borrowing during months of revenue shortfall is repaid during the months of surplus. Comparable loans in foreign currency are taken to smooth international transactions over time, which helps to limit short-term volatility in the exchange rate. The average level of short-term government debt related to domestic borrowings usually grows more or less at the rate of growth of overall domestic economic activity, while the foreign currency component of such debt grows roughly in proportion to the growth of foreign trade and payments. This type of borrowing does not lead to sovereign debt crises.

Governments often also borrow during economic recessions in response to unplanned declines in tax revenues and recession-related increases in expenditures. The alternative to borrowing is to cut expenditures or raise taxes in response to the revenue shortfall, which would aggravate the recession. All too often in recent years, developing countries with very limited borrowing capacity have had to follow such so-called pro-cyclical policies. The quid pro quo when instead undertaking "counter-cyclical" borrowing is that the government should repay the cycle-related debt during the next boom period, which entails running a budget surplus. That is, although the original duration ("tenor") of the loans undertaken during the downturn could be any length of time, perhaps even ten years or more, the government should either repay them during the recovery period or not roll over other loans as they mature. As a result, over the full economic cycle the net borrowing would be nil. Problems arise when the net borrowing over the full cycle is excessive. This could happen when a sequence of adverse economic shocks repeatedly postpones recovery, or when a permanent adverse change is mistaken for a temporary development. Excessive net borrowing could also be the result of policy failures of the borrowing government, such as not restraining expenditures during the boom when high demands are made based on the argument that now "you can afford it."

Governments also borrow for specific policy purposes, for example, to purchase military hardware, or for specific long-term investments, such as constructing or improving highways or ports. While the "useful life" of some military hardware may be several years or a decade, some infrastructure (with proper maintenance) will last a generation or more. Because such investments benefit residents over time, it is generally considered fair that the future beneficiaries of these investments bear some of their costs. Thus, instead of asking current taxpayers to bear the full cost, governments borrow and share the cost with future taxpayers through interest and principal repayments. Indeed, as infrastructure investments can increase economic growth, they can thereby also enhance the capacity of the borrowing government to service the debt out of the higher tax revenues it collects on the higher incomes. There is nevertheless an important caveat, in that very heavy borrowing for capital investment can place an excessive debt burden on the populace in the future.

The borrowings discussed thus far should all appear in the government's fiscal accounts (and in those of the central bank when it undertakes external borrowing on behalf of the government). Government debt may also arise in less transparent ways; for example, for policy reasons the government may guarantee the borrowing of another entity (a state enterprise, a public-private partnership, even a private company). As the government is usually deemed a better credit risk than any other domestic entity, a government guarantee lowers the interest cost or extends the maturity of the borrowing for the favored entity. In that sense, issuing a guarantee is an attractive policy tool, as it can assist the targeted recipient, and yet it is not an actual budget outlay. In the event of default by the borrowing entity, however, the government becomes responsible for the repayment of the loan—that is, the guarantee creates a "contingent liability."

Governments may also incur debts without guaranteeing a specific loan, as when they have to borrow to make up a shortfall in promised payments, as to retired civil servants, owing to an insufficient provision or a bad investment experience of their pension fund. In this case, the government guarantee is to the pensioners and exemplifies a class of contingent claims that can be labeled "unfunded obligations." Sometimes, governments even have to incur debts to make good on obligations on which there are at best only implicit guarantees. One example is borrowing to recapitalize the local commercial banks in a generalized banking crisis. In such cases, the government may buy a portion of the bad debt held by the banks using funds it borrows itself. The new financial resources transferred to the banks are meant to rebuild confidence in them, without which no market-based economy can function.[2]

In sum, most categories of government debt are intentionally incurred, although unfunded obligations and contingent liabilities can add to government debt in an unplanned way. It is usually difficult to forecast when or with what probability such contingencies would require new borrowing, but the probability is not zero. In that sense, official government debt statistics understate the fiscal condition of governments, albeit by an amount that is difficult to measure. More generally, economic shocks can turn what appeared to be responsible budgeting into a debt crisis. The latter arrives at the moment when a government's usual creditors lose interest in extending further loans.

The Art of Sovereign Debt Management

To assist governments in their debt management, the international policy community has been trying to specify guidelines for what the "sustainable" level of government debt might be. There is no global consensus yet on the factors to include in an operational definition, however, let alone how to monitor them, and certainly we are far from agreement on any general guidelines for maintaining sustainability. Given the proliferation of debt crises over recent decades, however, the International Monetary Fund (IMF) now prepares a standard report on sovereign debt as part of the mandatory annual consultations with governments of member countries on their macroeconomic policies. The report examines alternative economic scenarios and potential economic shocks and traces what happens in each case to standard debt indicators (for example, the ratio of total debt to gross domestic product and foreign debt to exports of goods and services). Examination of these "debt dynamics" is meant to signal under what kinds of economic circumstances a country might become vulnerable to a debt crisis, although, as noted above, actually having one requires that the usual creditors lose confidence and cease lending, which is impossible to foresee.

Regardless of how difficult it may be, a government is regarded as responsible for managing its own debt. It may take a very cautious approach to borrowing, which lowers the probability of a crisis. But this would be at the cost of forgoing the benefits from borrowing, such as moderating an economic downturn or enjoying the services of particular infrastructure investments. The amount of risk to carry is thus properly a political decision, which means it should be taken by the appropriate political authority of a government (the executive branch, the legislative branch, or both). The international community of states could decide to share in this risk by providing automatic credit lines to governments that are deemed to budget "responsibly" so that there would be some form of adverse risk insurance. Thus far, the international community has not chosen to do so. IMF lending usually comes after the crisis starts and is contingent on the debtor accepting a long list of policy conditions.[3] The risk and responsibility is left fully with the government.

Why Do Governments Service Their Debt?

At any moment in time, a government's debt is the cumulative result of the borrowing and repayment by it and all of its predecessors. When a government is considered legitimate and seems generally to represent the wishes of its people, the debt is viewed as the collective obligation of the people and should be serviced by current and future governments, as contracted. In fact, governments almost always do service their debts, as do individuals and enterprises. Defaulting on a debt is everywhere considered a serious violation of a contract and implicitly it is a violation of a relation of trust between the borrower and lender. Governments take great pains to avoid default for the same reason private-sector borrowers do: the government wants continued access to credit from all its creditors and on as favorable terms as possible. It also wants the counterparties to all its contracts to be confident that it will fulfill its obligations. Anything else threatens to make governing more difficult.

Nevertheless, sometimes the economic and social (and political) cost of uninterrupted debt servicing may exceed the cost of suspending payments. Thus, under some conditions, governments will stop servicing their debt. Similarly, a government could reach the conclusion that its previous history of borrowing was so economically and socially harmful that it decides to eschew future borrowing. In this situation, the government may also feel less impelled to service its already outstanding loans. Indeed, this argument was made in Argentina, following its default at the end of 2001. Argentina, however, "cured" its defaulted debt in 2005 and quickly returned to new borrowing in the financial markets.

When a new government is formed, it inherits and almost always accepts responsibility for all of the obligations of the previous regime. In the case of debts incurred for constructing infrastructure that continues to provide services (roads, school buildings, and so on), the change of regime should not matter. It was understood when the loans were incurred that they would have to be serviced over successive governments, and the services from the investments are enjoyed by taxpayers under the new as much as the old regime. If the infrastructure investment had been grossly overpriced or is deemed dangerous to public health and safety, however, the investment agreement, including its financing, might be revisited (indeed, the government that signed the initial contracts may equally challenge the deal if it comes to suspect malfeasance). Governments are nevertheless cautious in challenging investors in such cases so as not to discourage investors in other projects. Specific cases of fraud or bribery are more easily pursued than general claims that all lending to a previous regime constituted "odious debt" that should not be serviced. Concerns to bring such ethical considerations to bear are typically swamped by desires to maintain as many financing and policy options as possible.

CREDITORS

It is necessary to discuss the different classes of creditors separately, as they have different motivations, expectations, and behaviors in their acts of lending to governments, which might lead to different judgments about the obligations of debtor governments with respect to servicing each type of debt.

Commercial Banks: Bedrock of the Financial System
Inside the banks. The loan officers of banks are expected to regularly assess and monitor the sustainability of their clients' borrowing. Banks also maintain risk-management offices to ensure that the overall portfolio of loans extended is not excessively risky. This involves questions of both the mix of loans and the riskiness of individual clients. Moreover, as commercial banks are regulated institutions, the supervisory authorities are also obligated to monitor the riskiness of the portfolio of loans of the banks.[4]

In fact, banks are regulated because they tend to take on excessive risk when attracted by the prospect of profit. Because banks charge riskier clients higher interest rates, lending to them is more lucrative, at least as long as the borrowers service their debts fully and on time. Management may discount warnings coming from their risk managers, especially as most banks are corporations whose shares trade on the stock market and whose management is remunerated according to stock-price movements, which usually reflect short-term profit performance figures.

The responsibilities of loan officers and risk managers to their banks are the same whether their banks are lending to the government or to private clients. But the banks are more likely to voluntarily continue lending longer to their government when its debt indicators are worsening than they are to a private firm. One reason is the presumption, which is warranted by history, that the government is a less risky client than private entities. (Unlike private entities, governments have the unique authority to tax.)

Banks may also lend when they would rather not. Banks are not immune to politics. Governments can first pressure and then force domestic banks to continue to lend more and for longer than they would voluntarily and can press "forbearance" on the part of regulators who might otherwise stop the lending.[5] In any event, domestic banks that lend to their government in local currency are less likely to hesitate to continue to lend voluntarily as a domestic situation worsens than are banks lending in foreign currency. The concern in domestic currency lending is typically less about outright default by the government than erosion of the value of loans owing to inflationary money creation. But domestic banks can also have to accommodate themselves to political pressure—with which they can live as long as it is put on all of them together—to lend to their government in foreign currency (which means either borrowing abroad on their own account for lending to the government or selling some of their foreign currency assets to raise funds to lend to the government). They can tolerate the risk of such lending because of the moral hazard problem: the banks know that as long as they are all in the same boat, should there be a general domestic banking crisis owing to a government default on its foreign currency obligations, they will have to be bailed out as a group since functioning banks are essential to the economy.

A scenario of this sort played out at the international level in the 1980s, when the large "money center" banks based in the developed countries that had lent large sums to developing countries put the entire international monetary system at risk. When the bubble burst, rather than accept the bankruptcy of their client governments, the big banks joined together and in cooperation with the IMF and the major country governments continued lending for several years, while their regulators looked the other way.[6]

On the other hand, during normal times, bankers are more often in a position to press their governments to follow "responsible" macroeconomic policies as seen from their perspective—that is, low-inflation policies. They may exert pressure on governments for "sound" policies individually or through local business associations. In addition, after the 1980s debt crisis the major international banks have increasingly lobbied together globally, as through the Institute of International Finance, based in Washington, D.C.

Large-scale international bank lending and its crises. Private international lending only emerged as a major form of international financial transfer to developing countries in the 1970s. It primarily took the form of international bank loans in foreign currency to governments. Banks had traditionally lent to governments to finance capital-equipment imports, such as airplanes or locomotives. These export credits often were (and still are) guaranteed by an official agency of the exporting country, however, and have thus been of low risk to the banks. But beginning in the 1970s, the banks also made large-scale, multibank loans to governments for general fiscal deficit financing, to replenish foreign exchange reserves, or for other purposes of such kind. It was this latter type of lending that created much of the foreign bank debt that ultimately had to be restructured by overindebted countries in the 1980s and early 1990s.

In this type of lending, the currency of the loan is the central issue in the prospect of default. As noted above, a government can usually service its domestic currency loans through additional money creation, albeit at the price of additional inflation. A government cannot create foreign money, however, nor can it mobilize foreign money once it empties its reserves and loses access to new international credit. All it can do is notify the creditor banks that it cannot make its next payment and seek to restructure the obligations. In this regard, banks have to assess the credit risk in lending to a foreign government (the risk of nonpayment), and they charge a risk premium above a risk-free interest rate as compensation for taking on the perceived risk of nonpayment.[7]

Although 1980s-style multibank lending to developing country governments has largely been superseded by bond financing, it is useful to recall how the sovereign defaults to international commercial banks were resolved. The loan agreements themselves embody part of the story; that is, most of the large-scale bank lending was conducted in syndications in which many banks—sometimes up to 500 or more—would participate. Large governments would typically have several syndicated loans outstanding at the same time. The cross-default clause in each loan contract typically said that any default against one of the syndications was a default against all of them. Funds that were recovered on a defaulted loan also had to be shared with all the other banks in proportion to their share of the total bank debt. In short, the banks were pushed by their loan contracts to negotiate together with the defaulting government to resolve the situation. The lead managers of the loan syndicates usually led the negotiations, after forming ad-hoc Bank Advisory Committees (BACs) or London Clubs, so named because many of their meetings in the 1980s took place there.

A country's BAC would negotiate a debt restructuring deal with the government and then have to "sell" it to the other banks in the syndicates, oftentimes abetted by quiet or public pressure from governments of the creditor banks and the IMF. This negotiating structure for the banks also turned out to be efficient for the sovereign debtor, who only had to deal with a limited number of negotiators. But it did not indicate what the debt workout should look like. In the early years of the 1980s crises, the governments and banks seemed to have a common interest in avoiding a formal state of debtor default. The emphasis then was put on "concerted" or "forced" additional lending by the banks acting collectively so the loans could continue to be serviced.[8] They were buying time while they hoped for recovery and the sovereign's return to repayment capacity. But this ruse could not last. Inevitably, the question became how to share the losses from the actual insolvency.

There were essentially two sets of interests among the banks. Some of the banks had invested in the domestic sector of the debtor country and had long-term interests to protect. Their desire to recover on the defaulted debt had to be set against not wanting to jeopardize their other businesses in the country. Others had no long-term relationship with the debtor country and were only interested in recovering their funds. As the 1980s wore on, many of the latter banks lost patience and decided to cut their losses. They sold their shares in the loan syndicates at deep discounts to speculative investors in a new market in nonperforming debt. The investor who purchased his loan share at thirty cents on the original dollar of loan would make a very good profit if the final deal netted him sixty cents on the dollar. And so, eventually deals were struck among the remaining creditors and with the debtor.[9]

Today, London Clubs still form to deal with governments that encounter difficulties with their bank debt, but there is little interest in arranging any more forced lending. In the 1990s crises, the banking community instead looked to the multilateral lenders, especially the IMF, to provide governments with the resources to keep the loans of the banks "performing." By the end of the decade, however, governments of the major creditor countries reacted negatively to their experience with large-scale lending to stave off defaults of countries in crisis (although all the loans have been fully paid). Instead, they sought to limit the amount of official lending in such situations, preferring to see the banks take losses in acknowledgment of the risk of their lending. In the parlance of international financial diplomacy, this has been called "involving the private (creditor) sector in crisis resolution." The terms of this bank-government relationship continue to evolve, but whenever a London Club is formed today it is understood to require dealing with an insolvent government and that the creditors may need to take a "haircut"— that is, accept less than full repayment of their loans.

Purchases of Government Bonds
Large-scale syndicated bank loans are more common today for corporate financing, although they are still arranged for governments. Instead, the international bond market has retaken its historical (nineteenth-century) role as the primary modality for arranging large-scale foreign lending to governments. One reason for the increased popularity of bonds as a funding instrument is that it is easier for the banks as well as other creditors to buy (and sell) government bonds than it is to participate in loan syndications. Bonds are standardized financial instruments that are usually traded on markets, making them more liquid (that is, they can be sold more readily) than participations in syndicated bank loans (which could also be sold, but in a "thinner" market, one with fewer trades).

Usually, the first markets in financial instruments to develop in a country are the markets in government "paper," beginning with short-term notes and eventually involving longer-term bonds. The government is the best-known and least risky issuer in every domestic market. The buyers of its bonds are usually domestic financial institutions (banks, pension funds, insurance companies) and wealthy individuals.

An international market for government bonds in "hard" currencies (those of the highly industrialized countries) first reemerged in the postwar era with developed country issuers in the Euromarket. Developing country governments thus only had to gain acceptance as issuers in an already existing market that had already standardized financial instruments. In addition, from the beginnings of the "Eurobond market" in the 1960s until late in the 1990s, governments rarely defaulted on their foreign bonds, making them seem lower-risk credits than bank loans.

More recently, foreign demand has begun to grow for government bonds issued on the financial markets of the larger developing countries, albeit first for dollar-linked domestic currency bonds and other types of securities, and then local currency bonds themselves. The increased willingness of international financial investors to hold local currency bonds of emerging economies is indeed a major step in financial globalization.

Main players in the international bond market. Several of the major internationally active commercial banks of the 1980s (or their postmerger successors) now make up some of the most important intermediaries in the emerging-economy sovereign bond market. In this business, the commercial banks have joined in the core business of "investment banks" ("merchant banks" in the United Kingdom), which advise governments on how, where, and when to issue their bonds, help them to structure the bond offerings, take care of the initial marketing of the issue, and underwrite the issue as they effect their sale to first buyers. (The contrast is with commercial banking per se, when the banks lend their own money.)

International investors generally see government bonds as part of a portfolio of securities they hold. The trick for the portfolio manager (whether an individual or a firm) is to strike an appropriate balance among a variety of financial assets with different risk and return characteristics so as to earn some targeted average yield in exchange for an overall level of risk. The portfolio manager may buy and sell securities continually as he or she seeks to adjust to changing perceptions about the securities in the portfolio. In the developed countries, bond buyers usually see lending to their own governments as a safe albeit generally low-yield investment. Own-government bonds are thus a standard part of most investment portfolios in developed countries, although in different proportions of the total invested, depending on the investor's ability and desire to be exposed to risk in exchange for taking the chance for greater yield. Foreign government bonds, in particular those of emerging economies, are still viewed as high-risk and pay a relatively high return.[10]

Whether in developed or developing countries, it is considered the responsibility of the so-called buy-side institutional investor or purchasing household to choose its portfolio of investments wisely and not to subject the portfolio to greater risk than intended. There is a presumption that the institutional and individual investors are capable of doing this—that is, that they have the capacity to assess the financial situation of the issuers of the securities they hold, including those of their own government and any other government whose bonds they buy.

Private and independent bond-rating agencies exist to help the buy-side make its assessments. It is considered to be in the interest of the bond issuer that the market have credible information on its bonds—and indeed, the ratings industry lives off the fees paid by bond issuers for the assessments the agencies make of them. Moreover, government regulators of pension funds and other financial institutions heavily restrict the international bonds that the institutions they oversee can hold, often requiring that only the bonds that pass a particular hurdle rating ("investment" grade) qualify. Nevertheless, it is clear to all professionals in the market that the rating agencies are only making judgments of the probability of default on the bond. They issue no guarantee and have been charged—especially after the Asian financial crisis of the late 1990s—with being slow to react to changing circumstances that warranted a revised rating of the issues of a particular country or firm. Indeed, most institutional investors make their own assessments of the riskiness of any individual bond, using the rating agency's grading as only one input into their assessment.

Whatever the extent and reliability of the information available, those providing it—market research firms, research departments of merchant banks, rating agencies—are not held financially accountable if the information proves false, as long as the information was provided in good faith. The same holds whether institutional investors or households use the information to buy foreign or domestic currency bonds of their own government, of corporate issuers, or of foreign governments.

While the presumption that the buyer/investor is responsible for being well informed may seem reasonable, things become much less clear if financial intermediaries have misrepresented the true risks of the government bonds being purchased by a household or by a buy-side intermediary, such as a mutual fund. What if the issuing government then defaults on those bonds? If the distortion was intentional, the sell-side intermediary is presumably guilty of fraud and should make the buyer whole. If the government issuing the bonds has withheld information relevant to the buy-side decision, the bond-issuing government should arguably be held responsible. In the latter case, perhaps the government officials would be found guilty of a crime, and the public in the debtor country would be responsible to make the creditor whole. When there is no fraud, the principle of caveat emptor ("buyer beware") generally prevails.

What happens in a bond default? The bond itself is a contract between the issuing government and the holder of the bond by which the government promises to service the bond fully in accordance with its terms. The government that defaults on its bonds unilaterally breaks the contract and the contract stipulates what happens next. The default usually begins with the government advising the bondholders that it cannot make the next debt servicing payment falling due. Unlike bank loans, which are kept on the books at nominal value until a decision is made to declare them "impaired," there is no hiding from the loss in value of the bonds after the debtor's announcement. The bonds are available for trade continually on international markets, and at the end of each day the institutional investors "mark to market" (recalculate the value of their portfolios at the closing prices of each security held).

After a grace period, the bond may be "accelerated" by the bondholders—that is, the bondholders can vote to require the government to repay the whole bond immediately and fully, which of course it cannot do. Unlike some of the provisions in bank loan contracts that drive the lenders together, individual bondholders have strong incentives to try to collect what

Barry Herman

is owed to them individually, which at this point may start a "race to the courthouse" to try to attach assets of the debtor government existing within the jurisdiction of the court in lieu of the accelerated bond. There is usually very little to attach, however; for example, all diplomatic property is out of bounds. It is also never cheap to begin a legal proceeding against a defaulting government, and the outcome is always uncertain at best.

It is also possible for a government that anticipates trouble to ask its bondholders to restructure the coming repayment obligations.[11] Most emerging-economy bonds, however, have been issued under New York law, and until recently the standard contracts made such a negotiated restructuring of repayments virtually impossible, as they required approval of all bondholders. There has been a way around this—called "exit consents"—by which the government offers to swap the old bond on which it could not meet its obligations with a new bond, and as part of the deal the bondholders agree to change the nonfinancial terms of the old bond in such a way as to make the old bond virtually worthless. Typically, the government would consult the largest bondholders (who might form themselves into a committee) so that when the government makes its "exchange offer" it has a good chance of being accepted. This works because to change the non-financial terms usually requires only a simple majority of bondholders. With the recent introduction of collective action clauses (CACs) into developing country bonds issued under the laws of New York State, however, a practical new mechanism is being introduced (which existed all along in bonds floated in London under British law) by which the government can directly approach its bondholders to change the financial terms of the bond before (as well as after) it defaults. The bond contract will say what specific majority is required to effect the change and how the bondholders are to be mobilized. If accepted, the government then commits to fully meet the new terms.

Over the next ten to fifteen years, as new bonds with CACs increasingly replace maturing old bonds without them, it should become easier to mobilize the holders of individual bond issues to renegotiate with insolvent debtor governments. This is, however, a rather minor reform. In particular, it involves no built-in mechanism for bringing the holders of all outstanding bond issues of a debtor together to restructure their obligations (called the "aggregation" problem). It is of course attractive to a debtor if the bondholders form themselves into a single bondholders' committee with which it can negotiate, and large institutional investors that hold several different issues of a country's bonds may also have an interest in forming a single creditors' group.[12]

Even if CACs lead to better mechanisms for bringing bondholders together for negotiation with a sovereign debtor, this does not tell us the direction in which the negotiations themselves would move, in particular in light of the recent Argentine experience. It took four contentious years, during which a number of bondholders made fruitless attempts to bring the government to court, before Argentina's defaulted foreign bond debt was finally exchanged for new bonds worth about thirty cents on the dollar.[13] This experience would seem to make a more cooperative approach to negotiations more attractive to the creditors and the debtor in the next case of default. On the other hand, Argentina's unprecedented debt reduction may encourage defaulting debtors to toughen their negotiating stance, making for a more protracted negotiation.[14] So too might the very positive reception the international financial markets gave to two new Argentine bond issues floated almost before the ink was dry on the final restructuring of its defaulted debt.

In all such cases, bondholders risk more a partial than a complete loss in the event of sovereign default. A crucial ethical as well as economic policy question is how much loss the bondholders and other parties should bear under different sets of circumstances. Today there are no general principles to govern or guide how much loss should be asked of the bondholders, nor whether bondholders, the banks, nor any other commercial medium-term lenders should receive the same or different haircuts in a debt workout for a sovereign in financial crisis. If it is not obvious that the haircut should be the same for all, then which subcategories of each type of creditor should be treated differently, and in what ways? Another question that has vexed governments and private creditors is how the private creditor haircut should compare to that on debt owed to governments. Finally, would it be just if other parties who are neither the debtor country nor the creditors absorb some of the loss, especially if they could do so at a relatively low cost? (For example, in treating the debts of the poorest countries, bilateral aid donors

Barry Herman

have contributed amounts to cover poor-country obligations to the World Bank that were unrelated to the size of their own loans to the country.)

Government Creditors and the Paris Club

Government-to-government lending is a different category of international finance from private lending to governments. For many governments of developing countries, especially the poorest ones, official lending is the main source of foreign credit, but even middle-income countries owe some debt to other governments. Most of the loans to the poorest countries are highly subsidized. Many are offered as official development assistance (ODA), or for military equipment purchases, or for emergency humanitarian assistance (although the latter is probably mostly grant assistance now). While there are exceptions, such loans are usually repayable in the currency of the lending government. Most of the lending is of a medium-term nature, and a large part is contingent, wherein the creditor government guarantees the loan of a private lender (usually a bank), promising that the guaranteeing government will cover the obligations should the borrowing government default.

A large part of the loans and guarantees are of a commercial nature, primarily credits to promote the export products and services of the lending government's economy. But the lending or guaranteeing export credit agency is not a private or for-profit entity. Governments create such agencies for policy purposes, especially export promotion. Unlike a private corporation, the export credit agency does not need to report quarterly profits to the market, which investors can scan when deciding whether to buy, hold, or sell its equity shares. But the export credit agency is mandated to cover its costs (or not exceed its budgeted subsidy). Losses will displease its government overseers, thereby potentially threatening its resource stream and hindering the professional prospects of its managers. Its mandate entails a moderate subsidy of exports, but nothing more. Thus, officers of these agencies can be expected to have a responsibility similar to that of private creditors to be informed about the repayment capacity of the borrowing governments. Also, like private creditors, they will make great efforts to recoup their loans when a borrower defaults.

When a borrowing government defaults on officially guaranteed export credits, the guarantor government pays what is owed to the private creditors, takes over the obligation directly, and seeks repayment from the defaulting government. The creditor government equally will seek repayment of any of its direct loans on which the debtor government defaults, including ODA. It does not seem to matter in practice if the defaulted repayment is on an ODA loan, the collection of which might itself compromise the development capacity of the borrowing country. It seems that the pursuit of development assistance goals is overridden by the lending government's attempt to exercise its "creditor rights" in its credit recovery negotiations with the debtor.[15]

A borrowing government usually defaults on the loans of all government creditors at once. Each creditor wants to recover all of the funds owed to it, but the very act of default signals that the debtor cannot satisfy all of them. Rather than compete against one another to recover what they can, the main government creditors formed the so-called Paris Club in the 1950s, and have since then jointly negotiated their overall debt relief packages with each debtor government, guided by an assessment of the financial needs of the debtor as prepared by the IMF. In general, the Paris Club does not reduce the level of debt but instead postpones payments, capitalizes unpaid interest, and charges market interest rates on all the outstanding amounts.

In essence, the basic Paris Club agreement is thus a refinancing of the debt, buying time for the debtor economy to recover and resume the debt servicing. The club typically addresses only part of the problem at any sitting about a given country, rescheduling debt payments over a one- or two-year period, requiring a sequence of visits and agreements. This "short leash" approach is meant to add pressure on the government, on top of that of the IMF, to follow policies deemed corrective of the debt crisis.

The club has also made special "deep" relief arrangements, however, for certain politically important cases (such as Poland and Egypt in the early 1990s and Iraq and Nigeria most recently), and it has adopted different policy frameworks for dealing with special situations. The most notable is for the heavily indebted poor countries (HIPCs), which can receive substantial reductions in the stock of their debt, and the new Evian Approach, which opens the possibility of debt reduction in special cases for countries outside the HIPC process. The innovation in the latter, like the HIPC Initiative, is to offer "comprehensive" treatment (code for potential net reduction in claims) aimed at postrelief sustainability for countries with unsustainable debts that undertake what are deemed to be appropriate policies. Both the Evian Approach and the HIPC Initiative require a multistage process over several years before the final debt workout.[16]

The formal result of these and all regular Paris Club negotiations, called an "Agreed Minute," specifies only the general terms of the debt restructuring deal (such as how much debt will be postponed for how many years, or what percent of covered obligations will be written off in special cases). The debtor government then has to negotiate implementing agreements with each of the Paris Club members, in which the interest rate on postponed repayments, penalty fees, and precise loans to be affected are determined. These negotiations can drag on for many months—even a year—after the Paris Club decision and can impose a considerable administrative burden on the debtor government, since it may have to negotiate deals with as many as nineteen individual creditor governments. Under the short-leash approach, almost as soon as one set of bilateral negotiations ends, the next Paris Club negotiation can begin, making debt renegotiation a semipermanent job of senior finance ministry officials of (generally low-income) debt-distressed countries.

The debtor is also required by the terms of the Agreed Minute to seek comparable debt relief from all other government creditors and even the private creditors on which it defaulted. Creditor governments that are not part of the Paris Club are not bound by the agreement, however, nor are private creditors, and the debtor government is usually not in a position to press its case. Indeed, even the Paris Club creditors have not succeeded in doing more than exhorting those other creditors to match the relief in the Agreed Minute. As a result, the debtor may receive less relief overall than envisaged in the Paris Club arrangement and the IMF needs assessment on which it was based.

The debtor government is not in a strong position to press its own case in the Paris Club either. Many developing countries that come to the Paris Club (especially the poorer ones) have not had the capacity to estimate their own debt-relief needs. In any case, as noted above, the creditors are mainly guided by the assessment presented by the IMF, and it has been accused of regularly underestimating the level of needed relief. It is not clear if this reflects an inherent optimism based on the need to assume that the policy and output targets that accompany the IMF's recovery program for the country will be attained, or the IMF focus on how much relief the creditors say they are willing to grant. It is only clear that over time the Paris Club has acknowledged the need for deeper cuts in debts owed to its members by the poorest countries and that the IMF has produced the economic memoranda needed to underpin those cuts at each step.

Multilateral Institutions

The IMF was established to mitigate international financial instability. The World Bank and the regional development banks (the Inter-American Development Bank, the Asian Development Bank, the African Development Bank, and smaller subregional banks) were established to transfer financial resources to selected governments in amounts and on terms that the governments could not obtain without such assistance. All of these institutions are themselves creditors of developing countries, but given their different natures it is useful to discuss them separately.

The International Monetary Fund. The IMF is a credit union. Governments contribute their domestic currencies plus a certain amount of gold or hard currency, and in return are able to draw from the Fund's currency pool during times of need for balance-of-payments adjustment. Of course, the developed countries put very much more into the Fund than the poor countries, as there is no demand to draw the currencies of the latter group and all members want to be able to draw the currencies of the former. This fact provides the justification for "conditionality" in Fund lending: the owners of the drawn resources want more assurances than just promises that their resources will be returned. It also shapes the governance structure of the Fund. Decision-making power, determined by the voting rules for the executive board, is in proportion to the usable resources contributed.

While this governance structure has a certain logic, the Fund is also an international organization whose Articles of Agreement give it a mandate to help member countries manage their balance-of-payments problems in the interest of global financial stability and the growth of world trade and income. In this context, it is not immediately obvious that "one dollar, one vote" is the proper governance rule. Indeed, the reallocation of voting rights in the Fund has been under intergovernmental discussion for several years.[17]

For countries entering a balance-of-payments crisis, the IMF is the one international "lender of last resort." It lends when no one else will, albeit not immediately and always with conditions and thus typically after a crisis breaks open.[18] The IMF can deploy quite substantial sums of money of its own and it can mobilize large sums from governments on an as-needed basis, especially in any case that is seen to threaten global financial stability. Moreover, once the IMF and the government agree upon an economic adjustment program (by approving a "stand by" or other lending arrangement), other multilateral creditors may step forward and proffer funds. An active IMF program is also a precondition for a Paris Club negotiation. Private creditors in cases of sovereign default have also looked to the IMF for leadership on when to negotiate with the debtor government.[19] In short, the IMF is regarded as the principal interlocutor of the whole international community with the debtor government on its adjustment policies.

All classes of international creditors of a government believe that while balance-of-payments crises—and external debt crises in particular—may occur for any of a variety of reasons, the workout requires policy adjustments by the government. While there may be cases in which this is not true (for example, a crisis caused by a temporary fall in commodity export prices that would resolve itself after prices recovered to a normal level), it is effectively presumed always to be true. The IMF thus demands policy changes as the quid pro quo for the use of its funds. It also closely monitors the government's policy agreement, releasing its loans only in periodic tranches after being satisfied at each point with the pace of implementation of the program.

IMF adjustment programs have long been subject to strong criticisms by various international actors, however, if not by the creditors. The complaints go beyond the fact that the IMF imposes stringent constraints on developing economies. The stronger complaint is that the IMF often gives poor advice, demands inappropriate policies in exchange for the funds it provides, and is congenitally overoptimistic about recovery. Indeed, time after time, governments—especially the poorest ones—do not complete their Fund programs. The standard defense of IMF policy prescriptions is that the policies would have succeeded if the governments had followed them more assiduously. The reply to that defense is that were governments to have done so, they would have fallen, owing to the political disruptions and economic stresses that implementing the programs engendered. Indeed, for over thirty years the IMF has only lent to developing and "transition economies" (Eastern Europe and successor countries of the former Soviet Union), although it was established for all its members to use. Developed countries have not been willing to subject themselves to IMF "conditionality" as it is now being practiced. If IMF programs were such as to be acceptable in developed countries, adjustment programs in developing countries might look somewhat different.

In addition to concerns about the effectiveness of IMF policy advice, many of the poorest countries accumulated so much debt to the IMF while purportedly attempting to follow its advice that they arrived at a debt crisis vis-à-vis the IMF itself. This is especially troublesome because until recently the IMF never countenanced any relief of member obligations to itself. The "preferred creditor" status of the IMF is a conventional practice and not part of the Articles of Agreement of the Fund. Nevertheless, other creditors, including the private sector, accept it. They do so precisely because the Fund serves as the international lender of last resort and as the globally mandated agent for correcting balance-of-payments problems. Thus, an inability to service IMF debt is a sign of deep financial distress. It means that the country could not service its IMF debt even after receiving all the relief that nonpreferred creditors would accord it.

In fact, the IMF provides some relief from obligations to it of the poorest countries under the international initiative for the HIPCs. It has financed the relief through special operations, in particular using the investment income on the net proceeds from off-market gold sales in 1999.[20] The relief, however, was not enough. Indeed, the governments of the major creditor countries acknowledged this in 2005, and by the end of the year a new Multilateral Debt Relief Initiative (MDRI) had been arranged under which almost all debts owed to the IMF, the World Bank, and the African Development Bank by specified poor and heavily indebted countries would be cancelled in 2006.

The World Bank and regional development banks. The major multilateral development banks were mostly created between the 1940s and 1960s, a period when most governments in the world could not borrow from foreign private sources.[21] Governments joined the World Bank and the regional development banks by purchasing shares denominated in hard currency, with the biggest and richest countries purchasing the largest number of shares.[22] With this strong equity backing mainly from the shareholding of the developed countries, the banks issued their own bonds in the world's largest capital markets at interest rates very close to those of the shareholding developed country governments. The banks have in turn lent these funds for long-term investment projects to developing country members at only a small markup over their own interest cost. The lending decisions have been made by the executive boards, whose composition reflects the shareholdings of different governments in each bank, as must have seemed natural to the bankers and finance ministry personnel who created them. Today, more effective participation of the borrowing governments in decision-making in these institutions is an accepted goal, as in the IMF, as discussed above.

Since the poorest countries could not afford loans on the terms resulting from the resources raised from bond sales, the shareholders of the multilateral banks organized highly subsidized lending "windows," most notably the International Development Association (IDA) of the World Bank. These loans were initially funded by contributions from donor governments in proportions and amounts agreed at each triennial refunding exercise,[23] although they are also funded today from repayments of old loans. The loans have a longer tenor than standard World Bank loans (up to forty years instead of twenty) and a service charge of 0.75 percent in lieu of interest (plus a running commitment charge of 0.50 percent to pay before any funds are drawn). A major focus of interest today is the extent to which even these loans are too expensive for some countries so that only grant financing is warranted for them. Indeed, the IDA is increasingly providing grants instead of loans to the poorest countries.

The difficulty that HIPCs have had in servicing their IMF debt applies equally to their servicing of debts owed to the multilateral development banks. Like the IMF, but for a different reason, these institutions are also regarded as preferred creditors, and until the start of the HIPC Initiative they had not allowed any rescheduling or postponement of their own obligations. The argument against permitting such rescheduling or postponement is that such a practice would worry the buyers of World Bank and other development bank bonds, since they would view the revenue stream of the bank as potentially compromised by debtors not fully servicing their loans. The bond buyers would then demand a higher interest rate to buy new bonds, and all the borrowers from the development banks would suffer. It was thus arguably in the interest of all the borrowers that each borrower service every dollar of its debt on a timely basis.

The primary flaw in this argument is that the poorest countries borrowed only from the highly concessional windows, which were not funded from bond issues. It is hard to imagine that bondholders would not distinguish Mozambique from Mexico. The second flaw is that when it came time for someone to actually cover the obligations that the poorest countries could not pay to the IDA and comparable windows of the regional banks, part of the funds came out of the profits of the banks from their lending to the other countries. This is to say that those somewhat better-off developing countries have paid part of the cost of debt relief for the poorest countries (the rest has come from voluntary donations from the richer countries). Thus, insisting that every penny of debt servicing owed to the multilateral institutions be financed, with no outright forgiveness of the obligations of the HIPCs, has at least partly come at the expense of the non-HIPCs.

Special rules for HIPCs. One way or another, countries qualifying under the HIPC Initiative obtain increasingly deep debt relief from most of their creditors, and the recent MDRI agreement recognized the need to do more. The IMF plays a central role in overseeing this process, as it does for non-HIPCs, although it shares this responsibility more closely with the World Bank in the case of the HIPCs. This is probably because the Bank takes the lead in mobilizing the donors to put up the resources for multilateral debt relief (and that the initiative was started by its former president). But it is probably also because unlike debt relief for other countries, relief under the HIPC program requires that the government develop in consultation with its civil society a package of structural reforms and pro-poor policies that it incorporates into a Poverty Reduction Strategy Paper (PRSP).[24] Debt relief for HIPCs, in other words, is conditioned on the adoption of an agreed set of social policies that are beyond IMF mandates, in addition to the standard economic policies demanded of other debtor governments.

The HIPC/PRSP process starkly raises an international political question: to what extent should sovereign states be subjected to international policy preferences? The powers conferred on the IMF to intervene in national policies are based on the shared global need to contain international financial instability because of the potential it has to damage any and all IMF member countries. (And even here there is no formal compulsion; rather, countries announce their policy changes in "letters of intent" addressed to the IMF.) The founders of the IMF at the Bretton Woods conference had their eyes on the experience during the Great Depression and thus agreed to create a powerful institution that could assert a global adjustment imperative into a national policy context owing to the international impact of national policies. While such IMF influence over the developed countries has atrophied, it retains a strong voice over developing countries. It is hard to justify this asymmetry. If the "global public good" argument that drives IMF interventions is valid, it should apply universally, and it should apply only to policies that pertain to concerns about international financial stability.

In contrast, the goals in establishing the World Bank—also agreed at Bretton Woods—and its regional partners were different and the implications for international policy interference more limited. First and foremost, the goal was to overcome an international financial market "imperfection" and promote the transfer of private financial resources to developing countries through the intermediation of the development banks. As the banks added concessional lending, they expanded into transferring official aid resources to low-income countries under what was intended to be less political "multilateral"—as opposed to "bilateral"—control. The banks, like banks everywhere, needed to assess how their funds would be used and whether they had sufficient confidence they would be repaid. As the development banks are public institutions, however, the staff also had to ensure the loans accorded with the policy priorities of their oversight boards. Here was the slippery slope, as the donor-dominated boards became increasingly ambitious over the years as to what policies the borrowing countries should follow.

One constraint on donor government and development bank power, in this regard, was that there was a measure of competition among donors, from which the recipient governments could choose the most appealing aid offers for their needs. Unfortunately, some aid-receiving countries had more capacity to choose and use funds well than others, and not all donors made offers to all countries. Today, there is less diversity in donor government views, and in the name of enhancing donor coordination the World Bank has strengthened its leadership role among donors, especially as regards assistance to the HIPCs. To the degree that the donors comply (and some still have differing views), the aid-receiving countries face more of a monopoly over aid provision and less donor competition. To be fair, in creating the PRSPs, the development assistance community created the opportunity for local political processes, including domestic civil society participation, to shape the single aid package. Unfortunately, it also seems fair to say this has not yet been very effective in many HIPCs.

Moreover, the "aid relationship" encapsulated in the PRSPs that is being described here—and that through global agreement, as at the United Nations World Summit in September 2005, meant to focus on achieving the Millennium Development Goals—has in practice been subordinated to other policy priorities of the donors and creditors. Thus, each time from 1996 to 2004 when the official creditors asked themselves how much debt relief the HIPCs needed to reach debt sustainability, they completely couched their analysis in financial terms, focusing on what they regarded as relatively safe levels of ratios of debt to exports or output or fiscal revenue. They also underestimated how much relief was needed. Furthermore, they pressed for domestic policies that would financially benefit the investors and export sectors of the donor countries.

But civil society advocates had been claiming for years with some reason that despite HIPC relief, low-income countries were still servicing their debt at the expense of anti-poverty and development programs. They called on the aid-giving governments to instead set their relief targets in light of the social opportunity cost of debt servicing, which warranted deeper relief than had been accorded based on purely financial terms.

One may say that this argument finally carried the day in 2005 with the MDRI and that the opportunity exists for domestic political processes in a number of countries—in particular, where civil society organizations are able to play their advocacy and monitoring role—for local priorities to shape the use of the budgetary funds freed up by the MDRI. Yet it also remains to be seen to what extent the MDRI frees additional resources on a net basis for development in the HIPCs (that is, one needs to monitor the degree to which other flows are not cut back). And it should be recalled that MDRI applies only to a limited number of poor countries. In addition, the neoliberal conditions for obtaining debt relief have not been relaxed. In sum, while there has recently been important progress, the tension over whether financial or development priorities should govern official debt relief is not yet fully resolved.

DO THE PIECES COHERE AS A FAIR GAME?

Although the present arrangements for HIPCs and other countries clearly concentrate power on the side of the creditors, it should be noted that they are actually less unbalanced than the case of private corporate bankruptcy proceedings, where creditors hold almost all of the power over the disposition of the bankrupt enterprise. Defaulting on obligations to creditors is considered a serious breach of property rights, which are considered an essential aspect of a well-functioning market economy.

A question that is central to recent debates on sovereign debt crises is whether the treatment of sovereign governments should be modeled on U.S. bankruptcy laws, which embody an option to allow the bankrupt entity a "fresh start." The proposal is not to model sovereign bankruptcy on the U.S. treatment of bankrupt corporations, in which power is very heavily concentrated in the creditors, as noted, but rather in the treatment of municipalities facing bankruptcy.[25] When municipalities and other sub-sovereign public entities in the United States go bankrupt, a separate part of the U.S. bankruptcy code (Chapter 9) is applied. Some have suggested that the model ought to be adopted to deal with sovereign insolvency too, since it seems more evenhanded in its treatment of creditors and debtors. Sub-sovereign public entities within the United States, however, are responsible to the states. At present, there is no comparable responsible authority at the global level over sovereign governments, nor is there a comparable legal system or enforcement mechanism. Strictly speaking, then, Chapter 9 is an inapplicable model, though the question remains whether arrangements that share some of its features would improve on the present process for resolving sovereign debt crises.

Instead of a bankruptcy regime, the "international community," as represented by the IMF and World Bank, plays something like the role of central overseer/umpire, most explicitly in the HIPC debt workouts. The Fund and Bank executive boards, which include developing countries—if only with a minority voice—as well as developed countries, can be said to coordinate the official creditors, who account for almost all of the debt, as such poor countries usually have only limited amounts of defaulted private debt. Many people believe the process has not worked well. The relief accorded has been halting and inadequate. It is given in stages, like the tranches of IMF adjustment financing, albeit over a longer period of time. And when the final arrangement is agreed and the relief becomes "irrevocable," only some of the creditors cancel the obligations straightforwardly; others commit to cover the debt servicing as it falls due year in and year out for decades to come, as necessary, which is less assured.

Not surprisingly, there have been many strong criticisms of the HIPC process, not least that it has not been successful in bringing about sufficient debt relief to enable HIPCs to enter onto sustainable development paths. The HIPC Initiative was ten years old in 2006, and as of late 2006 only twenty of forty countries that have been targeted as potential beneficiaries had reached the "completion point" in the process. Moreover, as noted above, even that amount of relief was considered insufficient, and it is being supplemented by the MDRI. But then after the "final" completion point, the multilateral institutions and government donors will again offer new loans to the borrowers and perhaps begin a new cycle of debt buildup leading to debt forgiveness. The alternative would be to provide more assistance in the form of grants, but the major creditor governments also do not seem willing to increase the level of grant assistance adequately to replace potentially unsustainable borrowing. Moreover, one could say that the entire mind-set in which the HIPC Initiative operated has been wrong. It is as if the relief was a reward for adhering to an adjustment program rather than an acknowledgment that the country was insolvent and its obligations unpayable (or payable only at the expense of essential public expenditures for development).

In the case of non-HIPCs in debt difficulty—and post-HIPCs should they again require relief at some future time—there is no effective international coordination mechanism for the debt workout. There is the mixture of private and official creditors discussed above. Each class of creditors seeks the best deal it can get when a restructuring is necessary: commercial banks through a London Club, bondholders through various bondholder committees, government creditors through the Paris Club, and others independently. There is no forum in which to put the pieces together in a coherent way, see if they add up to what the state needs, and adjust the terms as necessary so that the state's needs are met.

Not having such an international mechanism may actually serve a purpose for the international community. It makes it easier to postpone what would otherwise be an essential international conversation on what principles should guide such a comprehensive debt-restructuring process, on where *justice* would lie in treating the debt of countries in crisis. That is not a sufficient excuse, however. Let us have this conversation. What would be a fair treatment of unsustainable sovereign debt?

NOTES

[1] In the United States and the United Kingdom, where most international borrowing is arranged, sovereign governments are considered immune from lawsuits except when they engage in "commercial activity." Government borrowing is considered such an activity (and explicit waivers of sovereign immunity are standard clauses in loan or bond contracts). This only means, however, that a private creditor can sue a sovereign debtor in court in New York or London. Winning a settlement is rare, and collecting on it is far rarer still.

[2] It is widely held that taxpayers are justified in insisting on government regulation and supervision of privately owned banks in a market economy precisely because of this contingent claim on them owing to the essential public service that banks provide. The concern is that the failure of a single bank not spook confidence in banks in general and provoke a systemic crisis. This is an additional argument to the perhaps more standard one that deposit insurance should be coupled with official supervision to reduce the claims on the insurance fund from failed banks.

[3] The exception is a small loan of essentially the country's own foreign-currency membership payment, called the "reserve tranche."

[4] In light of the greater complexity and speed of banking transactions today, regulators have increasingly focused oversight on the methods ("models") used for risk management instead of the contents of a given loan portfolio itself at the moment of the regulators' visit, especially for the larger, internationally active banks.

[5] Vulnerability to pressure to continue lending is especially the case for banks that are government owned, many of which still exist in developing countries.

[6] This only ended after shareholders in the banks and regulators increasingly expressed alarm about the "distressed debt" the banks were holding half a decade after the crisis began and the Brady Plan developed a mechanism under which banks agreed to accept less than face value on their loans. Many of the banks then ceased to make further such loans to governments.

[7] The risk-free rate was typically the rate that the major banks charge each other for loans in London, the world's deepest financial market. As sovereign bank loans usually paid interest semi-annually, the interest rate would be calculated as the six-month London inter-bank offer rate (LIBOR) plus the preset risk premium.

[8] Left to their own devices, each bank could have waited for the other banks to lend the funds to prevent a formal default; only by bringing the banks together and jointly agreeing to lend the country the funds to continue to service the loans could outright default be avoided, which thus became known as "concerted" or "forced" lending.

[9] In the final set of debt workouts for the 1980s crises, the IMF and international development banks lent additional funds to the governments to help them purchase so-called zero coupon U.S. Treasury bonds (these bonds pay the total sum of their interest upon maturity of the bond). As the value of these bonds at maturity would equal the debts falling due, they guaranteed repayment and sweetened the final restructuring deals. There were also "rolling guarantees" of interest payments in a number of the agreements, in essence insuring the "next" payments falling due.

[10] From the developing country government's perspective, the interest rate on foreign-issued bonds in hard currency may be a small fraction of that paid on domestic currency bonds, where the interest rate and inflation environments are very different.

[11] In fact, the simplest way to accomplish the same thing would be to newly borrow enough funds to cover the payments falling due and repay that new loan later; thus, asking to restructure a bond means the government's reputation has already sagged so much that it has lost "access" to the market and cannot issue new bonds.

[12] One contentious issue between governments and private creditor representatives (as expressed in discussions of a prospective "code of good conduct" for countries and their private creditors) has been who should pay for the expenses of a creditor committee. The reader may imagine how the different sides of this dispute aligned themselves.

[13] Based on detailed estimates by Federico Sturzenegger and Jeromin Zettelmeyer, "Haircuts: Estimating Investor Losses in Sovereign Debt Restructurings, 1998–2005," IMF Working Paper No. 05-137, July 2005.

[14] Having defaulted at the end of 2001, Argentina made a take-it-or-leave-it swap offer of new bonds for old valued by the market at about thirty cents on the dollar in early 2005, and its Congress essentially declared that any original bonds remaining after the swap would be null and void; Argentina had claimed its bondholders had all along refused to enter into serious negotiations despite trying to engage them. The bondholders, on their side, said it was hard to negotiate, since the government was asking them to absorb unprecedented losses, which most of them did, as in the end 76 percent of the bondholders agreed to the swap.

[15] This is neither to deny that ODA debt is in practice often treated differently in negotiated debt restructuring, nor that several creditor governments long ago converted all their ODA loans into grants; it is rather that the practice is not universal, and considerable bilateral ODA is still given as loans and repayment is insisted upon and renegotiated as part of debt restructurings after recipient governments default.

[16] Although the Iraqi and Nigerian cases can be claimed as falling under the Evian Approach, the reality is that political forces and not economics drove the analysis.

[17] Following global recognition of the governance issue when heads of state and government included it in the Monterrey Consensus at the United Nations International Conference on Financing for Development in March 2002, it entered the agendas of the ministerial committees that oversee the IMF and World Bank. In April 2006, the IMF committee requested that concrete proposals for reform of the IMF be presented at its next meeting in September 2006, when it endorsed a two-year program of "quota and voice reforms."

[18] The phrase "lender of last resort" is used in a different sense here than in discussions of national central banks providing short-term loans to replace liquidity in the commercial banks in a domestic banking crisis.

[19] The IMF insists, nevertheless, that it does not and should not intervene in actual debtor-creditor negotiations on the terms of relief. Private creditors agree with the Fund on this, and one of the reasons that they so forcefully resisted the IMF initiative to create the Sovereign Debt Restructuring Mechanism in 2003 is they feared that the IMF would manipulate the debt negotiations from behind the scenes.

[20] The IMF has a large stock of gold, mainly paid in by members in its early years. The gold is valued on the IMF's books at an artificially low price and so any sale at market prices provides very large capital gains. The constraint on selling the gold is that gold-producing countries fear it will reduce the market price of their gold exports. The 1999 sale was thus artfully designed so the gold never hit the market and the sale was almost immediately reversed when the buying governments (Brazil and Mexico) used the gold to make loan payments to the Fund, leaving the IMF with its original physical volume of gold intact, albeit with some of it now carried on its books at the current market price.

[21] The exception is the European Bank for Reconstruction and Development, which was created in 1991 to assist in the economic transition of the formerly centrally planned economies of eastern and central Europe and the former Soviet Union. Its primary mission is to nurture private-sector development in those countries.

22 Governments actually had to purchase outright only a fraction of the value of their shares as "paid-in capital," the rest being "callable."

23 The IDA completed its fourteenth replenishment in 2005.

24 In fact, many governments have prepared PRSPs with limited consultation, and in some cases World Bank staff themselves prepared PRSP drafts on an interim basis. While some fault the Bank for not pushing hard enough for civil society involvement (or for not taking challenging civil society views on board when expressed), the PRSP exercise seems a unique foreign intervention into borrowing country politics.

25 The argument has forcefully been made by Kunibert Raffer, this volume, pp. 127–50.

Fairness in Sovereign Debt
Christian Barry and Lydia Tomitova*

When can we say that a debt crisis has been resolved fairly? That is, what makes processes of debt restructuring, debt cancellation, or the enforcement of debt contracts more or less fair, or the outcomes of such processes better or worse? These are not idle questions. The recent economic collapse in Argentina and financial crisis in Turkey, and the persistent unsustainable debt burdens of many developing countries highlight the practically urgent problem of excessive indebtedness. High debt levels can limit a sovereign government's capacity to provide social services necessary for the well-being of its citizens, and divert resources and energy from the pursuit of long-term development strategies. In addition, after a government defaults, the mechanisms for managing the restructuring of sovereign debt usually act slowly, do not return the country to debt sustainability, and often leave the different classes of creditors as well as the people of the indebted country feeling as if they have been treated unfairly. This in turn can create disincentives for lending and investment that can be crucial to the prospects of developed and developing countries alike. An often overlooked but very important effect of financial crises and the debts that often engender them is that they can lead the crisis countries to increased dependence on international institutions and the policy conditionality they require in return for their continued support, limiting their capabilities and those of their citizens to exercise meaningful control over their policies and institutions.

These outcomes have been viewed by many not merely as extremely *unfortunate* and *regrettable*, but also as deeply *unfair*. And indeed, increasingly

* A version of this essay was published in *Social Research* 74, no. 2 (2006), pp. 649–69. It draws on two working papers by Christian Barry: "Ethical Issues Relevant to Debt," and "A dívida soberana como problema ético: algumas considerações preliminares." We are grateful for comments by Michael Cohen, Álvaro de Vita, Sakiko Fukuda-Parr, Ludmila Palazzo, Thomas Pogge, Kunibert Raffer, Sanjay Reddy, and Alys Willman-Navarro, and especially to Barry Herman and Robert Hockett for their detailed written comments. We are also grateful to the Ford Foundation for providing funding for the project "Ethics and Debt," and to the Carnegie Council for supporting our work.

potent popular movements have pressured governments, financial institutions, and the financial community to seek what they take to be fairer solutions to debt crises. Some of these resulting initiatives, including that for the Heavily Indebted Poor Countries (HIPC), have focused on defining sustainable debt levels for poor countries and designing policies to maintain debt at these levels. Other proposals, such as the Fair and Transparent Arbitration Process, which could serve a similar function (albeit without the same enforcement authority) at the global level to legal bankruptcy regimes under national law, have sought means of distinguishing between debts for which creditors deserve full repayment from those for which creditors either lack claims or have claims that are too weak to recover what they have lent.[1] Still others have instead recommended a contractual approach to sovereign debt crises, in which new clauses are introduced into bond contracts to enable debts to be restructured more easily and quickly.[2]

The merits of these programs and proposals for dealing more fairly with sovereign debt remain hotly disputed. In this essay, we try to take a step back from the political fray and examine some more fundamental considerations that seem relevant to assessing the fairness of current arrangements governing economic exchanges related to debt contracts and alternatives that have been (or might be) proposed to them.

Our discussion is organized into seven sections. First, we characterize briefly the concept of fairness and its role in social evaluation. Second, we clarify what sovereign debt is, and, third, the ethical statuses that particular sovereign debts can have. Fourth, we identify and describe the main features of current practices related to sovereign debt. Fifth, we describe an "ideal picture" of creditor/debtor relations. We argue that in such a scenario a broad range of ethical considerations can plausibly be invoked in support of practices that closely resemble those presently governing sovereign debt. Sixth, we draw attention to the many ways in which in reality the relations between sovereign debtors and their creditors differ markedly from the relationships between the creditor and debtor in the ideal picture. Because of this, many of the ethical considerations that would support present practices were relations between sovereign debtors and their creditors to resemble more closely those depicted in the ideal picture fail to do so under present circumstances. We conclude, moreover, that the remaining

Christian Barry and Lydia Tomitova

ethical considerations that might be advanced in support of the present system are at best quite inconclusive. Finally, we describe briefly specific reform proposals to current practices. While we will not attempt to prove that these proposals would necessarily make the rules governing economic exchanges relevant to sovereign debt more fair, we conclude, in light of our earlier analysis, that they must be given much more serious consideration than they have so far received in policy circles. Indeed, there are strong prima facie reasons to believe that some combination of these proposed policies might prevent or mitigate some of the most ethically regrettable outcomes of present practices and norms by changing the incentives of sovereign borrowers and those who lend to them.

THE CONCEPT OF FAIRNESS

Fairness and unfairness are core ethical predicates, which are broad in application, complex in structure, and morally deep in content. They are *broad in application*, since many different kinds of things are said to be fair or unfair. We speak variously of persons *being* unfair, for example, when they typically fail to consider the feelings of others. We refer to the conduct of agents (persons, firms, governments, and so on) as *treating* others unfairly—such as when these agents fail to deal with others evenhandedly or show them respect. We also sometimes claim that social institutions *affect* or *treat* agents or groups unfairly—for example, when they include rules that allocate scarce resources or valued occupations and positions of authority on the basis of such apparently ethically arbitrary characteristics as race, gender, or religious affiliation. Finally, we judge outcomes—such as the fact that some people are much worse off than others through no fault of their own, or perhaps that people whose conduct toward others is fair suffer terrible misfortunes while others who conduct themselves unfairly enjoy good fortune—as unfair.

The concepts of fairness and unfairness are *complex in structure*. Social institutions, such as laws governing what kinds of things can be owned, how they can be acquired, transferred, relinquished, and forfeited, the manner in which decisions concerning trade policy and the monetary system are made, and so on, can be judged to be *distributively* unfair—perhaps because they leave many badly off and a few very well off; *procedurally* unfair—perhaps because they systematically disadvantage some in economic competition; or *metaprocedurally* unfair—perhaps because these arrangements were first fixed when many who should have had some say in their content were excluded from voting or other forms of political participation.

The concepts of fairness and unfairness are also *morally deep* in content. To call an institution unfair is to claim that there are strong reasons to reform it, and to claim that a person is treating another unfairly is to claim that she has strong reasons to alter her conduct. Indeed, unlike reasons to act charitably, beneficently, or kindly, reasons based on fairness are usually taken to state quite stringent ethical requirements. This is perhaps particularly true with respect to the ethical assessment of social institutions. Reasons based on fairness to reform some social rule, such as electoral procedures that exclude many competent adults within a country from voting for political representatives, for example, are generally taken to be not only stringent but *decisive* unless undertaking such reforms will likely bring about still greater unfairness elsewhere in the social system.[3] More controversially, it has been argued that particular individuals may sometimes lack decisive reasons to work for the reform of an unfair institution when doing so will require of them significant personal sacrifice, or when they have not themselves contributed substantially to its unfairness.

Discussions of fairness with respect to sovereign debt relate mainly to two topics: (1) the conduct of sovereigns and other agents involved in borrowing and lending financial resources; and (2) rules governing the borrowing and lending of financial resources between sovereigns and other agents.

Topic (1) involves the assessment of various actors involved in sovereign borrowing and lending, and the specification of the ethical norms that should guide their contractual behavior, such as whether lenders should be more discriminating about the sovereigns to whom they should provide resources, and whether sovereigns ought to have made sounder borrowing decisions, been more honest in their dealings with creditors (and their own people), or acted more fairly in their decisions regarding domestic budgetary expenditures. Topic (2) relates to the assessment of rules that govern economic exchanges relevant to the practice of sovereign borrowing, and the ethical norms that should guide actors in designing them. These rules include those governing the kinds of contracts that sovereign borrowers and creditors are permitted to enter; the circumstances under which contracts entered into are to be considered legitimate; the conditions (if any) under which legitimate contracts of sovereign borrowers should no longer be considered to bind them to repay their creditors on the terms stipulated in them; and those determining the steps that creditors and others are permitted to take in order to enforce contracts that are considered to bind sovereign debtors (including informal practices, such as debt workouts).[4]

In the remainder of this essay we will emphasize topic (2). This is not because topic (1) is irrelevant or less important. Surely the conduct of agents involved in lending and borrowing *is* quite relevant to many of the regrettable features of the current situation. There is little doubt that were creditors to act (and to have acted) in their lending decisions less recklessly and with more regard to the harms their conduct imposes on others, and if sovereigns had made sounder borrowing decisions and used the resources acquired through these borrowings in a way that was more beneficial to their general population, the outcomes of present practices would be much better.

Indeed, it is partly because of the clear interconnections between these topics that we will emphasize topic (2). Determining whether the rules governing economic exchanges relevant to sovereign debt are unfair and developing a more informed view of what alternative arrangements might be fairer will enable us to provide a fuller ethical assessment of the actors involved in sovereign debt, since it is they who institute, benefit from, uphold, or contrarily seek to reform existing rules. For example, however decently a lender may conduct itself in its direct dealings with sovereigns— for example, avoiding loans to notably corrupt regimes that are unlikely to use resources to benefit their people—our overall ethical assessment of its conduct may not be particularly positive if it is actively engaged in lobbying its government to support rules governing debt workouts that seem on balance to treat sovereign debtors unfairly. Furthermore, our assessment of whether the rules governing economic interaction relevant to sovereign debt are fair will significantly influence even our *descriptions* of the interactions among different agents involved in borrowing and lending. Whether, for example, it is deemed to be a legitimate expression of national self-determination when the central bank of a country raises interest rates unilaterally, even when this harms the economic prospects of other countries, or is instead thought to exclude illegitimately those who can be significantly affected by political decisions from exercising some degree of influence over them, will significantly influence our assessment of the responsibilities of developing countries and the United States with respect to the 1980s debt crisis. If we affirm that such policies were indeed a legitimate expression of national self-determination, then the United States having undertaken it will be considered as part of the background circumstances that developing countries ought to have taken into account in deciding whether and on what terms to borrow, and equally their creditors in deciding to lend.[5] If, on the other hand, such policies are judged to have been illegitimately undertaken because they were procedurally or metaprocedurally unfair, then the claims of the United States (and perhaps other creditors) to amounts lent to developing countries may reasonably be viewed as weakened due to the fact that they have unfairly and significantly harmed the economic prospects of these borrowers through their domestic policies.[6] Indeed, if such decisions are deemed to have been illegitimately undertaken, these claims may be viewed as weakened even if evidence that such policies did cause such harm is inconclusive.[7]

THE MEANING OF SOVEREIGN DEBT

What is sovereign debt? To answer this question, we need to have a clear idea of what sovereigns are and what debt is. It is widely recognized that the idea of sovereignty (and thus of a sovereign) is contestable.[8] That the question of what debt consists in is also much more complex than may at first appear, however, is not often noted. It might be argued that A owes a debt to B when B has provided some benefit to A and has asserted a claim to repayment. This obviously won't do, however, since the mere fact that B claims that A owes it repayment for something does not show that A is indebted to B. Indeed, people make false and spurious claims all the time and it would be misleading to suggest that rejecting such claims amounts to "debt relief" or that by withdrawing them a creditor has thereby "reduced its claims" on a "debtor." It is more natural in such cases to claim that there

Christian Barry and Lydia Tomitova

were no debts to begin with, only invalid claims that have been rightly rejected. It may therefore be appropriate to define debt in terms of *ethically* valid claims. That is, A owes a debt to B only if B has a valid moral claim to repayment from A. This *moralized* understanding of debt has many things to recommend it. Indeed, speaking of "debt relief" and "voluntary" reduction of "claims" suggests, often misleadingly, that the creditors involved had morally valid claims to repayment and are therefore offering "assistance" to poor countries—to which they can attach whatever conditions they like. What is at issue, it may be argued, is whether these countries really have such debts in the first place, and not the conditions under which they should be "forgiven," since speaking in terms of "forgiveness" essentially assumes the validity of the creditor's claims.

While we are in sympathy with this account and believe that the concerns it expresses are very important, we fear that it may cause some confusion in evaluating the current debate on sovereign debt, which has been framed (for better or worse) in terms of the conditions under which (and terms on which) debts should be repaid. For this reason, we will understand the concept of debt in terms of the following definition:

A owes a debt to B if and only if:

(1) B has lent resources to A; and,
(2) B has a claim to repayment from A that has at least prima facie legal validity.

We will assume, moreover, that it makes sense to distinguish between legally valid and ethically valid claims. That is, while determinations of legal validity may depend in part on ethical considerations,[9] and while the fact that one has a legally valid claim may be seen as an important ethical consideration in determining whether one should be repaid, there are many contexts in which those who have legally valid claims to repayment lack ethically valid claims to repayment and in which those who lack legally valid obligations to repay nevertheless have ethically valid obligations to repay. Conflicts between legally valid and ethically valid claims and obligations will be most pronounced when legal systems are unjust or when they contain many "gaps," but it is unlikely that such conflicts can ever be completely removed.

We can distinguish between the ethical statuses of different types of debt. At the first level, a distinction can be drawn between those debts for which the debtor:

(a) has an ethical obligation to repay; and,
(b) has no ethical obligation to repay.

When an agent has an obligation to do something, this provides her with a reason to do it. However, obligations to do something do not necessarily provide decisive or under some circumstances even particularly weighty reasons to do it.[10] One may sometimes have conclusive reason not to honor one's obligations, such as when one fails to show up for an important professional meeting because of a family emergency. Even in cases where one does the ethically correct thing by failing to honor one's obligations, obligations matter, since one typically must make efforts to compensate those to whom one has failed to honor them.[11] Having missed the meeting, I must be willing to take pains to reschedule it (if possible) in a way that is convenient for others. Among those debts that the debtor is ethically obliged to repay, we can therefore distinguish between:

(i) debts that the debtor *ought* to repay;
(ii) debts that the debtor may *permissibly* repay or not repay; and,
(iii) debts that the debtor nevertheless *ought not* to repay.

Finally, it may be that one ought to repay debts even when she is not ethically obliged to do so, such as when failing to repay an invalid debt will hurt her credit rating and thus diminish opportunities for future borrowing that is essential to the economic prospects of her family. Among those debts for which the debtor is not ethically obliged to repay, a distinction can therefore also be drawn between:

(i) debts that the debtor *ought* still repay;
(ii) debts that the debtor may *permissibly* pay or not pay; and,
(iii) debts that the debtor *ought not* to repay.

Christian Barry and Lydia Tomitova

We can also distinguish between debts in terms of the attitudes that *creditors* ought to take toward them. I may have a valid claim that my employee repay a small loan that I have extended to him, but nevertheless do the right thing by forgiving it if he can repay it only at great sacrifice and I will in no way suffer from his nonperformance. We sometimes have "a right to do wrong."[12] Among those debts that the debtor is obliged to repay, a distinction can therefore be drawn between:

(i) debts for which the owner of the debt *ought* (in part or entirely) *not to demand* repayment (and thus to "forgive");
(ii) debts for which the owner of the debt *may permissibly demand* or *not demand* repayment; and,
(iii) debts for which the owner of the debt *ought to demand* repayment.

Among those debts that the debtor is not obliged to repay, we can similarly distinguish between:

(i) debts for which the owner of the debt *ought not to* demand repayment;
(ii) debts for which the owner of the debt *may permissibly demand* repayment; and,
(iii) debts for which the owner of the debt *ought to demand* repayment.

These last two possibilities ((ii) and (iii)) may seem odd, but they are not difficult to imagine, especially in the context of debts incurred by collective agents such as governments. We may think, for example, that country A has no obligation to repay a debt to country B because the debt was incurred by a murderous military dictatorship that used its resources to repress and impoverish the population. Suppose, however, that although this dictatorship is no longer in power it has been replaced by a corrupt and wasteful regime that consistently misallocates public funds in harmful ways. A creditor country may plausibly demand repayment from such a regime if it has strong reason to believe that these resources would do more harm than good if left in the regime's hands, especially if the creditor country uses these funds to lessen the suffering of the debtor country's residents or that of other unjustly impoverished persons.

TABLE 1

	Debtor has ethical obligation to repay			Debtor has no ethical obligation to repay		
Debtor	Ought to repay	May permissibly repay	Ought not to repay	Ought to repay	May permissibly repay	Ought not to repay
Creditor	Ought to demand repayment	May permissibly demand repayment	Ought to forgive	Ought to demand repayment	May demand repayment	Ought not to demand repayment

Finally, one can distinguish between the ethical status of a debt, and the ethical status of *particular claims regarding the terms* on which the debtor is obliged to repay it. It may be tempting to think that this distinction is not really important. After all, when a debt contract is made, it typically stipulates the schedule on which it is to be repaid. Insofar as there is an ethically valid claim to repayment of the debt at all, it might be argued, there ought to be an ethically valid claim to repayment on the terms under which it was incurred. This seems intuitively implausible, however. Suppose that I freely borrow resources from A on terms that I repay him in monthly installments over the course of the following year. Due to an accident, however, I find myself unable to work for a period of six months, after which I will resume earning a salary at the same level. If during the period of incapacitation I stick with the payment schedule stipulated in the initial agreement, I will be unable to afford physical therapy and pay for other basic necessities, which will raise the risk that I will never be sufficiently rehabilitated to resume work. It seems plausible to claim that the mere fact of my injury does not shield me from A's claim to repayment. Indeed, if it remains much more difficult than anticipated to repay A even after I resume full-time work, it may nevertheless plausibly be maintained that I am obliged to repay the full amount. However, it seems less plausible to claim that I am obliged to repay according to the original schedule.[13]

These considerations are relevant for evaluating issues that frequently arise in the debt context. When an agent is unable to keep up with payments or can only do so at unacceptable sacrifice, that agent is typically expected at least to continue to pay the interest owed on the principal. This means that, insofar as the agent is unable to pay according to schedule, the entire amount that will be paid out by the debtor to the creditor can grow. The ethical claim of the lender to "full" repayment thus becomes ambiguous, since it can refer to the principal (plus the interest attached to each monthly payment as stipulated in the original agreement) or it can refer to the principal, interest on monthly payments stipulated in the original agreement, and any additional interest and penalty payments that arise because the debtor does not meet its monthly obligations. If we believe that there are compelling reasons to diverge from the stipulated payment schedule even while honoring the obligation to repay the principal, then we may hold that creditors lack ethical claims to the additional interest that might otherwise be thought to be owed to them if the debtor is unable to meet its monthly payments.

The reasons for modifying the terms on which claims can be repaid may seem much more decisive when, unlike in our simple example, the lender's behavior unfairly and adversely affects the debtor in a way that makes it much more difficult for the debtor to meet its obligations as stipulated in the contract.

The discussion so far has identified the ethical statuses that debts may have, but has provided relatively little guidance about how to determine which status particular debts have or the fairness of rules governing economic exchanges relevant to sovereign debt. We have merely provided categories without indicating which kinds of considerations are relevant for determining which debts fall into which category. Next, we examine issues that are relevant to this task.

THE CENTRAL FEATURES OF THE CURRENT PRACTICE

Sovereign contracts are entered, on the borrower side, by national governments ("sovereign debtors") and, on the lender side, by national governments ("official/bilateral creditors"), international financial institutions, such as the IMF, World Bank, or regional development banks ("multilateral creditors"), or bondholders and commercial banks ("private creditors").[14]

Internal and External Sovereignty
When a finance minister or other public official makes the decision to borrow money in the name of the government, the debts incurred are

recognized and treated as an obligation of the country as a whole, which in turn raises revenues to service its debt (at least in part) from taxes imposed on citizens and other subjects taxable by the government.[15] When a new government comes to power, all of the debts that were obligations of the previous regime are treated as the new government's. Indeed, this is true even in cases of state succession and dissolution, as specified in the 1983 Vienna Convention on State Succession in Respect of Property, Archives and Debts. Since the debt is serviced primarily from tax revenues, the present and future citizens (and other subjects taxable by the borrowing government) are therefore held liable to repay it. As such, ministers or public officials (and the government more generally) thus enjoy not only *internal sovereignty*—unique power and authority within their state—but also *external sovereignty*—unique power to alter the claims of others on their present and future citizens and residents, and thus the privileges of these citizens and residents with respect to them.[16] Governments have nearly unlimited privileges in what they may legally borrow, although of course creditors are at liberty not to extend credit to them.

Unlimited Lending Privileges

Corollary to the external sovereignty of governments to borrow, creditors have the unlimited privilege to lend to whichever sovereign regimes they wish, in whatever amounts they deem fit, and on whatever terms they consider desirable. Their claims against the countries that have borrowed from them are in no way affected by either the nature of the political organization of the country to which they lend, the circumstances that it confronts, or the uses to which it puts the borrowed resources.

Three Features of Sovereign Debt Contracts

At present, debt contracts that are formed between sovereign borrowers and their creditors have three main features. First, they are *rigid*: debt is to be paid according to regular schedules, without consideration of changing circumstances of the creditor or debtor or of the environment in which they interact. Second, they are *neutral*: what sovereign borrowers choose to do with the resources they borrow has no effect on the claims of creditors upon them (and thus also the claims that they have on their citizens and other tax subjects). Third, they are *extensive*: no present or future citizen or tax subject of the debtor country is shielded from obligations to repay debts.

Pacta Sunt Servanda

Pacta sunt servanda, or "pacts must be respected," is the basic norm that underlies the present treatment of sovereign debt contracts. When a sovereign borrower defaults, it is treated as being in breach of contract and under obligation to repay the full amount of the loan, along with any interest that the contract stipulates must be added to the principal under such conditions. Unless a creditor decides to "forgive" a debt, then it retains full rights to claim it. There is no forum in which a debtor can bring a claim that its obligations under the contract should be considered invalid, or that it may permissibly act in contravention of its contractual obligations, unless the creditor has failed to disburse the resources as stipulated in the contract. Indeed, the principle of *pacta sunt servanda* is so entrenched in present practice that any discussion of the reduction of claims of creditors is described in terms of "relief," "assistance," and "forgiveness." Indeed, the strong presumption against voiding or fundamentally altering contracts—for example, in sovereign bankruptcy procedures—is evident in the two major policies that were implemented in response to the severe 1982 debt crisis. The Baker plan, which combined increased lending to restructure repayments falling due with "market-oriented reforms," and the Brady plan, under which nonperforming loans were swapped for bonds of reduced value, were both designed to restructure or refinance existing claims, even at a discount from original value, but avoid defaults or voided contracts.

While there are, of course, limits on what creditors can do to enforce their claims, there are powerful incentives for borrowers to repay them, even if they deem them to be in some way illegitimate.[17] And the general view of the private creditors is that domestic and international law should be reformed to make contracts more enforceable.[18] Their view is partly motivated by a desire to make *creditors themselves* more disciplined in entering into contracts. It is also a call to the intention of the G-7 countries (the major bilateral creditors) and the IMF to end the practice of providing "rescue" packages to debtor governments, even those of strategic importance. It is also motivated by a strong belief that a sovereign's failing to honor its contractual obligations involves the unfair treatment of creditors.

Governments that anticipate that they may have trouble servicing their debts are always at liberty to request that their creditors restructure the repayment obligations of their loans. Traditionally, bonds issued under British law could carry out such a restructuring of payments if a supermajority of creditors, specified in the bond contract, agreed. Under New York law, unanimity was required traditionally, but has been superseded by specified supermajorities under the collective action clauses. (Still, in both cases, the more usual mechanism is to swap a new bond for the old one, rather than reschedule payments on the old bond). On the other hand, in both jurisdictions a specified minority of dissatisfied bondholders can "accelerate" a bond when the issuer is in distress, in which case the bond would be fully and immediately repayable, usually precipitating default if it had not already occurred. In practice, there have been cooperative arrangements in which bondholders have agreed to voluntary exchanges of old bonds for new ones (as in the recent cases involving Uruguay and the Dominican Republic). There have also been contentious cases in which bonds were accelerated, forcing default (as in the case of Ecuador), and fiercely fought bond exchanges when eventually a deal was struck with enough creditors accepting the new bonds for the exchange to become valid (Argentina).

Indeed, when combined with the rigidity of sovereign contracts, *pacta sunt servanda* leads to so-called vulture funds—private investor firms, which purchase the strongly devalued debt of financially troubled governments for the sole purpose of seeking to profit from the distress of the borrower. One way is refusing to participate in future restructuring and instead seeking to recover the full value of the bonds by taking the government of the borrowing country to court. For example, in 2000, after four years in the courts, Elliott Associates, a U.S. hedge fund that bought "distressed" Peruvian bank loans for $11.8 million, forced the government to settle for almost $56 million.[19] Currently, Elliott Associates is suing the Republic of Congo (Brazzaville) to recover $400 million on a claim it purchased for $10 million.[20] Most recently, the High Court in London ruled that Zambia is to pay $20 million to Donegal International, a vulture fund which bought the Zambian debt from Romania for less than $4 million in 1999.[21] In the aftermath

Christian Barry and Lydia Tomitova

of Argentina's default, 24 percent of all private creditors refused to participate in a negotiated restructuring (in which Argentina paid 25 cents on each dollar it owed). Some thirty-nine suits have been filed by non-cooperating bondholders, in which they are seeking to recover $7 billion in currently defaulted bonds.[22] Among these is NML Capital, an offshore hedge fund affiliated with Elliott Associates, which has sued Argentina for the recovery of more than $170 million of bonds it bought at a deep discount.[23]

The emerging practice of inserting collective action clauses into bonds, which bind all bondholders by the decision of a supermajority to agree to some restructuring deal with a sovereign debtor, partly diminishes the rigidity of sovereign debt contracts, but it does not substantially diminish the centrality of the norm of *pacta sunt servanda*, since creditors *considered as a class* retain full rights with respect to how to treat a debt.[24] And, such clauses have been designed only for private, and not official creditors.[25]

The preeminence of *pacta sunt servanda* may also help to explain why no transparent criteria regarding eligibility for debt reductions exist.[26] Insofar as debt relief is conceived as involving the fully voluntary reduction of a rightful claim, then why should creditors not be permitted to exercise broad discretion with respect to their choice of beneficiaries and the terms on which such benefits are conferred?

CONTRACTUAL RIGHTS AND OBLIGATIONS: THE IDEAL PICTURE

What justifications might be given for *pacta sunt servanda* as the fundamental norm governing economic exchanges related to sovereign debt, for granting governments internal and external sovereignty, and for maintaining debt contracts that are rigid, neutral, and extensive? To examine this question, it is useful to explore some of the considerations in favor of allowing agents to make binding agreements with one another involving the provision of resources by one in exchange for certain rights to demand resources in the future from the other.

Let us imagine that there are two agents, A and B, who are faced with the choice of whether to make an agreement with one another. This agreement—in the form of a debt contract—would involve the provision of resources from A to B in return for B's promising to repay A according to a schedule agreed in advance.

Let us imagine that the interaction between A and B is characterized by the following conditions:

(1) *Rational Individualism.* A and B are simple, individual agents with ordered preferences, who generally act rationally to satisfy those preferences. Because of this, A and B are qualified to bear the full risk of loss and the full potential reward that their agreement may bring.

(2) *Formal Freedom.* Both A and B are *formally free* agents: neither has the right to unilaterally dictate the terms of their interaction.

(3) *Substantive Freedom.* They are *substantively free* agents: neither A nor B can, by dint of its superior power, exercise effective and unilateral control over the terms of their interaction. Both A and B have a range of meaningful conduct options, at least some of which involve refraining from engaging in financial transactions of the type that they are entertaining.

(4) *Informational Adequacy.* A and B are not only competent to understand the terms of the agreement that they are entertaining, but each has reasonably accurate information about the risks and potential benefits of making the agreement or refraining from doing so. A and B are roughly equal in the amount of information that they have or could potentially acquire about the risks and potential rewards of their agreement.

(5) *Stability.* The environment in which A and B interact is relatively *stable*—there are few unforeseeable changes that can occur which would fundamentally change the circumstances of A and B in general and in particular their capabilities to comply with the terms of the agreement that they are considering.

When the conditions characterizing the ideal picture hold, there is a broad range of ethical considerations that can be advanced in favor of allowing A and B to make agreements of the kind imagined, for taking B to have an obligation to repay according to the schedule stipulated in the agreement once it has been made, and undertaking measures to ensure that such agreements can be effectively enforced.

One common set of considerations are broadly "rule" consequentialist in nature, to the effect that people are, on the whole, much better off when agents are given wide discretion about which agreements to make, when they are taken to be obliged to keep agreements that they do make, and when such agreements are generally enforceable. There are at least four reasons why such considerations might be thought to apply. First, such a practice *allows* agents to enter into mutually beneficial agreements. If A lends to B because B promises to repay her at some later time, this is because A believes that she stands to benefit from such an agreement. And if B borrows from A in return for her promise to repay A later, this is because she too believes that she stands to benefit from such an agreement. Since A and B are rational, formally free, interact in a relatively stable environment, and have reliable and roughly equal information about the risks and potential benefits of proposed agreements, there is reason to think that they will generally enter into those and only those agreements that will indeed benefit them. Second, such a practice provides strong incentives for agents to make prudent decisions not only *ex ante* (when deciding whether to make agreements), but also *ex post* (when deciding how to manage their affairs after they have made them). An agent who is deciding whether to make an agreement will think twice about making false promises or breaking its promises if it knows that it will be held accountable for doing so. Third, absent such a practice, those who might provide resources to others that could be put to productive use will not do so since they will lack sufficient assurance that they will be repaid.[27] Finally, such a practice facilitates the provision of more reliable information to all agents about how others will act, ensuring greater predictability and thus facilitating well-informed future planning.[28] Human beings have interests in knowing what others will do and also in being able to provide reliable signals about what they will do, and such a practice serves these interests.[29]

There are also nonconsequentialist considerations that support aspects of these practices. For example, there seems to be a general connection between such practices and autonomy. Allowing persons, through consent or agreement, to bind themselves to do certain things for others is required if their autonomy is to be respected. As Joseph Raz has put it, "The ideal of autonomy is the vision of people controlling, to some degree, their own destiny, fashioning it through successive decisions throughout their lives."[30] Part of this control includes the power (in Hohfeld's terms) to alter the claims that others have with respect to one's future conduct. Keeping one's agreements, moreover, seems generally connected with showing respect for persons. In making false promises or breaking agreements agents seem usually to show inadequate respect for others who are often significantly and avoidably harmed by this conduct.[31] If B promises to repay A for resources that A has lent to her and later fails to do so, she induces false expectations in A that may lead to very dire (and avoidable) consequences for her.[32]

Making false promises or breaking agreements also seems to violate a duty of fair play.[33] B would gain from making false promises or breaking her agreement because she unfairly free-rides on practices that are sustained by others who keep their promises. What is worse, B getting away with this conduct may weaken confidence in the practices of agreement-making and promising, which in turn may reduce their benefits to all.[34]

There are still other values supporting these practices. The practices of promising and agreement-making arguably contribute to the ethical development of persons. Being able to bind myself through promises to do things for others strengthens my sense of agency in the world and my responsibility for the exercise of my agency. This value of granting freedom to make agreements (and trust on the basis of promises they involve) is well understood by parents, who sometimes grant greater freedom of this kind to their children than may be warranted because of its important role in their children's ethical development. Finally, the honoring of one's agreements might be linked to the maintenance of personal integrity. As Cheshire Calhoun has put it, "Persons of integrity treat their own endorsements as ones that matter, or ought to matter, to fellow deliberators. Absent a special sort of story, lying about one's views, concealing them, recanting them under pressure, selling them out for rewards or to avoid penalties . . . all indicate a failure to regard one's own judgment as one that should matter to others."[35]

Taken together, these considerations support granting quite a lot of weight to practices that grant agents broad liberties to make agreements,

Christian Barry and Lydia Tomitova

create stringent obligations for these agents to honor the agreements that they make, and ensure that such agreements can be enforced. Situations may of course arise in which the consequences of such practices will seem problematic. Imagine, for example, that after the time of making the contract, B makes imprudent choices that make it impossible for her to repay A without great difficulty and at great sacrifice of other important objectives that she values. Such a system will hold that she nevertheless has a stringent obligation to repay A, and that this obligation should be enforced. That this practice leads to such a regrettable outcome, however, does not seem to provide decisive reasons to reject it, especially since such cases are likely to represent exceptions in an otherwise well-functioning system. In extreme cases we may still hold that B ought to act against her stringent obligations. We may also claim that while not obliged to do so creditors ought nevertheless to forgive loans or at least offer generous terms for restructuring them.

CONTRACTUAL RIGHTS AND OBLIGATIONS: THE REAL PICTURE

The discussion above suggests that, were it to be shown that lending and borrowing relationships involving sovereign states relevantly and significantly resemble the relationships in the ideal picture, then current practices related to sovereign debt would seem well supported, even when these practices lead to regrettable outcomes.

Yet, if such regrettable outcomes arise very frequently, it seems unlikely that they are merely exceptions in a well-functioning system. Currently, the high incidence of severely indebted countries that are unable to pay up their debts without sacrificing significant portions of their budgets would suggest that there might be a serious divergence between the ideal picture and reality.

And indeed there is. With respect to all but the second condition (formal freedom), the current circumstances in which sovereign debtors and their creditors interact differ quite radically from the conditions characterizing the interactions of A and B in the ideal picture. Consider, for example, the following four types of differences that seem particularly relevant for assessing the fairness of current arrangements for dealing with external sovereign debt:

1. Sovereign debtors (and also usually creditors) are not typically individuals, but complex collective agents made up of many present and future individuals. Two aspects of these collective agents are particularly important to recognize. First, the individual agents who are empowered (via external and internal sovereignty) to agree to the contract and those who can potentially benefit from or be harmed by it are often different. Second, the interests of those who are collectively bound by the agreement are not always given adequate consideration by those entering the contract, nor are they (nor in the case of future persons or very young children *can* they be) adequately consulted about it.

Indeed, many debtor country governments are not even *minimally* representative of the interests of those they rule. With respect to debts contracted by governments of this kind, combining internal and external sovereignty with *pacta sunt servanda* seems extremely implausible: By what right should oppressive elites be entitled to run up debts in the names of those whom they impoverish (or worse) and bind the present and future citizens of their country to repay them?[36] The prevalence of debts that were *either actively acquired by* or *easily traceable to* nonminimally representative regimes also calls into question the unconstrained privilege to lend: By what right can a creditor provide resources to a dictator that she has reason to believe will be used to harm the people of his country, and which cost will later have to be paid by them?[37] And by what right can a creditor *escape* responsibility for compensating for the harms to which it has contributed, and in fact benefit from them?[38] For this reason, it seems far-fetched that granting external sovereignty to governments that are not even minimally representative while insisting on *pacta sunt servanda* will contribute to their "ethical development." Furthermore, should some future, more democratic regime refuse to pay debts that have resulted from reckless lending (or should the citizens launch a taxpayer revolt on the grounds that they should not be compelled to service invalid debts), it seems implausible to claim that they are failing to respect others. *They* never made promises to or agreements with anyone, nor had their interests reflected in agreements that were purportedly made on their behalf. For these reasons, considerations of "integrity" also seem out of place, since they can perfectly well treat their own endorsements as ones that matter, or ought to matter, to fellow deliberators but deny that they should be bound by the endorsements of others in agreements about which they were neither consulted nor considered.

Even with respect to regimes that are at least minimally representative, it is evident that the disincentives to reckless borrowing that are present in the ideal picture are much weaker with regard to debtor countries' governments, since those taking out the loans will not have to pay most (and in some cases any) of their cost.

2. While generally formally free, many debtors are often not substantively free in any relevant sense. This is so both because other agents, including creditors, can profoundly influence the terms of their interaction without their consent, and because they are often in so vulnerable a condition that refraining from entering into debt contracts with creditors (even particular creditors) is often not a meaningful option for them. As Joseph Stiglitz has recently pointed out, borrowers are typically much poorer than lenders, often they turn to them in times of crisis, and face an oligopolistic market for credit: "Credit markets are highly imperfect: borrowers typically have access only to a limited number (usually one, two or three) of sources of credit, while creditors face a large number of potential borrowers."[39]

These features of the relationships between creditors and sovereign debtors suggest that the practice of combining *pacta sunt servanda* with unconstrained rights to lend is highly unfair. By allowing creditors to demand nearly whatever terms the market will bear, this practice encourages lenders to take undue advantage of borrowers. Indeed, a strong case can be made that international financial institutions, developed countries, and creditors based in developed countries have indeed on occasion taken double advantage of developing countries. That is, they have sometimes encouraged them to borrow large amounts, encouraged them further to borrow still more money at higher cost to repay the earlier debts that they could not feasibly repay, and simultaneously encouraged (or demanded) further policy changes (such as capital account liberalization) that have arguably made their economies still more vulnerable and thus less able to service their debts and meet the needs of their people.[40]

3. It is very often the case that there are strong informational asymmetries between borrowers and creditors, and that borrowers have severely inadequate information about the risks that they may face. Developed countries, multilateral institutions, and private creditors have struggled actively since 2002 to determine what prudent levels of debt for these countries are, and how best to manage the risks that they face.[41] This is partly because of superior resources and expertise, but also (as mentioned above) because they influence the overall global economic environment to a greater extent. Current practice thus creates significant incentive problems. Those with more information can easily take advantage of those without such information. Creditors may encourage vulnerable developing countries to enter into debt contracts that they know are imprudent. Indeed, this is arguably what occurred in the period leading up to the 1980s crisis.[42]

There are, of course, some incentives for lenders not to make such loans, including the prospect that they will not be repaid. However, two factors somewhat diminish the significance of such incentives. The first is that creditors at least know that if a debtor encounters difficulties in meeting its payment obligations, they will likely enjoy a privileged position in any further negotiations with the debtor. Formally, at least, it will be up to them to forgive or restructure the contract, and to determine the terms on which this should be done. Given this privileged position, they may benefit significantly in the long term from such restructurings, not only relative to what they would have had without having made the agreement but also relative to what they would have had were the borrower to have honored the original terms of the contract.[43]

The second is that creditors themselves are collective agents, and those who are authorized to extend credit to borrowers can often reap the benefits of having done so without bearing the costs in case of default.[44] The financial manager who makes a debt contract with a sovereign may benefit himself by broadening his portfolio, yet be long gone when the sovereign becomes unable to repay the loan on the originally stipulated terms. Indeed, those who bear the significant personal cost of so-called nonperforming

Christian Barry and Lydia Tomitova

loans are often not those who extended the loan or even other members of their institutions, but ordinary persons whose pensions and other investments are linked to these contracts. In the case of Argentina, many institutional investors presented overoptimistic prognoses of the country's economic prospects, since increased holdings of bonds brought individual investment bankers, brokers, and money managers personal financial gain, as well as institutional profits in fees charged to clients for performing services.[45]

4. The global environment in which sovereign debtors and creditors interact is quite *unstable*—there are many changes that can occur which would fundamentally change the circumstances of debtor countries which are not only impossible for them to *control* but which are also quite difficult for them to *foresee*. Natural disasters or regional financial crises provide vivid examples of such instability.

Instability raises particularly serious questions about present practice when the lender's behavior adversely affects the debtor such that it is much more difficult for the debtor to meet its payment obligations. Suppose that the government of some very rich and powerful country G1 provides loans to the government of a weak and poor country G77 at time T_1. At time T_2, G1 decides to undertake a trade policy that blocks G77's ability to earn the foreign exchange to repay the loan, or some other set of policies that undermine G77's economic position. Consequently, G77 can no longer meet its monthly payments to G1 at time T_3 and is unable to pay down either the principal, or even pay the interest on the principal.

In some cases where the decisions of one agent greatly undermine the capabilities of agents who are indebted to it, we may wish to argue that this weakens its ethical claim even to the principal. In others, we may grant the validity to the claim to repayment of the principal, but hold that the lending agent's behavior weakened or invalidated its claims to repayment on the original terms. Of course, when we judge the lender to have affected the debtor's position through fair competition, or through the unintended side effects of ethically permissible policy measures, we may find the causal relevance of the lender to the debtor's position at a later time irrelevant; but it seems implausible to claim that greatly pressuring countries to liberalize their financial markets when the risks of doing so were known to finance ministers and central bankers of the G-7 should be conceived as part of fair competition or justified policy making.[46] Such instability also suggests that the rigidity of present sovereign debt contracts is questionable.

This section has shown how many considerations that might be invoked to support current practices relevant to sovereign debt have much less force than might initially have been supposed. It doesn't follow from this, of course, that significant reforms are ethically required or are even desirable to bring about. It may be that reforms which mitigate some of the regrettable outcomes of present practices may cause other (and perhaps even more serious) problems, and that proposed reforms may even have the opposite of their intended effect. Despite the evident problems with the current system, for example, it might still be defended on rule-consequentialist grounds. The importance of global capital flows to developing nations in today's globalized environment is significant, and any policy that established a wide range of doubt for creditors about which of their loans might subsequently be deemed void might cause more harm than benefit to developing countries and less advantaged persons within them.[47] Even regimes that are not minimally representative may borrow for legitimate purposes. For this reason reforms that significantly constrain their right to borrow (and others' right to lend to them) may seriously damage the interests of ordinary people living in the countries that they rule—especially if there are no foreseeable prospects for regime change—thereby harming the very people such reforms are intended to help. In the following section we will describe reform proposals that have features which provide reason to believe that they would help those currently disadvantaged by current practices, and do so in a way that would not impose undue burdens on others. Our purpose in outlining them is not to fully endorse any of them—this would require much more detailed empirical investigation of whether they could be feasibly brought about and maintained, and what their long-term effects would likely be—but to stimulate thinking about what appear to be promising alternatives to the existing status quo.

DEVELOPING ALTERNATIVE NORMS AND INSTITUTIONS

Our discussion of the ideal and real picture of contractual rights and obligations suggests two general approaches to remedying the problem of international debt. First, we can try to alter the actual nature of relationships of creditors and debtors so that they more closely resemble the relationship of A and B in the ideal picture. Second, we can try to alter features of present practices in a way that more adequately takes account of the differences between the actual nature of relationships between sovereign debtors and their creditors and the relationship between A and B, as sketched in the ideal picture.

The scope of the first approach is and will likely remain somewhat limited, since it is clear that many of the fundamental characteristics that distinguish present relationships between sovereign debtors and their creditors from the relationship between A and B in the ideal picture cannot be easily or substantially altered, and still others cannot be altered at all. Debtors and creditors will continue to be complex, collective agents, and for the foreseeable future they will possess unequal power and unequal access to information and will continue to interact in an environment that can be quite unstable. To be plausible, proposed reforms to current arrangements must be designed and implemented in light of these facts.

The second reform approach, which would involve changing features of debt contracts, limiting the internal or external sovereignty of borrowers, limiting the lending privileges of creditors, or departing from the norm of *pacta sunt servanda*, thus seems more promising (at least in the short term), since it might change the incentives of creditors and sovereign borrowers without wishing away enduring if often regrettable features of our present global order.

In reality any particular reforms will necessarily represent a mixture of these two general reform approaches—as indeed do the proposals we outline next. These proposals have various valuable objectives. However, since our concern here is with reducing the negative social consequences that arise under the present system, it is useful to think of them in terms of whether their primary intended systemic effects are (1) to deter lending that we may have good reasons, *ex ante*, to think would produce morally objectionable consequences (while encouraging or at least not discouraging lending that is likely to be beneficial in the long term to the creditor and debtor alike); or (2) to deal, *ex post*, with negative consequences that have arisen from lending (even those that were perhaps difficult to foresee).

Proposals of the first type generally involve constraining creditors' lending privileges and, in such way, diminishing borrowers' effective ability to borrow in certain ways and for certain purposes. They also seek to change the character of those contracts that are entered into, making them: (1) less neutral—by making creditors' claims and obligations in part contingent on what borrowers do with the resources that creditors have provided to them; (2) less extensive—by specifying circumstances under which present and future citizens may be shielded from repayment obligation; and (3) less rigid—by making repayment obligations contingent in specified ways on the circumstances of the creditor or debtor or of the environment in which they interact.

Proposals of the second type require that less decisive weight be given to the principle of *pacta sunt servanda* in certain circumstances.

Reallocating the Costs of Harmful Policy Advice and Lending

Two proposals, recently advocated by Kunibert Raffer, would reallocate the costs of harmful policy advice and of harmful lending.[48] Since the early 1980s, international financial institutions (IFIs) have assumed a significant role in giving economic policy advice to developing countries. They have also made extensions of loans to their client countries conditional upon implementing sectoral economic reforms, particularly through "structural adjustment programs." While the empirical assessment of the impact of these programs remains hotly disputed, there are aspects of them that seem to have been flawed, and of which IFIs were, or could have been, aware at the time—such as defining a country's level of sustainable debt. Recently, IFIs have themselves acknowledged that their projections of growth and exports, which are used to determine debt sustainability, were overoptimistic and failed to take into proper account the probability of external shocks that can affect export earnings and exchange rates.[49] And, according to the World Bank's Operations Evaluation Department, "the overall simple average of the growth rate assumed in DSAs [debt sustainability analyses] … is more than twice the historical average for 1990–2000, and almost six times the average for 1980–2000."[50] For example, in the run-up to the 1980s debt crisis, Latin

American countries' debt was deemed sustainable on the basis of the results of models that failed to take into account the possibility of a sharp drop in commodity prices during the mid-1980s.[51] The IMF and the World Bank have also acknowledged that some "completion point" countries—that is, countries that have fulfilled the requirements under the HIPC Initiative and are ready to see their debts cancelled and graduate from the program—such as Uganda have debt-to-export and debt-to-GDP ratios exceeding sustainable levels as defined under the HIPC Initiative, due to the drastic fall in commodity prices from the late 1990s through 2002, overoptimistic assumptions for economic and export growth, and in some cases new borrowings.[52]

Basing key criteria used for designing specific policy reforms on such flawed assumptions creates negative prospects for the success of IFI programs in restoring a country's economic viability. Indeed, though it is probably impossible to show conclusively, due to the complex nature of macroeconomic policy-making and the multiple actors involved in it, it is not implausible that in some cases in which a country's economic crisis worsened, such IFI programs may have contributed significantly to this outcome.

Under present rules, when a client country becomes insolvent, the repayment of obligations to IFIs takes priority over those to other creditors. The rationale that underlies their "preferred creditor status" is that the IMF and the World Bank provide loans to countries in especially difficult balance-of-payment situations, to whom no other creditors are willing to lend because of the high risk of their defaulting. Ensuring that the funds they loan out will be replenished allows IFIs to shoulder the high risk. However, this rationale can hardly be supported to the extent that IFIs contribute to increasing the risk of defaults with policy advice based on incorrectly designed programs. Protecting IFIs from losses comes at the expense of the poorest countries. Indeed, this creates a moral hazard: "When its strategy goes wrong, the IMF does not walk away. It stays, condemning the policies its former model pupil had to implement as inefficient and economically ill-advised, selling new advice, and helping with another program the country has to pay for."[53] It is reasonable to suggest that when IFIs work with a country to implement economic policy reforms, they ought to bear part of the risk of these policies being unsuccessful, and thus also some part of the costs when they turn out to be unsuccessful.

Because it is extremely difficult (if not impossible) to determine the precise share of responsibility of IFIs for situations of insolvency that arise following policy reforms advised by IFIs, a minimal reform that would also remove the moral hazard would be to demand that IFIs absorb the same share of unpayable claims as do the other creditors—rather than insisting that they should be paid first because they lend to countries with no access to capital. Indeed, it is not implausible to argue that IFIs should bear greater share of losses than private creditors, since unlike IFIs private creditors are not involved in giving economic advice to countries.

A serious concern associated with this proposal is whether the IFIs' credit rating will deteriorate and thus make it impossible for developing countries to obtain cheap loans when they urgently need them. However, acknowledging publicly that a country has defaulted on its obligations to the IFIs is little different from the present situation of countries being in de facto defaults that, though not acknowledged, are publicly known. Provided that de facto defaults have not diminished the IFIs' credit rating, it is not obvious why a formal, structured, and orderly mechanism of bankruptcy would. In addition, since 1986, when an external audit of the IMF indicated that the next audit will have to warn about the lower real value of some debts that were still booked at face value, the IMF has been building up "precautionary reserves," or loan loss provisions, in order to preserve its standing as a creditor. In 2003 the surcharge that the IMF imposed on the loans it makes to client countries to insure itself for the case of a default averaged 0.1 percent.[54] It seems plausible that these reserves will be put to use when actual losses do occur.

When it can be shown with some confidence that a creditor has inflicted harm on a debtor, and that this harm seems to have resulted from the creditor's negligence, creditors might both have their claims to repayment be considered null and void and also be made liable for compensating debtors financially. Introducing negligence standards into lending decisions and the design of economic policy programs by IFIs could create an incentive for IFIs to perform better—for example, it will deter them from basing debt sustainability levels on flawed growth and export projections. Again, the cited reason for the lack of such existing mechanisms is the need to maintain IFIs' preferred creditors status. However, the International Bank for Reconstruction and Development (the World Bank's arm that lends to middle-income and creditworthy poor countries) has itself admitted: "Too many projects have been selected either on the basis of political prestige or on the basis of inadequate regard for their likely economic and financial rate of return."[55] Where this has been the case, the ensuing failures or even damages to the borrowing country translate economically into costs of borrowing, albeit hidden since they are not reflected as points in the interest rate charged on the loans. Thus, if IFIs pay compensation for failing to act with proper care, or to observe professional standards, the total cost of borrowing that developing countries face might be lower, even after raising interest rates as insurance, because IFIs would act with greater care.[56] Like in domestic markets, it seems likely that the application of liability would be restricted only to cases where creditor negligence has resulted in substantial harm.

A permanent international court of arbitration could be established to adjudicate cases of alleged negligence of IFIs. For it, developing countries and international financial institutions would nominate the same number of members, who would then elect one further member to reach an uneven number of votes in order to avoid deadlocks. The right to file complaints would be conferred to NGOs, governments, and international organizations. The court will have investigative powers, and be able to invite outside opinion in the form of amicus curiae briefs.

One input to such a court's consideration could build on the several examples of public debt audits that have been undertaken by national parliaments or civil society groups, whose methods, although in need of improvement, warrant attention. These include the audits of national debt that were conducted in Argentina starting in 1982, Brazil in 2000, the Philippines in 2004, and Uruguay in 2005.[57] Moreover, the court's powers need not be limited to investigating conformity with existing IFI operating norms, but should also extend to examining the validity of these norms. A court should be able not just to hear a case of whether IFIs have complied with their existing guidelines for designing conditionality requirements under an economic program, but also to review the soundness of the guidelines. In such a way, it will contribute to repairing, where necessary, the rules with which creditors ought to comply. Damages for which the court finds IFIs to be liable could be covered in some cases by waiving repayment on part of the loans equivalent to the resulting damage. Notably, in cases for which it could be shown that the loans have been instrumental in harming them, additional transfers may be required. In such cases, simply releasing a government from obligations to repay funds that a corrupt predecessor regime used to enrich itself or that a dictator uses to further oppress those who oppose him or strengthen his grip on power—as was the case with the 1983 loan that the IMF provided to Mobutu's Zaire—cannot plausibly be viewed as compensating them adequately for the harms suffered.

Creating Disincentives to Lend to Repressive Regimes

Two proposals that would create disincentives to lend to repressive regimes and diminish the scope of internal and external sovereignty have been advanced respectively by Thomas Pogge and Jonathan Shafter. Most people would agree that lending to severely oppressive regimes, such as Nigeria under Sani Abacha, Argentina during the military junta rule, or indeed Myanmar's current government, is at the very least highly questionable because it contributes to their maintenance and undermines local activists' efforts for reform. The current system, because it ensures that creditors retain legal claims to repayment under all circumstances, does not create disincentives to lend to such regimes. However, Pogge has argued that such disincentives could be introduced if countries prone to political and military coups passed a constitutional provision during periods of democratic governance, stipulating that in case of undemocratic regime change, the loans incurred by this undemocratic government will not be honored by future democratic governments.[58] This mechanism will be self-enforcing for cases in which a military regime takes over and suspends a democratic constitution. For the more complex cases of a government becoming undemocratic over the course of its term, the proposal envisions an international democracy panel of independent experts outside the country judging in real time whether a particular country remains democratically governed.

Such reform, if instituted, poses the danger of undermining access to credit for fledgling democracies. Authoritarian regimes will sometimes reemerge despite the deterrent effect of a constitutional amendment. When this happens, the new authoritarian government will lack an incentive to honor the debts that may have been incurred by the previous democratic regime, since it is banned from international borrowing whether it repays

Christian Barry and Lydia Tomitova

them or not. The likelihood of such a scenario would make creditors apprehensive about lending to newly democratized countries. To solve this incentive problem, Pogge's proposal envisions the establishment of an international fund, backed by the major democratic countries, which could service debts of democratic governments in cases in which authoritarian regimes reject them. Indeed, the more financial backing that established democracies give to the fund, the less it may have to spend, since a fully credible fund will reduce the number of coup attempts. Indeed, it would create incentives for authoritarian regimes to become democratic in order to gain access to international resources, which is of special significance to countries in which regime changes rarely occur through elections.

In a similar spirit of raising the risk of lending to authoritarian governments, Shafter proposes a "due diligence model" of odious debt resolution, which envisions putting an international organization in charge of adjudicating *ex ante* that a certain regime is odious-debt-prone, subsequently creating a duty for creditors to employ reasonable best practices of due diligence to ensure that the proceeds of their loans be utilized for pre-specified public purposes.[59] They are free to extend the loan without such due diligence, but if they do so and the debts incurred are indeed harmful to the population of the borrowing country, the debtor is shielded from repayment obligations. To ensure that creditors have sufficient certainty that their loan is given with proper due diligence for the specific circumstances of a country, prospective creditors would submit an analysis of their loan proposal, including its intended uses by the borrowing government and the due diligence structures put into place to monitor the implementation of the proposal, to the international organization. If the proposal were to be approved, creditors would be ensured the validity of their claims against the borrowing government, so long as there is sufficient evidence that the creditor made a good-faith effort to comply with the pre-approved due diligence structure. Some actually existing or new international political body could conceivably be put in charge of evaluating proposals.

Reducing the Rigidity of Sovereign Debt Contracts
To account for the instability of the global system, Sanjay Reddy has recently suggested that debt contracts could be designed (and could be

demanded that they be designed) in a way similar to so-called contingent claims financial instruments, such as securities whose returns are linked to commodity prices or economic performance.[60] Such derivative-like securities would require lower payment during economic hardship, and higher payment in times of prosperity. When circumstances arise over which debtor countries have little or no control and which significantly and adversely affect a debtor's ability to repay its debts on a predetermined fixed schedule—such as natural disasters, plummeting world prices of a country's major export commodity, or rising interest rates as a result of another country's monetary policy—contingency claims clauses when written into contracts would describe a different set of repayment obligations. Such type of contracts in fact prevent potential moral hazard: by carefully specifying the contingencies that warrant reduced payments, the contracts eliminate debtors' abilities to manipulate events in such way as to "welch."[61]

Utilizing contingent claims instruments requires a system of monitoring and arbitration. Some third-party arbiter will be necessary in order to facilitate the operation of a system of legal definitions that can determine when the circumstances that could trigger a contingency claim have arisen. It might be feared that such a system would result in higher interest charges on loans to all borrowing countries, but this need not be the case so long as the specific characteristics of each country are known and publicly acknowledged.

Sovereign Bankruptcy

Sovereign bankruptcy proposals seek to amend the current situation in which the negative consequences of severe indebtedness are borne nearly entirely by the population of the borrowing countries (unless of course creditors agree to forgive its debts). One such proposal is the Fair and Transparent Arbitration Process (FTAP), which has been advanced in various variants by civil society organizations. It is based on the proposal for an international insolvency procedure modeled on Chapter 9 of the U.S. Bankruptcy Code, which governs the bankruptcy of municipalities.[62] The FTAP is a mechanism for the management of debt crises in a way that is "open, transparent, and accountable to citizens and taxpayers," in order to ensure that their interests are heard and given proper consideration and that their basic human rights (somehow understood) are given higher priority than creditors' rights. The FTAP is intended to be a neutral decision-making body, independent from both parties. It will consider the entire debt owed by a country, in contrast to the current practice of the debtor negotiating with individual classes of creditors for its respective types of debts. It envisions all types of creditors being subject to equal treatment, to address the concerns of private creditors that multilateral lending institutions are in a privileged position (and as is envisioned by the bankruptcy proposal advanced by the IMF, the Sovereign Debt Restructuring Mechanism).

The FTAP envisions the establishment of an ad-hoc international arbitration panel (which reflects the above principles), composed of an equal number of representatives from the creditor and debtor sides, who nominate by simple majority one additional panel member. In addition, a small technical secretariat may be set up to support the harmonization of countries' data, auditing, technical support to the arbiters, and the organization of the hearing of stakeholders according to procedural standards.[63] The benefit of an ad-hoc arbitration panel compared to a permanent court is that arbitrations do not usually use a precedent system, hence failure or success in one case will not prejudice a future case.[64]

The purpose of the arbitration court is to protect at the minimum the basic rights of the population of the indebted country. However, its final rulings could be informed by considering the full scope of relevant factors, including creditors' and sovereign debtors' due diligence. Even as its rulings do not set binding precedents, the court's mandate will ensure that its decisions have a measure of internal consistency—and would thus create incentives for creditors to avoid such behavior in order to diminish the overall risk they face without creating incentives for sovereigns to take out imprudent loans because they know that they will be "let off the hook" through arbitration later on.[65]

A major concern that has been voiced in relation to international bankruptcy mechanisms in general—including by some developing countries, such as South Africa and Mexico—is that it might diminish the availability of credit to developing countries. The validity of these concerns, however, is not immediately evident. As noted earlier, it could be argued that the current high indebtedness of many countries amounts to a de facto, publicly known (though not officially acknowledged) default. Indeed, any new lending at present is premised on canceling some of the existing debts.[66]

It is sometimes argued that despite the substantive promise of these proposals, the political space for their implementation is severely limited. Two proposals may help to improve the position of debtors under the current system, as well as create incentives to at least further consider proposals for reform.

Shift the Power Balance in Bargaining

Two suggestions are aimed at altering the power dynamics of negotiation and thus allowing debtor countries a wider range of alternative choices. One is to form debtor cartels, akin to creditor cartels such as the London and Paris clubs. Negotiating as a group, debtor countries of similar situations will be better able to reject a settlement that advantages creditors and would result in a fairer outcome.[67]

Another (relatively minor) proposal is to move the debt renegotiation forum from creditor to debtor countries. This will expose negotiators from creditor countries firsthand to political pressure from the populations of debtor countries and make them better aware of the consequences of a negotiation outcome that is perceived as privileging the interest of richer creditors. In the longer term, direct exposure to the political pressure in debtor countries would create a better perception of the constraints placed on debtor governments in fulfilling their obligations to foreign creditors at the costs of political dissent at home.

Alternatives to IMF Cancellation Conditionalities

Under existing programs for debt cancellation for the poorest countries, such as the HIPC Initiative and Multilateral Debt Relief Initiative (which resulted from the G-8's June 2005 decision on multilateral debt cancellation), qualifying countries must have complied with IMF-designed and monitored conditionalities in order to benefit from them. While IMF conditionalities may be motivated by legitimate reasons to ensure that the canceled resources are used for development purposes, they are seen as highly controversial by developing countries. Peer-run trust accounts that provide a check on governance but are not controlled by donor

Christian Barry and Lydia Tomitova

governments could provide an alternative to IMF-imposed conditional-ities.[68] As part of the condition for allowing a cancellation (and perhaps in the future, a bankruptcy settlement) to go forward, a country will be required to deposit an amount equal to its monthly debt payments into this trust account, from which the money will be transparently allocated to social expenditures on poverty alleviation, health care, and education.[69] Since payments into the fund will be made in monthly installments, potential abuses could be halted in time with in-progress audits. A further check on the fund's spending could be provided by an independent international arbitral body. This model may not be suitable for cases of countries in strong intraregional tensions.

CONCLUSION

We have not argued that bringing about these reforms is justified. Rather, we have described the ways in which these reforms might plausibly be viewed as addressing some of the apparently unfair features of present rules governing sovereign debt. We think these proposals are promising enough to warrant further intellectual and practical exploration. Whether they should be implemented cannot justifiably be determined in advance of such explorations. And it is therefore premature to judge whether or not, as some critics of these proposals have claimed, they are unworthy of consideration because they are politically infeasible to implement under current conditions. There are often various motivations for statements such as, "The sovereign bankruptcy option is simply too costly to contemplate under present institutional arrangements. Radical reform of those arrange-ments—creation of an international bankruptcy court—is patently unreal-istic. Discussing these ideas is a waste of breath."[70] Nevertheless, their effect is to advocate wrongly foreclosing discussion of these ideas, on grounds that it is unlikely that they could be implemented in the very short term. That reforms turn out to be infeasible because influential actors remain implacably opposed to them—even though it is likely that they will lead to improved social outcomes—does not imply that we should abandon discussing them. It suggests instead that we ought to find ways to pressure these actors to meet their ethical responsibilities.[71]

[1] See Kunibert Raffer, "Applying Chapter 9 Insolvency to International Debts: An Economically Efficient Solution with a Human Face," *World Development* 18, no. 2 (1990), pp. 301–13; Afrodad, "Fair and Transparent Arbitration on Debt" (2001), at www.afrodad.org/index.php?option= com_content&task=view&id=66&Itemid=54; and Erlassjahr, "A Fair and Transparent Arbitration Process for Indebted Southern Countries" (September 2001), at www.erlassjahr.de/content/languages/englisch/dokumente/ftap_englisch_rz.pdf.

[2] See Emerging Markets Trade Association, "Model Collective Action Clauses for Sovereign Notes," January 31, 2003, at www.emta.org/ndevelop/Final_merged.pdf; Arturo Porzecanski, "The Constructive Role of Private Creditors," this volume, pp. 307–19; and Group of Ten, "Report of the Group of Ten on Contractual Clauses," September 26, 2002; available at at www.bis.org/publ/gten08.pdf.

[3] That considerations of fairness seem to play such a foundational role, especially with respect to the assessment of social institutions, raises the question of whether and how this concept differs from the concept of justice (crisply characterized in Thomas Pogge, "Justice (Philosophical Aspects)," in Neil J. Smelser and Paul B. Baltes, eds., *International Encyclopedia for the Social and Behavioral Sciences* (Oxford: Pergamon, 2001), pp. 8055–61, to which the present discussion is indebted). While we are unsure whether and how the meaning of these concepts differs, we are skeptical that the truth or (if you are inclined to moral anti-realism) assertability conditions of sentences in which the predicates fair and unfair, or just and unjust respectively, differ or differ fundamentally. Does it make sense to say that a social institution, for example, was unjust but that it was fair or that it was fair but unjust?

[4] In this essay, by "contracts" we understand broadly any binding agreement, which includes both formal/legal contracts and informal/nonlegal practices that are customary when dealing with sovereign debts.

[5] See David Miller, "Holding Nations Responsible," *Ethics* 114 (2004), pp. 240–68; Alexander Cappelen, "Responsibility and International Distributive Justice," in Andreas Follesdal and Thomas Pogge, eds., *Real World Justice* (Berlin: Springer, 2005), pp. 209–22.

[6] Thomas Pogge, "Achieving Democracy," this volume, pp. 249–73; Sanjay G. Reddy, "Developing Just Monetary Arrangements," in Christian Barry and Thomas Pogge, eds., *Global Institutions and Responsibilities: Achieving Global Justice* (Malden, MA: Blackwell, 2005). It should be noted, however, that the claims to be repaid were mostly those of commercial banks, only some of which were based in the United States. Moreover, non-U.S. residents provided much of the funds lent (including from developing countries, recalling the role of petro-dollar recycling at this time). In addition, even the creditor institutions whose agents were U.S. citizens might reject the claim that they gave even implicit consent to the policy change; indeed, it foisted difficult times on them and ultimately losses. Finally, even claims of the U.S. government, as a direct creditor, might not necessarily be linked to the policy change, since the Federal Reserve arguably took that decision independently of the government.

[7] Christian Barry, "Applying the Contribution Principle," *Metaphilosophy* 36, nos. 1/2 (2005), pp. 210–27.

[8] Daniel Philpott, "Sovereignty," in Edward N. Zalta, ed., *The Stanford Encyclopedia of Philosophy* (Summer 2003 ed.), at plato.stanford.edu/archives/sum2003/entries/sovereignty/; and Stephen D. Krasner, *Sovereignty: Organized Hypocrisy* (Princeton, NJ: Princeton University Press, 1999).

[9] As argued in Ronald Dworkin, *Taking Rights Seriously* (Cambridge, MA: Harvard University Press, 1977); and Ronald Dworkin, *Law's Empire* (Cambridge, MA: The Belknap Press/Harvard University Press, 1985).

[10] Joseph Raz, *The Morality of Freedom* (New York: Oxford University Press, 1986); and Judith Jarvis Thomson, *The Realm of Rights* (Cambridge, MA: Harvard University Press, 1990).

[11] Thomson, *The Realm of Rights*.

[12] As put by Jeremy Waldron, "A Right to Do Wrong," *Ethics* 92 (1981), pp. 21–39.

[13] It is also important to note that even if we do hold that I am obliged to repay on the original schedule, and that the creditor may permissibly demand repayment in full, we may not feel that he may permissibly demand repayment on the original schedule. If the cost to him of allowing greater flexibility in repayment terms is slight, we may think that he acts very wrongly if he nevertheless insists on the original schedule.

[14] Through the 1980s, most of the long-term general purpose private foreign lending to governments constituted credit extended by commercial bank syndicates. Most of the bank loans that became "nonperforming" debt of crisis countries were converted into bonds of lower value in the early 1990s. Bonds then became the preferred general instrument for long-term sovereign borrowing, while loans from individual banks continued to be important in trade financing,

Christian Barry and Lydia Tomitova

project finance, and other needs. Though debtors are formally treated as a uniform class, we can distinguish among them in terms of the kind of credit to which they have access. For example, countries with low per capita income and undeveloped but resource-rich economies (such as Nigeria) will have some ability to sell bonds in international markets (because it is an oil producer), as well as access to multilateral lenders that lend on concessional terms such as the International Development Association, the concessional lending arm of the World Bank (because it is poor), and to official lenders (because of its strategic importance). In contrast, countries with low per capita income and undeveloped and resource-poor economies will generally only have access to government (or government-guaranteed private lending, as for export financing) and multilateral lenders. Middle-income countries with emerging markets generally have some access to all three types of creditors (though to what extent depends on the their particular levels of income per capita for multilateral lenders, their creditworthiness for private lenders, and on their perceived significance for official creditors).

[15] For a more detailed discussion, see Barry Herman, "The Players and the Game of Sovereign Debt," this volume, pp. 9–39.

[16] The terminology of powers, claims, and privileges is drawn from W. N. Hohfeld, *Fundamental Legal Conceptions* (New Haven, CT: Yale University Press, 1919). We owe the terms "internal" and "external sovereignty" to Thomas Pogge.

[17] Seema Jayachandran and Michael Kremer, "Odious Debt," *American Economic Review* 96, no. 1 (2006), pp. 82–92.

[18] Porzecanski, "The Constructive Role of Private Creditors." The recent reforms in the United States to tighten the conditions under which individuals may declare bankruptcy are also exemplary of this view.

[19] *Economist*, "Argentina's Debt Restructuring," May 3, 2005; available at www.economist.com/business/PrinterFriendly.cfm?story_id=3715779.

[20] BBC Newsnight, "Vulture Funds Threat to Developing World," February 14, 2007; available at news.bbc.co.uk/2/hi/programmes/newsnight/6362783.stm.

[21] BBC News, "Zambia Loses 'Vulture Funds' Case," February 15, 2007; available at news.bbc.co.uk/2/hi/business/6365433.stm.

[22] See Elliott Gotkine, "Argentine Restructuring 'Success,'" BBC News, March 4, 2005; available at news.bbc.co.uk/2/hi/business/4317009.stm; and Andrew Balls and Adam Thomson, "Argentina Urged to Deal with Hold-out Bondholders," *Financial Times*, April 29, 2005, p. 8.

[23] See the litigation involving NML Capital, Ltd. v. Republic of Argentina: 2006 U.S. Dist. LEXIS 29842 (S.D.N.Y., May 15, 2006); 2006 U.S. Dist. LEXIS 28247 (S.D.N.Y., May 10, 2006); and 2005 U.S. Dist. LEXIS 5387 (S.D.N.Y., March 31, 2005). See also NML Capital v. Rep. of Argentina, U.S. Court of Appeals for the Second Circuit, Summary Order, May 13, 2005; available at www.clarin.com/diario/2005/05/13/um/fallo.pdf.

[24] For a critique of collective action clauses, see Thomas Palley, "Sovereign Debt Restructuring Proposals: A Comparative Look," *Ethics & International Affairs* 17, no. 2 (2003), pp. 26–33.

[25] And of course also by the nature of the debt contract these conditions are stipulated in advance. To see model CACs, see Group of Ten, "Report of the Group of Ten on Contractual Clauses," September 26, 2002; available at www.bis.org/publ/gten08.pdf; and Emerging Markets Trade Association, "Model Collective Action Clauses for Sovereign Notes."

[26] Kunibert Raffer and Hans Singer, *The Foreign Aid Business: Economic Assistance and Development Co-operation* (Cheltenham, UK: Edward Elgar, 1996), ch. 10, point out that creditors have arbitrarily decided on thresholds, countries, and amounts of debt reductions. They note that creditors had until recently maintained that no debtor country was eligible for reductions at all, insisting on full repayment, while claiming that countries would "grow out of debts." For criticism of the eligibility criteria of the HIPC Initiative, see Raffer and Singer, *The Foreign Aid Business*, ch. 11; UNCTAD, "Debt Sustainability: Oasis or Mirage?" (New York: United Nations, 2004), available at www.unctad.org/en/docs/gdsafrica20041_en.pdf; and Eurodad, "What Goes Down Might Not Come Up: How Declining Commodity Prices May Undermine the HIPC Initiative" (October 2001); available at www.eurodad.org/uploadstore/cms/docs/What_Goes_Down_Might_Not_Come_Up.pdf.

[27] David Hume, *A Treatise on Human Nature* (Oxford: Oxford University Press, 1740/1978).

[28] Russell Hardin, *Trust and Trustworthiness* (New York: Russell Sage Foundation, 2002).

[29] Thomas Scanlon, *What We Owe to Each Other* (Cambridge, MA: Harvard University Press, 1998).

[30] Joseph Raz, *The Morality of Freedom* (New York: Oxford University Press, 1986), p. 369.

[31] Niko Kolodny and R. Jay Wallace, "Promises and Practices Revisited," *Philosophy & Public Affairs* 31, no. 2 (2003), pp. 119–54.

[32] Ibid.; and Scanlon, *What We Owe to Each Other*.

[33] H. L. A. Hart, "Are There Any Natural Rights?" *Philosophical Review* 64 (1955), pp. 175–91. John Rawls, "Legal Obligation and the Duty of Fair Play," in Samuel Freeman, ed., *Collected Papers* (Cambridge, MA: Harvard University Press, 1999), pp. 117–29.

[34] Kolodny and Wallace, "Promises and Practices Revisited."

[35] Cheshire Calhoun, "Standing for Something," *Journal of Philosophy* 92 (1995), p. 258.

[36] Ashfaq Khalfan, Jeff King, and Bryan Thomas, "Advancing the Odious Debt Doctrine" (Montreal: Centre for International Sustainable Development Law, 2003); available at www.cisdl.org/pdf/debtentire.pdf; and Jonathan Shafter, "The Due Diligence Model: A New Approach to the Problem of Odious Debt," this volume, pp. 275–95.

[37] Pogge, "Achieving Democracy."

[38] Kunibert Raffer, "International Financial Institutions and Financial Accountability," *Ethics & International Affairs* 18, no. 2 (2004), pp. 61–77.

[39] Joseph Stiglitz, "Ethics, Market and Government Failure, and Globalization," paper presented to the Vatican Conference, Ninth Plenary Session, Pontifical Academy of Social Sciences, Casina Pio IV, May 2–6, 2003, p. 5; available at www2.gsb.columbia.edu/faculty/jstiglitz/download/2003_Ethics_Market_and_Government_Failure_and_Globalization.pdf.

[40] Bank for International Settlements, "71st Annual Report: 1 April 2000–31 March 2001," available at www.bis.org/publ/ar2001e.pdf; Ann Pettifor, "Resolving International Debt Crises Fairly," this volume, pp. 321–29; Raffer, "International Financial Institutions and Financial Accountability"; Joseph Stiglitz, *Globalization and Its Discontents* (New York: W. W. Norton, 2002). Indeed, U.S. law traditionally has regarded with suspicion loans to poor persons in distress, such as by payday lenders or check cashers.

[41] Stiglitz, "Ethics, Market and Government Failure, and Globalization," p. 5.

[42] Raffer and Singer, *The Foreign Aid Business*.

[43] This factor should not be overstated, however. Most bondholders of Argentinean debt, for example, would not accept the assertion that they were in an effectively privileged position with respect to the Argentine government, even if they retained a formally privileged position.

[44] Though it is generally not discussed, this problem also applies to the case of official lenders whose governments are undemocratic—such as the case with lending by the former communist regimes of Eastern Europe, and as it might some day arise with respect to China.

[45] Paul Blustein, "Argentina Didn't Fall on Its Own: Wall Street Pushed Debt Till the Last," *Washington Post*, August 3, 2003, p. A1; www.washingtonpost.com/ac2/wp-dyn/A15438-2003Aug2?language=printer.

[46] Raffer, "Risks of Lending and Liability of Lenders."

[47] See, e.g., Jack Boorman, "Reviving Troubled Economies," this volume, pp. 297–305; and Shafter, "The Due Diligence Model."

[48] Raffer, "International Financial Institutions and Financial Accountability."

[49] IDA and IMF, "The Challenges of Maintaining Long-Term External Debt Sustainability," April 20, 2001; available at www.imf.org/external/np/hipc/2001/lt/042001.pdf; and IMF and IDA, "Debt Sustainability in Low-Income Countries—Proposal for an Operational Framework and Policy Implications," February 3, 2004; available at www.imf.org/external/np/pdr/sustain/2004/020304.pdf.

[50] Madhur Gautam, "Debt Relief for the Poorest: An OED Review of the HIPC Initiative" (Washington, D.C.: World Bank Operations Evaluation Department, 2003), p. 28; available at siteresources.worldbank.org/IDA/Resources/HIPC_OED_review.pdf.

[51] UNCTAD, "Debt Sustainability," refers this claim to William R. Cline, *International Debt Reexamined* (Washington, D.C.: Institute for International Economics, 1995), cited in Stijn Claessens et al., "Analytical Aspects of the Debt Problems of Heavily Indebted Poor Countries," Policy Research Working Paper 1618 (Washington D.C.: World Bank, 1996).

[52] UNCTAD, "Debt Sustainability," p. 21; and IMF and World Bank, "The Enhanced HIPC Initiative and the Achievement of Long-Term External Debt Sustainability," Washington, D.C., April 15, 2002.

[53] Raffer, "International Financial Institutions and Financial Accountability," p. 75.

[54] Ibid., p. 73.

[55] IBRD, "Toward Sustained Development in Sub-Saharan Africa: A Program of Action" (Washington, D.C.: IBRD, 1984), p. 24, quoted in Raffer, "International Financial Institutions and Financial Accountability."

[56] This is not to discount the significance from a point of justice that the parties harmed would be able to receive compensation for damages. The systemic contribution of this reform, however, is to reduce the incidence of such cases arising.

Christian Barry and Lydia Tomitova

57 Alexandra Fontana, "Opening the Books: Brazil's Experience with Debt Audits," Eurodad, September 2005; at www.eurodad.org/uploadstore/cms/docs/Brazil_Debt_Audit discussionpaper.pdf.

58 Pogge, "Achieving Democracy."

59 Shafter, "The Due Diligence Model."

60 Sanjay G. Reddy, "International Debt: The Constructive Implications of Some Moral Mathematics," this volume, pp. 81–98.

61 For an extensive treatment of this point, see Robert Hockett, "Just Insurance through Global Macro-Hedging," *University of Pennsylvania Journal of International Economic Law* 25 (2004), pp. 107–257. In the United States, "income-contingent" student loans were pioneered by James Tobin in the late 1960s. In the 1970s, Yale University implemented such a plan, called the "Tuition Postponement Option."

62 Kunibert Raffer, "Applying Chapter 9 Insolvency to International Debts."

63 Erlassjahr, "A Fair and Transparent Arbitration Process for Indebted Southern Countries."

64 Afrodad, "Fair and Transparent Arbitration on Debt." Some civil society organizations call for charging the IMF with the provision of loans during the arbitration process (when participating creditors are not willing to lend to the country) and giving priority to the repayment of these loans over all others. Pettifor, "Resolving International Debt Crises Fairly."

65 The strive for consistency between rulings while rejecting prior decisions' binding precedential value is followed most prominently by the International Court of Justice. See Ian Brownlie, *Principles of Public International Law* (New York: Oxford University Press, 1999).

66 See Erlassjahr, "FTAP Working against Debtor Countries? Some Remarks on Counterarguments Raised by Those Who Are to Benefit," February 2003; at www.erlassjahr.de/content/publikationen/e_ftap0302_againstdebtor.php.

67 Sony Kapoor and Meenoo Kapoor, "Financing Development towards the MDGs: What Needs to Be Done?" Heinrich Böll Foundation North America, July 2005; available at www.boell.org/docs/Boell_FinancingDevelopmentTowardsMDGs.pdf.

68 This proposal is outlined in Noreena Hertz, *The Debt Threat: How Debt Is Destroying the Developing World* (New York: Harper Business, 2004); and Sony Kapoor, "Unblocking the Path to Broader Debt Cancellation Using Trust Funds," Presentation, "Ethics and Debt" Conference, The New School, November 1–2, 2005. The idea of peer trusts goes back to Paul P. Streeten, who proposed an emulation of the Marshall Plan model of self-monitoring by recipients in the mid-1990s. See Kunibert Raffer and Hans Singer, *The Foreign Aid Business*. NEPAD already administers a peer mechanism whose goal is to provide an overall check on governance.

69 Indeed, this idea may help to address the problem of how to deal with cases of countries whose debts may be illegitimate, yet creditors may be deemed ethically obliged to demand repayment because they have strong reason to believe that these resources would do more harm than good if left in the regime's hands.

70 Barry Eichengreen, "Predicting, Preventing and Managing International Financial Crises," Testimony, House Banking Committee, U.S. Congress, September 1998; available at financialservices.house.gov/banking/91498eic.htm.

71 For a more detailed discussion of the relevance of feasibility concerns in assessing proposals for institutional reform, see Christian Barry and Sanjay Reddy, *International Trade and Labor Standards: A Proposal for Linkage* (New York: Columbia University Press, forthcoming).

International Debt: The Constructive Implications of Some Moral Mathematics

*Sanjay G. Reddy**

C an current norms and institutional arrangements in regard to the accumulation and discharge of international sovereign debt be mo- rally justified? If not, what sorts of modifications to these norms and arrangements would be required for such justification? These are live questions, as may be attested to by anyone who pays heed to contemporary debates over international economic relations. Some of the most active de- bates have centered on the moral obligations of creditors who are faced with poor countries that are heavily indebted. Some of these poor countries appear to be sacrificing the present and future well-being of their popula- tions in order to undertake debt service, sometimes for debts which were accumulated by predecessor regimes of questionable legitimacy for purpo- ses of questionable value. In this essay, I attempt to address the questions raised above in a preliminary manner, presenting some suggestions as to the shape of possible reforms.

A central proposition to be assessed holds that *states are capable of incur- ring and sustaining obligations over time.* This (perhaps apparently innocuous) proposition, which we will refer to as the proposition on the moral agency of states, refers not only to the empirical capability of states to enter into legal obligations, but also to the ability of states to take on responsibilities that are morally binding. The proposition is normative in content, since obligation is a normative concept.

* I would like to thank Christian Barry, David Grewal, Robert Hockett, Michael Pollak, Jedediah Purdy, Kunibert Raffer, Athanassios Tolis, and Lydia Tomitova for their valuable written comments. I would like to thank for their helpful suggestions the participants at the conference "Ethics and Debt," held at the New School, New York, N.Y., November 1–2, 2005. Nicholas Tenev provided helpful research assistance.

It is helpful to assess a proposition of this kind from the perspective of normative individualism, the view that it must in principle be possible to derive moral propositions concerning collective agents (such as states) from moral propositions concerning individual agents. In particular, the perspective of normative individualism suggests that we can attempt to understand how the obligations that we attach to a state may derive, or may fail to derive, from the moral properties of individuals and their capability to enter into certain kinds of relationships (generating moral obligations as a consequence).

THE DOMESTIC CASE

Moral intuitions concerning the obligations of states to fulfill the terms of their international debt contracts frequently appear to be heavily influenced by the analogy to domestic contracts (involving individual persons or firms). It is commonly accepted that an individual ought to fulfill contractual obligations that she entered into in the past, except in exceptional circumstances. This moral presumption derives from basic considerations of personal integrity. It is thought to be essential to moral personhood itself that a person must take responsibility for her own words and actions. It is also thought that the threads that link a person to her future self (generally) preserve this requirement of moral responsibility.[1] This presumption gives rise to a burden to fulfill promises (at least in the absence of sufficient countervailing reasons). It would be very strange to imagine a system of moral reasoning in which there was *no* such requirement for individuals. The burden to fulfill promises can give rise to a prima facie obligation to fulfill past promises, both on the part of individuals and on the part of entities constituted by the actions of individuals (such as firms). Other related considerations, such as a burden on individuals to refrain from taking unfair advantage of others, may also play a role in creating a requirement to fulfill contractual obligations (on the fulfillment of which other persons have come to depend).

In addition to these deontological considerations, there are also consequentialist considerations that underpin the presumption that contractual obligations of specific kinds (such as debt contracts) should be fulfilled.[2]

Sanjay G. Reddy

These consequentialist considerations appear also to have an important role to play in the justification of a burden on contracting parties to fulfill their obligations. Where specific exemptions from such a burden are recognized (in bankruptcy law, for instance), this is in large part because it has been thought that good consequences are generated by the upholding of such exemptions.[3] The consequentialist reasoning involved in the upholding of rules has been extensively explored in the philosophical literature, such as that on rule utilitarianism, and in the literature of related fields, such as law and economics.

Both deontological and consequentialist forms of moral reasoning appear implicitly to underpin the common presumption that domestic debt contracts ought to be fulfilled, as summarized in the legal slogan *pacta sunt servanda*—"pacts must be respected."

THE ANALOGY AND DISANALOGY TO THE DOMESTIC CASE

The simplicity of the analogy to the domestic case and its familiarity from everyday life is undoubtedly in part responsible for the influence of that analogy. In fact, the case of a state incurring and maintaining international obligations over time is both analogous and disanalogous to the case of domestic contracts.

Even in the emblematic case of individual persons, whether a contract of any kind (including a debt contract) is deemed to generate binding obligations may depend on diverse considerations, including the structure of the choice situation faced by the individual, and in particular whether it can be viewed as one that is characterized by sufficient freedom of choice for consent to be inferred.[4] These considerations will also be pertinent to determining whether the contractual arrangements entered into by states ought to be deemed similarly binding for deontological reasons.

Unlike individuals, states cannot, generally speaking, be described as having a temporally bounded existence. It is widely accepted that individuals' net debt obligations—that is, debts that fully exhaust the value of an estate—cannot legitimately be intergenerationally transferred, for example, from parents to children. There is no parallel principle in relation to states. Indeed, it does not make semantic sense to present such a principle since states are not generally conceived as having a temporally bounded existence. Of course, firms are also not generally conceived as having a temporally bounded existence. The implications of this observation for the identification of obligations (in particular for those that are deontological in nature), however, may be different for firms and for states.

In the case of firms, claims upon net assets and liabilities (established through ownership, management, and employment) change primarily on the basis of explicit contractual agreement between the parties. The set of persons who live within the boundaries of a state, who are citizens of a state, who are beneficiaries of the state's actions, and who are taxed or otherwise imposed upon by the state, may also change over time, and socially recognized implicit or explicit claims upon net assets and liabilities change accordingly. Explicit contractual agreement may not always be involved in such change, however.

It is critical to recognize the complexity of moral assessment in such a setting. Consider Figure 1, which represents lives lived in a country over a period of time. The horizontal axis represents time. Each discrete value along the vertical axis represents a distinct individual, and each bar represents the life lived by that person. Each life has its own starting point and duration. This diagram therefore represents overlapping cohorts in a population and represents the fact that persons are born at different times and die at different times. The members of each cohort, although they are born at the same time,

FIGURE 1:
LIVES LIVED

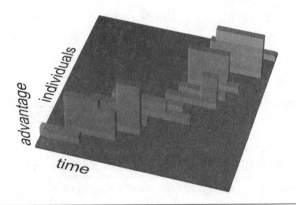

may live different lengths of time. Of course, this diagram only represents a slice of time. People live and die before and after the period represented here. Of course, the number of individuals living in a typical country is vastly greater than such a diagram allows us to represent.

On this diagram, the points at which people are born and the points at which they die are represented. The level of well-being of each person—the overall level of advantage or disadvantage—experienced by each individual at each moment in time is also represented in the diagram. The third axis (coming out of the page) of the diagram represents the level of advantage or disadvantage experienced by a person at a moment in time. The resulting diagram represents the lives lived (encompassing life spans and advantages experienced by each person at each moment in time during those life spans) of the members of the society.

Now imagine that the society to which all of these persons belong enters into a debt contract. The immediate consequence of this debt contract is that resources are made available, and that they can then be spent.

How the resources are spent will determine the level of advantage experienced by different persons at each point thenceforth. Of course, repayment obligations will eventually be incurred, which will cause subsequent decreases in advantage (relative to the counterfactual in which there are no such repayment obligations) at some point in the future. The burdens induced by repayment will be allocated across persons in accordance with social, political, and institutional factors, such as the features of the taxation and fiscal expenditure systems. In figure 2, this pattern is represented graphically, for an arbitrary case.

It is important to note that when the debt contract is entered into, some people may have already been alive for longer periods of time than others, so a larger proportion of their lives may have already elapsed. Additionally, even if two persons were born in the same age cohort and have already lived the same length of time, the length of time they can expect to live subsequently may differ. The reasons for this are diverse and may have to do with systematic variations in the advantages or disadvantages experienced by different groups of people as well as idiosyncratic factors associated with individual health.

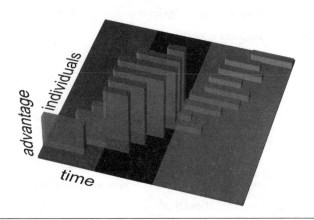

When a state enters into a debt contract, therefore, the extent to which different individuals will benefit from the resources that are garnered through undertaking a debt, and the extent to which different individuals will bear the ultimate obligations of repayment, will differ because of variation in the timing of individual lives and variation in the extent to which, at each moment in time, individual persons experience increased advantage as a result of the resources collectively garnered or experience decreased advantage as a result of the collective repayment obligations incurred.

An issue which is worth mentioning, although it is bewilderingly complex, is that the number of persons and the identities of the persons who are alive are likely to be endogenous—that is, determined by the amount of debt contracted and the manner in which that debt is both spent and repaid. When persons' lives begin and when they end depend in various ways on the availability of material resources and upon private and public decisions concerning the use of these resources. This dependence adds a tremendous amount of complexity to any kind of assessment of the impact of debt, of which one must be at least aware.[5]

A rather simple-minded, purely consequentialist approach to the analysis of alternative public policies which affect the debts accumulated, the use of the resources garnered, and the repayment obligations they impose might simply aggregate the advantages experienced under distinct alternatives from a single point in time onward. Such an approach (for example, a utilitarian approach) might consider different counterfactual policies or rule systems and ask how they affect the sum total of advantages experienced by all persons over time, or the mean level of advantage experienced by each person alive, or some other aggregative criterion that is held to be of interest. Even a simple-minded exercise of this kind may be inordinately difficult, however, due to the presence of the various complexities discussed here.

MORAL AND ECONOMIC CONSEQUENCES OF THE DISANALOGY

One way to view the disanalogy between the case of international (sovereign) debt and that of domestic debt is that the former involves a mesh of interpersonal externalities which are both intragenerational and intergenerational in nature. For example, the persons who enter into the debt contract may not be the persons who either benefit from the resources that are garnered thereby or who will bear the burden of repayment within any one age cohort, while future age cohorts that bear the burden of repayment may not be the beneficiaries of resources garnered in the past through debt. At least two preliminary conclusions arise straightforwardly as a consequence of the existence of such externalities.

The first preliminary conclusion is that any attempt to argue on *exclusively* deontological (that is, nonconsequentialist) grounds for a strong obligation for states to abide by international debt contracts is likely to be implausible. The arguments of this kind that pertain to individuals or firms (derivative of those that pertain to individuals) cannot be straightforwardly transferred to states, since doing so would entail attaching deontological obligations to some agents based on the actions of other agents entirely. If one takes the standpoint of normative individualism, as I have argued for doing, then such an ascription is far from immediate.[6]

The second preliminary conclusion is that consequentialist arguments for embedding a strong obligation for states to abide by debt contracts into the international regime are likely to depend on a range of empirical claims. These empirical claims may not always be easy to assess. On the one hand, the recognition and enshrinement of such obligations may make it more likely that certain beneficial consequences (in particular, secure access of states to credit markets) may result. On the other hand, the interpersonal externalities (both intragenerational and intergenerational) that are present in the creation and discharge of sovereign debt may give rise to inefficiencies and inequities that could be diminished under other rules.

The pervasiveness of the externalities that are involved is at the heart of contemporary debates. The externalities can be of many kinds, and can have important implications for our judgments of the moral acceptability of the outcomes that are likely to result, whether we adopt consequentialist or deontological evaluative perspectives.

Consequentialist Assessment

The existing rules regulating sovereign debt often make it possible for individuals to enter into contracts that cause *other* individuals to be assigned the obligation to repay. The alignment of incentives in a structure of this kind is very poor, as those who decide whether to borrow and who benefit from borrowing may not pay the full cost of doing so. The result is often an inefficiently large amount of debt.[7] The resulting distribution of burdens may also be inequitable. From this perspective, the existing rules concerning sovereign debt cannot be considered the unique embodiment of principles required to be adhered to in order to bring about an efficient outcome. Indeed, they may even be at odds with such principles. In standard general equilibrium theory, there are no states; there are only individuals. If it is possible for certain individuals or groups of individuals to enter into contracts which impose costs on other individuals, then inefficient outcomes will result. In order to attain efficient outcomes, it is necessary to put in place rules which enable these externalities to be internalized. If that is not possible, then the best possible—"constrained optimal"—rule systems will be those which balance the inefficiencies arising from such externalities against other goals, such as ensuring that poorer countries have adequate access to international credit markets. In either case, there will also be reasons to favor rule systems that have desirable *distributional* properties—helping to achieve a more desired distribution of advantages within and between age cohorts—in addition to minimizing inefficiency.

Sanjay G. Reddy

Deontological Assessment

As noted above, present rules governing the accumulation and discharge of sovereign debt may be difficult to rationalize in the presence of certain kinds of interpersonal externalities. The recent debate on odious debt—in which governments subsequently deemed illegitimate take on debt and employ the resources garnered for purposes that later seem inappropriate or ill-advised—is best understood in this light. It is difficult to argue for deontological obligations to repay debt according to an inflexible schedule in the presence of such externalities. For deontological obligations to repay to be present despite the existence of intragenerational and intergenerational externalities, it is necessary to argue either that individuals incur obligations as a result of their being bound by a collective decision-making apparatus to which they implicitly or explicitly consent and which has the power to give rise to such obligations, or that they have been beneficiaries of the debts incurred by others to an extent sufficient to generate obligations to repay. Although such conditions may sometimes obtain, it is unlikely that they are reliably present in empirical cases. Certainly, the existing international norms concerning the accumulation and discharge of sovereign debt appear not to take explicitly into account the preconditions for such deontological moral obligations to be deemed to exist.

A NEW DIRECTION: CONTINGENT REPAYMENT

It has been argued that the proposition on the moral agency of states—the claim that states are agents capable of incurring and sustaining obligations over time—must be assessed in light of the pervasive intragenerational and intergenerational externalities that arise in this domain, and that an exclusively deontological account is unlikely to provide a fully satisfactory perspective concerning the conditions under which states possess moral obligations to fulfill prior debt contracts. In order to arrive at a morally justifiable theory of sovereign debt, or of the kinds of obligations that could be incurred by states generally, it is necessary to permit consequentialist criteria to also play an important role in the assessment.

The stereotypical core feature of a traditional debt contract is that it gives rise to a fixed schedule of repayment obligations. Those repayment obligations are not circumstance- or process-contingent, by which I mean that they do not depend on the states of the world that ultimately arise or the specific actions and events that have given rise to these states. Contracts that provide for repayments to vary contingently with the circumstances that arise and the actions or events giving rise to those circumstances, or with subsequent revelations about prior circumstances and the actions or events that gave rise to those circumstances, would be at variance with this norm. Arguably, they would not be *debt* contracts at all, but rather should be described as contingent claims instruments. I will not refer to such contracts as modified debt contracts, however, putting aside this terminological issue.

Can modified debt contracts be structured so as to address partially the concerns that I have raised? A preliminary observation is that, from a general equilibrium theory standpoint, a world in which it is not possible to enter into state-contingent contracts will generally give rise to inferior outcomes as compared to a world in which it is possible to enter into such circumstance- and process-contingent contracts. Its outcomes can be improved upon (in the Paretian sense) through the introduction of circumstance- and process-contingent contracts.[8] Such contracts can provide for a more efficient distribution of risks. For example, under such contracts, if a very "bad" state of the world (from the standpoint of the debtor) arises, then the rate of repayment can be suitably reduced, and if a very "good" state of the world arises, the rate of repayment can be suitably increased, rather than demanding an inflexible and rigid repayment schedule. Debtors may be willing to pay higher rates of return to creditors in good states of the world in return for the privilege of paying less in bad states of the world, and this may also be attractive to creditors. This Paretian rationale for the introduction of contingent repayment schemes does not require sophisticated moral reasoning. It may be arrived at purely on the basis of conventional welfarist economic considerations, even in the absence of distributional judgments or nonwelfarist moral considerations.[9] The introduction of these additional moral perspectives, however, can certainly make it possible to arrive at more specific conclusions than might otherwise be attainable.

Sanjay G. Reddy

Quite apart from efficiency considerations, the introduction of circumstance- and process-contingent modified debt instruments may make it possible to align better the sovereign debt repayment obligations formally ascribed to nations under law with understandings of the circumstances under which it is morally justifiable to demand payments. In the next section, I will describe some concrete examples of how this can be done. It will be important to note that in doing so I am in no way challenging the legal slogan *pacta sunt servanda*; rather, I am calling for the introduction of contractual forms (or changes to the background understanding governing contracts) which will permit this slogan to be more comprehensively adhered to in practice—by limiting the need for ad-hoc debt restructuring and default while giving rise to outcomes that are more morally justifiable than those often brought about by the demand for adherence to an inflexible schedule of debt payments.

It may be objected that circumstance- and process-contingent contracts of the kind I explore here are often equivalent to contracts which "bundle" together traditional debt contracts and insurance contracts or state-of-the-world contingent securities. From this standpoint, there is nothing that can be achieved by modifying the traditional debt contract that cannot be achieved by combining a traditional debt contract with a suitable state-of-the-world contingent security. Although this is true under abstract conditions, in practice there are missing markets for such securities, in part for the very reasons that state-contingent modified debt contracts are rarely observed in practice. The demand for such securities may be insufficient to bring such markets into existence for various reasons, including the existence of the intrapersonal and interpersonal externalities that make such securities morally desirable—these externalities may limit the interest of decision-makers in hedging against risks of future adverse macroeconomic outcomes (which may beset *other* persons in the same or a subsequent generation), or in otherwise entering into contracts which include forms of circumstance and process contingency. The apparent relative absence of macroeconomic mechanisms for insurance against variations in public revenue and national income has been widely noted.[10] It is partly due to this absence that recurring debt crises, brought about by adverse macroeconomic events (such as commodity price shocks and interest rate shocks), the possibility of which may have been reasonably anticipated, appear to be an endemic feature of the international economy. Of course, if this problem of missing markets could be corrected, the need for modified debt contracts incorporating contingent repayment might correspondingly diminish. That recognition creates no embarrassment for the argument made here.

POSSIBLE CRITERIA FOR CONTINGENT REPAYMENT

Modified sovereign debt contracts might permit repayment obligations to be made contingent upon both states of the world and the actions or events giving rise to those states of the world. The possible role of such modified debt contracts is best illuminated through a few (far from jointly exhaustive) concrete examples.

Factors Affecting Revenue and Payments

Modified sovereign debt contracts can in principle allow repayments to be made contingent on factors that influence the foreign exchange revenue of countries and their foreign payment obligations. Such factors are often proximately linked to the occurrence of payments difficulties.

A historical case of some importance is offered by the widespread and deep developing country debt crisis that arose in the early 1980s. It is widely thought that the conjunction of a number of distinct factors was responsible for the occurrence and timing of the debt crisis and that these factors included the sharp increase in world interest rates in the early 1980s, significantly linked to measures taken by the U.S. Federal Reserve Board with the apparent intent of reducing U.S. inflation.[11] Although the Federal Reserve acted with the apparent goal of furthering domestic U.S. interests (perhaps especially those of the creditor class in the United States, which was threatened with losses due to unexpectedly high U.S. dollar inflation), there was a broader consequence—creditors in the United States and other developed countries were exposed to the risk of default on the part of developing country debtors who found that it was extremely expensive for them to re-finance their debt at the new, higher interest rates. This was an instance in which the group of creditors (or an institution associated closely with them) was at least partially responsible, it may be plausibly argued, for the problems of the debtors. In a situation of this kind, it seems difficult to make a strong moral argument that the payments required of debtors should have been inflexibly held to a previously agreed schedule.

Another reason for the occurrence of the debt crisis in the 1980s was that the prices of many primary commodities exports had become low by historical standards—a development which had not been adequately anticipated. Modified debt contracts can in principle be made contingent upon such prices. There are some existing examples of debt contracts incorporating such contingency. Contracts for capital services in Islamic banking are precisely of this kind. Perhaps more relevant to this discussion is the use by Nigeria since 1992 of "oil warrants," which are warrants attached to Nigerian government bonds that require the government to make payments to the warrant holder that vary with the current oil price, as well as the prior and similar use by Venezuela of oil-price-indexed obligations.

Basic Requirements of Populations

The extent and nature of the claims that a creditor might make of a debtor could be made to depend on explicitly normative as well as nominally empirical criteria. For example, debt repayment might be made contingent on the ability of the debtor to finance the basic requirements of the population.[12] Similarly, resources garnered through debt and demonstrably expended in the form of investment (with the capacity partially to benefit future generations) might be treated differently from resources which have been used demonstrably to finance present consumption. To the extent that such a demonstration is possible, contracts can be written which permit discrimination between these two cases. In particular, creditors may be held partially responsible for sustained financing of a pattern of expenditure that is unsustainable or morally indefensible.

Odious Debt

There has been considerable discussion in recent years (reviving that initiated by Alexander Sack in the 1920s) of whether certain sovereign debt obligations should be treated as "odious" and accordingly subject to special provisions concerning debtor repayment. For instance, Thomas Pogge, Seema Jayachandran and Michael Kremer, and Jonathan Shafter (the latter in this volume) have separately advocated that the debt contracts entered into by certain kinds of regimes ought not to be viewed as creating a binding repayment obligation on successor regimes.[13] The underlying rationale for such schemes may be viewed as having both consequentialist and deontological components. Illegitimate regimes may be more likely to spend resources in a manner that not only fails to benefit their populations but also lacks the capacity to create morally binding obligations on behalf of their citizens. A framework of international law that recognizes such a principle is one that implicitly makes debt repayment obligations contingent on whether past states of the world (in particular those in which debt was contracted and refinanced) have possessed specific features (such as debtor regimes that were nondictatorial).

FEASIBILITY CONCERNS

Contingent claims instruments, which condition the amount of repayment on the state of the world that arises and on the manner in which that state of the world arose, will require a system of legal definitions of relevant contingencies, a system of monitoring these contingencies, and third-party arbitration or other mechanisms of adjudication. In recent years, the impressive expansion of derivatives markets has demonstrated that the definition and monitoring of contingencies of diverse kinds is feasible if there is sufficient interest in these activities.[14]

An analysis of the incentives generated by the existence of, and participation in, contingent debt contracts must be at the core of any analysis of their likely effects. An argument that might be advanced against such contingent claims instruments is that they would cause an increase in the perceived—and, indeed, actual—risk of lending to developing countries as well as attendant increases in interest rates and other barriers to borrowing, potentially shutting countries out from the credit market and diminishing their ability to finance their development programs. It is crucial here to consider whether these modified debt contracts would be introduced as alternatives (alongside traditional debt contracts) or as part of a revised background framework of international legal norms. If the former, then this worry need not be of great concern, since countries that would face large increases in interest rates could opt out of modified debt contracts in favor

Sanjay G. Reddy

of conventional ones. If the latter, then there is reason for concern. The former approach is unlikely to be wholly satisfactory, as countries may well choose conventional debt contracts precisely as a result of the presence of the intragenerational and intergenerational externalities that we have identified above, which may centrally influence decisions as to whether to take on debt, how much debt to take on, and how to spend the resources thus garnered. Some incorporation of norms concerning contingent claims into the background framework of international law appears to be indispensable. This is, after all, the argument of those who have favored the introduction of odious debt provisions in the international legal arena. Similar arguments may apply to other instances in which contingent claims may be morally desirable. It is important to see that the argument that the introduction of such norms may raise the costs of borrowing for certain countries, although pertinent, cannot be decisive.

A central issue here is that of the scope of informational externalities. For example, if it is not possible to distinguish between countries that are likely to use the resources garnered through international debt in a "presentist" manner to finance current consumption (perhaps of a small elite) and countries that are likely to use those resources in an investment-oriented manner that benefits future generations, then both kinds of country may face higher interest rates because of the perceived and actual risk that contingent repayment provisions will lead to creditors forfeiting at least some repayment in at least some cases. Potential good borrowers would be deprived of resources which could benefit present and future generations in those countries. This is a nontrivial problem which has to be dealt with, as *ex post* inefficiencies will result if it is not possible to separate these cases.

One kind of solution which could be considered involves mechanisms for countries to identify themselves as of a specific type through provisions that assure transparency and make monitoring feasible. Such provisions already exist in limited form in the International Monetary Fund's surveillance of countries' macroeconomic situation and the reporting requirements implicitly imposed by private credit rating agencies. The IMF's Policy Signaling Instrument offers countries the ability to undergo IMF conditionalities and surveillance purely in order to demonstrate to the private markets that they possess good policies and provides them with the

IMF seal of approval without providing a line of credit or additional resources. This is an interesting example of a mechanism through which countries seek to ensure that they are pursuing sound macroeconomic policies in order to attract credit and investment on favorable terms.[15] It is not difficult to imagine the broadening of monitoring instruments of this kind to encompass the (morally and economically salient) information required. Mechanisms that employ third-party certification to ensure that basic labor standards have been adhered to in the production process present another example.[16] In any event, this issue is unlikely to be of great relevance to the poorest countries, most of which at present are not deemed sufficiently creditworthy to borrow on private international credit markets, and which borrow almost exclusively from official lenders. Official lenders can *choose* to provide borrowers credit at interest rates that they themselves determine.

Of course, changes to the background interpretative framework of international legal norms to permit contingent repayment will not be an unalloyed good either for debtors or for creditors. For debtors, such changes entail limitations on the prerogative of states to borrow at will and for any purpose that they wish, regardless of their regime type. For creditors, they entail limitations on the presumption of repayment according to an inflexible schedule, regardless of who is the recipient of a loan, for what purposes it was spent, and the actions undertaken by different actors or the circumstances that have arisen in the world. Changes to the interpretative framework of international legal norms in this direction entail greater risk sharing between debtors and creditors, as well as the sharing of responsibility for the attainment of normative ends. To advocate this incremental shift in the direction of the sharing of risk and responsibility is not in itself intended to authorize either an infringement on legitimate prerogatives of sovereignty or on such rights to property as may be deemed to exist, but rather to recognize the complexities that enter into the ascription of moral obligations to states. Such sharing of risk and responsibility entails in many instances nothing more than a codification of existing ad-hoc practices in regard to debt relief and the abrogation of responsibilities by successor regimes.

The animating force for the exploration of possible institutional alternatives to the current system of stereotyped debt contracts stems from the

Sanjay G. Reddy

observation that existing norms concerning the accumulation and discharge of debt by countries give rise to inflexible demands to repay which are often difficult to rationalize morally—and therefore difficult to accept.

NOTES

1 I do not comment on the question of how these intertemporal threads should be conceived, for example, in terms of invariance of personal identity or of psychological connectedness and continuity (on which see Derek Parfit, *Reasons and Persons* [Oxford: Oxford University Press, 1984]).

2 I make the conventional distinction between deontological (i.e., process-related) and consequentialist (i.e., outcome-related) moral considerations for purposes of convenience. In doing so, I do not take a view on whether moral considerations conventionally viewed as deontological can in fact be viewed in terms of consequential evaluation within a framework that is adequately rich (as argued, for instance, in Amartya Sen, "Consequential Efficacy and Practical Reason," *Journal of Philosophy* 97, no. 9 [2000]).

3 Whether a specific instance of derogation from the formal provisions of a contract should be viewed as an "exemption" (as contrasted with an implicit clause of the contract) may depend on the extent to which it is part of the common background understanding of the contracting parties. For instance, the possibility that a domestic debt contract may be made subject to the provisions of bankruptcy law may be thought to be part of the common background understanding of the contracting parties, and thus to constitute an implicit provision of the contract rather than an exemption.

4 The determination of whether the freedom of choice is present may depend on diverse considerations, including the availability of distinct alternatives, the ability to choose for oneself among the distinct alternatives, and the nature of the alternatives themselves. See the distinction between the freedom to choose and choosing freely in G. A. Cohen, "Why Do Workers Choose Hazardous Jobs?" in *History, Labour, and Freedom: Themes from Marx* (Oxford: Oxford University Press, 1989); and the discussion of procedural and substantive freedom in the context of international agreements contained in Christian Barry and Sanjay Reddy, *International Trade and Labor Standards: A Proposal for Linkage* (New York: Columbia University Press, forthcoming).

5 There is an extensive literature addressing pertinent issues under the name of the "nonidentity problem." See, in particular, Parfit, *Reasons and Persons*.

6 It has been proposed that there are such instances, e.g., when the individuals to whom obligations are being attached participate in a shared framework of collective decision-making that meets particular tests (such as implicit or explicit consent to the decision-making structure itself) or when they are beneficiaries of an action taken by others. See, e.g., David Miller, "Holding Nations Responsible," *Ethics* 114, no. 1 (2004), pp. 240–68. It is important to note that such attribution requires, at the least, special preconditions.

7 The inefficiency arises from the fact that lower borrowing combined with appropriate transfers of income between persons could in principle bring about a Pareto improvement.

8 See Andreu Mas-Colell, Michael D. Whinston, and Jerry R. Green, *Microeconomic Theory* (Oxford: Oxford University Press, 1995), ch. 19 ("General Equilibrium Under Uncertainty"), and the broader literature on Arrow-Debreu securities and related concepts.

9 I employ the term "welfarist" to refer to a focus on subjective preference satisfactions as the sole informational basis for evaluation.

10 See Robert J. Shiller, *Macro Markets: Creating Institutions for Managing Society's Largest Economic Risks* (Oxford: Oxford University Press, 1993); and Robert J. Shiller, *The New Financial Order: Risk in the 21st Century* (Princeton: Princeton University Press, 2003). See also Sanjay Reddy, "Safety Nets for the Poor: A Missing International Dimension?" in Giovanni Andrea Cornia, ed., *Pro-Poor Macroeconomics: Potential and Limitations* (New York: Palgrave Macmillan, 2006).

11 See Harold James, *International Monetary Cooperation Since Bretton Woods* (Oxford: Oxford University Press, 1996), on the debt crisis. More generally on the early 1980s as a period of high world real interest rates, see Menzie Chinn and Jeffrey Frankel, "The Euro Area and World Interest Rates," Santa Cruz Center for International Economics Working Paper Series 1016 (Center for International Economics, University of California at Santa Cruz, November 2003); available

at ideas.repec.org/p/cdl/scciec/1016.html; and Jong Eun Lee, "On the Characterisation of the World Real Interest Rate," *World Economy* 25, no. 2 (2002), pp. 247–55.

[12] Kunibert Raffer (in this volume, pp. 127–50) has argued for the recognition of principles in international law that provide for the legitimate interests of creditors to be balanced against such basic interests of populations during debt workouts.

[13] Thomas Pogge, *World Poverty and Human Rights* (Cambridge: Polity Press, 2002); and Seema Jayachandran and Michael Kremer, "Odious Debt," *American Economic Review* (forthcoming).

[14] See also the discussion in the works by Shiller, n. 10.

[15] It should not be necessary to underline that in providing the example of the IMF's Policy Signaling Instrument I am not suggesting either that it is in itself attractive or that the IMF would be the appropriate agency to do such monitoring more generally. For a description of the Policy Signaling Instrument, see International Monetary Fund, "The Policy Support Instrument: A Factsheet" (August 2006); available at www.imf.org/external/np/exr/facts/psi.htm.

[16] See National Research Council, *Monitoring International Labor Standards: Techniques and Sources of Information* (Washington, D.C.: National Academy of Sciences, 2004), esp. ch. 3, "Information from Nongovernmental Labor Monitoring Systems."

Sanjay G. Reddy

Should They Honor the Promises of Their Parents' Leaders?

*Axel Gosseries**

S hould the foreign debt of the world's poorest countries be cancelled? In this essay, I am concerned with whether a generational perspective makes a difference in answering this question. I will show that it does, and that alternative accounts of repayment obligations are possible. I argue that a distributive theory of justice is not only appropriate to address the challenges to justice raised by long-term sovereign indebtedness, but that it is also superior to the solution offered by the odious debt doctrine. Unlike the odious debt doctrine, a distributive view is capable of taking into account the separateness of generations. More specifically, I also argue that the need to preserve creditors' incentives to lend to the poor in order to ensure that the latter keep having access to credit for important development purposes requires the adoption of a narrow, problem-specific view, which focuses on the distributive impact of the loan transaction, rather than a broad distributive view, which looks at the general distributive situation of the two descendent communities.

GENERATIONS AND SOVEREIGN DEBT

Generations are "birth cohorts," or groups of individuals born during the same period. Throughout this essay, I examine the stylized case of two countries, one of which has borrowed money from the other. That is, at a

* I would like to thank Lode Berlage, Jasques Drèze, Marc Fleurbaey, Frédéric Gaspart, Jean-François Gerkens, Alain Marciano, Victor Muniz-Fraticelly, Hervé Pourtois, Philippe Van Parijs, Kunibert Raffer, Clark Wolf, two referees, as well as Christian Barry, Barry Herman and Lydia Tomitova for their comments and suggestions on earlier drafts of this chapter. Earlier versions of the essay were presented at conferences at The New School, New York, N.Y., November 1–2, 2005; Centrum voor Economie en Ethiek, Katholieke Universiteit Leuven, Belgium, February 16, 2006; and GREQAM, Aix-en-Provence, France, March 17, 2006. Many thanks to the audiences for very useful comments.

particular time—and thus within a single generation—the governments of two countries enter into a contract that entails the immediate, nonrecurring transfer of resources from one to the other. Under the contract, the borrower government promises to repay the borrowed resources, plus some interest, on a particular payment schedule. I refer to these two governments (along with the populations they represent) as "the borrower" and "the lender," and to the governments (and their respective populations) of the nonoverlapping generation that succeeds the borrower's and lender's generation as "the borrower's descendant" and "the lender's descendant."[1] The central question is then: Given that the borrower has borrowed money from the lender, under which conditions (if any) and to what extent would it be fair to cancel the remaining debt owed by the borrower's descendant to the lender's descendant? And if it is the case that debt should be canceled, on which grounds?

The question of canceling the foreign debt of the poorest countries raises issues of both *inter*generational and *trans*generational justice (in addition to *intra*generational issues that will not be addressed here). For an issue of *inter*generational justice to arise, it suffices to have two individuals or communities, each of them being part of a different generation. In contrast, for a question of *trans*generational justice to arise, there need to be at least three individuals or communities—as, for example, in the case of historical emissions of carbon dioxide[2]—and typically four persons or communities, two in each generation—as in the case of reparations for slavery. The question of whether a generation has transferred sufficient resources to the next one is about what one generation owes another, and is thus a problem of *inter*generational justice. In contrast, the question of whether the descendants of one community owe something to the descendants of another one (who are in the same generation) due to what happened between their respective ancestors entails a problem of *trans*generational justice. Arguments regarding the acceptable level and use of the public debt—such as whether it is acceptable for a generation to impose liability on its descendants for a debt if it was not contracted for the purpose of investments that will primarily benefit the members of the later generation—typically belong to the sphere of *inter*generational justice. However, they can sometimes be of a strictly *intra*generational nature as well, such as when the concern is about the

Axel Gosseries

distributive impact within the current generation of canceling a domestic public debt.[3] In such a case, the concern is with the impact of such cancellation on poverty and inequality within the current generation.

WHAT IS ODIOUS DEBT?

The odious debt doctrine, as formulated by Alexander Sack in 1927, seeks to specify when a government ought to be held liable for debts incurred by preceding governments of the same state. Although this essay is not concerned specifically with odious debt, Sack's doctrine provides a good starting point for two reasons. First, it constitutes a relatively clear doctrine, capturing some of the key intuitions of justice at play in the broad debt cancellation debate. Second, Sack's own intuitions are not primarily concerned with distributive justice questions, such as what the long-term effects will be on the least well-off if the debt was paid or not paid. I use Sack's doctrine in order to render more salient the specificities of the approach I defend—and not as a progenitor of the view developed here or as a possible way of implementing it.[4] Thus, relying on the odious debt doctrine allows me to bracket initially questions of distributive justice in my examination of debt cancellation. I will then move away from it in a stepwise manner, shifting to both a generational and distributive perspective on debt cancellation.

Two Provisos

Sack's odious debt doctrine aims at identifying when a new government is legally obligated by an earlier government's debt contracts. For a debt to be "regular," it must meet two characteristics. First, the debt needs to have been contracted in a regular way by a regular government, which refers to any "supreme power effectively existing within the limits of a given territory" (the so-called *regular government* proviso).[5] Second, the debt "must have been contracted, and the money raised through it used to care for the needs and in the interests of the State" (the *public interest purpose and use* proviso).[6]

On a close examination of the doctrine, it turns out that in order for a debt not to be owed, the violation of the regular government proviso is neither necessary, nor sufficient. First, it is not necessary because even if the contracting government was regular, a successor government may "provide evidence demonstrating that such or such debts contracted by the former government were not contracted in the interests and to the advantage of the state and—this being important only in this case—that the lenders knew that these sums of money would be meant for 'odious' ends."[7] In such a case, the successor government would not be liable for repayment, despite the regularity of the loan, unless "the lenders, in turn, … prove that, despite such an 'odious' purpose of the loan, a purpose known by them, all or part of its product has in fact been used in a manner useful for the state."[8] That is, even if a loan that was intended for odious purposes nevertheless led to benefits for the state, a successor government would be liable to some extent for its repayment if it led to benefits for the state despite the irregularity of the loan.

Second, while the violation of the regular government proviso may suffice in practice to render the debt not legally binding (because of rules of evidence embodied in Sack's doctrine), it is not always a sufficient condition for freeing the debtor. This is because, even in the case of irregular loans, creditors may still "prove that the state effectively enriched itself as a result of these loans."[9] This possibility also shows that, in theory, the violation of the public-interest-use proviso is both sufficient and necessary to invalidate a debt. Moreover, the word "odious" is not used by Sack to refer to the general quality of the former borrowing government. Instead, it primarily characterizes the purpose and/or the use of the specific loan at stake.[10] Hence, the centrality of the public-interest-use (or "non-odious" use) proviso explains why Sack's doctrine is generally referred to as a doctrine of "odious debt" rather than as one of "irregular debt."[11] A debt will only be referred to as odious in the case of a violation of the public-interest-use proviso.[12]

Three Underlying Intuitions

Three types of justice considerations are present in Sack's odious debt doctrine. First, the implicit ideas of consent to accepting a loan and prior commitment to repaying a debt provide a presumption toward the repayment of debts acquired in "regular" ways. While Sack's notion of a regular government is far less stringent than the idea of a democratic government, his theory nevertheless rests on the notion of consent and prior commitment: representatives make a promise on the citizens' behalf that a certain debt will be repaid by them. Following this logic, then, the reason why someone has to repay a debt back lies in this very same person's commitment to repayment, in this case expressed through representatives.

Second, the idea of public interest implies that the citizens of a country as a group should have benefited to some extent from the loan in order to owe anything back. This could lead in turn to a fully commutative reading of the two provisos—that is, in principle, citizens can only owe repayment if they have consented to the initial transfer and have benefited from that transfer in some sense. In other words, there can be no obligation without prior consent and no obligation without beneficial counterpart. Yet, even if the initial loan was not contracted by a regular government in a regular way, the lender can always try to show that the borrower benefited from the loan. As a result, the obligation to repay the loan could not be grounded on a prior and valid unilateral commitment from the borrowing state. It would derive instead from the need to avoid unjust enrichment.[13] The borrowing country would then owe repayment because canceling repayment would lead to a situation in which, all else being equal, the borrowing state would have enriched itself at the expense of the lending state. There is thus a clear distinction between at least two grounds for insisting upon repayment—consent and enrichment.

Third, for the cases in which only the public-interest-use proviso is violated, no money would be due back provided that the successor government can prove that the lender knew that the purpose of the loan was odious.[14] This translates into an intuition of justice that carries the expectation that lenders should not act with "hostility" toward the borrowing state's population.[15]

It is also relevant to mention two intuitions of justice that are *not* present in the odious debt doctrine. First, the doctrine does not take into consideration the respective wealth of the parties. This essay aims to fill in this absence, by separating considerations of distributive justice from other considerations relevant to determining obligations to repay debts. Second, the doctrine is not concerned with whether the deal struck by the initial lender and borrower was fair at that time. For example, it does not look at whether there was a gap between the specifications of the contract at stake and the average interest rate or terms of repayment at that time in the market for similar loans.

Amending the Two Key Provisos

For the purpose of addressing the significant debts of poor countries, I introduce two amendments to Sack's doctrine. First, instead of a regular government proviso, I will use a more stringent "legitimacy proviso." Sack explicitly states that a government can be regular without being democratic. I assume that since only a democratic government can be properly regarded as having a mandate from the people, only a democratic government can be said to validly bind the people it represents.

Second, instead of a public-interest-use proviso, the content of which remains relatively undefined in Sack's doctrine, I will rely on a "fair use" proviso, allowing for an explicit reference to substantive theories of justice such as utilitarianism, libertarianism, liberal egalitarianism, sufficientarianism, and so on, as opposed to a commutative approach that would be partly in line with Sack's legal doctrine.[16] This could a priori be significant considering the intergenerational dimension of justice (but will turn out not to be so). Moreover, for the fair use proviso to apply, it is not necessary that the lenders knew that it would be, or would likely be, violated. Dropping the "knowledge by the lender" part of the proviso will fully make sense from a generational perspective, since the lender's knowledge should not be seen as relevant to the responsibility of the lender's descendant, as will become clear below.

CAN THERE BE AN INTERGENERATIONAL MANDATE TO REPAY DEBT?

The fact of generational succession presents an important challenge to the legitimacy proviso, since it implies that some borrowing decisions will necessarily lack the prior approval of people who do not exist at the time of contracting. I argue that such a prior approval is required, and that no currently existing arrangement can be said to grant the consent of future people.

The notion of prior approval begs the question of who is entitled to make decisions for the country. In a democracy, this boils down to the

Axel Gosseries

question of who should be entitled to vote.[17] One possible principle for answering this question is that all those who are potentially affected by a government's decision should be allowed to vote (the all-affected principle). The idea of being affected can be understood in a more or less broad way.[18]

With respect to generations, the problem is that their members will be affected both by decisions taken while they are alive as well as by decisions made before they came into existence, because the validity of laws extends in most cases beyond the lives of those who voted for them.[19] This means that even under a very narrow interpretation of what it means to be affected, such that it entails the exclusion of expatriates from the voting population in their country of origin, the inclusion of future generations among the voting population could still be justified.[20] If they were to have a say in all the decisions that could potentially affect them, members of each generation would have to participate not only in decisions taken while they are alive, but also in those taken by earlier generations (including constitutional decisions). Beside the obvious difficulty of granting a vote to people who are not yet alive (a problem to which I will return), I turn briefly to two possible objections to the desirability of such an extended franchise, assuming it were an available option. The first objection claims that extending the franchise to the next generation is *unfair* since it would be equivalent to granting it a plural vote. The second objection claims that the extension of the franchise is actually *unnecessary* because, were no generation to benefit from it, this would not lead to any inequality in political power among generations.

Would the Enfranchisement of Successor Generations Be Unfair? The Expatriates Analogy

Let us address the first objection. The situation of a given generation with respect to its predecessor is analogous to the situation of expatriates toward their compatriots still residing in the country of origin. Asking whether a generation should be entitled to participate in the decisions taken by its predecessor is analogous to asking whether expatriates should still benefit from a right to vote in their country of origin, in addition to having the right to vote in their host country. The problem with answering in the affirmative is that some people would be entitled to vote in two constituencies whereas others only in one. Thus some could end up with a more extended franchise than others, globally speaking. This extended entitlement may be problematic from the perspective of equality in the right to vote.

At least two answers can be offered to this objection. The first one consists in the claim that expatriates are more affected than other people, because they are subject to the laws of two constituencies (and to a more significant degree than tourists, for instance). Thus, if they are affected to a larger degree than others, their influence on the decisions affecting them should be proportionally larger. In theory, this would amount to moving away from a strict rule of *one person, one vote* toward an equality of proportional influence, allowing those who are affected by more than one jurisdiction to have a proportionally larger aggregate voting weight than those affected only by the decisions of one jurisdiction.[21] And in practice, this could justify systems such as that extant in the Cook Islands. A Cook Islands expatriate can not only vote in her host country, but also on her island of origin. Her vote on the islands, however, will be valued less than the vote of a citizen who still resides there. The group of expatriates is in fact entitled to elect only a small set of representatives out of a larger assembly. This is a nice way of dealing with a practical problem. Insofar as dual citizenship generally entails the right to vote in two countries, it could appear unfair if only some inhabitants of the planet have dual citizenship and others do not. A Cook Islands strategy, however, will give extra weight to expatriates, albeit a lesser weight than in the case of a full dual vote. What, then, would an intergenerational version of the Cook Islands model amount to? Future people would of course vote for their own representatives in the future. Yet, in addition, they could be given *some weight* in today's decision-making procedure as well, for instance, by being granted 5 percent of the total vote, be it only for some subject matters that are likely to affect them significantly, such as energy policy, research choices, or cultural heritage decisions.

The second possible answer to this first objection is that there is no problem with granting an extra right to vote to expatriates as long as it is granted to all citizens, including those who remain in the country. In theory, a system of *one person, one vote* is just like a system of *one person, two votes*. Promoters of dual citizenship (or of a double right to vote) would simply need to specify, then, that they are willing to promote dual citizenship under the condition that *all* would benefit from a right to vote in two constituencies. The specificity of the intergenerational context is that each and every generation is an expatriate in a sense. The intergenerational equivalent of dual citizenship for *all* (or of a double right to vote for all) would then amount to requiring that the rule according to which each generation should have a right to take part in the decisions of the previous generations be enforced across all generations.

Thus, in the generational context, claiming a right to vote for successor generations regarding the decisions taken at the time of their predecessors need not lead to a violation of equal voting rights (be it in its "strict," "double for all," or "proportional" version). One implication is that if state procedures cannot lead to at least the consultation (in some sense) of future generations, the decisions of such a state cannot be seen as deriving from a mandate from both current and future people. As a result, future generations could not be regarded as legitimately bound by decisions from earlier governments.

Is The Enfranchisement of Successor Generations Necessary?
The Complete-Life Objection
For those defining the boundaries of the voting population by reference to the idea of being "affected by," it is clear that granting the right to vote to a successor generation whenever the current generation is about to take decisions makes perfect sense. Yet, one may object that if the goal is to guarantee some form of equality of influence (whether strict or proportional), such a scheme would not even be needed. For although each generation is affected by the decisions of its predecessors, disenfranchising each and every generation when it comes to the decisions of its predecessors would not necessarily lead to any inequality of influence, so long as each generation were equally excluded.

In fact, the disenfranchisement of future generations can be compared to the exclusion from the right to vote of those below a certain age (typically sixteen or eighteen) or those above a certain age (such as sixty). Excluding dead people from the right to vote is equivalent to setting an upper (and unavoidably variable) age limit defined by each person's age at death. Thus (leaving aside significant ontological problems) disenfranchising future generations is equivalent to excluding all those below the age of zero. What the complete-life approach may then claim is that these forms of exclusion do not necessarily lead to any inequalities of influence because they are applied to everyone in reference to their respective complete lives. In principle, this view could consider it acceptable to grant to each individual only a single opportunity to vote during his or her whole life.

A major weakness of such an argument, however, is that some cohorts may suffer more than others from the consequences of choices made by earlier cohorts. These earlier cohorts may be more myopic than others, in the same way as some generations over the age of sixty may come across people under sixty who would be especially gerontophobic. The impact of the exclusion of various classes of people (of the dead, of individuals over sixty years old, of children, of future generations) will thus vary across cohorts, depending on the behavior of their respective neighboring cohorts. Hence, while such exclusions do not seem prima facie discriminatory when we consider equality between people's complete lives, they actually are. Hence, it is not true that excluding future generations from the voting population consistently through time does not generate any differences in impact.[22] It is thus preferable to extend the franchise rather than reduce it, because doing so would better guarantee that equality of influence effectively buffers the effects of disparate behavior among neighboring generations.

Is the Enfranchisement of Future Generations Possible?

Among other possible objections to enfranchising future generations, let me mention two more. First, could a community-based approach dissolve the need for a mandate from future generations? According to a community-based approach, it is because we are a single family or nation that we would have to honor the promises made by our ancestors as our own. Very briefly, this approach raises at least two serious difficulties. First, it would likely lead to an excessively traditionalistic society in which decisions by earlier generations automatically bind later ones (just as one person's consent would bind that very same person at a later time). Moreover, such a community-based view, understood at the moral level, would imply a rejection of the separateness of persons, which does not fit with many people's basic moral intuitions. Of course, this does not necessarily mean that a legal doctrine of state continuity cannot have other justifications, be they of a prudential or even of a justice-oriented type. Moreover, the rejection of a communitarian approach should not be confused with a generational model that is restricted to nonoverlapping generations. The assumption is simply that all individuals, whether from the same or different generations, should be treated as separate units of moral concern. Moreover, the existence of generational overlap does not change anything due to the fact that decisions made at a given time are still imposed on all those who have not reached the age of electoral majority at that time.

Finally, does the fact that many international loans are repaid within the same generation and/or the fact of serial debt restructuring undermine the relevance of a generational approach to sovereign debt? For example, since most IMF loans must be repaid within five years and most World Bank loans are expected to be repaid within twenty years, one could be tempted to conclude that the generational approach will only be of significance if what we take as a standard length of a generational gap is shorter than the average expected repayment term.[23] If it were so, one would rightly conclude that the intergenerational approach is irrelevant since debts are constantly renegotiated and endorsed by new generations, which entails that this would actually be *their* debt. This objection is not final however, even in cases in which the terms fixed for reimbursement are very short. For, considering the fact of debt restructuring, it is clear that in many of the cases, renegotiations are made against the background assumption that what was promised by our ancestors is still owed in principle. Similarly, new debts are often contracted with the sole aim of repaying earlier debts, in many instances, by earlier generations. Hence, new endorsements of past debts through restructuring or through contracting new debts to repay past ones will always be forced in some sense, and hence not chosen by the new generation that is supposed to pay back.

This being said, I have just argued that future generations should not be seen as democratically bound by the decision of an earlier government if they were not part of the population that granted a mandate to authorities that contracted the debt. And it is yet more serious because such a mandate can never genuinely obtain in principle (at least beyond generational over-lap) because of time's arrow. Let me now add two further remarks.

First, various countries have set up institutions aimed at representing the interests of future generations. This is the case, for example, in Israel where the Knesset had a commissioner for future generations.[24] Without denying their usefulness, the status of such institutions should be properly under-stood. Rather than seen as truly representing future generations, they should be understood as alarm mechanisms, or watchdogs constantly calling the at-tention of contemporaries whenever the interests of the coming generations are especially at stake. Of course, if guardians for future generations and the like are not to be seen as true representatives, they should not be put in op-eration to exercise proxy votes, for instance, through an intergenerational version of the Cook Islands expatriates model, nor a veto over present deci-sions. Given this difficulty, it is much more appropriate to confer to such institutions the right to demand further explanations from parliament or to be heard before certain types of decisions by public authorities are taken. In some cases, they turn out to have real weight in practice. Naturally, it is ex-tremely important for such institutions to base their actions on clear sub-stantive principles of intergenerational justice, especially as those they are supposed to represent are not present to confirm or deny their conjectures, nor to question the principles they may invoke in their name. So much could be done (or not) in the name of future generations that explicit prin-ciples should always be invoked and argued for.

This problem, moreover, cannot be alleviated by a move from an actual mandate that could take two forms, as in the example of the Israeli Knesset, to a hypothetical mandate. The predictive version would require the current generation to anticipate what the future generations would want its prede-cessors (not) to do now. The hypothetical legitimacy test for present deci-sions would then require asking whether the coming generations *would* have voted for this measure, had they been allowed to do so now. However, even the best attempts at predicting the future will likely amount to wild guesses. Alternatively, one could ask what future generations *should* accept as current decisions. This prescriptive (rather than predictive) test would then consist in asking whether future generations should have voted for a certain measure. This test is much more plausible than the predictive one because it entails reliance on substantive theories of justice, rather than predictions of future events in the presence of little, if any, available information. In fact, the very idea of a mandate could be dropped altogether and simply replaced by the need to act in an intergenerationally fair way. When actual consent cannot be obtained, rather than invoking a hypothetical consent in support of given policy choices, it is more appropriate to defend on its own merits the set of principles belonging to a substantive theory of justice that we believe should guide our actions. This is also in line with the claim that a hypothetical social contract is no contract at all.[25] Hypotheticals, though useful heuristic devices, should not be considered instruments of real democratic representation.

Implications

Thus, as a matter of principle, although an intergenerational mandate would be needed for a generation to be able to bind the next ones, such a mandate cannot obtain. I consider in turn two types of issues. First, does this impossibility mean that any obligation for a generation to pay back the debts of its predecessors simply becomes meaningless? Second, what follows from the perspective of the odious debt doctrine?

To answer the first question it is useful to consider four basic accounts of justice. According to a commutative account of justice, one owes something to another because one has promised something to that other person. In addition to a promise and its accompanying consent, there should also be some equivalence between the values of what is owed by one party and what has been promised in return by the other.[26] In contrast, according to a rectificatory, or harm-based account of justice, the reason why I owe something to someone does not derive from any specific prior commitment. Rather, it results from the fact that I have worsened a person's condition through my conduct, characterized as harmful and wrongful. To connect these accounts with legal doctrines, commutative justice is very much at home in contract law (contractual liability) whereas rectificatory justice finds its locus in tort law (extra-contractual liability) and in criminal law. Following the harm-based account, one could owe something to someone one has harmed even if one has never been in contact with that person before the harmful conduct took place. This is not the case with respect to obligations grounded in promise or consent. What matters here is that one needs to be causally responsible, through wrongful conduct, for a harmful situation in order to be bound by an obligation in the rectificatory case.

Contrast these two accounts of justice with two others: distributive and aggregative. A distributive account of justice (such as egalitarianism or sufficientarianism) is concerned with the distribution of wealth (however understood) among people in a society. On such an account, a person may owe something to another even if the former has never promised anything to, nor has harmed the latter. This obligation may be discharged, for example, through the payment of taxes. According to standard accounts of distributive justice, the mere fact of suffering from bad luck due to a strictly natural event (such as a congenital disease or a natural disaster) may generate obligations on the part of those who did not suffer such bad luck. Similarly, an aggregative account will assert the presence of obligations for persons even when they have not made prior promises or engaged in harmful conduct toward those to whom the obligation is owed. However, in contrast to a distributive account, an aggregative one will be concerned with the maximization of wealth (however understood) in society, not with its distribution as such.

What is crucial is that the two former intuitions of justice should only lead to considering someone bound by an obligation if this very same person did something that she should not have done or if she did not do what she committed herself to do. In contrast, if we are primarily concerned with the distribution of wealth among members in a society (as distributive justice would) or with the maximization of wealth in a given society (as aggregative justice would), one can owe something without any prior commitment or action on one's side. This feature is of key importance in the intergenerational context in which the factor that allegedly harms a future generation has to do with the (in)action of an earlier generation.

Promise-based and harm-based intuitions of justice are not fit for resolving the question of obligations for international debts. We should turn to other available criteria, such as the ones offered by distributive or aggregative accounts of justice. For, first, the obligation to compensate for *harms* inflicted by previous generations should not be grounded on rectificatory considerations, since the current generation cannot be held causally responsible for its ancestors' past (in)actions. This insight is crucial in examining the validity of claims to reparation voiced by descendants of slavery's victims in the United States or of claims to compensation for the damage to the global climate resulting from historical emissions of carbon dioxide.[27] Second, the obligation to honor fully or in part *promises* that were made by ancestors should not be grounded in considerations of commutative justice, since the current generation cannot be said to have granted a mandate to such past representatives. This insight is crucial for the present debate on sovereign debt cancellation, as well as for other sorts of prior commitments by earlier generations, such as in pay-as-you-go pension schemes. In those, one generation (G1), upon retiring, makes a commitment through the policies of its elected representatives to the next generation (G2), which is economically active at that time, that the following one (G3) will pay the pensions of G2 members when they retire. Here as well, obligations regarding pensions cannot be grounded in commutative, promise-based considerations of justice, since G1 is not authorized by G3 to grant consent on its behalf. This does not mean that G3 would have no obligation to pay G2's pension, or, by analogy, that descendants of beneficiaries of the slave system have no obligation to give reparations to African Americans, or that a subsequent generation does not have an obligation to repay the debt contracted by its ancestors. It simply means that the obligation cannot be derived from a promise that manifests consent to be bound. Nevertheless, an obligation may be found in a distributive or aggregative account of justice.

Moreover, the distributive account is likely to be able to incorporate the intuition at play in concerns for avoiding unjust enrichment, insofar as some have become rich in a way that carries costs for others. More specifically, the very fact that the enrichment of one party results from a morally objectionable action by an earlier generation is not as such necessarily relevant. However, if such a harmful (past) action led to some losses for members of the current generation, then this may be considered as relevant. For example, it is fair to presume that the descendants of slave owners would be relatively worse off today had their parents not taken advantage of the labor of slaves.

Finally, since obtaining a mandate from future generations is impossible, the legitimacy proviso of the odious debt doctrine, as modified above, will thus never be met whenever it is not the same generation that borrows and pays back. Hence, in such a version of the odious debt doctrine, any such debt may end up not having to be paid back, unless the lenders can prove that the borrowers' descendants enriched themselves at the lender's descendants' expense. Thus, it is necessary to ascertain whether the other proviso, i.e., the public-interest-use proviso of the odious debt doctrine, can be incorporated into a distributive approach.

A SPECIAL CASE FOR A NARROW DISTRIBUTIVE VIEW

What can we say about the borrower's descendants' obligation to the lender's descendants in regard to the debt contracted by the borrower from the lender? Having excluded both the harm-based and the promise-based accounts as possible intuitions to deal with a problem of transgenerational justice, I look at the possibility and implications of a distributive account, leaving aside a close examination of the aggregative option. Initially, I assume that the relative wealth of the two groups of descendants is unknown—that is, that the background distribution is unknown, rather than that the borrower's descendants are poorer overall than the lender's descendants—though I will then relax it. The central issues to decide will then be whether a narrow or a broad distributive view is most adequate in the case of canceling sovereign debt.

The Narrow (Problem-Specific) Distributive Approach

The unknown background distribution assumption helps illuminate the importance of examining whether, on which ground, and to what extent the borrower's descendants should pay back the lender's descendants, despite not being bound on commutative grounds by the borrower's promise. Adopting such an assumption has two consequences. The mere possibility of the lender's descendants being overall poorer than the borrower's descendants sheds a different light on the problem than usual, the general case in the political debate on the matter being generally that the borrower's descendants are much poorer than the lender's descendants.[28] Hence, *first*, the unknown background distribution assumption encourages the adoption of a symmetric approach that is concerned not only with how the borrower's descendants fare, but also with how the lender's descendants do. This makes sense since, from a generational perspective, the lender's descendants are no more responsible for the lender's actions than the borrower's descendants are for the borrower's conduct. Hence, adopting a generational perspective that emphasizes the lack of actual consent by a subsequent generation raises serious concern with rigid contracts that allocate the risk in such a way as to impose the full burden on the lending side in case of default by the borrower. This also means that the standard justifications for putting the burden on lenders, namely that the lenders are in a better position to avoid or absorb the costs of default because they would have an incentive to verify from the start the ability of the borrower to repay or because they tend to be overall richer than borrowers, do not hold in this case. This is so because the incentives would not be felt by the lender's descendants and would thus be unable to influence the lender's conduct, or because it is not prima facie apparent that the descendants of the borrower would be less well-off than the descendents of the lender. *Second*, the unknown background distribution assumption requires the adoption of a narrow (or also interactive or problem-specific) distributive approach since we only know about the transfers directly connected with the borrowed money, and nothing about the general distributive situation of the two descendent communities involved. In other words, the narrow approach rests on the premise that had the lending and borrowing exercise not taken place, the borrower's descendants and the lender's descendants would find themselves in a distributively fair situation.

Due to the lending action of the lender, were the borrower's descendants not to repay anything to the lender's descendants, the latter would find themselves worse off than in the counterfactual baseline situation (absence of loan) that we have assumed to be distributively fair. The fact that the lender's descendants would thus have to bear the opportunity cost arising from the lender's lending does not necessarily entail, however, that interactive justice always requires that the borrower's descendants should then transfer something back to the lender's descendants.[29] Actually, *three* typical cases can be envisaged, assuming that the lender's descendants are worse off due to the lending than in the counterfactual situation, that the opportunity cost they suffer equals in current value the money that was lent, and that the populations of the two groups of descendants are equal in size.

First, setting aside any possible unfairness of the initial deal between the borrower and lender, imagine a situation in which the borrower's descendants inherited at least some durable goods that were realized from the loan. Note that merely dividing this gain by two and requiring the borrower's descendants to transfer the equivalent of half of it to the lender's descendants would ignore the *net opportunity cost* from lending suffered by the lender's descendants—that is, the difference between the opportunity cost of making the loan and the actual benefit derived from lending the money. Interactive justice would instead demand that the borrower's descendants transfer to the lender's descendants the equivalent of half of the lender's descendants' *net* opportunity cost as it results from the lender's lending *plus* half of the gain from borrowing that the borrower's descendants benefited from as a result of the borrower's borrowing action. If the size of what the borrower's descendants inherited as a result of the loan is equal in current value to the net opportunity cost to the lender's descendants, then the borrower's descendants should reimburse fully the lender's descendants in the same way as the naive, generation-blind commutative approach would require—that is, half of the net opportunity cost, plus half of what the borrower's descendants actually inherited as a result of the borrowing. But this would be the case only in the very specific circumstances that have been assumed here, as well when the opportunity cost suffered by the lender's descendants equals in current value the money that was lent. The gain to the borrower's descendants may, of course, be larger than the value of what was borrowed, in which case the sum to be transferred to the lender's descendants will have to be larger than the opportunity cost suffered by the latter. And if the gain is smaller than the value of what was borrowed, the borrower's descendants will be entitled to transfer to the lender's descendants less than the latter value. These scenarios illustrate two clear divergences from the generation-blind commutative approach.

Further divergences come to light once we consider a second type of case, in which the borrower's descendants gained nothing from the borrower's operation—for example, because the latter spent it all in nondurable goods or in funding events with no positive spillover effects for the borrower's descendants. In such a case, the borrower's descendants should transfer to the lender's descendants half of the lender's descendants' opportunity cost from making the loan. The transfer would have to be directed toward the lender's descendants despite the fact that the borrower's descendants gained nothing from the borrower's borrowing. This illustrates the way in which the narrow distributive account differs from the unjust enrichment account: unlike the latter, the former is equally concerned with the impoverishment suffered by the lender's descendants as with the one suffered by the borrower's descendants.

A third type of case arises when the borrower's descendants are worse off than if the borrower had not borrowed anything, due for example to the fact that the borrower's leaders would have used that money for sustaining their illegitimate power or for advancing their position in a civil war that only became worse as a result. Even in such a case, the borrowers' descendants may still have to transfer money to the lender's descendants if the losses they incurred as a result of the borrowing are smaller than the opportunity cost incurred by the lender's descendants as a result of the lender's lending. If, on the contrary, the loss to the borrower's descendants resulting from the borrowing action is larger than the lender's descendants' opportunity cost, the direction of transfer would be reversed, and the lender's descendants will have to compensate the borrower's descendants (on top of not being reimbursed at all). This would be done on purely distributive grounds, and not on the ground that the lender's descendants would somehow be responsible for what the borrower's descendants had to suffer as a result of the borrowing.

Clearly, these outcomes are different from the ones that would obtain under the presently operating naive, generation-blind commutative approach. The narrow distributive principle that would govern a just transfer can be therefore stated as follows:

> If the borrower's descendants gained from the borrower's taking out the loan, they should transfer to the lender's descendants the equivalent of half of the lender's descendants' net opportunity cost from the lender's making out the loan plus half of the additional gain that the borrower's descendants realized as a result of the borrower's borrowing. If the borrower's descendants lost from the borrower's taking out the loan, the community with the smaller loss should transfer to the other half of the difference between their respective losses.

Thus, a narrow distributive approach to the problem may require less from the borrower's descendants on some occasions than would a naive, generation-blind commutative approach. Yet, it may also be more demand-ing of the borrower's descendants. This would be the case whenever the ad-ditional benefit to the borrower's descendants resulting from the borrower's borrowing was larger than the opportunity cost for the lender's descendants of the lender's lending. And it will definitely require more from the borrower's descendants than a non-naive commutative view that takes generations into account, which would maintain that the borrower's de-scendants owe nothing to the lender's descendants since they did not prom-ise anything in the first place.

The Broad Distributive Approach[30]

The narrow approach may initially appear attractive because it allows us to adopt a distributive approach, especially in a context in which neither a promise-based nor a harm-based one seem to be appropriate. And still, it preserves a focus on a specific problem, which may be politically crucial in cases in which negotiators are unwilling to take advantage of a specific issue to deal with general injustices. As a second-best distributive approach, it might thus look like the right approach.

Still, as a first-best approach, such a problem-specific distributive ap-proach is quite unattractive. For there is no good reason, political feasibility aside, to restrict the focus to the distributive impact of the loan transaction, rather than to the general distributive situation of the two descendent com-munities. Why be concerned about the opportunity cost of lending for the lender's descendants if the lender's descendants inherited more generally from the lender much more than what the borrower's descendants inherited from the borrower, with a gap significantly larger than the size of the op-portunity cost of the loan? If the lender's descendants incur losses from the lender's loan, it can be seen as bad luck. However, the fact that the bor-rower's descendants inherited less on the whole than the lender's descend-ants is also brute bad luck for the borrower's descendants—be it due to the borrower's intergenerationally unfair use of what it inherited from a still earlier generation, to the borrower's intergenerationally unfair spend-ing of the money raised through borrowing, to the fact that, despite full dedication to intergenerational justice, the borrower itself had inherited

Axel Gosseries

comparatively little from earlier generations, or to natural events that during the borrower's lifetime affected its wealth.

To put things differently, if the actions of the borrower and the lender are to be treated as if they were natural events with causal impacts on the respective situation of the borrower's descendants and the lender's descendants, it is hard to see why other natural events and more generally *all* the circumstances inherited by each of the communities should not also be considered relevant. A global evaluation of what the borrower's descendants and the lender's descendants inherited is thus required. Both the size and direction of transfers between the borrower's descendants and the lender's descendants would then have to be determined exclusively on the basis of the ability of such transfers to cancel out the general distributive injustices arising between the borrower's and lender's descendants. Hence, the broad distributive principle can be stated as follows:

> The borrower's descendants should keep paying the debt to the lender's descendants until the per-capita wealth inherited by the borrower's descendants from the borrower equals the per-capita wealth that the lender's descendants inherited from the lender and acquired from the borrower's descendants' debt repayment. And the same holds conversely for possible transfers between the lender's descendants and the borrower's descendants.

Under this principle, the borrower's descendants may sometimes have to transfer more than what they would owe on naive, generation-blind commutative grounds, in order to end up with a situation in which the lender's descendants benefit from general circumstances equivalent to those of the borrower's descendants. This does not mean that such a theory of distributive justice should operate without any commutative component. When it comes to relationships among contemporaries, it is clear that commutative justice leads to autonomous obligations, as when one set of individuals promises to complete some actions to the benefit of some of its contemporaries. But whenever (and to the extent that) the necessary requirements of a non-naive commutative theory are not met (as in the transgenerational context), there is obviously no room for commutative obligations.

It is worth noting that not only is such a distributive approach able to face the problem of impossibility of an intergenerational mandate, required by an intergenerational interpretation of the legitimacy proviso. It also proposes a criterion that does not require any *direct* attention to whether the money has been used in a fair way. Of course, how much benefit ends up in the hands of the borrower's descendants will matter—but whether this is the outcome of a fair use is irrelevant here. Finding out whether the borrowed money has been used in an intergenerationally fair way is insufficient because what really matters are overall intergenerational transfers. As a matter of fact, it is even meaningless to state that the money has been used in an intergenerationnally fair way if we do not take into consideration the size and nature of the rest of the intergenerational transfers. Think about a state that cares about reducing its external debt while totally disregarding its environmental obligations toward the members of its next generation. Similarly, investing this borrowed money into something that will only benefit the current generation is not necessarily incompatible with intergenerational justice if other transfers take place that compensate for it.

The Incentive-Compatibility Argument in Favor of the Narrow Distributive Approach

In fact, the broad distributive approach raises a serious problem. Once we adopt a generational perspective, it entails in practice that if a country is overall very poor (poorer than its lenders), it is unlikely that it will have to pay back its debts, whereas if it is overall richer than its lenders, justice will require that it pay them back. If this were the theory to be institutionalized, lenders would systematically tend not to lend to the poor, or to do so at very high interest rates. This would be very problematic since access to credit is crucial to the poor, whether at the individual level or at the country level. Hence, in order to preserve the access to credit for the poor, we should adopt such a criterion according to which the overall wealth of the borrowing country would not necessarily be relevant. And this requires that the scheme proposed be to some degree incentive-compatible— that it be such so as not to produce strong disincentives for potential lenders to lend to poor borrowers.[31] It should be made clear, however, that the main concern with incentive-incompatibility is the lack of access to credit for the poor under such a system, and not that it would make

Axel Gosseries

ignoring incentive-compatibility less profitable for lenders to lend to poor countries.

We need a solution to outstanding debts that would not discourage lending to poor countries while remaining as close as possible to the general distributive approach. One possible solution, which exists at the domestic level in inheritance law regimes, is "acceptance under the benefit of inventory." This principle allows a successor to avoid liability for the decedent's debts by declining to accept any inheritance from the decedent. Similarly, a generation could have the right to decline accepting an inheritance from its predecessors in order to avoid liability for their debts, and it would have an interest in exercising it whenever the debts exceed the benefits. Yet, this approach, which could be coupled with a sovereign bankruptcy mechanism—the possibility for states to rely on the institution of bankruptcy as it is already applicable to firms or individuals—is problematic to the extent that it is one-sided. Avoiding liability for a debt means that others will have to suffer the consequences of its nonrepayment. Such a perspective thus contrasts with the symmetric approach advocated earlier. Note however that, as it applies as well in domestic inheritance law, wherein children inherit the assets but not the debts of their parents, while it is a non-symmetric approach case, the approach is one that is to some degree insensitive to the creditors' background circumstances.[32] Alternatively, among the possible candidates for guiding principles, we could move back to a strict *pacta sunt servanda*, if we could show that the interests of the least well off were best served in that way, whether or not combined with international distributive mechanisms such as foreign aid.

Yet, the narrow distributive principle presented above should certainly also be taken seriously as one of the incentive-compatible options, together with some set of legal institutions and conditionalities that would lead in practice to analogous outcomes while allowing for some degree of legal predictability. In other words, it may turn out that the narrow distributive principle would offer the best possible incentive-compatible approximation of what the broad distributive view would otherwise require, were the latter incentive-compatible. For example, we could certainly consider the insertion of the narrow distributive view as one ingredient in a more general state bankruptcy regime, as an *ex post* avenue, or, as an *ex ante* avenue, include conditions in making the loan that ensure that the situation in which the narrow distributive approach dictates nonrepayment would not arise. What matters is that the narrow distributive view would certainly not lend itself to problems of access to credit for the poor as much as the adoption of the broad distributive view would.

Two important remarks should be added here. First, the predictability of the borrower's behavior is probably an essential element of incentive-compatibility. All else being equal, whatever the principle adopted internationally, the very fact that the borrowing side pledges to act in accordance with some principle of repayment (which need not be equivalent to a mere *pacta sunt servanda*) would limit disincentives for lenders and help establish or bolster the reputation of the borrower. Second, the case for a narrow distributive approach does not directly have to do with the fact that it would be less demanding on lenders than a broad distributive one, hence politically easier to adopt. Rather, it has to do with the fact that, once put into place, the former's dynamic impact would not end up being detrimental to the least well off.

TAKING GENERATIONS SERIOUSLY

We have shown that some of the grounds for justifying an obligation to repay foreign debts do not survive an analysis that takes the separateness of generations (and hence of persons) seriously. This is certainly the case for harm-based or promised-based grounds in all cases where the harm or the promise was done by members of earlier generations. Still, such accounts of justice are present in, and indeed sometimes seem to dominate, the debt cancellation debate. This constitutes a sociological puzzle, and is surprising given that distributive views for debt cancellation are clearly available. Though the narrow distributive approach is relatively complex, it nevertheless turns out to be more defensible as a practical set of rules than a broad distributive one—not for reasons of political feasibility, but rather because it offers a way to avoid problems of disincentives on the lending side.

The odious debt doctrine is very different from both the broad and the narrow distributive approaches. Its regular government proviso is likely to be violated in most cases once the generational dimension is taken into account. As to its public interest proviso, while the doctrine certainly implies an assessment of the benefits to the borrower's descendants, it does not seem to be concerned at all about the costs to the lender's descendants. Hence, while Sack's doctrine could have radical consequences when it comes to a generational reading of its regular government proviso (redefined here as a legitimacy proviso), its more central public interest proviso may only lead to merely accidental convergences with the requirements of a distributive approach. For its underlying intuition is quite different from the distributive one.

Those endorsing general distributive goals while taking problems of incentive-compatibility seriously may thus want to give flesh to a view such as the narrow distributive one. It is beyond the scope of this essay to propose a practical approximation of what the narrow distributive approach would amount to in practice. Calculation problems may be quite significant, for example when it comes to assessing opportunity costs. Yet, there are reasons to believe that they will also be present in most of the other methods, including those that require the identification of unjust enrichment, as in the context of the odious debt doctrine, since actual benefits are not easier to trace back than opportunity costs on the lender's side.

NOTES

[1] Thus, I limit the analysis to bilateral interstate relationships. I believe, though I cannot show it here, that the argument of this essay could be applied *mutatis mutandis* to cases involving private lenders as well. One significant difference, however, is that membership in a country is usually not a choice whereas being, for instance, a shareholder in a private lending firm, is much more voluntary. In addition, as I show later, the conclusions will apply to the more typical case of overlapping generations as well.

[2] See Axel Gosseries, "Historical Emissions and Free-Riding," in Lukas Meyer, ed., *Justice in Time: Responding to Historical Injustice* (Baden-Baden: Nomos, 2004), pp. 355–82.

[3] See, e.g., Jean-Marie Monnier and Bruno Tinel, "Endettement public et redistribution en France de 1980 à 2004," in Rémy Pellet, *Finances publiques et redistribution sociale* (Paris: Economica, 2006), pp. 329–50.

[4] Moreover, the uncertainties as to the legal status of Sack's doctrine do not need to worry me here since I am not asking what the state of international law is but what its content should be.

[5] Alexander N. Sack, *Les effets des transformations des Etats sur leurs dettes publiques et autres obligations financières* (Paris: Sirey, 1927), p. 6. Sack explicitly specifies that whether this power is of a monarchic nature (absolute or limited), whether it is derived from the will of God or from the will of the people, and so on are irrelevant considerations here.

[6] Ibid., p. 157 (translation by the author).

[7] Ibid., p. 30 (translation by the author).

[8] Ibid., p. 30 (translation by the author).

[9] Ibid. (translation by the author).

[10] See, e.g., ibid., pp. 27, 30, and 157.

[11] Ibid., pp. 26–27.

[12] Note that while a careful reading of Sack's evidentiary proposal indicates the theoretical centrality of the public-interest-use proviso, he downplays its practical importance, treating it as "too arbitrary and too vague" because whether a given use can be considered as being in the public interest is unlikely to give rise to a consensus at the time of signing the contract, the borrower is generally free to dispose of the money in the way it finds most appropriate, and it is budgetarily hard to trace an

odious spending back to a given source of income (foreign debt being only part of it). See ibid., p. 157.

[13] This is clear from Sack's own writing as well as from authors he refers to, such as Gaston Jèze. See ibid., p. 28.

[14] This also means that the borrower's side will have to carry the full burden of its own inappropriate use if the lender did not know, a problem to which I return below.

[15] Ibid., p. 157.

[16] Ibid., pp. 162–63.

[17] Recent accounts on this include Gustaf Arrhenius, "The Boundary Problem in Democratic Theory" (2004, unpublished), p. 12, available at people.su.se/~guarr/; Claudio López-Guerra, "Should Expatriates Vote?" *Journal of Political Philosophy* 13, no. 2 (2005), pp. 216–34; and Robert Goodin, "Enfranchising All Affected Interests, and Its Alternatives," *Philosophy & Public Affairs* 35, no. 1, pp. 40–68.

[18] For a narrow interpretation, see López-Guerra, "Should Expatriates Vote?" Cf. Arrhenius, "The Boundary Problem in Democratic Theory."

[19] I have dealt with the mirror problem of taking the past generations' wishes into account in Axel Gosseries, *Penser la justice entre les générations: De l'affaire Perruche à la réforme des retraites* (Paris: Aubier-Flammarion, 2004), ch. 2. The reasons not to do so here are different. The problem is not only that we do not always know what they wanted (actually this is a less serious problem than in the future generations case) but that they can less easily be said to be harmed if we do not care.

[20] For the exclusion of expatriates, see López-Guerra, "Should Expatriates Vote?"

[21] For a similar proposal, see Harry Brighouse and Marc Fleurbaey, "On the Fair Allocation of Power" (February 2006), p. 28; available at mora.rente.nhh.no/projects/EqualityExchange/Portals/0/articles/brighousefleurbaeymarch2006.pdf. Note that rather than relying on a principle of equality of influence (or of political weight) or equality of proportional influence, one may rely on the idea of protecting potentially vulnerable minorities, here understood as future generations. When minority members are granted a larger weight per capita than majority members—for example, through mechanisms of qualified majority—it may be because we believe minority members will, by definition, be more affected by the majority's decisions. This would remain in line with the idea of equality of proportional influence. However, a principle granting special weight to minorities may also be grounded on distinct intuitions, such as giving special importance to seriously taking into account the diversity of opinions and arguments in an electoral district. Moreover, granting the status of a minority to the potentially large and at least indefinite amount of future generations is problematic as well for this "numerical" reason.

[22] For a detailed treatment of the complete life argument along these lines, see Axel Gosseries, "Are Seniority Privileges Unfair?" *Economics & Philosophy* 20, no. 2 (2004), pp. 279–305.

[23] Thanks to one referee for pressing me on this point.

[24] On existing institutions and proposals, see Jörg Tremmel, "Establishment of the Rights of Future Generations in National Constitutions," in Jörg Chet Tremmel, ed., *Handbook of Intergenerational Justice* (Cheltenham, UK: Edward Elgar, 2006), pp. 187–214; and Shlomo Shoham and Nira Lamay, "Commission for Future Generations in the Knesset: Lessons Learnt," in Tremmel, ed., *Handbook of Intergenerational Justice*, pp. 244–81. This Knesset commission has now ceased its activities.

[25] See, e.g., on Rawls's contractarianism, Ronald Dworkin, *Taking Rights Seriously* (London: Duckworth, 1977), pp. 168ff.

[26] For some commutative theories, the very existence of consent should be seen as a sufficient sign of equivalence.

[27] On carbon dioxide emissions, see Gosseries, "Historical Emissions and Free-Riding."

[28] Compare this to the historical emissions case where a priori the case is the reverse. Rich countries are also often larger polluters. To that extent, they can be said to "borrow" from poor countries an addition to their share of the environment's cleaning capacity. In the case of historical emissions of air pollutants, it is those who are generally poorer that are the "lenders" of cleaning capacity.

[29] I will not attempt to provide here a detailed methodology as to how to assess such opportunity costs. However, assessing what could or would happen, or have happened, in the absence of a given action is an extremely common problem, including at the international level. To provide just one illustration from another field, see the methodologies used to assess additionality (of emission-reduction projects) in the context of the Kyoto Treaty's Clean Development Mechanism, at cdm.unfccc.int/methodologies/PAmethodologies/approved.html.

30 For an example of a broad distributive approach, see Lode Berlage et al., "Prospective Aid and Indebtedness Relief: A Proposal," Center for Operations Research and Economics Discussion Paper no. 2000/0032, University of Louvain, Belgium (2000), p. 42.

31 To take an analogy with employment policy, the broad distributive approach would amount, in the absence of other redistributive schemes than employment regulation, to expect that less fortunate workers be paid more than more fortunate workers, which would certainly discourage employers from hiring these less fortunate workers. To the contrary, the narrow distributive view on wages would disregard people's background level of fortune. I owe this analogy to Eric Schokkaert.

32 This is also true about the operation of the principle in domestic law. I am indebted to Jacques Drèze for pointing this to out me.

Risks of Lending and Liability of Lenders

Kunibert Raffer

L
ike any other market, credit markets depend on functioning economic mechanisms and a framework predefining the rights and duties of market participants. They could not function without these.
Within this framework both debtors and creditors have rights and duties
and are subject to risk. So far, discussions on sovereign debts have focused
on debtor duties, virtually disregarding those of lenders—though there is
no reason why this one kind of debts should exempt lenders from any responsibility. The anomaly of shifting all responsibilities onto debtors,
unique to Southern sovereign debt, encourages economically and ethically
wrong behavior—and makes focusing on lender responsibilities mandatory.

Although *pacta sunt servanda* ("pacts must be respected") is a fundamental legal, economic, and ethical principle, all legal systems recognize circumstances where contractual rights can no longer be enforced, or indeed
cease to exist. It is well known, not least from credit relations, that any legal
system protects contracts only if both sides have complied with their legal
duties. Lenders, for example, have a duty of care. They have to observe professional standards, or make checks, such as whether persons signing for legal entities have the authority to do so. Tortious or illegal behavior makes
them liable to compensate for damages, and may void contracts. Guaranteeing human rights enjoys preference over perfectly legal claims and might
make them unenforceable, thus overruling *pacta sunt servanda*—except
when the borrower is a developing country.

Risk and liability are necessary systemic elements of the framework
markets need to function. Risk is the hazard of losing money, even without
any fault of the lender. It cannot be avoided and exists both with
sovereigns and other debtors. External shocks, individual catastrophes, or
unforeseeable events can change the debtor's circumstances drastically,
resulting in losses in spite of every possible precaution and state-of-the-art

analysis of creditworthiness. Even model creditors may lose money if external shocks, such as natural disasters, render debtors insolvent. Without any fault of creditors, such shocks change the terms of the initial contract. On the other hand, wrong creditor decisions may increase risk. Economically, risk serves as an incentive to assess carefully debtors' ability to service debts. Errors and negligence in assessment bring about losses.

By contrast, liability ensures the right of victims to receive compensation contingent upon conditions stipulated in law, such as negligent actions creating unlawful damage. Domestic liability and tort laws serve the purposes of compensating those suffering such damages and of deterring such behavior. Internationally, this legal principle applies equally, and it is the duty of governments to safeguard it, not least for economic reasons. One may argue that liability does not change the terms of contract, but creates a new counterclaim of debtors unlawfully hurt by lenders. Economically, though, creditors get less than stipulated. Net claims diminish.

Shifting all responsibilities onto debtors—as has occurred in sovereign lending—encourages economically and ethically wrong behavior. Over the past decades there has been a concerted effort to eliminate any lender responsibility.

This essay discusses the discrimination against Southern sovereign debtors presently denied all well-established debtor rights. I show that the perceived absence of creditor risk and the absence of liability, both grave market imperfections, have produced debts no decent legal system would recognize. This has aggravated the debt problem, triggering the discussion of concepts such as criminal or odious debts. Discrimination against sovereign debtors has distorted markets and infringed upon the rule of law, causing grave damages to debtors, but also causing losses to creditors that the mechanisms of risk and liability would have prevented. I analyze the fundamental difference between private creditors subject to laws and official creditors making the laws and obliged to defend decent legal and appropriate economic principles. Finally, I present briefly proposals for how to avoid repeating the disasters of the past.

Kunibert Raffer

RISKS OF LENDING

Losing money is part and parcel of lending, like grocers have to face the fact that some apples will rot before they can be sold. Fees and prices charged to clients must accommodate these costs. This is both economically and ethically justified. Well-managed lenders will, of course, lose relatively little, while those unfit for the market may be wiped out by losses.

Some risk can be avoided. Conscientious scrutiny of borrowers, lending limits, and checks into how prior loans were used and, if used improperly, stopping further loans reduce the total risk in the lender's interest. Additionally, these mechanisms perform important allocative tasks by ensuring that money is put to good use.

Risk makes creditors cautious; it is the main incentive against loose lending. This useful mechanism has been eliminated in sovereign lending, producing massive misallocations of funds. In sovereign syndicated lending, it was claimed that countries would always exist and thus always repay. This idea does not, of course, stand up to scrutiny, as the history of sovereign lending before the 1970s shows. Generally, sovereign debtors, including developing countries, were treated much more generously[1] before the Bretton Woods Institutions (BWIs) became debt managers.

Before 1945, risk was allowed to play its role and creditors were aware of the risk of sovereign lending. Economic mechanisms prevailed and debtor protection was accepted. Although gunboats were sent out once in a while, attempting to collect debts, much money was usually lost. Sovereign loans may be seen as the junk bonds of the past. Usually, after some negotiations and feet dragging, claims would be reduced. For example, the U.S. railways nearly routinely went bankrupt, leaving foreign creditors with worthless papers and the United States with the infrastructure. Established in 1868, the British Council of Foreign Bondholders has tried unsuccessfully to get compensation for damages suffered because of unilateral breach of contract.[2] In 1876 the representatives of private bondholders decided to use Egyptian insolvency law, including debtor protection measures, as the yardstick to solve Egypt's debt crisis. Tough nineteenth-century capitalists were more humane and successful than official creditors nowadays. The final outcome of Latin America's debt crisis in the 1930s may be seen as de facto insolvency.

Usually, without courts or arbitrators, percentages of nominal debts to be paid as final settlements were eventually agreed on. As Angus Maddison put it, "Debt default eased payments constraints."[3] After negotiations, Brazil's debts were reduced by over 75 percent in 1943. In Colombia, local governments (municipalities, possibly) pioneered debt default and central authorities followed later. Some big European debtors were themselves delinquent on their debts after World War I. The British and French governments defaulted in the 1930s, on the grounds that their peoples' needs were more important than legal obligations to creditors.[4] U.S. states, which are quasi-sovereign as regards borrowing, have a long record of defaulting. In the 1940s, nine U.S. states suspended interest payments on loans when the price of their main export good, cotton, left them short of resources. The term "repudiation" was apparently coined by Mississippi simply refusing to honor its debts in the nineteenth century. The London Accord of 1953 roughly halved the present value of Germany's foreign debt in a de facto insolvency, putting the country on the road to reconstruction and economic success. At the end of the 1960s, Indonesia was granted the same treatment with active support (after initial opposition) of the German government, which also went along with granting substantial debt reductions to Poland.

After 1970, however, a fundamental change occurred in international lending practices vis-à-vis developing countries. Receiving signals that their governments would protect them, commercial banks lent aggressively, disregarding the most elementary rules of prudent banking. OECD governments and multilateral institutions encouraged and applauded the "successful recycling of Petrodollars." In spite of quantitative evidence, OPEC has been used as a convenient scapegoat for the debt crisis.[5] Risk has eventually asserted itself, as both massive losses by the private sector and insufficient losses by multilateral institutions show. In the meantime, though, the mistaken belief of riskless loans influenced lending in a very damaging way, causing a massive misallocation of funds. Without proper checks and assessments, money was shoved into developing countries—and it is no wonder that most countries have little to show for it.

The Pertamina crisis of the early 1970s was a strong signal to lenders that risk would be eliminated. The Indonesian national oil company Pertamina had amassed uncontrollable debts, whose amount, the U.S. Senate

Committee on Foreign Relations[6] concluded, no one, including commercial banks themselves, seemed to know precisely. Agreements with the International Monetary Fund (IMF) put a ceiling on Indonesia's external borrowing and a specific subceiling on Pertamina's. Convinced that they would be bailed out, foreign banks rushed in to go on lending, using technical tricks (such as rolling over short-term loans, which were not subject to such ceilings) to circumvent borrowing restrictions. Even "direct representation"[7] and warnings by the U.S. embassy went unheeded. When the crisis broke, the U.S. government immediately helped. The Committee on Foreign Relations concluded that "the Indonesian situation" could be repeated at any time. Senator Sarbanes expressed fears that the Senate would soon be forced to vote for payments to debtor governments to bail out U.S. banks. The committee concluded: "Conceptually, the independence of private bank lending activities overseas would be fine if the banks were actually made to bear the ultimate risk." But intervention of creditor governments "calls into question the justification—the high degree of risk involved . . . for the high rate of interest banks charge to developing countries. Thus it is the creditor governments, not the banks, which are really bearing the risk."[8]

Offered a bailout, banks understandably took it. Only the rare saint, who would prefer on moral grounds not to accept perfectly legal rescue operations, can hold it against them. But the U.S. and the other governments that organized the bailout committed a fundamental mistake. Having the task and duty to provide proper frameworks for markets, they should not have eliminated risk. As this crisis was small, it would have been possible to signal very clearly that there would be no bailout. The problem of wiped-out equity would not have arisen yet. The opposite was signaled instead: do not worry, you may circumvent rules and act against our warnings, and we shall bail you out all the same. The Indonesian government picked up the bill, in spite of lender behavior. By thus conferring the illusion of protected, riskless lending, the official sector set the course for future crises. Rigging the market by eliminating risk and giving patently wrong signals to private creditors, the official sector bears great responsibility for the global debt debacle.

Once the IMF and the International Bank for Reconstruction and Development (IBRD) had established themselves as "debt managers," they propagated the illusion that everything would eventually be repaid. The illiquidity theory, the Baker Plan claiming that everything must be repaid, "forced lending" (commercial banks encouraged each other to lend the same percentages of new funds necessary to keep a debtor afloat as were their percentages of claims vis-à-vis that debtor), or the catchphrase "growing out of debts" (the idea that growth would soon render debts payable; that countries were illiquid, not insolvent) recall this phase. Eager to embrace a new raison d'être, the IMF offered its services as a debt manager, rigging the market further. Debt management after 1982 has increased unpayable, or "phantom" debts.[9] A speedy and market-friendly solution of the debt problem would have limited losses for creditors as a group. Now, as a group, creditors will have to accept larger losses than would have been necessary some twenty years ago in order to regain the sustainability of debtor economies. Because creditor structures have changed dramatically, however, not all creditors will necessarily be worse off. More recent entrants who have bought claims cheaply in the secondary market might gain. Regarding commercial banks, the main creditors in the early 1980s, one would have to calculate in each case whether the differences in interest rates compensated for final losses. If so, a lot of trouble and the costs of rescheduling have to be taken into account. It appears not impossible that (some) commercial banks did lose in the end. These losses were exacerbated by the fact that international financial institutions (IFIs) were able to secure themselves a privileged status of de facto preferred creditors, mostly in breach of their own constitutions.

Eliminating risk totally by political fiat is, of course, impossible. While still insisting on full repayment first (Venice Terms, 1987), economic facts eventually forced official creditors to accept reality. Thus, "100 percent debt relief" is meanwhile propagated by bilateral creditors for some countries. Although IFIs are still protected politically, they too have started to reduce their claims. As the G-7 decision at Gleneagles shows, IFIs remain largely able to shift risk onto others. After the demise of centrally planned economies in Eastern Europe, IFIs remain one of the last strongholds of unaccountable planning.

Substantial shares of present debt were caused by creditors delaying necessary reductions over decades. Although the IBRD declared "early recognition" of a solvency crisis and speedy settlement "*important for minimizing the damage*," lecturing that "protracted renegotiations and uncertainty damaged economic activity in debtor countries for several years. . . . It took too long to recognize that liquidity was the visible tip of the problem, but not its root," the IBRD joined other official creditors in delaying necessary and justified relief.[10] Official creditors inflicted damages on debtors and other creditors. It is difficult to argue that the IBRD did so unknowingly.

One main factor triggering the debt crisis in the 1980s was the introduction of variable interest rates during the 1970s. By stipulating a spread over the London inter-bank offer rate (LIBOR) or prime as the rate charged to countries, lenders shifted interest volatility risks onto borrowers. This is not necessarily against borrowers' interest, though. If fixed interest rates had been stipulated, lender charges would have had to include the specific volatility risk. If the stipulated variable rate is reduced by the costs of providing for interest rate variability (the difference vis-à-vis the fixed interest rate otherwise charged equals or is larger than the expected value of volatility costs), borrowers are not worse off. In cash-flow terms they are even more liquid. Whether developing countries actually benefited from comparatively lower rates would have to be answered by analyzing data. A functioning credit market, as opposed to sovereign lending, limits the amount of risk creditors can shift onto debtors. If interest hikes are too large, debtors are driven to insolvency. Functioning markets make creditors lose money in spite of shifting risk. This also applies to punitive interest rates: if they are too high, they push debtors into insolvency and cannot be cashed.

Interest rate differences should reflect specific risks. Very creditworthy debtors pay less interest than others. If countries would actually always repay, no risk would exist. Higher spreads charged to developing countries would have been unjustified and a sign of market distortion. Substantial losses suffered by commercial banks later prove that risk asserts itself, thus justifying spreads.

Good professional practice demands that part of the higher interest charged to riskier borrowers be used to build up loan loss provisions. In spite of differentiated interest rates, too many lenders did not provide sufficiently against risk. Because they held appropriate loan loss provisions, continental European banks were much less affected by the 1982 crisis than U.S. and Japanese banks. Without appropriate loan loss reserves, U.S.

money-center banks faced the risk of major defaults literally wiping out their equity. By contrast, Europeans could have realized losses immediately. Unsurprisingly, early calls for a reasonable solution came from European banks. A British banker, David Suratgar, was the first to advocate emulating U.S. Chapter 11 insolvency after 1982. The late Alfred Herrhausen, then CEO of Deutsche Bank, was among the most vocal advocates of negotiated debt reduction.[11] Heeding such proposals early on would have saved time, effort, and money.

Differences in legal frameworks explain this different behavior. While loan loss provisions are tax-deductible in continental Europe, the United States limited tax deductibility unduly. U.S. banks had to pay taxes on the money set aside against risk. This fundamental regulatory error discouraged economically appropriate behavior. The U.S. International Lending Supervision Act established the Allocated Transfer Risk Reserve "to cause all affected banking institutions to recognize . . . the risk and diminished value of certain international assets."[12] Authorities must therefore have been aware of the real value of nominal claims. Yet, they chose to destabilize international credit markets by unhelpful regulations.

Tax-deductible loan loss provisioning is a very efficient stabilizer with negligible costs to taxpayers.[13] To the extent that provisions reflect actual losses in the value of loans already suffered but not yet booked, they do not economically constitute taxable income. U.S. practice taxes illusory profits. It appears a paradox that otherwise anti-tax U.S. corporations have put up with this.

The precarious situation of U.S. banks was exacerbated by quarterly balance sheets and the perceived need to avoid reducing income by provisioning. Such fears were finally overcome when Citicorp set aside $3 billion in May 1987. The value of its shares increased because of this move. Markets reacted reasonably. In addition, especially U.S. banks were subject to what the literature called "legal risk."[14] Crises at quarters' ends during the 1980s were often triggered by awkward and economically debatable regulatory constraints, such as the ninety-days clause establishing an inflexible deadline for payments to be still considered in time, the impossibility of capitalizing interest arrears, or unpredictable and allegedly discriminatory decisions of regulators. Inflexible and antiquated U.S. regulations even brought about the only working "debtors' cartel" when debtors such as Mexico, Brazil, or Venezuela joined to help Argentina pay in time to save U.S. banks from having to classify loans as nonperforming.[15] On one occasion the hands of the clock were reportedly held back to "be able" to book payments "in time." Abolishing such legal harassment is in anyone's interest.

Inappropriate regulations made the bailout of U.S. money-center banks necessary, which rigged the market against smaller, domestic banks. The Independent Bankers' Association of America (IBAA), which represented roughly 7,000 members generally not involved in foreign lending, was troubled about the special protection granted by the IMF, the Treasury, and the Fed, "looking towards insuring that interest is paid in full," because "a special class of banks and a special class of loans is emerging that is not under market disciplines applicable to all other banks."[16] This hurt U.S. farmers' export interest, institutions serving them, and other banks. Kenneth Guenther put it in a nutshell: "It is patently unfair." It is also patent economic nonsense. Meanwhile, risk has asserted itself. Money has been lost. For more than a decade the private sector has accepted debt reductions, in sharp contrast to IFIs. A 45 percent reduction, as in the case of Ecuador's Brady deal, is definitely not negligible. The present statement by official creditors that there is a "necessity" to "bail in the private sector" is at severe odds with the truth.

Although responsible for aggravating debt crises, official creditors are much more intransigent than private ones. On purely logical-economic-political grounds this can be easily explained. Ethical considerations let us hope, of course, that such motives do not apply. Public creditors can use debt relief as a means of exerting pressure on Southern debtors. Unlike private creditors, they do not have to pick up the costs of protracted negotiations. Taxpayers have to. Public decision-makers gain without costs. For IFIs, crises mean more income and more political weight. If the fundamental market mechanism of risk were allowed to work, such motives could not prevail.

The private sector remained more pragmatic, as the case of a nonmodel debtor not under BWI control shows. Representing private creditors, British merchant bankers Morgan Grenfell negotiated a debt reduction with North Korea in 1988, which would have reduced the principal by 70 percent. This deal failed to be accepted by the majority of banks involved, which favored new negotiations.[17] Nevertheless, they accepted the principle of debt reduction as private creditors had done before 1945, only opposing the size of the cut as being too large.

RISKS COMPOUNDED BY LAWS

Basic legal principles, such as safeguarding human rights, increase risk by exempting economically recoverable resources. Insolvency laws change the terms of contract, often drastically, including for nonconsenting creditors. Insolvent debtors are by definition incapable of honoring all obligations. It is logically and economically impossible to fulfill contracts as stipulated. All civilized legal systems compound this factual creditor risk by granting debtor protection. There is a conflict between two fundamental legal principles, the right of creditors to interest and repayments (*pacta sunt servanda*) and the principle recognized generally (not only in the case of loans) that one must not be forced to fulfill contracts if that leads to inhumane distress, endangers one's life or health, or violates human dignity. Civilized laws give unconditional preference to human rights and human dignity. Debtors cannot be forced to starve themselves or their children to be able to pay more— unless they are developing countries. Although creditor claims are recognized as legitimate, insolvency exempts resources from being seized by bona fide creditors, aggravating the haircut creditors have to accept. It is important to emphasize that insolvency only applies to claims based on solid and proper legal foundations.

Insolvency changes contracts substantially. In the United States, general unsecured creditors can expect to receive nothing in four out of five bankruptcy cases, and 4–5 percent on average if they get anything at all.[18] Argentina's initial offer of 25 percent of face value, though 5 percentage points below the secondary market rate of Argentine debt, compares quite favorably. The final terms were a little more generous to creditors. Meeting President Bush in January 2004, Argentina's President Kirchner compared Enron paying its investors only "14 cents on the dollar"[19] with Argentina. In both cases *pacta sunt servanda* was overruled. Argentina caused an angry outcry. Enron's bankruptcy settlement did not but was considered a matter of course.

Kunibert Raffer

Laws may terminate, modify, or permit a party to terminate or modify contracts, explicitly allowing unilateral changes of contractual rights. Thus, section 365(a), 11 USC empowers the trustee (subject to the court's approval) to "assume or reject any executory contract or unexpired lease of the debtor." Pursuant to section 365(g) this "constitutes a breach of such contract," a perfectly legalized breach. Injured entities are given a prepetition claim for any resulting damages, and are treated as prepetition creditors with respect to this claim. Considering the statistical distribution of unsecured creditor receipts, a quick calculation based on Steven Schwarcz's figures renders an expectation value of about 0.01. The law itself annihilates perfectly legal claims. In the case of railroad reorganization (Subchapter IV of Chapter 11, Title 11 USC), section 1165 protects public interest "in addition to the interests of the debtor, creditors, and equity security holders." Section 1170(a)(2) permits courts to abandon railway lines if this is "consistent with the public interest." There exists a public interest in the preservation of rail transportation that mandates finding a balance between various interests, which economically means that creditors may have to lose more than without such balancing. The plan can only be confirmed (section 1173(a)(4), 11 USC) if consistent with the public interest. No creditor government has shown a similar public interest in avoiding that debt service increases infant mortality within Southern debtor countries.

The British Money Lenders Act of 1900 enabled courts to reopen any money-lending transaction when interest or charges were excessive and the transaction harsh and unconscionable, or otherwise such that courts of equity would give relief. Debtors needed not pay more than what the court thought to be fairly due. This act was replaced by the Consumer Credit Act in 1974, which made resistance to demands for debt repayment much more difficult.[20] Nevertheless, a couple whose initial debt of £5,750 had spiralled to over £380,000 had their debt "wiped out" because the loan agreement was unenforceable under this act.[21] Such changes of contracts are generally accepted and universally applied—except in the case of developing countries.

Examining domestic legal systems for general principles of law in search of international law rules, the Committee on International Monetary Law of the International Law Association concluded:

On the municipal level, bankruptcy laws and norms protecting debtors from enforcement measures affecting the right to a basic living standard would be relevant. As a State is involved, the special rights and obligations of the State on the national level have to be taken into account. An integrated perspective of these rules may suggest that obligations of a State cannot generally be enforced if basic rights of the population would be affected. Such considerations could be supplemented by reference to modern recognition of human rights in general, and of basic rights of the human person in particular.[22]

LIABILITY AND LACK OF LIABILITY IN INTERNATIONAL DEBT RELATIONS

All legal systems establish duties creditors must comply with in order to enjoy full legal protection of their contractual rights. Not complying with such duties may give rise to damage compensation payments. Establishing and enforcing these principles is the duty of governments, both with regard to domestic and international laws. While the private sector has no further duty but to abide by laws passed by others, governments have also the obligation to preserve the foundation of the rule of law, including international law, and to safeguard human rights. Creditor governments have not done so, but have abetted unlawful practices, such as the violation of membership rights of debtor countries by IFIs.

Their different roles and duties require us to distinguish clearly between private and official creditors. The former may have benefited from the absence of legal enforcement, the protection against the proper application of laws, or might even have broken laws occasionally. Public authorities actively engaged in not enforcing normal legal standards or violating the contractual rights of others are a totally different category. Official creditors have intervened into debtor economies, mostly in ways that cannot be described but as reckless and gravest negligence, creating damages that their victims have had to pay for.

Bilateral and Multilateral Creditors

The behavior of official creditors is characterized by the elimination of the market mechanism of risk and their contempt for the rule of law. Dominating debt management, official creditors have made "rules" conspicuously differing from universally accepted legal principles. They established a legal

Kunibert Raffer

double standard discriminating against developing countries, depriving the poorest of the globe of due protection of their human dignity. They led private creditors to act against economic, legal, and moral principles. Private creditors accepted this protection after 1982 also in order to survive under pressure of being wiped out due to economically unsound regulatory norms. Official creditors have inflicted damage on debtors, flouted contractual rights and obligations, even human rights, gaining politically and financially from their behavior and using these catastrophes to exert leverage with debtor countries. Obviously, *pacta non sunt servanda* when it comes to the rights of developing countries, an asymmetry destroying the foundations of markets and the rule of law. From an ethical point of view it is unjustifiable.

The debt crisis erupted in the early 1980s because a sudden change of economic policy in one creditor country—the United States—sent interest rates "sky-rocketing," as the OECD[23] described it. Creditor action pushed the debt service burden of developing countries over the brink. From an ethical point of view one may see this as weakening this creditor's claim to repayment, unless the interest hike is seen as a legitimate expression of national self-determination.[24] If lending to sovereigns were subject to civilized laws—as domestic debtor-creditor relations are—such creditor action would have driven debtors into insolvency protection. This creditor would have lost part of its claim, which seems justified. Other creditors not responsible for higher interest rates would also have lost money, such as private creditors, who have never had any influence at all on the level of any currency's interest rate. They cannot be blamed for the high interest rates around 1980. Their own borrowing became more expensive. Transmitting this effect via variable interest rates is not usurious.

Creditor governments have always restricted those exports where their debtors were most competitive. Their elaborated trade "barriers delay entry into the export-oriented industries, which are most accessible to developing countries."[25] We witness the unique spectacle of creditors simultaneously hindering their debtors to earn the necessary cash to pay as stipulated and demanding them to do so. This could not happen in any other creditor-debtor relation, because the law would protect debtors.

Finally, the capital weights of Basel I strongly encouraged those short-term flows that caused the typical crisis of the late 1990s, such as in Asia. Once again the public sector set the course for debt crises.

Unjustified euphoria of governments and IFIs encouraged and may even have triggered the new wave of bond lending after 1989. IFIs proclaimed the end of the debt crisis in Latin America, while their own statistics documented growing arrears.[26] Although a large chunk of loans went initially to the private sector, governments routinely had to bail out creditors once problems emerged. Again, risk-free lending was signaled.

The eagerness of the BWIs to acquire a new role as debt managers is one explanation for what happened after 1982. The IBRD did so in violation of its Articles of Agreement. Article III.4.vii stipulates that loans "shall, except in special circumstances, be for the purpose of specific projects." Article V, section 1(b) of the International Development Association's (IDA) statutes repeats this restriction literally. The shares of present program lending are certainly beyond what the phrase "except in special circumstances" could logically describe.

This would have been impossible, however, without the support of major shareholders, the G-7, and other European countries. One reason for that support might have been identified by Dani Rodrik, who interpreted the debt crisis as an opportunity seized "to wipe the slate clean and mount a frontal attack on the entire range of policies in use."[27] A crisis brought about by overspending and overlending in unregulated global credit markets and the sudden change of Northern economic policy was simply declared to stem from too little globalization, import substitution, and "inward looking" policies. Distinctions between bad and proper import substitution were not made, even though the Asian Tigers had used these discredited policies to good effect before they started neoliberal globalization, which caused the crash of 1997. The crash of globalized credit markets provided leverage for further globalization opening the South to Northern economic interests, but also for promoting petty political advantages. If one accepts Rodrik's explanation, "debt management" makes sense. Like economic efficiency, decent legal norms would have been a hindrance.

The public sector had recognized the problem of liberalizing capital markets years before the crash. The unfolding of the Asian financial crisis could be watched like a movie whose script is known. In 1999 the IBRD acknowledged having known "the relevant institutional lessons"[28] since the early 1990s, when an audit report by its Operations Evaluation Department described what had happened in Chile in 1982. Nevertheless, Asian countries were encouraged to adopt the same policies that led to Chile's crash. Any domestic law would see this as a clear case of liability.

Most Multilateral Development Banks (MDBs) have a statutory obligation to grant relief, but chose to violate their own articles of agreement. The IBRD's founders wanted lending to be subject to some market discipline, and designed mechanisms that would allow the Bank to shoulder its fair share of risk. Pursuant to Article IV(4)(c), member countries suffering "from an acute exchange stringency, so that the service of any loan contracted by that member or guaranteed by it or by one of its agencies cannot be provided in the stipulated manner . . . may apply to the Bank for a relaxation of the conditions of payment." Article IV.7 contains the obligation to reduce claims in the case of default. By contrast, other creditors, especially the private sector, have no similar obligation to grant debt relief. Logically, this supports the view that the IBRD and other IFIs are meant to grant relief well before others, that their statutes legally subordinate multilateral claims. Their task of fostering development would explain this decision of their founders.[29] All obey their statutory duty to establish loan loss reserves. So has the IMF without such duty. Debtors have already financed debt reductions, but are refused relief. IFIs have charged without delivering what has already been paid for, wrongly claiming that they cannot finance relief unless someone else bails them out.[30] The G-7 and other major shareholders support this incorrect policy in spite of preaching good governance and the rule of law to the very debtors whose rights they help infringe.

IDA rather than the IBRD is of importance for poor countries. Its Articles of Agreement, although somewhat vague, also foresee debt relief. Pursuant to Article V(3), titled "Modifications of Terms of Financing," IDA may "agree to a relaxation or other modification of the terms on which any of its financing shall have been provided." In the case of maturities of thirty-five, forty, or even twenty years with ten-year grace periods and "no interest charge" (IDA prefers to call its 0.75 percent interest rate a service charge), this leaves little realistic alternatives but outright reductions.

The IMF's practice of violating membership rights of developing countries has been supported by Northern governments. Although all IMF members have the statutory right to capital controls, developing countries have been forced to liberalize capital accounts. Asian countries had a right to control capital outflows in 1997—as the IMF had to admit when Malaysia exercised it—but by forcing members to finance large and sustained outflows by speculators the IMF clearly violated its own constitution. Forcing debtors to forgo their right to capital controls in open breach of the IMF's statutes makes increased stocks of international reserves necessary. These practically sterilized reserves could be used either for anti-poverty measures or for debt service.[31]

The persistent problem of wrong IFI estimates forming the base of "debt relief" has been raised repeatedly,[32] as well as the need to introduce damage compensation. One very telling illustration of errors in debt management may suffice. When classifying different countries in transition, the IBRD erred, putting an IDA country into the higher IBRD loans category.[33] The country suffered substantial damage because of loans at terms surpassing its servicing capacity. It was not even discussed whether compensation should be paid. Such lack of financial accountability, good governance, and creditor government interest in applying the rule of law universally have led to what Jeffrey Winters[34] called "criminal debts." IFIs disbursed loans to corrupt governments, such as Suharto's in Indonesia, knowing that large parts of these loans would be embezzled. Economically, embezzlement and capital flight would have been perceptibly lower without multilateral financing. Before the era of the BWIs such lending would in all likelihood not have obliged a debtor to full repayment.[35]

The concept of odious debts also illustrates creditor domination cum arbitrariness. The United States propagated it twice: first, to free Cuba from Spanish colonial debts, when it became an informal U.S. colony; and when Iraq was invaded. In both cases U.S. interest is evident. Conspicuously, this concept was neither discussed nor applied to dictators such as Nicaragua's Somoza, Zaire's Mobutu, or the fascist military juntas in Chile and Argentina—all of which enjoyed strong U.S. support and were characterized by substantial claims of U.S. creditors, unlike Cuba and Iraq. The present discussion of odious debts and the rather thorny question of what constitutes such debts would largely have been avoided if risk and liability had been allowed to fulfill their roles in sovereign lending.

What seems particularly worrying is that executive wishes in the United States may change court judgments. After Costa Rica had prevailed, based in part on the assumption that this was consistent with U.S. policy, the Second Circuit reheard the matter and reversed itself when the executive branch clarified as amicus curiae that supporting Costa Rica was not U.S. policy.[36] This reversal occurred in spite of the court's own legal arguments and what it had called "principles recognized by all civilized nations." Logically, this subordinates legal principles to administrative whim. Although it was always explicitly acknowledged that Costa Rica's capital controls were effected "in response to escalating economic problems," the court specifically named U.S. "interest in maintaining New York's status as one of the foremost commercial centers in the world" as one reason for the final judgment.[37] Grave economic problems were subordinated to this commercial interest, even though it seems unlikely that a different judgment would have done perceptible harm to New York's standing as a financial center. On the contrary, given that court judgment, one wonders why New York is so frequently the jurisdiction of choice. While it is perfectly understandable that creditors wish to avoid national courts, fearing that these might not be really independent from their governments, and would prefer courts weighing interests in the way this court did, it is difficult to understand why debtors do not insist on neutral jurisdictions, where the courts are not inclined to accommodate their government's wishes so fully.

Private Creditors

The law imposes duties and restrictions on creditors, such as duties of care. Checking whether a person signing on behalf of a legal entity actually has the authority to sign is one obligation of creditors. If the official signing has no authority, the contract does not bind the debtor. Although this is self-evident and such checks are routine for Northern corporate or sovereign debt, this principle has de facto been waived in sovereign lending with Northern government support. There is no valid reason for such discrimination. By basic legal principles substantial parts of sovereign debts are null and void.

Article 75 of the Argentine constitution, for instance, reserves the authority to incur sovereign debts to Congress. Article 76 prohibits Congress to delegate this prerogative to the administration.[38] Sovereign debts multiplied under the military dictatorship from $7.8 billion in 1975 to $46 billion in 1984 without one single loan raised in the proper, constitutional way. One may argue that the existence of a dictatorship violating human rights obliged creditors in particular to check whether all formal requirements had been obeyed. In the famous Olmos case, a citizen, Alejandro Olmos, sued the government "and others"[39]; the verdict by Judge Jorge Ballesteros on July 14, 2000, established irregularities in 477 credit operations.[40] No debtor—except developing countries deprived of self-evident rights—would be expected to "honor" such "contracts." Argentina's unilateral debt reduction, though second best from the point of view of economics and the rule of law, has meanwhile corrected the debt burden somewhat. Unfortunately, Argentina suffered strongly from these illegal debts. Creditors as a group suffered as well, because they lost more money in the end than they would have under an early solution or correct application of legal principles. Ultimately, private creditors had to pick up the bill. Protecting claims without proper legal foundations, the public sector is responsible for many of Argentina's troubles and for present creditor losses. While private creditors may have tried to cover up errors, the public sector has allowed them to do it, disregarding the very foundations of the rule of law. The IMF even financed a program in Argentina which "Directors viewed as deeply flawed,"[41] knowing that the policies demanded from the debtor would be "counterproductive."[42] Nevertheless, it gets paid in preference to private creditors.

When I proposed verifying debts as part of my international Chapter 9 approach,[43] as is routine in any domestic case, the need and even the possibility of doing so were denied by IFI personnel. Meanwhile the IMF demands specific checks regarding, "for example, the authority of an official to borrow on behalf of the debtor," echoing my demand, nearly in my own words.[44] Over decades this self-evident obligation was ignored. It still has no practical relevance. Neither the IMF nor any other creditor has encouraged debtors to consider such debts null and void and to act upon that conclusion.

The IBRD found that "governments in many of these countries were forced to assume the losses suffered as a result of the external debts of private banks and corporations, which further worsened the burden on the budget."[45] Chile in the early 1980s is one prominent example of such "socialized" debts, which had initially been incurred without any government involvement and while the government declared that it would neither intervene in private contracts nor bail out private debts. Banks tried to cover themselves after the crisis broke. Without protection by the public sector, however, this open breach of the law would not have been possible. The BWIs did not even criticize this practice of "retroactive guarantees" of already defaulted private debt. Although this *ex post* socialization made debt management more difficult, the BWIs and Northern governments insisted on punctual service of these illegal debts as well, thus anointing them with international respectability. In any case but Southern sovereigns, such debts would be legally null and void. The 1997 Asian crisis is another dramatic case of the state bailing out creditors after liberalizing capital flows.

Banks were accused of helping capital flight, thus rendering the economic situation of their debtors even more untenable. If risk and normal legal responsibility had not been eliminated, banks could not have had an interest in debilitating their debtors in such a way. This problem would not have arisen to the same extent.

All legal systems contain norms protecting debtors against either too cavalier attitudes by creditors or against creditors carelessly financing illegal activities, embezzlement, or fraud. Such laws may sometimes be quite strict. Reginald H. Green saw a legal basis to void contracts and related loans if they "were fraudulently procured (whether by bribery or false description of the project or of its suitability. . .) and the lender knew or had cause to know of the fraud."[46] Unless the debtor is a developing country, any creditor suspected of lending with full knowledge that employees (in the case of countries, politicians, or functionaries) would redirect these funds into their pockets would face troubles. In the Philippines, firms connected to the Marcos clan borrowed government-guaranteed loans to go bankrupt after disbursement, leaving the government to pick up the bill. According to the *New York Times*[47] such loans amounted to $9.59 billion, a very large chunk of the country's total sovereign debt. It is difficult to believe that this practice had gone unnoticed by creditors.

In 1922, Costa Rica refused to honor loans made by the Royal Bank of Canada to the former dictator Federico Tinoco. Chief Justice Taft, of the U.S. Supreme Court, was the sole arbitrator. While holding that Tinoco's government was a legitimate de facto government capable of binding the state to international obligations, he held that the Royal Bank of Canada simply "knew" that the funds in question were to be used for the personal expenses of the retiring ruler. This case thus stands for the principle that funds borrowed by the state must be for legitimate governmental use, and not for personal enrichment. Otherwise there is no obligation to repay.

Generally, domestic laws enforce much higher standards of lender accountability. For example, Lloyd's had to pay damages to a couple its manager had advised and encouraged to borrow to buy, renovate, and sell a house at a profit. Because the manager went beyond mere lending by adding advice, the High Court ruled that the manager should have pointed out the risks clearly and should have advised them against the project.[48] In several countries professional creditors may also be held accountable for damages created by negligently granted credits. Juan Pablo Bohoslavsky[49] is surveying laws and judicial practice in eight countries with regard to creditor liabilities connected to loose lending in order to extract common principles from national, domestic laws to form the basis for new principles of international law. According to this concept lenders are liable for damages they inflicted on other creditors by their lending with disregard for the most basic principles of risk evaluation, thus postponing the insolvent lender's crash, thereby increasing other creditors' losses. In particular, French, Belgian, and Italian jurisprudence have developed this concept.

CONCLUSION

Official creditors largely eliminated the most essential economic principles and the rule of law in sovereign lending after 1970. They established a framework violating human rights, destabilizing credit markets, and inflicting damages on the poor in particular, but also on private creditors. Delaying a solution of the problem of sovereign overindebtedness, official creditors have reaped political and economic gains. The Sovereign Debt Restructuring Mechanism[50] proves that strong forces within the IMF want to continue as before, even increasing the weight of wrong incentives. It is a highly self-serving scheme that would confer further privileges on the IMF and other IFIs, such as legal exemption for IFI claims, which would have a considerable ratchet effect protecting IFIs against the market and the rule of law. Fortunately, it was voted down.

Risk and liability must be reintroduced into international credit relations to allow markets to function. This can simply be done by international debt arbitration based on U.S. Chapter 9, which would put debtors and creditors on an equal footing, as is normal in the case of insolvent debtors.[51]

IFIs and bilateral creditors must be made liable for damages they cause unlawfully.[52] In short, the IBRD should obey its statutes and function in the way initially foreseen when it was founded. The European Bank for Reconstruction and Development proves that MDBs, if properly managed, can survive financial accountability and market risk. For the IMF there are two options: either returning to its origins (unconditional emergency financing, which could justify a preferred status) or continuing its present practice of policy advice plus conditional money. Then the Fund must be made financially accountable.

Reform of debtor-creditor relations must also abolish regulatory harassment of private creditors and inappropriate regulations to allow markets to function well. These changes could be made easily if creditor governments were prepared to do what they preach. These ethically, economically, and legally needed reforms would abolish a range of grave market imperfections, the present double standard of rights and duties, and establish a level playing field. Risk and liability must be allowed to play their role in international debt relations. Unfortunately, there still is a long way to go before basic legal principles such as human rights will be applied without regard to the nationality of those otherwise suffering under legal and economic discrimination.

NOTES

[1] Cf. Alberto Acosta, "La increíble y triste historia de América Latina y su perversa deuda externa," in Chris Jochnick and Patricio Pazmiño Freire, eds., Otras caras de la deuda, Propuestas para la acción (Quito/Caracas: CDES/Nueva Sociedad, 2001), pp. 17–40; Kunibert Raffer, "Schemes for

Resolving the External Debt Problem," in OPEC Fund for International Development, ed., *Financing for Development, Proceedings of a Workshop of the G-24 Held at Nigeria House, New York, September 6–7, 2001* (Pamphlet Series No. 33, 2002), pp. 147–51.

2 John M. Makin, *The Global Debt Crisis: America's Growing Involvement* (New York: Basic Books, 1984), p. 41.

3 Angus Maddison, *Two Crises: Latin America and Asia, 1929–38 and 1973–83* (Paris: OECD, 1985), p. 28.

4 Richard Fletcher, "Lessons of Recent Debt Reorganizations," in Khadija Had, ed., *The Lingering Debt Crisis* (Islamabad: North South Roundtable in Collaboration with UNDP Development Study Programme, 1985), p. 91.

5 See Kunibert Raffer and H. W. Singer, *The Economic North-South Divide: Six Decades of Unequal Development* (Northampton, MA.: Edward Elgar, 2001), pp. 133–37.

6 U.S. Senate Committee on Foreign Relations, *Bretton Woods Agreements Amendments Act of 1977, United States Senate, 95th Congress, 1st Session, Report No. 95-603* (Washington, D.C.: Government Printing Office, 1977).

7 Ibid., p. 22.

8 Ibid.

9 Kunibert Raffer, "Schemes for Resolving the External Debt Problem," pp. 142–47.

10 IBRD, *World Debt Tables 1992/93*, vol. 1 (Washington, D.C.: IBRD, 1992), pp. 10–11. Emphasis in original.

11 See, e.g., Alfred Herrhausen, "Die Zeit ist reif—Schuldenkrise am Wendepunkt," *Handelsblatt* no. 124 (June 30, 1989). Mindful of the United States, he proposed a period of up to five years with interest rates on already existing debts substantially reduced (with exceptions, such as trade financing) to allow banks with insufficient provisions to increase theirs before the haircut.

12 Edward Bransilver and Ernest T. Patrikis, "Lending Limits and Regulatory Constraints under U.S. Law," in Michael Gruson and Ralph Reissner, eds., *Sovereign Lending: Managing Legal Risk* (London: Euromoney Publications, 1984), p. 6.

13 Cf. Kunibert Raffer, "Tax-Deductible Loan Loss Reserves and International Banking: An Economist's Unbiased Analysis," *Working Papers in Commerce WPC 91/19* (Birmingham University, Department of Commerce, Birmingham Business School, U.K., 1991); more recently, Raffer, "Internationalizing U.S. Municipal Insolvency: A Fair, Equitable, and Efficient Way to Overcome a Debt Overhang," *Chicago Journal of International Law* 6, no. 2 (2005), pp. 363–82.

14 Bransilver and Patrikis, "Lending Limits and Regulatory Constraints under U.S. Law."

15 Kunibert Raffer, "International Debts: A Crisis for Whom?" in H. W. Singer and Soumitra Sharma, eds., *Economic Development and World Debt* (London: Macmillan, 1989), p. 54 (selected papers of a conference at Zagreb University in 1987).

16 Kenneth A. Guenther (then the IBAA's executive vice president), Letter to Senator Bill Bradley, July 31, 1986.

17 Kunibert Raffer, "Applying Chapter 9 Insolvency to International Debts: An Economically Efficient Solution with a Human Face," *World Development* 18, no. 2 (1990), p. 310, n. 4.

18 Steven L. Schwarcz, "Sovereign Debt Restructuring: A Bankruptcy Reorganization Approach," *Duke Law School Working Paper* no. 1 (1999), p. 145, n. 239; available at papers.ssrn.com/paper.taf?abstract_id=203671.

19 Eric Helleiner, "The Strange Story of Bush and the Argentine Debt Crisis," *Third World Quarterly* 26, no. 6 (2005), p. 956.

20 Raffer, "Applying Chapter 9 Insolvency to International Debts," p. 310, n. 3.

21 Phillip Inman, "Court Cancels Debt That Grew from £6,000 to £380,000," *Guardian*, July 28, 2005; available at www.guardian.co.uk/business/story/0,,1537428,00.html. Upholding the county court's decision, the court of appeals declined to say whether it agreed with the judge that the loan at an annual interest rate of 34.9 percent was "extortionate."

22 ILA Committee on International Monetary Law, "Committee Report, Warsaw Conference" (1988), p. 9, para. 21.

23 OECD, *Shaping the 21st Century: The Contribution of Development Co-operation* (Paris: OECD, 1996), p. 18.

24 Christian Barry, "Ethical Issues Relevant to Debt," International Affairs Working Paper 2006-05 (March 2006), p. 6, at gpia.info/docs/wkg_papers/Barry_2006-05.pdf.

25 OECD, *Development Co-operation, 1999 Report: Efforts and Policies of the Members of the Development Assistance Committee* (Paris: OECD, 2000), pp. 31–32.

26 Cf. Kunibert Raffer, "Is the Debt Crisis Largely Over?—A Critical Look at the Data of International Financial Institutions," in Richard Auty and John Toye, eds., *Challenging the Orthodoxies* (London: Macmillan, 1996), pp. 23–39. Warning of growing arrears and the

impeding crisis, this text, written in June 1994, was presented at the Development Studies Association Conference at Lancaster in September 1994, before the Mexican crisis.

27 Dani Rodrik, "Understanding Policy Reform," *Journal of Economic Literature* 34, no. 1 (1996), p. 17.

28 IBRD, OED, *1998 Annual Review of Development Effectiveness* (Washington, D.C.: IBRD, 1999), p. 2; see also Raffer and Singer, *The Economic North-South Divide*, pp. 150–51.

29 For details, see Kunibert Raffer, "International Financial Institutions and Financial Accountability," *Ethics & International Affairs* 18, no. 2 (2004), pp. 68–70; or Raffer, "Delivering Greater Information and Transparency in Debt Management" (paper presented at the 5th UNCTAD Inter-regional Debt Management Conference, Geneva, June 20–24, 2005); available at r0.unctad.org/dmfas/speakerspapers.htm.

30 Raffer, "International Financial Institutions and Financial Accountability," p. 68.

31 Adding insult to injury, IFIs have made these reserves "one of the widely-used targets of poverty reduction strategies in Africa." UNCTAD, *Economic Development in Africa: From Adjustment to Poverty Reduction: What Is New?* (Geneva: UN, 2002), p. 31.

32 See Raffer, "International Financial Institutions and Financial Accountability"; and Raffer "Delivering Greater Information and Transparency in Debt Management."

33 "Secretariat Report of the Consultation," Multi-stakeholder Consultations on "Sovereign Debt for Sustained Development" (Concluding Session, held in Conjunction with the Fifth UNCTAD Debt Management Conference, Geneva, June 20–22, 2005), p. 6; available at www.un.org/esa/ffd/09multi-stake-consul-flyer-debt-Report.pdf.

34 Jeffrey Winters, "Criminal Debt," written statement, "Combating Corruption in the Multilateral Development Banks," Hearing before the Committee on Foreign Relations, U.S. Senate, 108th Congress, 2nd session, May 13, 2004; available at foreign.senate.gov/testimony/2004/WintersTestimony040513.pdf. See also Raffer, "International Financial Institutions and Financial Accountability," pp. 64–65.

35 See Costa Rica's Tinoco case in 1922, described below.

36 Allied Bank International v. Banco Credito Agricola de Cartago, 566 F. Supp 1440, 1443–44 (S.D.N.Y. 1983); Allied Bank International v. Banco Credito Agricola de Cartago, 757 F.2d 516 (2d Cir. 1985); UNCTAD, *Trade and Development Report 1986* (Geneva: UN, 1986), p. 142; and Raffer, "Internationalizing U.S. Municipal Insolvency," p. 365.

37 757 F.2d 516 (2d Cir. 1985).

38 Letter by Congresswoman María América González and Congressman Mario Cafiero to the Securities and Exchange Commission, Washington, D.C., c/o Mr. Russell Clause, dated July 29, 2004 (with official letterhead Cámara de Diputados de la Nación).

39 See Ann Pettifor, Liana Cisneros, and Alejandro Olmos Gaona, *It Takes Two to Tango: Creditor Co-responsibility for Argentina's Crisis—and the Need for Independent Resolution* (London: Jubilee Plus, NEF, 2001), pp. 8–9.

40 Letter by González and Cafiero.

41 IMF, Independent Evaluation Office, "Report on the Evaluation of the Role of the IMF in Argentina, 1991–2001" (2004), p. 81; available at www.imf.org/External/NP/ieo/2004/arg/eng/index.htm.

42 Ibid., p. 91.

43 Raffer, "Applying Chapter 9 Insolvency to International Debts," p. 309.

44 IMF, "The Design of the Sovereign Debt Restructuring Mechanism—Further Considerations" (November 27, 2002), p. 68; available at www.imf.org/external/np/pdr/sdrm/2002/112702.pdf; and Kunibert Raffer, "What's Good for the United States Must Be Good for the World: Advocating an International Chapter 9 Insolvency," in Bruno Kreisky Forum for International Dialogue, ed., *From Cancún to Vienna, International Development in a New World* (Vienna: Kreisky Forum, 1993), p. 68; available at homepage.univie.ac.at/Kunibert.Raffer.

45 IBRD, *World Debt Tables*, vol. 1 (Washington, D.C.: IBRD, 1988).

46 Reginald H. Green, "External Debt, Internal Debilitation: The Philippine Context," Institute of Development Studies, Brighton, U.K. (1988), mimeo.

47 Fox Butterfield, "Marcos Fortune: Inquiry in Manila Offers Picture of How It Was Acquired," *New York Times*, March 30, 1986, p. 12.

48 John Gapper and Richard Gourlay, "Damages Win Leads Lloyds to Rethink Advice," *Financial Times*, September 5, 1995, p. 9.

49 Juan Pablo Bohoslavsky, *Responsabilidad por concesión abusivo de crédito soberano* (European Ph.D. thesis at the Faculty of Law, University of Salamanca, 2006).

50 For details, see Kunibert Raffer, "The Present State of the Discussion on Restructuring Sovereign Debts: Which Specific Sovereign Insolvency Procedure?" in UNCTAD, ed., *Proceedings of*

the *Fourth Inter-regional Debt Management Conference and WADMO Conference 10–12 November, 2003* (New York: UN, 2005), pp. 69–74; available at ro.unctad.org/dmfas/pdfs/raffer.pdf; and Kunibert Raffer, "The IMF's SDRM—Simply Disastrous Rescheduling Management?" in Chris Jochnick and Fraser Preston, eds., *Sovereign Debt at the Crossroads, Challenges and Proposals for Resolving the Third World Debt Crisis* (Oxford: Oxford University Press, 2006), pp. 246–67.

51 For details, see Raffer, "Applying Chapter 9 Insolvency to International Debts"; Raffer, "International Financial Institutions and Financial Accountability"; and Raffer, "Delivering Greater Information and Transparency in Debt Management."

52 See Raffer, "International Financial Institutions and Financial Accountability."

Kunibert Raffer

National Responsibility and the Just Distribution of Debt Relief

Alexander W. Cappelen, Rune Jansen Hagen, and Bertil Tungodden[*]

The Highly Indebted Poor Countries (HIPC) Initiative is the largest multilateral effort aimed at providing debt relief. According to the World Bank, as of June 2006 "nominal debt service relief of more than US$59 billion has been approved for 29 countries through the HIPC Initiative, reducing their Net Present Value of external debt by approximately two-thirds. Of these countries, 19 have reached the completion point and have been granted unconditional debt service relief of over US$37 billion."[1] In this essay we address the question of whether this program is consistent with a view of justice commonly known as liberal egalitarianism. Liberal egalitarianism holds that agents should be held responsible only for free and informed choices, which in an international context can be understood as saying that a population should be held responsible only for policy choices to which they have given their informed consent. Liberal egalitarianism is an attractive view of justice because it combines two moral ideals that are considered to be fundamental by most people: first, the egalitarian ideal that inequalities resulting from factors outside an agent's control should be eliminated, and second, the liberal ideal that inequalities resulting from factors under an agent's control should be accepted.[2] Liberal egalitarian ethics has implications for many aspects of debt relief policy, including the question of what the overall level of debt relief should be. We focus, however, on its implications for how resources made available for debt relief should be distributed among poor countries.

* We thank the participants at the Ethics and Debt conference in New York, the editors, and two anonymous referees for valuable comments. Financial support from the Research Council of Norway is gratefully acknowledged. The usual disclaimer applies.

An important motivation for engaging with these questions is the observation that there is considerable variation in the per capita debt relief given to poor countries in the HIPC Initiative. (Data for the eighteen countries that had completed the program as of the end of 2005 are given in Figure 1.) This variation follows from the fact that the objective of the HIPC Initiative is to bring the debt of the participating countries down to a "sustainable" level.[3] We want to examine whether these differences and the resulting distribution of debt relief is fair. Furthermore, if the distribution of debt relief is judged to be unfair, it is important to ask whether donors compensate by adjusting other aid flows.

These types of questions are equally relevant for more recent initiatives, such as the write-off begun in 2006 of more than 40 billion U.S. dollars (USD) of debt owed by the poorest nations to the International Monetary Fund (IMF), the World Bank, and the African Development Bank. Within such an initiative, it is important to ask to what extent the resulting distribution of debt relief and aid is just.

The task of achieving a just and efficient distribution of debt relief, and a just and efficient distribution of aid more generally, raises a number of complex challenges. First, one needs to formulate more precisely how to

FIGURE 1
DEBT RELIEF PER CAPITA IN HIPC IN CONSTANT 2000 U.S. DOLLARS

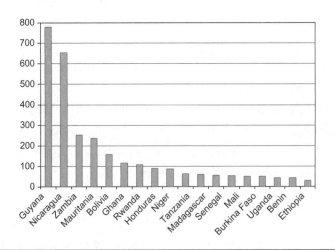

Source: Authors' Own Calculations.

Alexander W. Cappelen, Rune Jansen Hagen, and Bertil Tungodden

measure a country's overall situation. Second, one needs to take into account a country's effectiveness in applying international aid. And finally, one needs to take into account incentive problems. All these issues have been extensively discussed in the development literature. It is by now well established that a country's per capita disposable income is far from a perfect measure of its status, that countries may use aid more or less effectively, and that the possibility of debt relief in the future might induce countries to undertake excessive borrowing.[4] Nevertheless, in order to achieve a sharp focus on the question of what constitutes a *fair* distribution of debt relief and aid, we will narrow our framework and avoid detailed discussion of these issues. To simplify, we will take a nation's disposable income per capita to be the relevant outcome, and we will assume that all recipient countries are equally effective in their use of international aid. Furthermore, we will not study the incentive effects of a fair distribution of debt relief and aid. In the implementation of any debt relief and aid program, fairness needs to be balanced against incentives, but in order to do so we first need to understand the nature of both sets of considerations.

We argue that the HIPC Initiative is not at all consistent with liberal egalitarian commitments. More generally, we show why the debate on debt relief must move beyond a discussion of whether countries should be held responsible for their sovereign debt. That question of just distribution of debt release needs to be superseded by a more careful and broader classification of which of the factors affecting a country's situation it should be held responsible for and which it should not. Though it is beyond the scope of this essay to outline a detailed proposal in this respect, we will show how a liberal egalitarian framework can be used to evaluate critically the justice of such debt relief programs as the HIPC Initiative.

NATIONAL RESPONSIBILITY AND INTERNATIONAL EQUALIZATION OF PER CAPITA INCOMES

Liberal egalitarians draw a distinction between what agents should be held responsible for (responsibility factors) and what they should not be held responsible for (nonresponsibility factors). A liberal egalitarian approach to justice can thus be seen as consisting of two parts: the liberal principle that morally relevant inequalities due to differences in responsibility factors should be accepted, which we call the *principle of responsibility*; and the egalitarian principle that morally relevant inequalities due to nonresponsibility factors should be eliminated, which we call the *principle of equalization*. By way of illustration, in the context of income distribution, if we assume that talent and effort are the only factors that affect a person's pretax income and we hold people responsible for their effort but not their talent, then a liberal egalitarian framework justifies inequalities in income due to differences in effort but not inequalities in income due to differences in talent.

In the context of sovereign states and given that we focus on inequalities in per capita disposable income, we may formulate the following versions of the two principles defining the liberal egalitarian framework.

The principle of international equalization: International inequalities in per capita disposable income due to differences in nonresponsibility factors should be eliminated.

The principle of national responsibility: International inequalities in per capita disposable income due to differences in responsibility factors should be accepted.

We believe that these two principles are extremely attractive. Many standard approaches to debt relief violate one or both of them, however. Consider, for example, the view that debt relief should be given to those countries that are most effective in their use of international aid. Given that a country's ability to use aid in an efficient manner typically depends on factors they are not responsible for, such as historical, geographical, or climatic conditions, giving aid in order to maximize the benefits from aid would violate the principle of international equalization. Similarly, as long as we think that countries should be held responsible for some of the factors that affect their development status, the view that debt relief always should be distributed equally among poor countries would violate the principle of national responsibility.

It is not obvious, however, how these two principles should be interpreted more generally and how they can be combined. In particular, the implications of the liberal egalitarian framework for considerations of international debt relief depend upon what factors countries are viewed as being responsible for and which factors they are not seen as being responsible for.

Alexander W. Cappelen, Rune Jansen Hagen, and Bertil Tungodden

What Should Nations Be Held Responsible For?

According to international law, governments are generally responsible for repaying the sovereign debts incurred by their predecessors. It has been argued that so-called odious debts constitute an exception to this general rule. According to the "odious debts" doctrine, debts are odious and thus not legally enforceable claims when the population has not consented to the transaction; when it has not benefited from it; and when the creditor was aware of the absence of consent and benefit.[5] This doctrine, however, is controversial among international lawyers. Furthermore, we argue that from a normative point of view it is too strict as a criterion for determining when debt is illegitimate.

The liberal egalitarian framework holds that agents should be held responsible only for free and informed choices, which in an international context can be understood as saying that a population should be held responsible only for policy choices to which they have given their informed consent. This is fully in line with the first condition of the odious debt doctrine. The liberal egalitarian approach, however, does not take into account the questions of benefit and creditor awareness when deciding whether a population should be held responsible for their sovereign debt. Certainly, whether a country has benefited from the sovereign debt will be of relevance for the further analysis of how to deal with illegitimate debt in the distribution of debt relief and aid, but this is an independent issue that should not be confused with the question of whether we should hold the country responsible for its sovereign debt. A country might be responsible for debt it has not benefited from and not be responsible for debt it has benefited from. Similarly, within a liberal egalitarian framework, there is no basis for arguing that whether we hold a country responsible for sovereign debt should depend on the degree of creditor awareness of the country's situation at the time the debt was contracted. It may very well be the case that the degree of creditor awareness should affect the total amount of transfers from rich to poor countries and the distribution of the cost of a debt relief program among rich countries, but these are again very different issues that should be clearly distinguished from the question of whether the debtor is responsible for its debt.

It is also important to note that the liberal egalitarian approach is much broader than the odious debt approach. It does not confine itself only to considering whether countries should be held responsible for their sovereign debt but makes a more general classification that covers *all factors* that affect a country's situation. Factors that fall paradigmatically into the non-responsibility category include geographical or climatic conditions and colonial history. The paradigmatic example of factors that are viewed as responsibility factors would be national policies that the population has consented to in a well-functioning democracy.

A problem with the consent approach to responsibility in an international context is that there is often strong disagreement within a country about many policy decisions, including decisions on contracting sovereign debt. Even in well-functioning democracies with informed voters there will typically be a minority—and sometimes even a majority—that disagrees with the national policy. Holding a country responsible for its policies will therefore, without other initiatives, necessarily involve holding individuals who disagree with these policies responsible as well. This is clearly not an unproblematic implication, and we might think that this kind of group responsibility should be apportioned differently among the individuals in society.[6] We will not pursue a further analysis of this problem here; in what follows we will study the implications of the following liberal egalitarian view on responsibility: Nations (and the individuals within them) should be held responsible for national policies that are formulated and decided through democratic procedures, but not for factors outside democratic control.

Implications for Debt Relief

It may be tempting to think that all it takes to justify giving priority to debt relief within a liberal egalitarian framework is to establish that a country should not be held responsible for its sovereign debt. To see that this is a fallacy, however, consider the hypothetical situation where *all* factors affecting a country's situation, including the debt level, are viewed as non-responsibility factors. In this case, the principle of national responsibility is vacuous. Any inequality among the poor countries would be due to differences in nonresponsibility factors, such as climate and natural resource

Alexander W. Cappelen, Rune Jansen Hagen, and Bertil Tungodden

holdings, and the principle of international equalization would not provide any justification for a particular focus on the most indebted countries.

More important, most people would reject the view that countries are responsible for all factors other than debt level that affect their situation. This, however, is the only position that could justify a single-minded focus on indebtedness in the distribution of international aid. If factors other than debt levels also are viewed as nonresponsibility factors, then justice requires that these factors, at least ideally, be taken into account when distributing international aid or debt relief. Clearly the current debt relief initiatives are not about ideal justice. But even in a discussion of second-best policies, we need to have a clear picture of the ideal world in order to be in a position to evaluate the various policies available to us.

Even though debt relief initiatives typically have been justified by the claim that countries are not responsible for their sovereign debt, it is interesting to note that the justification of a debt relief initiative does not necessarily have to rely on such a view. To illustrate this point, consider a situation where the actual consequences of sovereign debt partly depend on factors we do not want to hold countries responsible for. In this situation, if we hold countries accountable for the actual consequences of their sovereign debt, then we will sometimes also hold them responsible for their nonresponsibility factors. This will in turn violate the principle of international equalization, since countries that are identical with respect to all responsibility factors might end up with different net disposable incomes per capita.

Consequently, given a liberal egalitarian framework, the principle of national responsibility has to be interpreted differently. There is a substantial technical literature on how exactly to formulate the principle of responsibility within a liberal egalitarian framework, but the general idea is that agents should be responsible for the *fair* consequences of their choices.[7] Consequently, the liberal egalitarian framework may justify a focus on the most indebted countries even if they are held responsible for their sovereign debt, if the countries have not experienced the fair consequences of borrowing.

This last point shows the importance of clearly separating the question of whether a country should be held responsible for its sovereign debt and the question of whether a country has benefited from it. The odious debt doctrine only justifies a focus on whether a country has benefited from its sovereign debt if the population did not consent to the transaction. But as the liberal egalitarian framework makes clear, to focus on the lack of benefit may be equally appropriate within a framework where we hold the country responsible for its sovereign debt but acknowledge that the outcome of a debt transaction has been affected by factors beyond the country's control.

THE DISTRIBUTIONAL IMPLICATIONS OF THE HIPC INITIATIVE

The World Bank and the IMF launched the HIPC Initiative in 1996 and re-structured it in 1999. Its aim is to bring in as many creditors as possible, in-cluding multilateral ones, to grant debt relief to poor countries with high debt levels that demonstrate a willingness to undertake reforms deemed necessary to reduce the likelihood of future debt problems as well as to re-direct public spending toward social expenditure.[8] To be eligible, a country must meet three requirements. First, it must be poor enough to qualify for assistance from the concessional facilities of the World Bank and the IMF.[9] Second, its net present value (NPV) of the public and publicly guaranteed (PPG) external debt must exceed 150 percent of the country's exports after the application of "traditional" debt relief, granted by the bilateral creditors organized in the so-called Paris Club. Countries that are very open to trade, however (that is, their export-to-GDP ratio is at least 30 percent) or gen-erate a lot of government revenue from trade (at least 15 percent of GDP) are also eligible if their PPG external debt exceeds 250 percent of govern-ment revenue, even if it does not exceed 150 percent of exports. Third, countries must establish and maintain track records of policy reform with respect to both macroeconomic stability and poverty reduction.

In 1999, the HIPC Initiative was replaced by the so-called Enhanced HIPC Initiative, the adoption of which allowed both more countries to qualify and greater relief for the participants. Moreover, the fixed three-year period between the granting of eligibility for the program (the "decision point") and the actual according of relief (the "completion point") became flexible and performance-related. In combination with the provision of in-terim relief after the decision point, this brought faster debt relief. Finally, while performance initially was wholly focused on macroeconomic stability

Alexander W. Cappelen, Rune Jansen Hagen, and Bertil Tungodden

TABLE 1

DECISION POINT YEAR STATISTICS FOR HIPC COUNTRIES HAVING REACHED THE COMPLETION POINT

Country	Decision point	Completion point	GDP per capita	Aid per capita exclusive of debt relief	PPG debt per capita	Per capita net present value of debt relief
Benin	Jul. 2000	Mar. 2003	362.4	33.5	231.7	42.6
Bolivia	Feb. 2000	Jun. 2001	1008.9	55.3	497.3	156.5
Burkina Faso	Jul. 2000	Apr. 2002	230.7	13.2	111.8	49.1
Ethiopia	Nov. 2001	Apr. 2004	99.0	16.4	82.6	30.1
Ghana	Feb. 2002	Jul. 2004	303.4	24.5	290.5	107.7
Guyana	Nov. 2000	Dec. 2003	939.0	111.9	1488.0	778.7
Honduras	Jun. 2000	Apr. 2005	921.6	64.7	684.6	86.1
Madagascar	Dec. 2000	Oct. 2004	249.8	19.2	276.7	53.9
Mali	Sep. 2000	Mar. 2003	223.5	23.5	246.4	49.7
Mauritania	Feb. 2000	Jun. 2002	355.2	72.4	809.8	235.2
Mozambique	Apr. 2000	Sep. 2001	208.3	38.0	256.9	114.4
Nicaragua	Dec. 2000	Jan. 2004	778.8	109.3	1083.1	652.3
Niger	Dec. 2000	Apr. 2004	167.4	17.9	135.8	61.8
Rwanda	Dec. 2000	Apr. 2005	234.9	41.2	149.0	90.3
Senegal	Jun. 2000	Apr. 2004	458.9	38.4	335.0	51.2
Tanzania	Apr. 2000	Nov. 2001	269.4	23.8	177.7	60.1
Uganda	Feb. 2000	May 2000	253.3	31.2	131.2	43.1
Zambia	Dec. 2000	Apr. 2005	327.5	62.0	450.0	252.8

Notes: All data in constant 2000 USD.

Sources: Own calculations based on data from World Bank, "World Development Indicators on CD-ROM" (Washington, D.C.: World Bank, 2005); OECD, "International Development Statistics Online" (Paris: OECD, 2006); and IMF and IDA, "Heavily Indebted Poor Countries (HIPC) Initiative—Status of Implementation" (Washington, D.C.: IMF and IDA, August 19, 2005), available at www.imf.org/external/np/pp/eng/2005/081905.htm.

and structural reforms, in line with the original goal of debt sustainability, it was broadened to include planning for poverty reduction and targets for social spending, thus adding a poverty dimension to the program. Prior to the decision point, the country must now have a three-year track record of satisfactory macroeconomic policy performance, as well as having prepared a plan to clear arrears to foreign creditors and at least an interim Poverty Reduction Strategy Paper (PRSP).[10] To qualify for the full amount of debt relief potentially available, the country must have completed a PRSP, implemented it satisfactorily for a year, carried out structural and social reforms agreed to with the World Bank and the IMF, and maintained macroeconomic stability through an IMF-supported program.

As of November 2006, there were twenty-nine countries in the initiative, of which twenty had completed the procedures and exited from the mechanism. In addition, eleven countries are considered potentially eligible for the program. In this essay, we look at the eighteen countries that had reached the completion point and exited from the initiative as of the end of 2005.[11] We focus on the latter since these are the countries for which the total committed debt relief is fully known. The countries in our sample are listed in Table 1 together with the month in which they entered (the decision point) and exited (the completion point) the mechanism. The economic data pertains to the year of each country's decision point, which is 2000 for sixteen of the eighteen countries. Our measure of debt relief is the present value at the decision point of the commitments made by creditors at the completion point. To be comparable, the other data must therefore also be for the year in which the countries were allowed into the program. For ease of interpretation, we show the data in constant 2000 USD. As shown in the regressions below, however, adjusting for purchasing power parity (PPP) does make a difference even in a sample consisting only of developing countries.[12] As may be seen, although all of the countries are classified as "poor," there is a tenfold difference in the GDP per capita of the poorest (Ethiopia) and least poor (Bolivia) country in the sample. The ratio of the per capita PPG debt of the most indebted country (Guyana) to the least indebted one (Ethiopia) is approximately eighteen to one.

The first observation to make is that there is a positive correlation (0.61) between per capita debt relief and per capita GDP as reported in Table 1 that is significant at the 1 percent level; that is, richer participating countries

TABLE 2
REGRESSIONS FOR DEBT RELIEF PER CAPITA

	1	2	3	4
Debt per capita	0.61*** (0.08)	0. 61*** (0.11)	0.52*** (0.09)	0.52*** (0.15)
GDP per capita	−0.17 (0.11)	−0. 17 (0.15)	0.01 (0.15)	0.01 (0.23)
Constant	−23.60 (33.80)	−23.60 (27.32)	−196.19 (143.73)	−196.19 (147.15)
R^2	0.87	0.87	0.90	0.90
Number of observations	18	18	18	18

Notes: Regressions 1 and 2 are based on data in constant USD. Regressions 3 and 4 are based on data adjusted for purchasing power parity. Standard errors in parentheses (robust standard errors in regressions 2 and 4). *** means the coefficient is significant at the 1 percent level.

Alexander W. Cappelen, Rune Jansen Hagen, and Bertil Tungodden

TABLE 3
REGRESSIONS FOR PER CAPITA AID EXCLUDING DEBT RELIEF

	1	2	3	4
Debt relief per capita	0.10*** (0.02)	0.10*** (0.02)	0.11*** (0.02)	0.11*** (0.02)
GDP per capita	0.03*** (0.01)	0.03*** (0.01)	0.02 (0.02)	0.02 (0.01)
Constant	14.36*** (4. 34)	14.36*** (4.16)	65.62** (22.96)	65.62*** (19.74)
R^2	0.89	0.89	0.88	0.88
Number of observations	18	18	18	18

Notes: Regressions 1 and 2 are based on data in constant USD. Regressions 3 and 4 are based on data adjusted for purchasing power parity. Standard errors in parentheses (robust standard errors in regressions 2 and 4). *** means the coefficient is significant at the 1 percent level; ** at the 5 percent level.

get more relief in absolute terms. This could be a result, however, of a positive correlation between debt per capita and GDP per capita. It is therefore interesting to check whether the correlation between income and debt relief remains positive and significant if we control for differences in debt levels. Table 2 reports the regressions, where we see that an additional 100 USD in sovereign debt per capita corresponds to an increase in debt relief of about 60 USD (regressions 1 and 2). The number is somewhat smaller if we express the variables in PPP terms instead of USD (regressions 3 and 4). It is still sizeable, however: the point estimate implies that about one-half of any difference in debt per capita among the eighteen HIPCs is in effect forgiven. Moreover, contingent on debt levels, there does not seem to be any statistically significant correlation between per capita debt relief and GDP per capita. Thus, the HIPC program does not bring greater debt relief to poorer countries.

Donor governments and civil society organization often disagree on whether debt relief should be viewed as a part of the total aid flow to poor countries. Civil society organizations have campaigned widely for measuring debt relief separately from aid. Independent of how one answers this question, however, it is of interest to study how the distribution of debt relief interacts with the overall distribution of aid. We thus construct a measure of per capita aid excluding debt relief by subtracting Debt Forgiveness Grants from the net Official Development Assistance each country receives from all donors.[13]

In Table 3, we regress this variable on debt relief and GDP, both measured per capita. In the first two regressions there is a statistically significant effect of income on per capita aid excluding debt relief. Contrary to what one would have expected from previous studies, it is positive.[14] The effect is very small, however, and becomes statistically insignificant when we use the PPP data. These results indicate that at best donors do not compensate relatively poor HIPC countries for their poverty. Moreover, there is a strongly positive effect on other aid flows from debt relief regardless of whether the data is adjusted for purchasing power or not; that is, countries that get less debt relief are not compensated by higher levels of conventional aid. To the contrary, they also receive smaller non-debt-related transfers. The effects are large. We see that another 100 units of debt relief yields an additional 10–11 units of regular aid.[15]

The HIPCs are typically highly indebted because they have received a lot of aid in the form of loans, and the HIPC Initiative might therefore be construed as a retroactive adjustment of aid terms. For this to be an explanation of why high levels of debt relief go together with high current levels of other forms of aid, however, the allocation of aid must be fairly constant over the long run. And over the short run, at least, aid flows tend to be highly volatile and reflect current donor preferences and constraints.[16]

DISCUSSION

The HIPC Initiative does not bring greater debt relief to the poorest countries. If justice simply consisted in equalizing income, then this would imply that the HIPC Initiative is unfair. The ideal of liberal egalitarian ethics is not simply to equalize income, however, but also to hold agents responsible for factors under their control. In this section we evaluate the HIPC Initiative against the two liberal egalitarian principles of justice.

It is useful to distinguish three ways in which the design of the HIPC Initiative violates the principle of international equalization and the principle of national responsibility. First, the criterion of debt sustainability introduces a critical level for the debt-over-exports ratio. The aim of the program is to reduce the debt level for countries that are above this level, but not for countries below it. For any view on what factors a country should be held responsible for, this feature of the HIPC Initiative violates either the principle of international equalization or the principle of national responsibility,

Alexander W. Cappelen, Rune Jansen Hagen, and Bertil Tungodden

or both. The design of the HIPC Initiative implies that countries are not responsible for policies or institutions that increase their debt-to-exports ratio if it is already above the critical level, but are fully responsible for such policies as long as the ratio is below this level. There are obvious efficiency arguments against the use of such threshold values, but here we are only concerned with the unfairness it introduces. To the extent that debt and exports are determined partly by factors under national control, such as democratically determined economic policies, and partly by factors outside it, such as climatic conditions or natural disasters, the HIPC Initiative implies that countries are responsible for too little if they are above the critical level and for too much if they are below this level. To illustrate this point, consider two equally poor countries that are on different sides of the debt sustainability threshold. The country that has a debt ratio above the sustainability level will not be held responsible for national policies or institutions that move it further away from debt sustainability. A country that has a debt ratio below the sustainability level will not be compensated for some factor outside its control that moves it closer to (but not beyond) the critical level of debt sustainability.

The specific debt sustainability criterion—that is, the debt-over-exports ratio—is a second source of unfairness in the HIPC Initiative. Countries with small export sectors relative to the size of their economies will typically benefit from such a definition, but there seems to be no compelling normative reason why this should be the case. Factors that determine the share of exports in GDP, such as population and geographic size, are to a large extent outside a country's control. Countries with larger export sectors relative to their economies will thus be held responsible for factors outside their control. This problem has been addressed partly by introducing other criteria allowing economies that have a high exports-to-GDP ratio to be included in the program. Moreover, the possibility of being granted additional relief at the completion point ("topping up") provides some protection against adverse exogenous shocks. The general point, however, is simply that this ratio does not capture all the relevant differences in a country's ability to sustain a given debt level.

Finally, the HIPC Initiative, and a single-minded focus on debt relief more generally, can be seen as unfair because it contributes to a distribution of total aid that is unfair. The correlation between foreign aid and debt relief implies that different sources of poverty are treated very differently. Poverty that is due to sovereign debt is to a large extent eliminated, while poverty that is due to other sources is to a large extent accepted. From a fairness point of view, taking the liberal egalitarian framework as the point of departure, this pattern can only be justified if one takes the extreme position that poor countries should be held fully responsible for all factors affecting their situation except for sovereign debt. While there are good arguments for why poor nations sometimes should not be held responsible for their sovereign debt, it is hard to see why the same arguments should not also apply to many other factors that affect a country's net disposable income. If highly indebted poor countries are seen as not responsible for their sovereign debt, then it is unreasonable to hold the same countries responsible for such factors as geographical and climatic conditions or colonial history.

It is beyond the scope of this essay to answer the question of how a debt relief program should be designed so that it would satisfy both these principles. It should, however, be pointed out that the answer to this question would depend critically on a careful analysis of what factors nations should and should not be held responsible for. In a country without any democratic history, it could be argued that the country could not be held responsible for any factors, not even their economic policy. In such a situation it is hard to see why debt should be singled out as different from any other source of poverty. If no factors are viewed as responsibility factors, then we should simply try to equalize the effect of nonresponsibility factors by giving debt relief and other types of aid to the worst-off countries. More realistically, we would want to hold even poor nations responsible for some factors, such as certain national policies and institutions. Democratic regimes should at least be held responsible for decisions they make—for example, about tax and trade policy. The challenge is then to ensure they are held responsible only for such decisions without at the same time holding them responsible for factors outside national control.

NOTES

[1] World Bank, "The Enhanced HIPC Initiative", available at web.worldbank.org/WBSITE/ EXTERNAL/TOPICS/EXTDEBTDEPT/0,,contentMDK:20260411~menuPK:64166739~pagePK: 64166689~piPK:64166646~theSitePK:469043,00.html.

Alexander W. Cappelen, Rune Jansen Hagen, and Bertil Tungodden

2 The contemporary focus on the relationship between these two ideals in the philosophical literature can be traced back to the seminal work of John Rawls, *A Theory of Justice* (Cambridge, MA: Harvard University Press, 1971), but the ideas of Rawls have been developed further, notably by Richard Arneson, "Equality and Equal Opportunity for Welfare," *Philosophical Studies* 56 (1989), pp. 77–93; Gerald Cohen, "On the Currency of Egalitarian Justice," *Ethics* 99 (1989), pp. 906–44; Ronald Dworkin, "What Is Equality? Part 2: Equality of Resources," *Philosophy & Public Affairs* 10 (1981), pp. 283–345; Marc Fleurbaey, "Equal Opportunity or Equal Social Outcome," *Economics and Philosophy* 11 (1995), pp. 25–55; John Roemer, *Theories of Distributive Justice* (Cambridge, MA: Harvard University Press, 1996); and John Roemer, *Equality of Opportunity* (Cambridge, MA: Harvard University Press, 2000).

3 David Andrews, Anthony R. Boote, Syed S. Rizavi, and Sukhwinder Singh, "Debt Relief for Low-Income Countries: The Enhanced HIPC Initiative" (Washington, D.C.: IMF Pamphlet Series, no. 51, 1999); available at www.imf.org/external/pubs/ft/pam/pam51/contents.htm.

4 See Amartya Sen, *Development as Freedom* (Oxford: Oxford University Press, 1999); Craig Burnside and David Dollar, "Aid, Policies, and Growth," *American Economic Review* 90 (2000), pp. 847–68; and William Easterly, *The Elusive Quest for Growth* (Cambridge, MA: MIT Press, 2002).

5 Ashfaq Khalfan, Jeff King, and Bryan Thomas, "Advancing the Odious Debt Doctrine" (Quebec: Centre for International Sustainable Development Law, 2003); available at www.odiousdebts.org/odiousdebts/publications/Advancing_the_Odious_Debt_Doctrine.pdf.

6 For a general discussion of the issue of group responsibility, see Kaushik Basu, *Prelude to Political Economy* (Oxford: Oxford University Press, 2000).

7 Marc Fleurbaey, "Three Solutions to the Compensation Problem," *Journal of Economic Theory* 65 (1995), pp. 505–21; and Walter Bossert and Marc Fleurbaey, "Redistribution and Compensation," *Social Choice and Welfare* 13 (1996), pp. 343–55.

8 For a description, see, e.g., Andrews, Boote, Rizavi, and Singh, "Debt Relief for Low-Income Countries"; and for assessments and evaluations from various angles, see Romilly Greenhill and Elena Sisti, "Real Progress Report on HIPC" (London: Jubilee Research, 2003), available at www.globalpolicy.org/socecon/develop/debt/2003/09realprogresshipc.pdf; Matthew Martin, "Assessing the HIPC Initiative: The Key Policy Debates," in Age Akkerman and Jan Joost Teunissen, eds., *HIPC Debt Relief: Myths and Reality* (The Hague: FONDAD, 2004); and World Bank, "Debt Relief for the Poorest: An OED Review of the HIPC Initiative" (Washington, D.C.: The World Bank Group, 2003), available at lnweb18.worldbank.org/oed/oeddoclib.nsf/0/86dd1e3dca61e0b985256cd700665b1c?OpenDocument.

9 The International Development Association (IDA) and the Poverty Reduction and Growth Facility (PRGF), respectively.

10 According to the IMF Web site, the five core principles of the PRSP approach are that the poverty-reduction strategies should be country-driven, results-oriented, comprehensive, partnership-oriented, and have a long-term perspective. See IMF, "Poverty Reduction Strategy Papers (PRSP)," September 2005; available at www.imf.org/external/np/exr/facts/prsp.htm. Critics have questioned whether actual PRSP processes conform to these principles. In a major concession to these critics, the explicit endorsements of PRSPs by the executive boards of the World Bank and the IMF are no longer required for PRGF lending.

11 Cameroon reached the completion point in May 2006 and Malawi in August 2006.

12 Adjustments for PPP aim to make economic data comparable across countries by expressing them in terms of some common denominator. Here we use the most widely used denominator, which is called an international dollar. The international dollar by construction has the property that it has the same purchasing power over a country's GDP as the U.S. dollar has in the United States.

13 These two data series are taken from the online version of International Development Statistics, which is based on data collected by the Development Assistance Committee of the OECD from its member countries as well as other sources. While the subtraction of the principal and interest due in the decision-point year that has been canceled might also remove some debt relief that is unrelated to HIPC from our data, this is unlikely to matter given the scale of that program.

14 That poorer countries get more aid is one of the main findings of the aid allocation literature. See Alberto Alesina and David Dollar, "Who Gives Foreign Aid to Whom and Why?" *Journal of Economic Growth* 5 (2000), pp. 33–63; Peter Boone, "Politics and the Effectiveness of Foreign Aid," *European Economic Review* 40 (1996), pp. 289–329; Peter Cashel-Cordo and Steven G. Craig, "Donor Preferences and Recipient Fiscal Behavior: A Simultaneous Analysis of Foreign Aid," *Economic Inquiry* 35 (1997), pp. 653–71; and Lisa Chauvet, "Socio-Political Instability and

the Allocation of International Aid by Donors," *European Journal of Political Economy* 19 (2002), pp. 33–59.

[15] These results continue to hold even if one tries to correct for the fact that our measure of debt relief is not directly comparable to the flow concept of aid and that, as pointed out in Cohen, "On the Currency of Egalitarian Justice," the NPV of the debt relief exaggerates the gain to a country, since presumably much of the debt would not have been serviced in any case.

[16] See Ales Bulir and A. Javier Hamann, "Aid Volatility: An Empirical Assessment," *IMF Staff Papers* 50 (2003), pp. 64–89; and Stephane Pallage and Michel Robe, "Foreign Aid and the Business Cycle," *Review of International Economics* 9 (2001), pp. 641–72.

DATA APPENDIX

The source for most of the data is the World Bank's "World Development Indicators on CD-ROM," 2005. The exceptions are the aid data, which are taken from the OECD's "International Development Statistics Online," and the data on the net present value of committed debt relief to the HIPC countries that have reached the completion point, which are from Table 1 in IMF and IDA, "Heavily Indebted Poor Countries (HIPC) Initiative—Status of Implementation." As the net present values of debt relief are in terms of the decision-point year only, we use data from that year for the other variables too. Where necessary, the raw data have been converted into per capita values using population data from "World Development Indicators on CD-ROM," 2005. Data in current USD have been converted into purchasing power parity (PPP) values by using the ratio of the PPP conversion factor to the official exchange rate. Aid excluding debt relief is calculated by subtracting the item "Debt Forgiveness Grants" from the flows of net Official Development Assistance.

TABLE A1
SUMMARY STATISTICS FOR THE PPP DATA

Variable	Obs.	Mean	Std. Dev.	Min.	Max.
Population (mill.)	18	14.8	15.0	0.8	65.8
GDP	18	1495.8	978.6	516.6	4043.0
Total debt	18	1943.6	2003.8	408.8	7792.0
PPG debt	18	1600.4	1638.0	340.8	6407.2
Net present value of debt relief	18	647.9	905.6	114.3	3352.8
Aid excluding debt relief	18	171.3	126.6	45.7	481.7
Total aid	18	187.5	148.0	48.5	565.5
Debt relief share	18	36.0	15.3	12.6	60.6

Note: Per capita values.

Alexander W. Cappelen, Rune Jansen Hagen, and Bertil Tungodden

Judeo-Christian Tradition on Debt: Political, Not Just Ethical

Ton Veerkamp

any civil society groups that deal critically with the situation of highly indebted developing countries draw their inspiration from principles arising from religious traditions and work within religious networks, such as the World Council of Churches. This essay seeks to inform questions about the resolution of today's debt crisis against the background of this engagement. The approach is valuable both because of the moral richness of religious teaching, and because of the historical practice of translating moral religious principles into political action on debt. The first section interprets how the basic documents of the Judeo-Christian tradition dealt with the debt problem in an ancient agrarian society. The second section asks what role appeals to ethics generally can perform in a political controversy, especially concerning the debt problem. The final section links solutions to the debt problem of individuals in ancient Judean society to debt problems of countries in modern societies. It argues that the linkage can help in finding political solutions for problems of our times.

SOLUTIONS TO PERSONAL DEBT PROBLEMS IN ANCIENT JUDEAN SOCIETY

The consideration of debt in the ancient biblical texts, although it pertains to the debt of people or households, can help illuminate the question of the debt burden of the governments of poor countries. It sheds light on the ethical principles and political action that might be applied in seeking solutions to the debt problem.

The Torah as the Constitution of Ancient Judea
After the breakdown of the Hebrew monarchy in Jerusalem in 587 BC, the Babylonians drove the elites of Jerusalem and Judea into exile and killed

many of them. Only the poor and a few pro-Babylon leaders stayed in the countryside of Judea. In order to enable a rudimentary agricultural production to resume, the Babylonians decreed a land reform: "they gave those, who had nothing, vineyards and fields" (*Jeremiah* 39, 10). Since the Babylonians had severe problems in their own country, they had no opportunity to settle the confused situation in Judea. There was no longer a state authority and the new landowners had to find a set of elementary rules for social life.[1]

The type of society that emerged during this time in Judea can be called a regulated anarchy.[2] During the same period, 570–520 BC, the core of the *Torah* was formulated.[3] It is unclear how much of the compilation of principles and laws in the *Torah* reflected actual practice and how much was, in effect, proposed reform, but in many respects it spoke directly to the problem of social organization. Chapters 12–26 of the biblical book *Deuteronomy* comprise the main law document of this regulated anarchy: no central authority, no central political institutions, no taxes, no duty to pay tribute to a foreign power, and no regular army.[4] One of the outstanding features of the regulations of *Deuteronomy* 12–26 is the institution of the seventh year as the Year of Release: "Every creditor shall release what he has lent to his neighbor, his brother" (15, 2).

Social Structures

The basic social unit of production was the *beth av*, House of the Father, an extended family, headed by the father, and including those descended from him and their dependents.[5] The chiefs of the several *beth av* are seen as members of clans (*mishpachah*), the clans being descendants from the twelve sons of Jacob, called *Israel*. This legend legitimates a social structure of Brotherhood.

The clan structure of ancient Judea was strictly patriarchal. The wife of the patriarch belonged with other possessions to "all what is his" (*Exodus* 20, 17). The social order of Judea was egalitarian, but equality was limited to the equality among the several *beth av*, and not among individual persons. The "brothers," the chiefs of the family clans, were supposed to assist the "brother who is falling down,"[6] that is, the *beth av* in the process of losing its means of production and living (*Leviticus* 25, 25, 29, 39). Since every *beth av* ran the risk to "fall down," this system was a *political* system of mutual assurance in response to the dangers to subsistence in a semi-arid agricultural area. It was, in short, an egalitarian ideology of brotherhood and freedom from serfdom. This system of "brotherhood" was thus defined by the principles of autonomy and equality, which were shared by all members of ancient Judean society.

Liberation from Serfdom as the Central Paradigm of the Judean Constitution
The story of Exodus, the liberation of the Jewish people from the oppression in Egypt, is central in the *Torah*. And yet the Kingdom of Judah that arose around 1,000 BC and was not fully destroyed until about 400 years later came to be characterized by landlordism. The ownership of the fertile soil was a matter of the royal House of David and of a few influential families. The population, especially in the countryside, had the status of serfs, who worked on the large estates of the elites. Old Testament prophets had strongly criticized the loss of freedom and property among peasant families.

In the situation of a regulated anarchy, after the destruction of the monarchy in Judea, the traditional story of Exodus gained new strength, since Egypt was the chief ally of the oppressive regime of the last Davidic Kings. Freedom of the people was the central issue, freedom to live with the extended family on the soil and in the house, which are the unalienable heritage (*nachalah*) of the *beth av*. First task of this regulated anarchy was the protection of freedom. The Name of the Judean God, denoting the core of the Judean social order, was pronounced as "the One, who brought out the people from the land of Egypt, from the house of serfdom" (*Exodus* 20, 2). All laws of the *Torah* ultimately have freedom as their real focus, although the relation between some of the detailed cultic prescriptions and freedom is hard to understand. But there can be no doubt about the great importance of freedom to self-reliance and freedom from exploitation by other human beings, especially by those of one's own people. So the protection of the new freedom is the main task of all social and political institutions designed by the *Torah* for ancient Judea.

At the end of this period, the Persian Empire under King Darius I (521–486 BC) supplanted Babylon and allowed the installment of a semi-autonomous government in Jerusalem. It decreed the reconstruction of the temple that the Babylonians had destroyed as the central political and cultic institution of Judea. A number of descendants of the exiled Judean elites returned to Jerusalem. The political reorganization of Judea as a part of the Persian Empire was the end of the system of regulated anarchy. The impression from the books of some of the Prophets (Trito Isaiah, Zechariah, Malachi) is that Judea in the first half of the fifth century BC was a corrupt and unjust society.

One of the reasons for the deterioration of social life after the return to Judea was the fact that the Persian Empire required tribute to be paid in coined money instead of in kind or bullion. The governments in the provinces with restricted home rule had to exact taxes in coined money from the population. Such money could only be earned on markets, so the *beth av* now had to produce cash crops, not just food crops. Many small farms were not able to meet the new conditions. They had to borrow money for the tribute of the king (*middah hammelek*) (*Nehemia* 5, 4), their "fields and vineyards" functioning as securities to the lenders. In case of default they lost their farms to the lenders. In Persian times, the tribute to the imperial government was moderate compared to what other central governments, such as of the Assyrian or Babylonian empires, required, but the tribute-based monetization of the Judean economy worsened the situation of small farms.

The Reforms of Nehemia: the System of Brotherhood
"A great outcry of the people and their wives against the Judean brothers occurred" (*Nehemia* 5, 1). The majority of the *beth av* were not able to pay their debts to other members of society and to the imperial government. Typically, in all ancient oriental societies, debtors who defaulted had to sell their property, and when the yield was still insufficient to meet the claims of the creditor, the debtors had to sell members of the family on the slave market, using the proceeds to satisfy the creditors. First to be sold were the young unmarried women or girls (*Nehemia* 5, 5).[7] In all ancient societies, debts were the main origin of serfdom and it was widespread.[8]

This outcry can be seen as a popular movement against the exploitation of defaulting indebted *beth av* by the elites of the province. As Persian governor of Judea, Nehemia, himself a Jew, had the main task of keeping or

Ton Veerkamp

restoring the social and political stability of the province. Rebellion in this province could trigger off rebellions in the neighboring Egyptian region, where the empire had vital interests.

Nehemia had two options: mercilessly suppress the outcry or accept the claims behind the outcry of the popular movement. The peaceful pacification of the Judean province seemed to him politically the best way. The claims of the *Torah*, which were substantially identical with the claims of the popular movement, had to be enforced on the elites of the society. Nehemia wanted to make the *Torah* the constitution of the semi-autonomous province of Judea and have it accepted by the acclamation of a "great assembly" (*qahal gadol*) of the people. The story, told in *Nehemia* 5, 8, and 9, may substantially have been historical: Jewish politicians, backed by the imperial government, renewed political and social life based on an egalitarian economy. Nehemia decreed a debt release and redistribution of the land, the main economic resource of Judean society.

Elements of Social and Economic Legislation during 440–330 BC in Judea
Nehemia's striving for an adequate response to a popular movement—the restoration of the ability of every *beth av* to self-sustaining production—resulted in a policy of debt release and redistribution of economic resources as a condition for a "fresh start" of the society and its members. Importantly, Nehemia's ad-hoc reaction was institutionalized by a constitutional process. He forced the elites of Judean society to act according to the regulations of the *Torah*, especially of *Deuteronomy* 15, 1–11. The detailed social legislation in Chapter 25 of the book *Leviticus* can be seen as an adaptation of the developments in Judean society of the fourth century.

The Year of Jubilee was a central feature of the social legislation. While lending and borrowing are necessary elements of every economy, lending is only possible when debts are paid back. The political question was what to do when debts cannot be paid back. First, Judea declared owning land as the sole privilege of the God of the Judeans (*Leviticus* 23, 23f.). No *beth av* owned its land; it had only usufruct. The Year of Jubilee prescribed the limitation on all contracts concerning the use of land, since private property in land, the basic economic resource in Judean economy, did not exist. The same limitation applied to the use of labor. Buying or selling land was rather handing over usufruct for a limited period of time, a number of crop cycles until the Year of Jubilee. The same restriction applied to all other contracts involving right to usage over time; in particular, debt contracts or contracts of servitude also ended in the Jubilee Year.

In principle, then, every *beth av* that "fell down" was to be given an opportunity for a "fresh start." There is no evidence that the Year of Jubilee was put into regular practice and Leviticus extended the traditional institution of the seventh year as "year of release" (*Deuteronomy* 15, 1ff.) to a period of forty-nine years. The fiftieth year is the Year of Jubilee. However, there is some scattered historical evidence of attempts to set a time limit on contracts of servitude, "setting free all Hebrew slaves." "Free" meant free of every obligation (*chafschi*). Moreover, the slave was to be compensated for his service—"furnish him out of the flock, threshing floor and vat" (*Deuternomy* 15, 14)—because "this service was worth twice as much as the wage of a hired worker" (*schakir*) (*Deuteronomy* 15, 18).

This practice was new in ancient society. Liberation of slaves in ancient economies was an act of trade or of grace, but not of law and justice. The rule was that a slave should pay for his liberation, when he wants to be set free. He was "private property," and liberation was handing over this private property from his master to himself. The master could set him free without demanding purchase money, but this occurred only at will. The *Torah* on the contrary established not only the *right* of being released but also of being rewarded for the services the Hebrew slave performed.[9]

Jeremiah 34, 8–22 tells of an abortive attempt to free slaves during the reign of King Zedekiah (597–586 BC), the last of the kings of Judah.[10] Clearly, periodical liberation had to be enforced by state authorities; apparently it did not function.[11] Also, the extension of the period of seven years to forty-nine years in *Leviticus* practically meant a lifelong servitude for most of the Hebrew slaves. The sense of the Year of Jubilee was the general conviction that every claim was connected with the proviso of "God"—that is, of the social system of autonomy and equality. The combination of debt release and land reform was the central issue of the Year of Jubilee: every *beth av* should be able to return "each to his property, each to his family" (*Leviticus* 25, 10). This was the inspiration, if not necessarily consistent practice.[12]

Ton Veerkamp

Periodical Debt Release and Lenders' Incentives

The ancient Judean economy was mainly a subsistence economy. Most of the goods that people needed for survival were produced by the *beth av* itself and the rest were obtained through barter and purchase on credit. Loss of land owing to debt default was devastating. As soon as a household lost its land, it ceased to be a full member of society. People without land were people without rights.

This phenomenon was by no means a specific Judean problem; indebtedness was a central problem in all the ancient societies. Indebtedness led almost always to enslavement of the debtors. Since no economy functions without the possibility to lend and to borrow, the egalitarian system of ancient Judea had to find means to deal with the debt problem of the *beth av*. Even in a society in which the autarchy and self-reliance of the productive units are predominant, situations will occur in which they can no longer carry out their task of self-reliant survival. Sickness of important family members, bad harvest, adverse weather, plagues like locust-swarms, and so on require the assistance of other members of society. The help consists in providing goods, mainly grain, for survival and for sowing. The grain has to be returned after the new harvest.

In most cases, agriculture in ancient Judea was self-sustaining: crops were sufficient for survival, new sowing, and a small portion for barter. As in most subsistence economies, however, there was often insufficient surplus to pay back the assistance received; lenders took risks. The *Torah* demanded the willingness to lend in cases of emergency (poverty): "You shall not harden your hearts or shut your hand against your poor brother, but you shall open your hand to him and lend what is sufficient for his needs, whatever it may be" (*Deuteronomy* 15, 8). The willingness to lend had to be stressed, since the borrower could seldom offer securities (collateral) sufficient for the requirements of debt service.

This is an important economic problem. On the one hand, the needy must receive assistance. On the other hand, the needy were obligated to repay, often could not, lost everything, but could be made whole again. Thus the periodical debt release necessarily decreased the willingness to lend. The *Torah* sees the incentive problem for lenders: "Take care lest there be a base thought in your heart and you might say: the seventh year is near, the year of release, and your eye grows hostile to your needy brother, and you give him nothing" (Deuteronomy 15, 9). *Deuteronomy* sees no political solution to the problem; it appeals morally to the unwilling lender: "The needy poor cries to the Lord against you: this will be a sin in you" (ibid.). The extension of the period of seven to forty-nine years in the book *Leviticus* did not eliminate the problem of lender incentives: toward the end of the forty-nine years every inclination to lend would also cease.

Forty-nine years is a long period, and regulations had to be found to deal with debt problems within that period. Since the general consent was that members of an autonomous and egalitarian society should not, in case of debt default, lose their basic means of living and their freedom, society required that relatives of the defaulting debtor "redeem" the debtor. If there were no solvent relatives, the debtor had to hand over his property to his creditor. The creditor, however, did not become the new owner of the land of the debtor; he had only the usufruct—a number of crops—until the debt was paid. The debtor had no other means of payment than his labor. He and his family were obliged to work for his creditor. The status of these people was something between free man and slave. They were to be treated as a "brother and sister," but as not-free members of the extended family of the creditor. Yet neither the debtor nor members of his family could be sold on the slave market.

Disapproval of Interest

To meet the risk of lending to defaulting debtors, lenders required payment of principal and a surplus. Risk is the perennial justification of interest. The Hebrew word for interest was *tharbith* or *marbith* ("making many"). Taking interest was described as *noschek* (bite)—that is, interest was something "bitten off" from somebody. Contemporary Hellenic philosophers also despised the practice of taking interest.[13] The reason is that while every debtor must produce an output sufficient for survival and a surplus, the reality was that only under extraordinarily favorable circumstances would a surplus be attainable, since economic growth was not the normal state of affairs. Thus peasants would frequently not be able to pay their debts, especially with interest added to the principal.

Ton Veerkamp

When ancient creditors required interest rates of up to 50 percent,[14] successful debt servicing would become an illusion and most debtors would end up losing their property and freedom. Allowing the taking of interest could thus put an end to the egalitarian society of free producers and lead to a society of a few great landlords and a majority of serfs, as in Hellas and the Roman Republic. In ancient Judea, the social system of Brotherhood saw freedom from serfdom as the most essential good of social life. It breaks down when taking interest is common practice. Since the status of debt default and serfdom could be the fate of any *beth av*, the general disapproval of interest was of a political nature. It was driven by concern to protect a way of life and a potential threat to each household, not a code of individual morality.

Judea's concern with the preservation of the system of Brotherhood was shared across time and religions. The medieval church also prohibited interest, and considered Christian society as a holy family. In Islam the *umma*, the community of the true believers, was also a sort of family; even today fundamentalist Islamic regimes address their citizens as "brothers and sisters." Islam strictly condemns interest and complicated ideological constructs have been necessary to reconcile Islam with a capitalist economy, in which interest is a basic element.

A Note on Equality

Since we have no statistics on income, income distribution, and production in ancient Judea, we do not have measures of inequality. However, inequality in ancient Judea was certainly present; farms differed in soil quality, access to water, size of the extended family (labor power), and so on. On the other hand, the techniques of production were probably similar for all *beth av* and in most cases the yearly product of the *beth av* was probably on average slightly above the subsistence level. One might roughly characterize this economy as an equality of poverty; rich peasants would have been rare.

The political target of egalitarian policy was equality in opportunity: every *beth av* should be able to sustain itself and should in case of default be awarded a "fresh start." We find in the historical documents no answer to the question of whether this model of debt release and land redistribution actually functioned. The detailed regulations of *Leviticus* 25, 25–55, show that the temple courts decided on juridical cases related to land property and debts. This means that the society in the fourth century BC tried to practice the regulations of the system of Brotherhood and was confronted with complications that needed juridical clarification.[15]

After the collapse of the Persian Empire, this system ceased to exist, although it was never forgotten. The remembrance of the system of Brotherhood was kept alive by the sacred books of Israel. And since the Hebrew Scriptures were translated into Greek, the universal language at the time— the origins of that translation dating from the middle of the third century in the Jewish community of Alexandria—this remembrance is the legacy of mankind.

Final Breakdown of the Autonomy of the Egalitarian Judean Society

In Hellenist times, inequality in income and opportunity became a feature that Judea had in common with the surrounding societies. Judea became part of Ptolemaic (Hellenist) Egypt. Egypt was in constant war against other Hellenist empires in Syria and in Greece, and the need for money was acute. The central government in Alexandria divided the kingdom into several tax provinces. The collection of tribute was leased to private persons. They paid the tribute in advance and afterward extracted it from the population in their tax provinces. This business was only profitable when they charged the population a tax collection fee, in essence a surtax. Under these circumstances, small farms defaulted and a system of rich landlords and widespread slavery arose, replacing the system of Brotherhood of ancient Judea.

The privatization of tribute ruined almost all traditional societies in the Hellenist Empires in the East during the third and second centuries BC. This led to many traditionalist revolts of which the Judean revolt led by the Hasmonean family of Jehuda, called *Makkabi* (the Hammer), after 170 AD was the best known. The revolt aimed to restore the traditional egalitarian Judean society. Autonomy was the ability of traditional society to live according to its own laws (*autos nomoi*) and was under the new circumstances the necessary condition for equality.[16]

Tribute in the Judean economy worked as in all other small economies of that time—like heavy external sovereign debt. The government under Jonathan, brother of Jehuda Makkabi, negotiated a new agreement on the tribute,[17] which was substantially lower than the former. More autonomy meant less tribute, that is, less external debt. The basis for this new agreement was the political and military power of the government under Jonathan.

Christianity

Finally, all governments in the ancient Near East were overthrown and replaced by the "super-government" of the Roman Empire. In New Testament times, autonomy was the predominant problem since the military power of the Roman Empire was absolutely overwhelming. Many people no longer expected help from local revolutionary leaders but only from Heaven. This caused the emergence of various kinds of messianism not only in Judea but also in other regions of the ancient East.[18] In fact messianism replaced politics—and in some cases also ethics. According to messianic faith, there is no human political alternative, no need for rules of right conduct: the Messiah must and will come.[19]

Nevertheless Christianity (the word Christian originally meant messianist) kept the sacred Books of Israel and also its social visions as a basic element of faith. The heritage of the egalitarian features of the *Torah* has been living in many Christian movements up to the Theology of Liberation in Latin American during the twentieth century. In Christianity, the backdoor to politics was never definitely closed.

ETHICS AND POLITICS

The regulations of the *Torah* have not served as political guidelines for over 2,000 years. The society for which they were formulated no longer exists. Rules for proper conduct derived for an egalitarian peasant society would not be legislated by societies based on other principles. No longer serving as political regulations, the system of Brotherhood could only survive as ethical maxims. That is, these prescriptions, derived from religious moral principles, now function only as rules for right conduct based on logical argument or appeal to a higher authority or other form of inspiration. In practice, ethics rooted in religious teaching serves mainly as rules for individuals in an accepted game; the game itself is not usually contested. And, aside from the various philosophical traditions that inform ethical thinking, people can also develop very different "personal" moral codes. Is this all that can be said about religious ethics?

The Ethical Deadlock

In trying to develop an ethical approach to the problems of heavily in-debted countries, one would like to start by presupposing that all actors share a common set of basic values that they interpret in a common way, and that they would rank their normative priorities similarly when they conflicted in any given situation. Reinhold Niebuhr wrote in 1932 that "a sharp distinction must be drawn between moral and social behavior of indi-viduals and of social groups, national, racial, and economic; and that this distinction justifies and necessitates political policies which a purely indi-vidualistic ethic must always find embarrassing."[20] There are two reasons it might be embarrassing: people might have to compromise on the values they individually hold in reaching political agreement or they might dis-agree on the facts in light of which the situation must be evaluated. Both have occurred and it is not always easy to tell which one (or both) is behind any specific disagreement.

This dilemma can be seen in discussions between Third World advocacy groups and creditor country politicians or private lenders about whether the debts of poor countries should be paid or cancelled. One side stresses the issue of poverty; the other the functioning of the international financial system on the basis of the principle that debts must be paid, as a special instance of the general principle of *pacta sunt servanda*, or contracts must be fulfilled.

Third World groups claim that payments of debts cause misery and death among the poor, and this fact should override the principle of *pacta sunt servanda*. The first claim is subject to empirical disputes, and the second is a question of whether, even if the first claim is true, it should be allowed to trump the values expressed by the other side.

On the other side, holders of bonds issued by lending governments are normally private institutions, primarily in the financial sector. The manage-ment of commercial banks may feel a moral responsibility to fulfill expecta-tions of their depositors, who want rewards for their deposits. As buyers of bonds, banks similarly expect rewards and feel obligations. They might well

Ton Veerkamp

perceive Third World advocates as unrealistic and say, Our business is not charity; our business is to carry out the wishes of our depositors. Creditors typically claim that national governments should be responsible for their own poor, and that debt cancellation (breaking contracts) presages the breakdown of the international legal system, which is detrimental to everyone, even the poor who live in countries that will lose access to credit. As with the claims of Third World advocates, it is an empirical question whether these statements are true, as well as a question of whether, if they are true, they should dominate other considerations.

The political system is the arena in which such parties should be able to come to agreement on such specific problems, even if for different reasons (including for reasons that some individuals might find "embarrassing," as Niebuhr wrote). Such a political system in a pluralistic society should comprise a set of processes that would be seen as "legitimate" and would be valued. Within those processes, the contending people might reach agreement and the outcome could be called "fair" because the processes for reaching it were deemed fair by the different parties. This would only be the case if the contending parties find that their basic interests are met in the agreement. Fairness embodies at least implicit acknowledgment of basic and legitimate interests.

Fairness (or the lack of it) is in the meantime also an important notion in civil society advocacy on the problem of external debt. It is no accident finding the word "fair" so often in documents of civil society groups working on debt. One thus finds, for example, that a prominent proposal from the Jubilee movement for a new process to resolve sovereign debt problems is called a Fair and Transparent Arbitration Process.

In the case of Christian movements, evoking fairness is also a commentary on the limited agreement on how to respond to social injustice. For example, while adherents to Catholic Liberation Theology have espoused as a main doctrine of their faith a "bias for the poor," the mainstream Church has narrowly interpreted how to act on that principle. It emphasizes taking actions that are individual and charitable, in contrast to the political and structural foci of Liberation Theology.[21] One finds parallel disputes between groups such as Kairos Europa and mainstream Protestant churches, and they are much debated within the World Council of Churches.

In other words, mainstream Christian Ethics, as such, would not compel the "rich" to give from what they have to the "poor" what they need. A rich individual who experiences Christianity as an incentive for his individual behavior may give freely from what he has to a poor person or charitable institution what he/it needs. In the view of the "radicals," while this attitude may save a life in a particular case, it cannot solve the problem of poverty as such. Within both of the Catholic and Protestant traditions, the mainstream view is shared by a vast majority of the population, and the radical view is a position of a minority.

In sum, very often the discussion between many Christian groups and the nominally Christian executives in finance and business turns out to be an unprofitable discussion between two doctrines (or two different interpretations of a single doctrine) that each side considers to be comprehensive, between the biblical doctrines of justice and utilitarianism, between the doctrine of the cake justly cut and the doctrine of the cake eternally growing, between the radical creed of Christian ethics and mainstream individualism.

Moral Arguments and Political Movements

Despite these difficulties, the argument of this essay is that ethical social change is possible if it can be made political. It is helpful to analyze a concrete example. In 1980–86, German Churches cancelled some of their accounts with Deutsche Bank, Germany's most powerful bank, because of its intensive business with the Apartheid regime in South Africa. The churches disapproved the policy of the South African government on ethical grounds. Deutsche Bank was not really impressed. Churches—the institutions themselves—were not powerful enough to hurt Deutsche Bank. But there was another element: political momentum. The action of the Churches in Germany raised consciousness among their Christian believers about the character of the Apartheid regime. Moreover South Africa's church leaders, playing an important role in the resistance against the regime, felt encouraged by the action of the Churches of Germany and other nations. Most importantly, the new idea of what is ethically acceptable spread in South Africa itself and turned into political power, and it was this power of the anti-Apartheid movement in South Africa that finally toppled the system.

Ton Veerkamp

In other words, appeals to ethical arguments can play an important role in raising consciousness and thus in building support for political movements.

Examples can also be found in the resolution of external debt crises themselves. The relatively successful agreements between Argentina and its creditors have been due to a great deal to the massive protests of the population of that country since December 2001. The Argentinean government could convincingly argue that debt business as usual would only stiffen the resistance of the people and eventually result in interior chaos, detrimental to all parties in the debt debate.

In each case, it was not moral persuasion per se that brought about the change, but the political strength that came from the numbers of people who accepted the moral argument—or who supported the demanded policy for other reasons—and became willing to act politically. Niebuhr sums up this observation:

> It may be possible, though it is never easy, to establish just relations between individuals within a group by moral and rational suasion and accommodation. In inter-group relations this is practically impossible. The relations between groups must therefore always be predominantly political rather than ethical, that is, they will be determined by the proportion of power which each group possesses at least as much as by any rational and moral appraisal of the comparative needs and claims of each group.[22]

The World Council of Churches organized a workshop on debt in June 2003 that produced a document whose final chapter read: "At core, the debt problem is one of profoundly unequal power relations."[23] Power was the decisive factor in the attempt to restore or maintain the system of Brotherhood in ancient Judea. Power will also be the decisive factor in attempts to realize an ethically more acceptable form of society. One may eventually convince individuals to change their attitude to political and social problems, but to convince a commercial bank to release debts for ethical reasons alone is without the slightest chance: Banks have no ethics, they have balance sheets, or at least that seems to be how their managing boards operate.[24] As long as a bank sees some little chance to collect an outstanding debt, it will not release the debt. Only if a refusal to negotiate debt release would hurt the affairs of the bank by damaging its reputation would it consider a change of its policy. Being able to hurt an institution, such as an international commercial bank or an international financial institution, or even one's own government—as developed country governments extended many of the loans that the poorest countries cannot pay—one must have adequate political power.

RELATING JEWISH-CHRISTIAN TRADITION TO THE PROBLEM OF EXTERNAL DEBT

Could debt release and redistribution of economic resources in ancient Judea, which were the determinant vehicles of a consistent social policy, offer an orientation to formulate a new policy concerning the present problem of the heavily indebted countries and of the economic inequality in our world?

The Lesson of Nehemia

Nehemia reacted to a popular movement: He was confronted with a serious domestic conflict that eventually could destroy the political stability of the Judean society and harm vital interests of the Persian Empire that entrusted him with the task of maintaining law and order in the province. The popular movement put him under political pressure and he had to react politically. His reasons might have been "moral" or even "embarrassing," in Niebuhr's terminology, but we can applaud the actual actions. Nehemia had two options: crushing the popular movement or acting according to the complaints of the people. In the first case, he would back the cause of the Judean elites; in the second, the cause of the Judean people. Nehemia chose the side of the people, be it for reasons of political opportunity—the popular movement being too strong—be it for reasons of inner convictions, or both. Anyway the option chosen had to work politically at least as well as or better than the other. In every decision of this kind political relationship plays the decisive role.

The "outcry of the people" was a political coalition of the indebted *beth av*. A single debtor could never have impressed governor Nehemia enough to initiate a process of fundamental political and social reform. A coalition of debtors could. Similarly, internal political pressure made it possible for Argentina's government to take a strong stand against its foreign creditors after 2001. In the same way, a coalition of Latin American countries could

Ton Veerkamp

deploy much more power to reach a really new political approach to the debt problem. However, such a coalition could only be built upon the cooperation of the popular movements in the indebted countries.

This way of thinking about ethical positions and political power has been recognized in the international social forums organized by NGOs in recent years. It is seen, in particular, in the AGAPE Document of the World Council of Churches (WCC), resulting from church activities in many countries in the North and South.[25]

These initiatives are promising signs that such coalitions of popular movements could eventually be forthcoming. However, the question is what can be really fair, just, or good under profoundly unequal power relations. Fairness in the biblical narrative was not the decisive concept. Nehemia understood that massive indebtedness would eventually destroy society and create a state of political instability. He also understood that traditional conceptions could prevent social and political instability. Forgiving debts was politically wise.

The same rationale applies to Africa today. Indebtedness may not have been the sole or even the main reason for the murderous political instability of western Africa in recent years, but the continuation of the debt situation will prevent this region from returning to stability. The private and public creditors of African governments must be politically as wise as Nehemia and understand that an unstable Africa, Latin America, or Indonesia are threats to their own business, not to speak of a threat to world peace. This wisdom will not fall from heaven. New policies often begin in the streets with popular action.

Debt Release

The *Torah* required that after a fixed period of seven or forty-nine years *all* debts be cancelled. The debts the *Torah* is speaking of are always debts that threatened survival or at least a life in freedom. When we talk about sovereign debt in the light of these *Torah* prescriptions we must think of debts that destroy the sovereignty of the indebted country, that is, of debts that deprive the country of the possibility to make policies in favor of their poor citizens. Such debts must be cancelled. Any conditionality must aim at restoring sovereignty of the country, as the *Torah* aimed at restoring the autonomy of the indebted *beth av*. Structural adjustment programs, imposed by the international financial institutions as *conditio sine qua non* for restructuring outstanding debts—let alone their cancellation—do not fulfill the Biblical condition: restoring freedom and autonomy (sovereignty) of the *beth av* or the indebted country.

The *Torah* knew the possibility of bailing out or redeeming (*Géulah*) debtors by their relatives. For our problem this seems not to be relevant. But one might think of an international fund that could help in alleviating debt burdens. Also, at the WCC workshop, the African Forum and Network on Debt and Development called for the establishment of an International Arbitration Court on Debt.[26] Other thoughtful procedural proposals were made and discussed, such as by Ashfaq Khalfan, Jeff King, and Bryan Thomas, who advanced an Odious Debt Doctrine, stating what "odious debt" is and why it should not be repaid.[27] Expectations of a new spirit of "brotherhood" may be very unrealistic at this time. The mentioned ideas, however, are possibly a sign that a more realistic and wise attitude to the problem of sovereign debt is possible.

Redistribution of Economic Resources

The two main elements of the Nehemian reforms were forgiving the debt and giving back the land to the debtors who lost their land in the course of their indebtedness. Similarly, debt release for countries is only a *fresh start* for the peoples of indebted countries when the unequally distributed economic resources are redistributed. These two elements were invariably parts of all biblical regulations in the area of the economy, the decree of Nehemia, the institution of the seventh year, and Year of Jubilee.

Indeed, the groups engaged in finding alternatives to the present institutional management of the debt problems of developing countries were also to be found among the demonstrators during the WTO meeting in Hong Kong in December 2005. Consistent with their concerns over debt, these groups advocated a new economic system, distributing the economic resources more fairly. The ideology of unlimited free trade benefits the interests of global enterprise, of the European Union, and of the United States, cementing the present situation of unequally distributed resources. Those

Ton Veerkamp

advocacy groups in Hong Kong saw the same linkage between debt release and redistribution of economic resources as Nehemia did.

The Problem of Interest

Another constant element is the prohibition of interest. An ancient farmer, being obliged to pay principal and interest, was forced to work more than necessary to keep himself and his extended family alive. Since Biblical times, when interest kept the debtor in a lifelong dependency to the creditor and gave him no chance of recovery, it was forbidden to take any interest from a debtor.

Interest is transferring the results of the labor of individual or collective debtors to individual or collective creditors. In the case of collective debtors like heavily indebted poor countries portions of the national production will be transferred to the creditors, thus diminishing the benefits of any economic growth. Paying interest is redistribution of economic resources from the poor to the rich countries. This can be hardly seen as a contribution to political stability, not to speak of solving the problem of poverty.

In the same light we should consider the question of repatriating of enterprise profits produced in poor countries. Free repatriation of profits belongs to the core of the WTO philosophy of free trade. These profits are basic elements of economic growth, and economic growth is necessary though not sufficient for the elimination of poverty. Interest and profits have the same root in that both represent a surplus in the production process after having allowed for the replacement of used materials/machines and for the basic needs of the workers. They differ, however, because share owners will be rewarded only if profits are actually being made; money lenders will in any case take their interest payments, regardless of whether the borrower makes profit. This is the reason why Islam thinks sharing profits with a creditor is legitimate, while interest is not.

Those who desire to see interest forbidden and profits refunded to those who produced them in fact want the end of capitalism. Abolition of capitalism may in the long run be a respectable goal; it does not, however, solve the present and urgent problems of heavily indebted countries. Nevertheless, we might consider some form of refunding of interest and profits. In negotiations, debtors may request that parts of interest due be invested instead in projects of social infrastructure for education and health care, and that profits be reinvested in the country in which they were produced. South Korea successfully applied the instrument of domestic reinvestment of profits mainly of Korean but also of some Japanese enterprises in the period 1970–80. State-directed growth was only a necessary condition for solving the problem of poverty in the country. The fair distribution of growth was also required and an "outcry of the people" was needed to realize this. Violent demonstrations and strikes of Korean workers in the period after 1980 enforced a more fair distribution of Korean wealth.[28] Ethics may start the job; politics must finish it.

A PARABLE

While some of the books of the Bible are historical, the biblical *Book of Job* is literary fiction. It is a parable of the impossible communication between the poor and the wealthy. It tells the story of a poor man, who fell down in a state of appalling poverty, living in and from trash and rubbish. He discusses his situation with wealthy friends. In more than thirty agonizing chapters, these men try to communicate but Job cannot make his case understandable: being poor *and* not being responsible for his poverty. The final "discussion" between God and Job ends with resignation: "Therefore I reject, I am disgusted—in dust and in ashes" (*Job* 42, 7). The story itself ends with a conversion of God himself (*Job* 42, 8ff.). If we take the conception of God as a concentrated formula for social order, the story wants a renewal of the traditional social order of the *Torah*. In the fiction God converts. In reality the breakdown of communication between the poor and the wealthy resulted in the Maccabean revolt. This revolt was nothing but a social revolution, seeking the revival of traditional society.

There are no poor countries but only poor people. The difficulty is not only the communication between heavily indebted poor countries and the countries of their creditors, but also of the communication between the poor and the wealthy within both blocks. This communication is now more problematic than a quarter of a century ago. Our situation is not yet the situation of Job and his friends, a situation of complete breakdown of communication between the poor and the wealthy. Those who are thinking

Ton Veerkamp

about the problems of sovereign debt try to hold the lines of communication open. If ethics can raise consciousness of the problems, that widespread poverty threatens world peace, it will play an eminently political role. It lies within the reach of political possibilities to avoid global conflict.

NOTES

[1] The Jewish exiles in Babylon lived in communities that supported themselves according to the counsel that the prophet Jeremiah gave them: "Build houses and live in them; plant gardens and eat their product. Take wives and sons and daughters... Seek the peace of the city... because in its peace lies your peace" (29, 5ff.). The task of the prophets in Babylon was to organize the social structure of the Jewish communities according to the prescriptions of the Torah and to prevent assimilation to the Babylonian way of life.

[2] The German sociologist and ethnologist Christian Sigrist uses this expression to characterize civilizations without a central authority. See Christian Sigrist, *Regulierte Anarchie* (Frankfurt/Main: Syndikat, 1979).

[3] The *Torah* comprises the *Pentateuch* or *Five Books of Moses*, and includes the main historical narrative and laws of the Jewish people.

[4] There are essentially three sets of laws in the *Torah*, each derived from various sources and practices. The one in *Deuteronomy* is apparently an adaptation of the so-called *Book of the Covenant*, Exodus 21, 1-23, 19, which may have its origins in the political (prophetical) opposition movement under the last kings of Judea, late seventh century BC. All dating of Old Testament texts however is highly hypothetical. See Frank Crüsemann, *Die Tora: Theologie und Sozialgeschichte des alttestamentlichen Gesetzes* (München: Chr Kaiser, 1992).

[5] See the basic analysis of Hans G. Kippenberg, *Religion und Klassenbildung im antiken Judäa* (Göttingen: Walter De Gruyter, 1978).

[6] The meaning of the Hebrew root *makak* was originally "falling down," that is, being ruined.

[7] Married women belonged to their husbands; they could only be sold with the husband and his family. Girls, on the other hand, had apparently less working power and less value for the *beth av* and were the first to be sold in case of indebtedness.

[8] The other main source was war; prisoners of war ended almost always as serfs.

[9] The Bible is not an idyllic book. The *Torah* prescriptions limited the rights of slaves only to slaves from the Judean people. Other slaves were treated like private property (*achuzzah*) (*Leviticus* 25, 45). Moreover, there was an additional stipulation on freeing Jewish slaves. If a slave did not want to be set free in the Jubilee year "for he loves you and your household and is happy with you... then he shall become your slave in perpetuity" (*Deuterotomy* 15, 16–17). On the other hand, a slave who was set free without giving him land could end up in a worse situation. Being a Hebrew slave (*ebed*) offered security that a hired worker (*shakir*) never had.

[10] In fact, the rule of setting free all Hebrew slaves every seventh year existed at least since the social reform of King Josiah (640–608 BC).

[11] *Jeremiah* reports that because the freed slaves were taken back by their former masters, against God's will, Judah would be destroyed: "I hereby give the command—declares the Lord—by which I will bring [the Babylonians] back against this city. They will attack it and capture it, and burn it down. I will make the towns of Judah a desolation, without inhabitant" (*Jeremiah* 34, 22).

[12] The *Mishna*, a summary of discussions among the great rabbis of the first century AD and written down in the first half of the third century AD, has some detailed prescriptions on redeeming of fields in the Year of Jubilee (e.g. Mishna Ararkhin 7 and 9). Since the Israelites lived all over the ancient world, a universal land reform could not be carried out, but the detailed legislation by the rabbis indicate that *Géulah* (redemption), in one way or another, did function, even in the Jewish communities after the second destruction of Jerusalem.

[13] Aristotle, *Politica*, ed. David Ross (Oxford: Oxford University Press, 1957), p. 19. Interest (*tokos*), "makes something more (*auto poiei pleon*)," and was regarded by Aristotle as something "against nature" (*para physin*).

[14] Between 58–56 BC Brutus "lent the city of Salamis a considerable sum at 48% interest" (M.I. Finley, *The Ancient Economy*, London: Chatto and Windus, 1973), p. 54. This is an example of sovereign debt, the "private sector"—Brutus—being the creditor. In Roman times, public authorities issued bonds that were bought by wealthy individuals. Those debts could only be paid back by extorting tribute from conquered provinces.

[15] An example is the different treatment of real estate in townships and in the countryside. A house in a village was always a farmhouse; losing it meant losing life, and so had to be redeemed. In contrast, the law on the redemption of houses and land in townships could be deregulated, *Leviticus* 25, 29–34, and a kind of real estate market was admitted.

[16] The regime of the Hasmonean family turned out to be just another Jewish form of Hellenist rule. See Elias Bickerman, *From Ezra to the Last of the Maccabees* (New York: Schocken Books, 1962), esp. pp. 153–65.

[17] *First Book of Maccabees*, 11, 34f.

[18] S. K. Eddy, *The King Is Dead: Studies in the Near Eastern Resistance to Hellenism, 334–31 BC* (Lincoln, NE: University of Nebraska Press, 1961).

[19] The Gospel of St. John has no place for "ethics"; it knows "love" (*agape*), but that means solidarity among the members of the sectarian group for which the Gospel was written. Also the doctrine of St. Paul of the justification not by works but by faith alone has a connotation of a nonpolitical, nonethical life. In his early epistles, St. Paul expected the quick arrival of the Messiah. Later he had to define some rules of conduct, the beginning of "Christian ethics."

[20] Reinhold Niebuhr, *Moral Man and Immoral Society* (New York: Charles Sribner's Sons, 1960 [1932]), p. xi.

[21] Recently, in particular, Pope Benedict XVI called for the Catholic Church to continue to be directly involved in "charity," while ruling out its direct involvement in bringing about "justice," which necessarily involves the "world of politics," albeit seeing a Church role in helping "the lay faithful" clarify their thinking as they take part in public life. See *Deus Caritas Est*, Encyclical Letter, The Vatican, December 25, 2005, pp. 26–29.

[22] Niebuhr, *Moral Man and Immoral Society*, p. xxiii.

[23] Rogate R. Mshana, ed., "The Debt Problem for Poor Countries: Where Are We? A Report on Illegitimate Debt and Arbitration" (Geneva: World Council of Churches, 2004), p. 141.

[24] Admittedly, as noted earlier, bankers would say it differently, that their ethical obligation is first and foremost to their depositors (and shareholders).

[25] World Council of Churches, "Alternative Globalization Addressing Peoples and Earth (AGAPE): A Background Document" (Geneva: World Council of Churches, 2005); available at www.oikoumene.org/fileadmin/files/wcc-main/documents/p3/agape-new.pdf.

[26] Mshana, ed., "The Debt Problem for Poor Countries," pp. 1–45.

[27] Ibid., pp. 92–104.

[28] See Hartmut Elsenhans, "Strategien aus der Entwicklungskrise," *Zeitschrift für internationale Kulturaustausch* 41, no. 1 (1991), pp. 483–99; Amartya Sen, *Development as Freedom* (New York: Oxford University Press, 1999); Guk-Yueng Yi, *Staat und Kapitalakkumulation in ostasiatischen Ländern: Ein Vergleich zwischen Korea und Taiwan* (Saarbrücken: Verlag Breitenbach Publischers, 1988).

Ton Veerkamp

Making the Case for Jubilee: The Catholic Church and the Poor-Country Debt Movement

Elizabeth A. Donnelly

T he pledge by the Group of 8 (G-8) in July 2005 to cancel all the debt owed by eighteen, and ultimately more, heavily indebted poor countries to the International Monetary Fund (IMF), the World Bank, and the African Development Bank was the most recent victory in a series of campaigns by a broad-based coalition of churches and NGOs that had begun more than twenty-five years before. In the late 1990s, the movement grew considerably and achieved its most extraordinary mobilization in the Jubilee 2000 campaign, which successfully touched masses of people around the world with a moral message that politicians could not ignore. There are not many instances in modern history in which moral appeals based on religious principles drive political change (albeit limited). The civil rights movement in the United States may be one example. The struggle against apartheid in South Africa may be another. The anti-debt movement may be a third.

To better understand why the appeal has been so strong, this essay examines the ideas and ethical argumentation of the Catholic Church that have guided its involvement in the global debt campaign since the early 1980s. The focus is warranted because the Church played a leading role from the earliest days of the campaign by virtue of its size and vast array of resources. Its actors on the debt question have included individual Catholics, parish-based justice and peace groups, church personnel (especially missioners), religious orders and their social action offices, relief agencies, academics and universities, national episcopal conferences, the Vatican's justice and peace office, and Pope John Paul II. The global coalition's most extensive and best-known moral arguments for debt reduction originated at Catholic bishops' conferences and the Vatican. Statements from the Church leadership especially were addressed to both Catholics and non-Catholics among the general public and policy-makers. By stimulating discussion in policy circles, they strengthened the legitimacy of the fundamental claim that excessive sovereign debt servicing was unjust. The essay looks more closely at the two most widely disseminated and influential Church statements—by the Vatican and by the U.S. bishops—which have served as benchmarks in the Church's long engagement with the anti-debt campaign.

THE MORAL MESSAGE IN THE APPEAL FOR DEBT CANCELLATION

Emblematic of the appeal of debt cancellation was Carmen Rodriguez, who headed the Catholic Charismatic Movement in a sprawling shantytown parish south of Lima, Peru. She and other lay leaders of her diocese prepared for the new millennium in a rather unusual way. In early 1999, they participated in workshops offering economic and theological perspectives on the theme the Peruvian Catholic bishops had chosen for that year's Lenten observance: debt relief. They went door to door and gathered some 90,000 signatures on a petition, calling for a one-time cancellation by the end of 2000 of the unpayable debt of highly indebted poor countries. More than 1.8 million Peruvians in just three months' time and 17 million people from over 160 countries signed the petition, which was organized by a coalition of churches, antipoverty groups, and other civil society organizations as part of the Jubilee 2000 campaign. The delegation presenting the petition to German chancellor Gerhard Schröder, who accepted it in the name of the G-8 leaders in Cologne in June 1999, included such disparate figures as Archbishop Oscar Rodriguez Maradiaga of Tegucigalpa, Honduras, and Bono of the Irish rock group U2.

Jubilee 2000 organizers, led by such groups as Christian Aid U.K., Oxfam, the European Network on Debt and Development, a Washington-based coalition of church and anti-poverty groups, and Catholic national episcopal conferences, relief agencies, and the Vatican, argued that heavily indebted countries devoted an inordinate portion of their national budgets to making interest and principal payments on their debt, leaving too little available for desperately needed outlays for health, education, housing, and job creation. Invoking a biblical prescription for periodic debt relief, the coalition urged the international community to mark the millennium by recognizing a period of "jubilee" for poor countries, in which government debts would be canceled and the freed-up resources used to alleviate poverty. Of particular concern were thirty-six low-income and twelve middle-income countries the World Bank categorized in 1998 as "severely indebted."[1] The coalition also protested the disproportionate burden placed on the poor by structural adjustment programs, mandated by the IMF and the World Bank as conditions for debt rescheduling and reduction. Such programs have regularly featured deregulation of the private sector, the privatization of government-controlled industries and services (causing cuts in jobs and wages), and cuts in government budgets, which have typically slashed food subsidies and spending on health and education.

NGOs and churches had been working to alleviate the harmful consequences of debt and structural adjustment since the late 1970s, with efforts at national, regional, and then global collaboration, leading to a functioning transnational network by the late 1980s.[2] Efforts in the 1980s principally focused on large, middle-income countries, especially in Latin America, whose possible default on commercial bank loans threatened the stability of the international financial system. Limited debt reduction, followed by rapidly expanding international private-sector investment in "emerging market" countries in the early 1990s, largely defused the crisis in the eyes of creditor country policy-makers and the international media. The poorest and most heavily indebted countries were largely bypassed, however, and the growing civil society network turned its attention to pressing for debt relief for these countries, which tend to owe the vast majority of their external debt to bilateral and multilateral creditors, rather than commercial lenders.

Subsequent government crises in the late 1990s and early 2000s in Ecuador, Argentina, and other middle-income countries showed that the euphoria of investors for emerging markets would not save those countries from being vulnerable to new external debt crises. The anti-debt movement thus found itself needing to refocus on the lack of a coherent and comprehensive international mechanism for dealing with countries' unsustainable debt burdens. In other words, under existing solutions, debts were not being adequately reduced. A concrete proposal for "financial architecture reform" was thus advanced within the Jubilee movement, as in the joint call of the large networks of Catholic relief and development agencies for a "fair and transparent arbitration process."[3] While it has yet to win broad international acceptance, its appeal embodies essentially the same moral outrage as in the straightforward call for debt cancellation for the poorest countries: the international community expects developing countries—and especially poor people in those countries—to bear the consequences of excessive debt burdens, and that is immoral.

RELIGIOUS SOURCES OF THE MORAL MESSAGE

Throughout the campaign, the moral inspiration has been the biblical call for jubilee. According to the concept found in *Leviticus* 25 and *Deuteronomy* 15, justice required that the Jewish people should periodically—sometimes said to be every seven years and other times every fifty years—free slaves, redistribute land to its proper owners, and cancel debts in order to respect the human dignity of debtors and restore the bonds of community fractured by exploitation, greed, and the vicissitudes of economic activity. The case for jubilee debt cancellation, made throughout the 1980s, became a vital and effective frame for the campaign in the second half of the 1990s: activists identified the year 2000 as the jubilee year, and people around the world saw substantial debt cancellation as a fitting and sufficiently grand way to celebrate the new millennium.

The call to jubilee as articulated in the Catholic tradition is grounded in Catholic social teaching, a tradition encompassing ethical norms from the Bible, the work of such major theologians as Augustine and Aquinas, and social encyclicals and letters promulgated by popes and, more recently, national bishops' conferences. Its key principles are that each person is endowed with essential human dignity as a child of God, and individuals and institutions are obliged to protect and promote the dignity of persons. Also, people are social in nature, created by God as one single family, and must be committed to promoting the common good, the sum total of those conditions in society that make it possible for all persons to achieve their full potential, with the understanding that governments also have the duty to promote the common good. This ethics of solidarity, in which all assume

Elizabeth A. Donnelly

responsibility and work together for the effective realization of the unity of the human family, must not only be proclaimed at the level of principle but also be translated into concrete policies and institutions. All people of good-will are thus challenged to exercise a preferential option for the poor in examining the social impact of economic and financial policies and institutions. If the latter are organized in such a way as to injure the poor and exacerbate their poverty, one should consider them to be a form of institutionalized violence and social sin that should be addressed. In this analysis, the debt overhang is a structural block preventing the realization of the sustainable, integral human development valued in Catholic social teaching. Debt relief, then, must be linked to poverty alleviation.

Catholic social teaching also advocates subsidiarity, the principle that, whenever possible, individuals and local institutions should take responsibility for policy solutions. Subsidiarity has dual implications for the debt question: civil society in debtor countries must participate in decision-making on debt, and problems that cannot be solved by individuals, civil society, or national governments must be addressed by international structures. Thus, national debt crises are part of a growing list of issues on which people are called to greater international solidarity because of increased international economic interdependence.

The Catholic tradition also evaluates the debt question by theories of justice. While commutative justice implies a moral presumption that contractual obligations such as debts should be honored, distributive justice (the requirement that the allocation of income, wealth, and power in society be evaluated in light of its effect on persons whose basic material needs are unmet) may require that debts be canceled. Moreover, social justice (the imperative that all persons should be able to be active, productive participants in the life of society and that society should develop the full range of social, economic, and political institutions that enable individuals to do so), a key element of Catholic social thought, adds theological weight to the call for relief from debt.

These ethical principles nevertheless leave open the question of whether policy changes should be reformist or radical. Indeed, a reformist/radical cleavage has marked the debt network since the mid-1980s, increasingly lining up on a North (reformist) versus South (radical) axis. Catholic and non-Catholic activists alike have consistently had sharp debates over policy and strategy, most basically on the question of whether to reject SAP conditionality entirely and demand complete and unconditional debt cancellation, or accept with qualifications substantial debt reduction with reformed conditionality geared toward poverty alleviation. Nevertheless, with activists conscious that splitting the movement would seriously weaken it, the dominant tendency has been to seek common ground and maintain a steady critique of target institutions while welcoming incremental improvements in policy.

HOW CHURCH VIEWS DEVELOPED: 1970S TO 1980S

The "Mexican Weekend" of August 1982, during which the Mexican government threatened to default on its international debt, was the event that triggered widespread public attention to the debt crisis. Some of the first transnational expressions of concern about the impact of government debt on the poor came earlier, however, in the late 1970s, as U.S. and European missionaries working in debtor countries returned to their home countries and urged churches and NGOs to take up the issue. Many activists had experienced firsthand the devastating effect of the crisis on their parishioners and friends in debtor country shantytowns, and had been deeply imbued with the injunction of Latin American liberation theology to examine and confront "sinful structures" that contribute to poverty. Thus, arguments made by the U.S.-based Debt Crisis Network and its counterparts in Europe emphasized moral outrage at the debt overhang's implications for the poor as well as the degree to which it eviscerated efforts to tackle poverty. For example, Rev. Thomas Burns, a Maryknoll priest who has worked in a shantytown outside Lima for over twenty-five years, put it succinctly in his March 1987 testimony to the U.S. Congress: He was baptizing more dead babies since the institution of IMF-imposed structural adjustment in Peru.[4]

In England, Oxfam activists launched a successful media campaign, DATAA, in 1984 to educate people on the "five forces" that connected Britain with world hunger, focusing on one theme each year: debt, aid (not enough and of the wrong type), trade (scales weighted against poorer countries), agriculture (European Community policies on surplus production

Elizabeth A. Donnelly

and of manipulated world markets), and arms (the extravagant trade in weapons). Oxfam's 1986 campaign focused on debt. Coming on the heels of the 1985 Live Aid concert, which had generated attention to and monies for famine relief, Oxfam pointed out that for every dollar of emergency aid given to the African relief effort, about two dollars was paid to the West by the poorest twenty-nine African countries in debt repayments.[5]

The mid to late 1980s saw the leadership of many Catholic and Protestant national church bodies and the World Council of Churches draft statements evaluating the ethics of the debt crisis. Several of Latin America's national Catholic bishops' conferences issued statements condemning the disproportionate burden that economic adjustment policies placed on the poor of their countries.[6] In their 1986 major pastoral letter on the U.S. economy, the U.S. Catholic bishops joined their Latin American counterparts in deploring the social impact of the debt crisis, and advocated a two-tier solution: longer repayment periods, lower interest rates, and modification of IMF adjustment requirements for middle-income debtors; and extensive debt cancellation for the poorest, chiefly sub-Saharan African countries.[7] The U.S. bishops followed up their 1986 letter with congressional testimony on developing country debt by the chairman of the economics pastoral drafting committee[8] and by a principal advisor to the episcopal conference on international issues.[9] The U.S. bishops also established a subcommittee, which, after consulting with leading government, multilateral, and commercial bank officials, drafted an in-depth statement in 1989 updating and expanding the bishops' previous analysis.[10]

Other national bishops' conferences in creditor countries also took up the issue. For example, the German Catholic bishops issued a detailed statement on the social impact of the debt crisis.[11] In addition, together with the Evangelical Church in Germany, they issued a joint statement and presented testimony before the German parliament, bringing together a Protestant biblical analysis of the jubilee theme and the Catholic common good tradition.[12]

The highest level of the Catholic Church supported this outpouring of local and national religious engagement on debt crises. Pope John Paul II repeatedly raised the debt issue on his many trips to both creditor and debtor countries, in his public sermons, in talks with officials representing national governments, international organizations, commercial banks, and local churches, and in two of his encyclicals, "Sollicitudo Rei Socialis" (1987) and "Centesimus Annus" (1991). Because of his office, personal charisma, and well-covered activism on East-West and North-South relations, he drew the most media attention to the issue from the mid-1980s through the late 1990s. At the pope's request, in 1987 the Pontifical Commission for Justice and Peace, the Vatican's think tank on international development questions, issued a more explicit examination of the ethical dimensions of the debt.[13] The commission's president, Cardinal Roger Etchegaray, traveled to Washington to discuss the statement's recommendations with top officials of the World Bank and the IMF.

THE VATICAN AND U.S. BISHOPS' STATEMENTS

By the second half of the 1980s, the debt crises in developing countries were on the agenda for discussion in Catholic churches around the world and in Church officials' dialogues with key policy-makers. It is worth looking in more detail at the 1987 Vatican statement and at one of the national bishops' statements, the 1989 U.S. bishops' statement, as they arguably had an impact on the thinking of the leadership of several major U.S.-based banks, the U.S. government, and international financial institutions based in the United States, the IMF, the World Bank, and the Inter-American Development Bank (IDB). For example, extensive interviews in the early 1990s with the top leadership of the IMF, including past and present managing directors and deputy managing directors, and major country executive directors, revealed that they were most conversant with these two statements. IMF Managing Director Michel Camdessus, a practicing Catholic and longtime close friend of Cardinal Etchegaray, had been asked to review and comment on drafts of the Vatican's 1987 statement, as had his predecessor, Jacques de Larosiere.[14] A comparison of the two statements reveals that the U.S. bishops, addressing more particularly their country's role in the crises, were slightly more critical of major public- and private-sector actors than was the Vatican, and made a stronger case for the need for structural change in the international economy.

The Authority of the Two Statements

The Pontifical Council (formally Commission) for Justice and Peace (PCJP), an advisory body that grew out of the social justice concerns of the Second Vatican Council in the 1960s, prepared the Vatican statement. The PCJP is a standing committee whose members and "consultors" are appointed by the pope to study matters bearing on justice, peace, and human rights. It collaborates with others within the Catholic Church, as well as with the academic and intellectual world, and other religions and secular organizations. Among other concerns, the council "promotes ethical reflection on the evolution of economic and financial systems." It formulates ethical principles and guidelines in the areas it examines, drawing on the Church's social teachings, with a view to spreading knowledge of those teachings.[15] While officially the PCJP advises the pope, it effectively serves as a means to open discussion within the global Church, giving visibility and urgency to issues on which the Vatican expresses concern.

To address the complex issue of sovereign indebtedness, to which Catholic development and relief agencies, bishops, and missionaries, among others, had been seeking greater Church attention, the PCJP departed from usual practice by drawing heavily on the work of laypeople, namely a group of European Catholic bankers and international organization personnel who had been meeting for ethical reflection in Paris. The PCJP leadership integrated much of a 1985 report the group had drafted into the Vatican statement. This explains the fairly detailed and technical policy language unusual for Vatican documents.[16] The debt statement provided continuity with previous Vatican statements in its broad tone at the level of principle, and its moderate analysis and recommendations.

The text draws almost exclusively on papal and curial teaching.[17] The statement does not review biblical themes that might shed light on the issue of indebtedness. The entire document makes only two references to the New Testament, both in the form of ancillary recommendations implying that a Gospel-based ethic would require a more radical approach than the principal one suggested by the document.[18] The statement's drafters are less explicit as to the sources drawn upon for its policy analysis and recommendations, other than to mention that the text "has made use of many studies on the international debt that have already appeared."[19]

The second influential statement was drafted by the U.S. Conference of Catholic Bishops (USCCB), a coordinating body of the Catholic Church in the United States. Originally established by the U.S. bishops in 1919 as the National Catholic Welfare Council to work for peace and social justice after World War I, the USCCB, like similar bishops' conferences in other countries, now organizes and carries out a wide range of religious, charitable, educational, and social welfare work. The USCCB is intentionally called a "conference" to emphasize that it is a consultative rather than legislative body. In this regard, when it takes positions through statements, they are meant to be teachings of the U.S. bishops collectively; it is up to individual bishops to decide whether they want to take action on those declarations. The USCCB largely works through some fifty committees that focus on different specific issues, one of which is the Department of Social Development and World Peace. This committee developed the 1989 statement on developing country debt and others that were subsequently issued.[20]

The U.S. bishops' statement on debt, issued two years after the Vatican statement, reflected continuity with earlier USCCB statements, such as the 1983 war and peace pastoral[21] and the 1986 economic pastoral, in drawing upon a multiplicity of sources, following an explicitly consultative methodology, and acknowledging a plurality of views within the U.S. church. The sources include the Bible, papal speeches and encyclicals, the PCJP statement, the 1971 Catholic bishops' synod on justice in the world, their own 1986 economic pastoral letter, the 1989 UNICEF annual report, comments from debtor country bishops and the UN secretary-general, and World Bank studies. Reflecting their consultative approach, the U.S. bishops explain that they chose to write the letter partially in response to the requests of their fellow bishops in developing countries and U.S. missionaries working there. They also consulted "chief executives of U.S. banks, officials of government and international financial institutions, leaders of developing countries, theologians and other experts and policy makers."[22] Furthermore, in a departure from tradition, the subcommittee formed in 1988 to explore the debt question was composed of just one bishop and three laymen. At the time the latter three were senior executives of social science institutes or foundations; one was a former banker and one a former congressman.

Finally, the U.S. bishops were willing to acknowledge and publicize the fact that different views existed within the Church as to an ethical assessment of the debt crisis. The U.S. bishops only partially distinguish themselves from more radical views, mirroring the process and resulting document of the U.S. bishops' 1983 war and peace pastoral, in which they adopted a just war framework but also put forth the pacifist critique of their positions.

Ethical Perceptions and Principles

The PCJP statement declares that the church "hopes to enlighten the moral conscience of the decision makers, but she does so without proposing action programs which would be outside her field of competence."[23] Nevertheless, three-quarters of the statement proceeds to offer moderately detailed short-, medium-, and long-term policy recommendations to the four sets of actors it identifies as co-responsible for both the crisis and its resolution: creditor country governments, debtor country governments, public- and private-sector creditors, and multilateral financial organizations.

The ethical motivation for the PCJP statement is expressed succinctly. The body of the text refers to the "serious, urgent and complex" nature of the crisis due to its impact on living conditions, development, and the international financial system. The most explicit and strongest moral concern, however, was offered in the introductory presentation made by Cardinal Etchegaray and Archbishop Jorge Mejía, the PCJP president and vice president, respectively, when the statement was released: "Debt servicing cannot be met at the price of the asphyxiation of a country's economy, and no government can morally demand of its people privations incompatible with human dignity."[24]

These ethical judgments led the PCJP to formulate six ethical principles, broadly cast as general rules to guide the relevant parties' response to the crisis: create new norms of solidarity; accept co-responsibility; establish relations of trust; know how to share efforts and sacrifices; foster the participation of all; and identify emergency and long-term measures.

The U.S. bishops' letter is approximately the same length as that of the Vatican, but is differently weighted. A third of the document is devoted to a much more detailed discussion of the crisis, with greater focus on the

United States' role in its origins and management.[25] The bishops also seek to "put a human face on the reality and injustice hidden by the figures, the reports and the proposals—what the Latin American bishops described to us as 'an iron ring around the necks of our people.'"[26] The statement reviews the causes and the evolution of the crisis and proposed current solutions to it, suggesting that few of the latter "address the basic concern of social justice: Why should the poor in debtor countries, who had nothing to say about accruing the debt and have received little or no benefit from it, have to bear the greater burden of its payment?"[27] The bishops determine that the debt problem, "with its human consequences, is economically unsound, politically dangerous and ethically unacceptable."[28]

The bishops then take up more radical ethical arguments made by "many advocates, especially in the religious community," who consider the debt, "in the aggregate," to be unjust. According to this line of argument: first, even though there may have been a contract in the beginning, the debt has increased and become more burdensome over time in ways that were unforeseeable; second, the debt was accrued without participation by or benefit to the poor who suffer most from the austerity measures imposed to service it; third, it has been paid already many times over through the unusually high interest rates; fourth, most of the renewed borrowing, beyond the initial loans, has been undertaken almost entirely to service the debt, rather than for genuine development; and finally, a considerable part of the borrowed funds was expended on dangerous and wasteful armaments or on programs benefiting the elites. In some cases it was simply returned to the industrialized world in the form of foreign investment—what has come to be called flight capital.[29]

In more detail, they cite the arguments made by "many voices in the church" who make a moral claim that the debt should not be paid. The U.S. bishops agree that "in terms of social justice" such a case "may be possible to make," and yet they also posit that "a moral presumption exists in personal and social relations that debts should be paid." The bishops believe, however, that this presumption "must be tested against a further series of questions" regarding the justice of the contractual arrangements between developing country governments and their creditors. These include the legitimacy of the governments that contracted the original debts (some

Elizabeth A. Donnelly

having come to power through military coups or fraudulent elections), the record of what has been paid to date in debt service at high interest rates, and the internal social costs borne by debtor countries in servicing their debts. The bishops conclude that given the variety of situations, both "the nature of the original agreements and the attempts of some debtors to repay them lead us to the conviction that no single principle can govern all the different situations of indebtedness."[30]

In short, while the bishops do not endorse the radical view, neither do they definitively disassociate themselves from its conclusion: "One does not, however, need to accept the argument that the debt is illegitimate to urge that there be relief from payment or even forgiveness in whole or in part, in order to lessen the suffering of those most vulnerable to the effects of the debt burden."[31]

The bishops make this alternative case for relief by reviewing pertinent themes from Catholic social teaching, the Vatican debt statement, and earlier papal teaching, and they also integrate biblical themes, such as the treatment of the most vulnerable (widows and orphans) as a measure of the moral character of the early Hebrew community, the Jewish institution of the jubilee year, and Jesus' use of stories about debtors treated mercifully as being revelatory of the quality of God's love and how people should treat each other. The bishops explicitly acknowledge that such images "do not provide either a formula for addressing the complexity of international debts or even clear principles for adjudicating a fair resolution of this major institutional question." Biblical themes, rather, "provide a starting point, a way to understand creditor-debtor relations, which a purely empirical assessment of the debt problem will never offer."[32]

This brings them to emphasize human *rights* as well as *needs*. The biblical images suggest, they argue, that "those who are in debt retain their dignity as well as their basic human rights, which make demands upon creditors; debtors cannot be reduced to a situation of abject poverty in order to pay debts."[33] They imply that respect for the human rights of the poor entails meeting their basic human needs, in accordance with the integration of social and economic as well as political and civil rights in Catholic notions of human rights.

In short, one may say that alleviating extreme poverty drives their central statement of principle, which they then affirm:

> We believe that in many instances the presumptive obligation to repay should be overridden or modified because of the social costs imposed on the poor. When the social costs erode personal dignity, causing hunger, homelessness, sickness and death, the principles of justice point not toward repayment by the debtors, but toward remission, even if partial, by creditors. Remission in complex cases like this does not mean "forgiveness" for all states. A range of remedies is possible and necessary; a scale of redress is needed to judge different situations. At times partial forgiveness will be a fair response, as we noted in "Economic Justice for All," or at times renegotiation or partial rescheduling.[34]

The bishops then offer eight "criteria on how the principles of justice, solidarity and the common good can be used in contributing to the resolution of Third World debts."[35] They advocate solutions to the crisis that promote the participation of the poor in the economy and respect for human rights, an equitable sharing of responsibility, attention to external factors beyond the control of debtor countries, and the ability of debtor countries to pursue "independent, self-reliant, participatory, sustainable development."[36]

Different Policy Recommendations

The PCJP offers relatively extensive policy recommendations, which it divides into immediate emergency measures for those countries unable to meet their payments and whose populations are particularly suffering, and medium- and long-term "adjustment measures" organized according to the four groups of actors previously cited. It offers two main recommendations for short-term measures. First, in what the PCJP terms an "ethics of survival," it urges that the parties "foster dialogue and cooperation," "avoid payment defaults which could destabilize the international financial system," and "avoid breaches between creditors and debtors as well as any unilateral termination of prior commitments; respect the insolvent debtor and do not burden him with immediate and intolerable demands which he cannot meet." It recommends that the parties consider other avenues, such as debt rescheduling and partial or even total remission, "with the Gospel as the source of inspiration."[37] Second, the PCJP suggests that "coordinating structures" be set up as quickly as possible "to foresee, prevent and attenuate such crises." They suggest that the IMF is particularly well suited to lead the design of such measures. It is also in this context, however, that the statement offers its most stinging criticism of IMF-imposed adjustment policies: "In numerous cases, however, the IMF's decisions have been ill-received by the leaders and the general public of countries in difficulty; the decisions in question may seem to have been imposed in an authoritarian and technocratic way without due consideration for urgent social requirements and the specific features of each situation. It would be advisable to bring out clearly that dialogue and service of all concerned are values which guide the actions taken by the IMF."[38] This quotation was most often cited, with bitterness, by some of the people interviewed by the author at the Fund.

The PCJP urges industrialized country and developing country governments, creditors (states, commercial banks, and multinational companies), and multilateral financial organizations to play an active role in international efforts to address the crisis. Policies advocated include not only debt rescheduling and the resumption of lending, but also measures to bring down high interest rates, combat protectionism and erratic exchange rate fluctuations, and increase investment and aid monies for the debtors. The multilateral financial organizations should, among other things, "acknowledge the need to increase the representation of developing countries and their participation in the major international economic decisions that affect them," tailor loan conditions more carefully to each country, and "foster dialogue between creditors and debtors for a rescheduling of debts and a reduction of the sums due in one or even more years if possible."[39]

The USCC policy recommendations to international actors are much briefer, and focus more pointedly on the need for negotiations of fundamental changes in the structure of the international economic system on a par with those preceding the establishment of the Bretton Woods system, this time with greater developing country participation.[40] The remaining recommendations are geared toward U.S. actors. The statement urges the executive and legislative branches to act on the intention, announced by President George H. W. Bush in July 1989, to forgive bilateral sub-Saharan African debt, and to modify banking regulations in order to encourage commercial banks to pursue debt reduction. It also appeals for U.S. leadership in the IMF and the World Bank in favor of "policies less tied to the highly questionable development model of structural adjustment," with "genuine flexibility and a case-by-case approach" versus the "rigid and uniform conditionality to which the IMF and the World Bank seemed in fact to be committed," and for action by commercial bankers toward "effective debt relief, which can include at least partial forgiveness of debt" as a matter of "obligatory," "realistic" justice rather than charity.[41]

It is hard not to see the USCC recommendations as bolder than those that emerged from the PCJP. The PCJP may be thought of as legitimating breaking the ground that the USCC later plowed. Also, the imperative to call for strong measures was more pressing after two additional years of unresolved debt crisis. The growing voices in global civil society calling for radical reforms were also better heard by 1989. Indeed, in addressing those views, the U.S. bishops were led to a more explicit questioning of the morality of the outstanding debt itself, and to a stronger call for extensive debt forgiveness and efforts to restructure "an international economic system that is becoming increasingly unworkable and inequitable."[42]

TOWARD JUBILEE 2000

Network activists continued throughout the 1990s to press for further bilateral and multilateral debt reduction. They welcomed incremental improvements in creditor country policies customarily announced at annual summits of the major powers, but they also offered detailed analysis of shortcomings and demanded further action. The decade also saw a marked improvement in the capacity of civil society groups in debtor countries to document the impact of the debt overhang on the poor and press for cancellation. Zambia provides a good case in point.

A View from the South: Zambia's Churches
If Latin American Catholic churches drove the major involvement of the global Church in international debt policy in the 1980s, the focus in the 1990s turned to Africa. In some sub-Saharan countries, a strong civil society movement emerged, with Catholic and other churches at the center. In the case of Zambia, the Catholic Episcopal Conference joined with the other two national church bodies—the Christian Council of Zambia (mainline Protestant) and the Evangelical Fellowship of Zambia

(evangelical Protestant)—to issue a joint pastoral letter in August 1998 to much local publicity. It states:

> Zambia's total debt is clearly unpayable. Zambia *cannot* pay back because the debt burden is economically exhausting. It blocks future development. Zambia *will not* pay back because the debt burden is politically destabilizing. It threatens social harmony. Zambia *should not* pay back because the debt burden is ethically unacceptable. It hurts the poorest in our midst.[43]

The Jubilee Zambia campaign noted at the time that the country owed more than $6.5 billion, more than $650 for every Zambian. During the 1990s, the country paid out approximately 20 percent of GDP in debt service, but budgeted only 2–3 percent of GDP for health and education.[44] The gross inadequacy of the education budget was starkly indicated by the fact that in the late 1990s it was more likely for a Zambian teenager to be illiterate than for a Zambian between the ages of thirty and thirty-five.[45]

As to the origin of Zambia's excessive debt, the director of the Jesuit Centre for Theological Reflection in Lusaka, which hosts the Zambian Jubilee 2000 campaign, Dr. Peter Henriot, S.J., has cited "minor" and "major" causes. The minor causes in his view are poor management of the economy, including corruption, especially in recent years. The major causes are a chronic trade imbalance caused by generally weak prices of copper, the principal export commodity, and high prices for needed oil imports, coupled with the consequences of irresponsible lending by creditors, high interest rates caused by industrialized countries' macroeconomic policies, and exacerbation of economic decline and social hardship due to the conditionalities imposed under SAPs.[46] Campaigners also have charged that the structural economic reforms adopted by Zambia beginning in 1992 were dogmatically imposed by the World Bank and the IMF with great hardship: "Privatization of para-statals proceeded with harsh impact on employees; trade liberalization opened borders and closed industries; budget cuts meant rising fees for education and health, and declining enrollment and services."[47] In addition, Henriot has pointed out a special factor in the case of Zambia that further questions the notion that its government should be held responsible for the debt: a substantial portion of the external debt can be attributed to the moral position taken by President Kenneth Kaunda not to cooperate with apartheid in South

Africa. As a consequence of that decision, economic disruption and dislocation due to border closings, destruction of infrastructure, and the inescapable need to host refugees forced Zambia to borrow heavily in the 1970s.[48]

In addition to calling for debt cancellation, Jubilee Zambia was sensitive to the need for civil society involvement with the government so that freed funds would be spent wisely and ethically. They thus campaigned vigorously for a transparent, accountable, and participatory process of allocating debt relief resources and contracting future debt—in effect, conditionality from below. In particular, the campaign has argued that Zambia should receive no debt cancellation unless the government puts into place an effective "debt mechanism." This mechanism, the campaign argued, should entail, first, accountable management of debt relief resources, so they actually are dedicated to poverty eradication. In this regard, the Zambian government formed a Heavily Indebted Poor Country (HIPC) Expenditure Monitoring Team in 2003 composed of representatives from several accounting and auditing groups and civil society groups, including Jubilee Zambia. Jubilee Zambia charged that the team was slow to organize and play an effective role, however. The campaign has proposed a tripartite committee of members of parliament, officials from relevant government ministries, and representatives of civil society groups to establish priorities in targeting HIPC funds and monitor their allocation and distribution. They suggest a social fund similar to that of Uganda's be established, in which debt relief resources would be placed to be distributed to poverty eradication programs in an accountable and transparent way. Second, the mechanism should entail transparent contraction of new debts, with clear priorities and limits, parliamentary approval and public awareness of large loans that the Minister of Finance and National Planning had instead been able to contract without consultation or approval of parliament. Again inspired by the limited success of the Ugandan parliament preventing the contraction of some questionable loans, the campaign has argued that the purpose and beneficiaries of a loan, conditions attached to it, and expectations of repayment should be subject to public scrutiny.[49]

Elizabeth A. Donnelly

A GLOBAL CAMPAIGN GATHERS MOMENTUM

During the second half of the 1990s, the debt cancellation movement grew increasingly global in scale and interaction, as coalitions like that in Zambia could exchange information more readily via the Internet. It gained fresh energy and impetus as the upcoming millennium provided a fixed goal for debt cancellation. British groups, led by the overseas relief agencies of the Anglican and Catholic churches, launched the Jubilee 2000 U.K. campaign in April 1996.

The campaign took the existing jubilee-inspired analysis that had infused previous campaigns, but provided new energy and coordination with the focus on the year 2000. According to Ann Pettifor, the seasoned and astute South African–born political organizer, who was hired to lead the staff, the original idea for the campaign came from Professor Martin Dent. He suggested that the most worthy way to celebrate the millennium would be to make substantial progress in improving the lot of the poor who bore the greatest burden of indebtedness, and that the most efficient way to do so would be to cancel their countries' debts; the year 2000 was targeted as the jubilee year.[50] U2's lead singer, Bono, who joined the campaign in 1998, perhaps argued this idea most colorfully:

> The most inspiring thought I bumped into last year was the concept of Jubilee 2000, a call to cancel third world debts going into the next millennium and to give crippled nations a chance to get up off their knees and walk again. . . . Without a real commitment to do something about the dire circumstances of a third of the population of the planet, all new year's eve 99 will amount to is an up drawbridge scenario, a fancy dress ball at the castle where we all play Louis 14 pissing across a moat of champagne on the poor.[51]

The U.K. network was the first to establish the campaign's goal of a one-time cancellation of the unpayable debts of the world's poorest countries by the end of the year 2000; some sixty-nine national Jubilee 2000 networks were subsequently formed.[52] The movement took inspiration from and widely quoted the call of Pope John Paul II for debt relief in his 1994 statement on preparations for the next millennium, "Tertio Millennio Adveniente" (51): "Christians will have to raise their voice on behalf of all the poor of the world, proposing the Jubilee as an appropriate time to give thought . . .

to reducing substantially, if not canceling outright, the international debt which seriously threatens the future of many nations."[53]

The campaign used simple but powerful statistics to communicate both the scale of the crisis and the efficacy of debt cancellation for reducing poverty. For example, it cited that whereas the 1985 Live Aid concert raised $200 million for Africa, this is also the sum that Africa pays each week in debt service; that, spread over twenty years, the cost of canceling the debts of the fifty-two Jubilee countries is only one penny a day for each person in the industrialized countries; and that canceling the debt could save the lives of 7 million children a year.[54] In making its case, the Jubilee 2000 U.K. campaign drew a parallel between the debt crisis and the Atlantic slave trade: "It, too, was a system of international oppression, accepted for generations as a normal and necessary part of trade and life. And it, too, resulted in the West benefiting from the resources of the southern hemisphere while southern countries, and particularly sub-Saharan Africa, were devastated."[55] And, just as it took the concerted effort of thousands of ordinary people to abolish the slave trade, so too would it require the mobilization of many to convince creditor governments to cancel the debt: "Justice demands that richer countries give up unfair privileges, held at the expense of the poor. If creditors agree to remission of debts, the removal of a restraint on growth could allow poor countries to compete on fairer terms and reduce their dependence on the rich parts of the world."[56]

The increasingly global Jubilee campaign thus continued the efforts of its predecessor organizations in pressing for total debt cancellation while also critiquing the specific initiatives of creditor governments and the multilateral institutions, pushing for further reforms.

In fact, a consensus was forming among creditor authorities that the debt crisis in the poorest countries had gone on long enough. In September 1996, the leadership of the World Bank and the IMF launched the HIPC Initiative, the first comprehensive plan to reduce the debt of qualifying poor countries to "sustainable" levels through additional reductions in bilateral government debt and—for the first time—reductions in debt owed to multilateral institutions. While the overwhelming majority of the forty-one countries that potentially qualified in 1999 for HIPC debt relief were in sub-Saharan Africa, they also included Bolivia, Guyana,

Honduras, and Nicaragua. By mid-1999, however, only four of the HIPC countries had advanced to a point in the review process at which they actually received debt relief. Campaigners pushed for deeper, broader, and faster debt reduction.

CONTINUING CATHOLIC CHURCH ACTIVISM ON DEBT

The Catholic Church made a number of crucial contributions to the Jubilee 2000 campaign. One way was through its access to key Catholic policymakers, such as IMF Managing Director Michel Camdessus. This was significant, especially as the IMF had initially opposed the HIPC proposal, which the new president of the World Bank, James Wolfensohn, was championing. In addition, the Church hierarchy used its convening power to sponsor important conferences discussing the moral dimensions of debt, which arguably helped advance the HIPC Initiative as well as subsequent assessments of its shortcomings.

For example, on February 12, 1996, Cardinal Basil Hume of London hosted a private seminar on the ethics of multilateral debt reduction attended by church leaders from three continents, Camdessus and other senior executives of the IMF and the World Bank, senior politicians, academics, and journalists. In his welcoming address, Hume asserted two of the ethical principles that the Church believed to be applicable: "the need to acknowledge a co-responsibility for both the causes of, and the solutions to, the debt problem"; and that "there should be an equitable sharing of the adjustment efforts and necessary sacrifices, taking into account the priority to be given to the needs of the most deprived peoples."[57]

A second important example took place in October 1998, when shortcomings in the initial HIPC Initiative were increasingly being realized. Then, the PCJP, the U.S. Catholic Conference, and Seton Hall University cosponsored a major conference on the ethical dimensions of international debt, which drew over sixty leading officials from debtor and creditor country governments, multilateral institutions, NGOs, foundations, private-sector financial institutions, and universities. Participants included World Bank President James Wolfensohn, IMF Managing Director Michel Camdessus, and then Deputy Secretary of the U.S. Treasury Lawrence

H. Summers. This was the first time that debt campaign leaders met collectively with such senior officials. The spirited and forthright discussion included an exchange of views on the morality of various dimensions of the debt issue, including the efficacy and appropriateness of different types of conditionality, which countries should receive debt cancellation, and the relative merits of debt relief versus other policies in achieving poverty reduction.[58]

The Catholic Church also contributed to policy debates by continuing to issue statements. In April 1999, for example, the U.S. bishops issued a follow-up statement to their 1989 analysis, which restates their earlier teaching and incorporates new realities leading up to the Jubilee year.[59] They affirmed their earlier analysis of the causes of the debt overhang, and updated their description of its deleterious impact on the poor. They also broadened their moral assessment of the issue, adding "care for creation," criticizing the environmental degradation that can result when export-oriented sectors such as logging, mining, or mono-cropping are overemphasized in order to generate hard currency to make debt repayments. They firmly stated that debt relief must be tied directly to poverty reduction: "Funds made available through debt relief must be used to improve the living conditions of the poor and the most vulnerable."[60] They then develop seven criteria from Catholic social teaching to help evaluate and guide decisions about debt relief. Debt relief programs should: first, include the full range of poor countries that now have to make unacceptable sacrifices to human development in order to repay their debt; second, ensure that resources freed through debt relief are, in fact, used for poverty reduction; third, foster the active participation of civil society in decision-making processes; fourth, ensure economic reform policies associated with debt relief make adequate provision for those adversely affected and have poverty reduction as a central goal; fifth, include mechanisms of accountability, so as to overcome corruption and other obstacles that prevent debt relief from benefiting the poor; sixth, be fully funded, with costs shared equitably among creditor governments and international financial institutions; and seventh, be part of a much broader, coordinated effort to promote sustainable development for the poorest countries.[61]

Elizabeth A. Donnelly

THE COLOGNE INITIATIVE FOR THE JUBILEE YEAR

The Cologne Summit in June 1999, virtually on the eve of the millennium, provided the answer of the G-8 to what had become widespread criticism of the HIPC Initiative and the increasingly massive mobilization on debt. In the Cologne Initiative, the leaders agreed in principle to cancel an additional $45 billion of the bilateral and multilateral debt owed by the forty-one potentially qualifying countries. This was to be added to the $55 billion already committed through operations under the Paris Club of bilateral creditors ($30 billion) and the HIPC Initiative ($25 billion).[62] Also, countries would now begin receiving debt relief after demonstrating compliance with IMF-mandated structural adjustment for three years, down from six years under the original HIPC Initiative. Furthermore, the G-8 leaders directed the IMF and the World Bank to assist qualifying countries in the drafting and implementation of poverty reduction plans "for the effective targeting of savings derived from debt relief, together with increased transparency of budgetary procedures to protect social expenditures." The leaders also recommended, but did not require, that the IMF and the World Bank consult civil society groups in the design and implementation of such programs.

The G-8 leaders were not proposing to write off the debt owed to multilateral institutions, but to pay it down with bilateral donations, profits from other operations of the multilateral institutions (earnings on loans to other developing countries), and in the case of the IMF, what became an off-market sale of almost 13 million ounces of its gold reserves. The latter also helped fund additional IMF concessional loans through its Enhanced Structural Adjustment Facility, renamed the Poverty Reduction and Growth Facility.

While Jubilee 2000 leaders especially welcomed the explicit link between debt relief and poverty reduction, the call for civil society participation, and greater transparency of budgetary procedures to protect social expenditures, they nonetheless objected to several features of the plan. First, the amount of relief was still insufficient. Campaigners suggested that the IMF and the World Bank could afford far more extensive relief without jeopardizing their mission[63] and questioned the definition of "debt sustainability," which was the basis for calculating the amount of debt reduction countries should receive. They also argued that the IMF and the Bank make overly optimistic assumptions in forecasting future export earnings, growth rates, and investment patterns for debtor economies, thereby underestimating the amount of relief needed even under their own methodology.[64] More profoundly, however, Jubilee campaigners such as Peter Henriot argued:

> "Sustainability" should be measured in terms of true *social indicators*, not mere economic indicators. That is, the ability of a country like Zambia to service its debts should be looked at within a wider socio-economic context, especially taking into account poverty levels and the impact of HIV/AIDS. Then debt levels are sustainable if the sustainable development needs of a country are first being met.[65]

Second, Jubilee 2000 feared that too few countries would receive relief. The Jubilee 2000 U.K. campaign estimated in June 1999 that of the forty-one potential HIPC countries, perhaps twenty-four would qualify for some reduction in debt service payments by the end of the year 2000, and that the reduction would be significant for only sixteen of these.[66] No additional debt relief was offered to countries, such as Lesotho, that did not qualify as HIPCs but also had high debt servicing requirements that impeded government action on poverty reduction. In addition, campaigners argued that countries emerging from armed conflicts or natural disasters required special treatment.

Third, campaigners opposed the Cologne Initiative's granting to the IMF and the World Bank *more* control over the debt reduction process. Countries receiving debt relief would still be required to undergo IMF-sponsored structural adjustment, a process that network critics had consistently charged exacerbated poverty and contributed to environmental degradation.[67] Many Jubilee 2000 supporters expressed skepticism that civil society groups would be adequately consulted—or that their expressed views would actually be taken into account—in IMF and World Bank adjustment programs for their countries, as well as any poverty reduction programs.

CONCLUSION

In the years since the millennium celebrations, the global anti-debt coalition has continued to focus world attention on the debt crisis in developing

Elizabeth A. Donnelly

countries, which despite international policy initiatives is still oppressing many countries. In part, the anti-debt campaign has adopted a new language since 2000, albeit one invented in intergovernmental circles as the campaign to reach the Millennium Development Goals (MDGs), which are specific social targets to be realized by 2015 based on the commitments adopted by all the world's leaders meeting at the United Nations in September 2000. As this language embodies the commitments of the official creditors, global civil society's use of it helps strengthen its own voice. But the language of civil society, like its demands, is broader, as we have seen.

Indeed, the campaign continues to push against the ever-reluctant creditors, even as the latter implicitly accept what the debt advocates have been telling them. This can be seen clearly in the reaction to the steps that leaders agreed to at the 2005 Gleneagles Summit of the G-8. Thus, on the one hand, the coalition welcomed the Gleneagles pledge to cancel the remaining multilateral debt of eighteen eligible HIPC countries, in effect, accepting finally the argument of Henriot and others that debt sustainability means that debt servicing should not impede countries from achieving the MDGs.[68] In the case of Zambia, for example, the debt was dramatically slashed from $7 billion at the beginning of 2005 to less than $1 billion in 2006. The major task now for campaigners in Zambia and the other qualifying HIPCs is to assure that the freed-up funds do go toward poverty eradication.

On the other hand, the global coalition continues to protest that debt cancellation for additional countries (up to twenty are eligible) would require them to implement harmful economic reforms under HIPC. Also, too many impoverished countries do not qualify and will continue to spend more on debt service than on education and health care. The Jubilee USA Network, citing a recent study by Christian Aid and others, estimated that the eighteen countries that immediately qualified constituted fewer than a third of those countries that needed full cancellation to meet the MDGs, and that the $40 billion to be canceled represented less than 10 percent of debt cancellation required to meet those goals. The network also called on the G-8 to include the IDB among the multilateral creditors covered in the agreement, pointing out that the four Latin American countries among the eighteen qualifying HIPC countries, Bolivia, Guyana, Honduras, and Nicaragua, would pay a total of $1.4 billion in debt service to the IDB over the next five years. And finally, the agreement did not deal with the odious debt contracted by such undemocratic regimes as the apartheid government in South Africa, Mobutu Sese Seko in what is now the Democratic Republic of Congo, and Ferdinand Marcos in the Philippines.[69]

At the same time, many of the religious and secular groups active on debt cancellation since the 1980s have long been keenly aware of the need to press for a multipronged approach to combating extreme poverty; they strategically chose to focus on one issue—debt cancellation—as a unified, concrete way to celebrate the new millennium. Now they have turned to broaden their campaigns. In particular, they have increasingly focused on the interrelationship of trade and debt, for example, calling for a dismantling of agricultural subsidies and import quotas in creditor countries, such as those benefiting U.S. cotton producers and EU sugar producers at the expense of their debtor-country competitors. Coalitions such as the ONE campaign in the United States and the Make Poverty History campaign in the United Kingdom have shifted to multifaceted initiatives to achieve the MDGs by 2015, especially the first goal of eradicating extreme poverty and halving the proportion of people suffering from hunger. Along with further debt cancellation, the campaigns call for fair trade and a substantial increase in poverty-focused official development assistance to provide such basic needs as health, education, and clean water, combat HIV/AIDS, empower women, and promote integrated rural development in support of small farmers. It is expected that they will continue to argue that debt cancellation, if not a prerequisite, is an essential requirement if the world is to meet the MDGs.

The movement also continues to press for reforms of the international financial architecture, in particular so that a mechanism that all would view as fair, transparent, and comprehensive is used to restructure developing country debts whenever the need arises. That is, even if the debt burdens that currently exist were removed, no one believes countries could always avoid debt crises in the future. There is now no such mechanism and there is far less confidence than there once was in the informal leadership of the IMF in the separate debt renegotiations that a debtor government undertakes with its different classes of creditors. Indeed, there is little coherence in the entire international financial and trading system regarding development, despite pledges to work toward such coherence, most notably in the UN Conference on Financing for Development in Monterrey, Mexico, in 2002.

While the struggle thus continues, the prospects for continued Catholic hierarchy leadership on the issue have recently become uncertain. Pope Benedict XVI spoke of his concern for African poverty in his first Sunday homily after his April 2005 election, and affirmed in his first encyclical that the Church will continue to contribute its reasoning in political life as to "the authentic requirements of justice" and the formation of just social structures.[70] He was less encouraging, however, with regard to the engagement of the institutional Church in the practical application of ethics to policy reform, as opposed to acts of charity.[71] Thus, it remains to be seen whether he will be the vigorous advocate for economic justice for the poor that his predecessor was. Recently appointed bishops in both creditor and debtor countries have not been as active on these issues as their predecessors, and their moral authority, especially in industrialized countries, has been seriously eroded by the sexual abuse crisis that erupted in early 2002. The U.S. bishops' conference, for example, has continued to post analysis and calls to action on debt-related legislation on its Web site, but debt cancellation has not been a high priority in the last four years as the bishops have attended to the internal Church crisis.

The key Catholic statements on debt were important ethical benchmarks in the international treatment of debt because of the strength of the institutional commitment to speak out as well as the force and moral authority of what was said. For the Catholic community, they represented a vigorous and considerable effort to apply the core concepts of Catholic social teaching—respect for the life and dignity of the human person, the common good, solidarity, the preferential option for the poor, subsidiarity, social justice, and care for creation—to the complexities of a pressing social issue. The making of such statements—and the attendant engagement of Church leaders in economic policy debates on behalf of the world's poor—should not be allowed to slip into historical obscurity.

NOTES

1 World Bank, "Partnership for Development: From Vision to Action" (Washington, D.C.: World Bank, 1998), p. 67.

2 For a history and assessment of the informal network of NGOs and churches that evolved into a more integrated but loosely affiliated coalition of groups collaborating on the Jubilee 2000 campaign, see Elizabeth A. Donnelly, "Proclaiming Jubilee: The Debt and Structural Adjustment Network," in Sanjeev Khagram, James V. Riker, and Kathryn Sikkink, eds., *Restructuring World Politics: Transnational Social Movements, Networks, and Norms* (Minneapolis: University of Minnesota Press, 2002), pp. 155–80.

3 See CIDSE and Caritas Internationalis, "The Case for an International Fair and Transparent Arbitration Process," Background Paper, September 2002; available at www.cidse.org/en/tg3/ftapfin.pdf.

4 "Impact of the Latin American Debt Crisis on the United States," Subcommittee on International Debt, Committee on Finance, U.S. Senate, 100th Congress, 1st sess., March 9, 1987, D125.

5 John Clark, "A Grassroots View of the Debt Crisis," *Food Monitor* 42 (Fall 1987), p. 11.

6 See, e.g., statements by the Mexican (1987) and Cuban (1986) Catholic bishops, reprinted in Edward Cleary, O.P., ed., *Path from Puebla: Significant Documents of the Latin American Bishops since 1979*, trans. Phillip Berryman (Washington, D.C.: U.S. Catholic Conference, 1989), pp. 330–48. Other Latin American bishops' conferences issued short reflections on the debt crisis as part of more comprehensive statements on socioeconomic conditions in their countries. See, e.g., the statement by the Ecuadoran bishops (1986) in Cleary, *Path from Puebla*, pp. 210–20. Individual bishops, most notably Cardinal Paulo Evaristo Arns of Sao Paulo, Brazil, also spoke out on debt.

7 United States Catholic Bishops Conference, "Economic Justice for All: Catholic Social Teaching and the U.S. Economy," *Origins, NC Documentary Service* (hereafter *Origins*) 16, no. 24 (November 27, 1986), p. 438.

8 Archbishop Rembert Weakland, O.S.B., "Viewing International Debt in Its Full Dimensions," *Origins* 16, no. 41 (March 26, 1987), pp. 722–26.

9 J. Bryan Hehir, "Third World Debt and the Poor," *Origins* 18, no. 36 (February 16, 1989), pp. 607–12.

10 Administrative Board of the United States Catholic Conference, "Statement on Relieving Third World Debt," *Origins* 19, no. 19 (October 12, 1989), pp. 305–14.

11 World Church Commission of the German Bishops, "The International Debt Crisis: An Ethical Challenge. The Role of the Federal Republic of Germany" (Bonn: Secretariat of the German Bishops Conference, May 16, 1988).

12 Joint Conference on Church and Development (GKKE) of the German Commission for Justice and Peace of the German Catholic Bishops' Conference and Church Development Service, an Association of Protestant Churches in Germany, "The International Debt Crisis Concerns Us All: Contributions to the Public Hearing of the Commission for Economic Development of the German Parliament," *GKKE* 16 (September 1988).

13 Pontifical Commission for Justice and Peace, "An Ethical Approach to the International Debt Question," *Origins* 16, no. 34 (February 5, 1987), pp. 601–11.

14 Interviews with Michel Camdessus, IMF Managing Director, July 2, 1992, and Jacques de Larosiere, Governor of the Bank of France, March 17, 1992.

15 See "Pontifical Council for Justice and Peace" at www.vatican.va/roman_curia/pontifical_councils/justpeace/documents/rc_pc_justpeace_pro_20011004_en.html.

16 Interviews with: Bernard Snoy, then Executive Director to the World Bank and IMF, July 2, 1992 (a founder of and participant in the Paris group); Rev. Philippe Laurent, S.J., March 13, 1992 (a social ethicist who served as the group's ecclesial advisor); Monsignor William F. Murphy, March 4, 1992 (former PCJP undersecretary); and Cardinal Roger Etchegaray, March 24, 1992 (then PCJP president).

17 The most oft-cited documents are Pope Paul VI's 1967 encyclical on development, "Populorum Progressio," and the 1986 "Instruction on Christian Freedom and Liberation," issued by the Vatican's Congregation for the Doctrine of the Faith.

18 PCJP, "An Ethical Approach," pp. 605, 608.

19 Ibid., p. 604.

20 See United States Conference of Catholic Bishops at www.usccb.org/whoweare.shtml.

21 National Conference of Catholic Bishops, "The Challenge of Peace: God's Promise and Our Response; A Pastoral Letter on War and Peace" (Washington, D.C.: U.S. Catholic Conference, May 3, 1983).

22 Administrative Board of the USCC, "Statement," p. 307.

Elizabeth A. Donnelly

23 PCJP, "An Ethical Approach," p. 604.

24 Ibid., p. 603.

25 The bishops point out that over 30 percent of developing country debt at the time was owed to U.S. commercial banks and the U.S. government, imposing a special responsibility on the U.S. Church to speak out. See Administrative Board of the USCC, "Statement," p. 307.

26 Administrative Board of the USCC, "Statement," p. 307.

27 Ibid., p. 308.

28 Ibid., p. 310.

29 Ibid.

30 Ibid., p. 312.

31 Ibid., p. 310.

32 Ibid., p. 311.

33 Ibid.

34 Ibid., p. 312.

35 Ibid.

36 Ibid., pp. 312–13.

37 PCJP, "An Ethical Approach," p. 605.

38 Ibid.

39 Ibid., p. 610.

40 Administrative Board of the USCC, "Statement," p. 313.

41 Ibid., p. 314.

42 Ibid., p. 313.

43 "Jubilee 2000: Cancel Zambia's Debt," ecumenical pastoral letter of the Christian Council of Zambia, the Evangelical Fellowship of Zambia, and the Zambian Episcopal Conference, August 7, 1998, in Fr. Joe Komakoma, ed., The Social Teaching of the Catholic Bishops and Other Christian Leaders in Zambia: Major Pastoral Letters and Statements (Ndola, Zambia: Mission Press, 2003).

44 Peter Henriot, S.J., "Should Zambia Pay Its Debt?" National Mirror, August 18, 2004.

45 Elizabeth A. Donnelly, "Seton Hall Conference Discussion Summary" (Conference on the Ethical Dimensions of International Debt, Seton Hall University, October 22–23, 1998), p. 3; available at www.usccb.org/sdwp/international/shusum500.htm.

46 Peter Henriot, S.J., "Governance Issues and External Debt Relief for Poor Countries" (unpublished paper, January 13, 2003); available at www.jctr.org.zm/publications/gov-debt.htm.

47 Peter Henriot, S.J., "Connecting Debt and Trade from a Development Perspective: Challenges for Ireland and the EU" (paper presented at the International Jesuit Network on Development conference "Debt and Trade: Time to Make the Connections," Dublin, Ireland, September 9, 2004), p. 3.

48 Henriot, "Should Zambia Pay Its Debt?"

49 Henriot, "Governance Issues and External Debt Relief."

50 Interview with Ann Pettifor, March 8, 2001.

51 Jubilee 2000 U.K., "New Year Brings Call from the Pope, Bono, and Salman Rushdie"; quote taken from Q, February 1999, p. 149; available at www.jubileeresearch.org/jubilee2000/quotes.html.

52 See Jubilee 2000, "How It Was Achieved," at www.jubileeresearch.org/jubilee2000/final/how.html.

53 Pope John Paul II, "Tertio Millennio Adveniente" (November 10, 1994); available at www.vatican.va/jubilee_2000/docs/index.htm.

54 Jubilee 2000, "How It Was Achieved."

55 See Jubilee 2000, "Who We Are," at www.jubileeresearch.org/jubilee2000/about.html.

56 Ibid.

57 Cardinal Basil Hume, "International Debt: An Introductory Address," February 12, 1996; available at www.catholic-ew.org.uk/briefing/9603/9603009.htm.

58 For a summary of the proceedings and alternative views on the causes of the debt overhang, allocation of monies to debt relief in relation to development assistance, which countries should receive debt relief, the efficacy of the HIPC Initiative, and the ethics of conditionality, see Elizabeth A. Donnelly, "Seton Hall Conference Discussion Summary."

59 Administrative Board of the United States Catholic Conference, "A Jubilee Call for Debt Forgiveness," April 1999; available at www.nccbuscc.org/sdwp/international/adminstm.htm.

60 Ibid., p. 8.

61 Ibid., p. 13.

62 The additional relief was to be deemed warranted by a revision in the criteria for "sustainable" debt, principally measured by two ratios: a net present value of debt of 150 percent of annual export earnings, down from 200–250 percent; and, for countries highly dependent on export income, a net present value of debt of 250 percent of annual government revenue, down from 280 percent.

63 Jeffrey D. Sachs, "A Millennial Gift to Developing Nations," *New York Times*, June 11, 1999; available at www.jubileeresearch.org/jubilee2000/news/sachs14jun.html.

64 In the case of Zambia, for example, the HIPC approach assumed 5.5 percent annual growth in the volume of exports, 5 percent annual GDP growth, a significant increase in foreign direct investment, and balance-of-payment support in the form of grants. Jubilee Zambia campaigners pointed out that these were unrealistic given Zambia's previous track record, economic volatility and decline, and an international environment marked by war.

65 Peter Henriot, S.J., "Is HIPC Good for Zambia?" (undated); available upon request at www.jctr.org.zm.

66 See Jubilee 2000, "G8 Cancels More Debt—An Important Step but Only a First Step," June 22, 1999; available at www.jubileeresearch.org/jubilee2000/news/cologne24jun.html.

67 As recently as September 2004, Henriot complained that "Zambia's policies on civil servant wages, further privatization and hiring of teachers are dictated not by national consensus but only by one thing: meeting the elusive HIPC completion point." Henriot, "Connecting Debt and Trade from a Development Perspective," p. 3.

68 Much of the intellectual and advocacy work can be traced to a series of papers involving the Catholic Agency for Overseas Development and other NGOs in the U.K. See Henry Northover, "An Alternative Approach to Debt Cancellation and New Borrowing for Africa," CAFOD, October 2003, and the references cited therein; available at www.cafod.org.uk/var/storage/original/application/phpQ5RYil.pdf.

69 Debayani Kar, "G-8 Deal: First Step on a Long Journey, Jubilee USA Calls on World Bank/IMF to Expand Country List, Cut Harmful Strings," *Drop the Debt*, Jubilee USA Network newsletter (Washington, D.C., Fall 2005), pp. 3, 4; available at www.jubileeusa.org/resources/newsletter0905.pdf.

70 Pope Benedict XVI, "Deus Caritas Est" (December 25, 2005), sect. 28a; available at www.vatican.va/holy_father/benedict_xvi/encyclicals/documents/hf_ben-xvi_enc_20051225_deus-caritas-est_en.html.

71 Cf. Thomas Massaro, S.J., "Don't Forget Justice," *America* 194, no. 9 (2006), pp. 18–20.

Elizabeth A. Donnelly

Argentina, the Church, and the Debt

Thomas J. Trebat

By the mid-1990s, Argentina appeared to have overcome decades of stagnation and inflation. It did this through a series of dazzling economic reforms under the guidance of the International Monetary Fund (IMF) that were held up by many as the gold standard by which reforms in emerging-market economies were to be judged. President Carlos Menem was invited to address the annual meeting of the IMF and the World Bank in October 1998, an honor accorded him by these institutions out of admiration for reforms put in place during his administration. Argentina privatized state enterprises, liberalized international trade, put its banking system on sound footing, vanquished endemic inflation, attracted back Argentine capital formerly shipped abroad, stimulated the creation of domestic credit markets, and created a sense of optimism in the investing public that had been all but forgotten for most of the twentieth century. Gains were also made in most social indicators, showing that growth and the reduction in inflation had generated broadly shared benefits. The number of urban Argentines living below the poverty line declined from 40 percent of the population in 1990 to 22 percent in 1994 before rising again to 29 percent by 1998, the year that gross domestic product (GDP) peaked.[1] Infant mortality declined. Primary school attendance reached 100 percent.[2] In short, in the 1990s the country was the "poster child" of the Washington Consensus and its free-market-oriented policies.

The 1998 celebrations, however, were premature. The debt crisis of 2002 and its chaotic aftermath transformed Argentina from the "darling of emerging-market finance to the world's leading deadbeat."[3] The social impact of the crisis was brutal. After several years of a grinding recession, the Argentine economy plunged by 11 percent in 2002 and unemployment doubled to almost 30 percent of the workforce, a figure comparable to unemployment levels reached in the United States during the Great Depression in the 1930s. The cumulative fall in GDP in Argentina was on the order of 20 percent from its peak in 1998, greater than output declines in Russia or in any of the Asian economies except Indonesia during similar financial crises in the late 1990s. More than one-half of the population (58 percent) were thrust below the poverty line and many of these fell into indigence.[4] In an atmosphere of political turmoil and social resistance, five different Argentine presidents held office in one brief interval of a few months.[5]

This essay evaluates the Argentine crisis within the moral framework of Catholic social teaching on the debt problems of poor countries. The rationale for examining Catholic social teaching is, first, the fact that Argentina is (nominally) a predominantly Catholic country in which the Church has intervened in political affairs. The Argentine Church has had a long history of antagonism toward the Peronist party, and some members of the Church hierarchy were openly favorable to the brutal military regime that ruled Argentina from 1976 to the early 1980s.[6] Nevertheless, during the period of the recession and the debt crisis in 2001–2002, opinion polls consistently ranked the Church as the most credible of institutions in Argentina.[7] Indeed, Church leaders increasingly expressed their views as the crisis deepened and, I will argue, those views were heard. Second, Rome and the broader hierarchy of the Church, dating back to the 1980s, wrote extensively on moral and ethical aspects of Latin America's debt crises during the infamous "lost decade of the 1980s." While the framework they developed at that time reflected the issues of the day, the Church's teaching was intended as a permanent guide to moral and ethical behavior for all participants (creditors and debtors, governments and private citizens) for use in future crises, and it was specifically worked out in the case of Latin America.

Thus, the essay seeks to bring together and interpret the Church's teaching in the light of the particular economic and social circumstances of Argentina in the early 2000s. The question is, then, how closely did the outcome of the crisis conform to what social justice, in the Church's interpretation, would have required?

To address this question, I first examine the Church's teaching on debt, probably the most comprehensive moral framework available for addressing international debt. Next, I look into the economic and political origins of Argentina's 2001–2002 social crisis, which resulted in an impasse with its creitors. The blame for the crisis could be assigned to mistakes by both debtors and creditors as well as to adverse international economic conditions. I then examine the written record of the Argentine Catholic bishops to ascertain how the local Church leaders themselves viewed the crisis. There was considerable Church activism as part of a broad civil society campaign in Argentina to force the government to prioritize problems of unemployment and poverty that had engulfed so much of the population—the arguments that the Argentine government used most prominently when negotiating the debt reduction deal with its creditors.

CATHOLIC SOCIAL TEACHING ON INTERNATIONAL DEBT

Much of the Catholic Church's teaching on international debt grew directly out of the Latin American debt experience of the 1980s. This infamous "lost decade" was also a time of social activism by many parts of the Church throughout Latin America. The intellectual leadership was often provided by the umbrella conference of Latin American bishops, the Consejo Episcopal Latinoamericano (CELAM), which engaged in serious economic and social assessments of Latin America in the 1980s and sought solutions to the 1980s crisis.[8]

In the view of Latin American bishops, Latin American society is one in which "a few enjoy a privileged economic, political, and cultural lifestyle while on the other side of the gap in society, many live in inhuman conditions." This comprises a "rupture of God's plan for mankind," leaving the Church in Latin America no choice but to protest the "sinful structure of the societies," and to orient Church teaching and action to be "in solidarity with the poor." Poverty is a "negation of the most fundamental rights of the suffering majority of the people"; "an insult to God the Creator and Redeemer whose image is in the millions of poor"; "a scandal occurring in a supposedly Christian continent"; an "undeserved misery inflicted by neighbors who do not even see the poor"; and a "contradiction of the fundamental essence of Christianity."[9]

The first Vatican statements on the debt problems of Latin America in the 1980s were references embedded in broader papal encyclicals and other official statements of the Holy See in Rome. They were later echoed and interpreted by various regional and national conferences of Catholic bishops. Almost all subsequent Church documents on debt have adhered to the fundamentals of the influential 1986 Vatican statement that dealt explicitly with questions of international debt and was elaborated with the involvement of Latin American members of the Church hierarchy, including Archbishop Jorge M. Mejía.[10]

In 1989, the U.S. Conference of Catholic Bishops (USCCB) issued a major statement on third world debt, as it was called at the time, that drew particular attention to the role and responsibility of the United States in resolving the problems afflicting Latin America during its lost decade.[11] Coming three years after the bishops' well-known pastoral letter on the U.S. economy, the statement was an attempt "to examine the moral and human aspects of this crisis and to explore how our nation's institutions and policies have contributed to the situation." Moreover, "because so much of the money is owed to U.S. banks, we have a special responsibility to serve the universal Church by speaking out. We believe these (ethical and human) aspects are too often neglected in public discussion of the debt, dominated as it is by economic, political, and even ideological concerns."[12] The statement argues that Catholic social teaching—rooted in the revelation of Scripture, rational reflection on human nature, and historical experience—offers a unique perspective for examining the problem of international debt.[13] Church teaching from John XXIII to John Paul II has stressed the importance of the moral quality of the political and economic reality of global interdependence. As a result, it argued, a *moral interdependence* has evolved among nations and peoples—since standards of justice and charity, traditionally applied to domestic societies, apply as well to relations among states and peoples across national boundaries. This view is rooted in the common creation, humanity, and destiny of the human race. Church teaching has often referred to this moral interdependence as one of "co-responsibility" for the social problems afflicting poorer nations and societies.

The interdependence of peoples must have a moral dimension to avoid grave consequences for the weakest, with the key consideration of morality of public actions being the impact on the weakest in society, the "widows and orphans" in the Hebrew ethical tradition. To the extent that the

Thomas J. Trebat

weakest in society suffer malnutrition, poverty, and premature death in order to permit the servicing of a country's international debt, a grave moral
failing occurs. The manner in which one treats debtors "is a test case of moral rectitude and spiritual sensitivity."[14] In the New Testament, the parables
of Jesus often refer to the merciful treatment of debtors as a measure of
rectitude.

The biblical imagery does not provide a clear road map of how to resolve
the debt crisis, but it does "provide a starting point, a way to understand
creditor-debtor relations which a purely empirical assessment of the debt
problem will never offer. The biblical lessons reject an interpretation of these
issues cast purely in terms of economic gain or power over others: Those who
are in debt retain their dignity as well as their basic human rights, which
make demands upon creditors; debtors cannot be reduced to a situation of
abject poverty in order to pay debts."[15]

Three "pillars" were suggested in order to examine the overall impact of
the debt. The first is the effect of the existence of large amounts of third
world debt, as it was called at the time, on the international common good.
This can create conditions whereby the policies of one country, such as a
decision by the United States to raise interest rates, can have negative effects
on citizens of other countries by raising the cost of borrowed capital and increasing the size of the debt. This is still an important issue in global finance
today, and it was especially so in the early 1980s when the bishops were
writing, as the United States then increased its own interest rates dramatically while most third world debt had been contracted at floating rates of
interest, tied to the U.S. interest rates. As U.S. interest rates rose, the debt-
servicing payments of the poor nations increased in lockstep.

The second pillar in examining debt is the implication for social justice.
The bishops argued that the rules of the international system do not equally
favor rich and poor nations; that is, the rules of the global trading system
have tended to reflect the interest and power of the more developed countries. In more recent times, this argument has been expounded by the critics
of globalization. Poorer nations, more limited in their ability to compete in
the global marketplace and often dependent for export earnings upon a
small number of commodity exports, can find their ability to service debt

unfairly hampered by rules that restrict access of their products to rich-country markets.

The third pillar refers to solidarity, arguing that the suffering of the poor and the weakest among us is the responsibility of all. Solidarity follows from the moral interdependence of peoples and refers to the moral imperative incumbent upon countries and private citizens alike to avoid actions that have grave consequences for the poorest, regardless of the national boundaries within which these vulnerable populations happen to reside. If the servicing of the debt creates intolerable social conditions for citizens in a poor country, the responsibility to address this problem rests with citizens of rich countries as well.

The Catholic writings on debt gave only limited consideration to the legitimacy of the accumulated debt, and whether any moral obligation existed to repay it at all. Reduced to its essence, a core argument could be made that since the poor had no voice in the decision to accumulate the debt and did not benefit from it, their interest should predominate and the debt should not be paid at all. Nonetheless, the bishops' view is more nuanced and more pragmatic, little inclined to encourage outright default by irresponsible governing officials: "We believe that a moral presumption exists, in personal and social relations, that debts should be paid." In other words, the Church teaching started from the relatively conservative premise that debtor countries have a moral obligation to repay contracted debts. It then went on to define as carefully as possible circumstances in which some debt relief, ranging from partial to a total elimination of the debt, was the morally superior outcome. On this issue of the external debt, as well as other economic matters, the thinking of the Church has not been to overthrow the market system of economic organization, but rather to point out and urge correction of its obvious shortcomings.

The moral issues of debt management for practitioners arise in the event that a poorer country cannot or will not continue to make full repayment of debt. In these circumstances, determining how much of the debt is in fact unpayable involves often very complex technical and financial considerations of a debtor's ability to pay, about which the teachings of the Church have little to add. These are matters to be thrashed out between debtors and creditors in tedious negotiations. The truly compelling issues arise when debtors and creditors cannot agree or when the agreement worked out creates even greater hardship for the citizens of the debtor country.

In such circumstances beyond the reach of ordinary creditor-debtor dynamics, how much of the debt should be paid? The various Church documents urge a more careful examination of the contractual arrangements that were made between the debtor and the creditor and the political and social context in which these arrangements were reached. The bishops acknowledged that "no single principle" could be useful in adjudicating all disputes, which necessarily involved a case-by-case approach, though the statements of the U.S. bishops reveal a set of guidelines when looking at these contractual arrangements. These include: Was the relationship between the debtor and the creditor one of reasonably equal bargaining power? Have human rights been fostered and protected in the country? Did the debtor country representatives have the best interests of their people in mind when the debt was contracted? Did the governments come to power through legitimate means or through fraudulent elections or a military coup? How was the borrowed money used—for investment projects with a long payoff period, or for capital flight or government corruption? Was the majority of it used simply to pay high interest rates charged by the creditors?[16] How much of an effort already has been made by the debtor country to fulfill the contract, and with what impact on the population, measured by the extent of social unrest and resistance?

After arguing that the Latin American debt situation of the 1980s was much more complex than that of poverty-stricken African states, whose debt was primarily owed to official lenders, the bishops observed: "In some cases, simple repayment is neither possible nor, in our view, necessarily demanded by justice. In all cases, the *internal record of performance* of the debtor government—the soundness of its economic planning and particularly its efforts on behalf of the poor—should be key criterion for how the external debt is adjudicated."[17] If the possibility of repayment is afforded only through a heavy social cost, then "the principles of justice point not toward repayment by the debtors, but toward remission, even if partial, by creditors. . . . A range of remedies is possible and necessary; a scale of redress is needed to judge different situations."[18] In order to find the proper scale of redress, a cooperative effort is required between all those major actors who, separately and jointly, are "co-responsible" for finding a solution that alleviates the burden on the poor. Thus, co-responsibility is added as a requirement for creditor and debtor governments, banks and other private creditors, and multilateral institutions, especially the World Bank and the IMF.[19] And indeed, on several occasions, Church authorities, often at the initiative of the Latin American conference of bishops, held meetings with the heads of the principal multilateral lenders, including the IMF, the World Bank, and the Inter-American Development Bank, as well as with senior representatives of commercial banks, many of whom were Catholic laypersons.

WHAT SORT OF SOLUTION? ETHICAL GUIDELINES FOR RESOLVING THE DEBT

Once the need for debt relief is established, as the Church argued was the case for Latin American countries in the 1980s, how are we to judge the morality of the resulting efforts to reschedule or partially forgive the debt? The bishops gave considerable thought to the ethical principles that should inform debt negotiations:

- The primary objective must be to revitalize the debtor country and to improve the life of the poor in that economy; in particular, some immediate benefit from debt relief should be obtained, especially for the poor.
- Co-responsibility requires that the burden imposed by the solution be borne by both creditor and debtor countries, particularly by the wealthier sectors within these societies and not by the poor disproportionately.[20]
- The solution should address the issue of government corruption, which may have been among the aggravating factors behind the accumulation of the debt in the first place.
- It should attempt to relieve external factors beyond the control of the debtor country that would tend to aggravate or perpetuate the burden of the debt, such as adverse terms of trade, unstable commodity prices, global interest rates, and unpredictability in the global flow of capital to the debtor country.

- It should be judged in terms of the ability of the debtor economy to recover: "the debtor country should not be compelled to choose debt service over self-reliant development."[21]
- A just and lasting solution also requires changes in the *structure* of the global economy as well as in the behavior of the major actors. Without entering into much detail, the bishops spoke favorably of changes in the global "architecture"—for example, new global monetary arrangements with a greater voice for the poorer nations and a global bankruptcy court.[22]

In addition to these guidelines, the U.S. bishops argued for a special responsibility of the U.S. government and people in finding a just and equitable solution, particularly in view of the U.S. trade and budget deficits, which were imposing a large cost on Latin America by weakening the value of the U.S. dollar (in which their export earnings were denominated) and, especially, by keeping U.S. interest rates at elevated levels, thereby raising the costs of debt servicing. The bishops argued:

> Real solidarity means that we cannot accept that the world's poor be required to sacrifice in order to sustain the lifestyle of the world's more affluent people. . . . We urge our commercial bankers, including the many who are Catholic, to understand and accept co-responsibility for the solution of this urgent and crucial problem. This is not a matter of what is often, but inaccurately, termed charity, but of justice. Justice is neither sentimental nor optional; it is realistic and it is obligatory. . . . Debt relief is necessarily a complex and technical matter, but it need not be as drawn out and arduous as it has been in the past. We urge U.S. bankers to place considerations of justice and co-responsibility above those of short-term financial gain or loss. . . . We are not interested in assessing blame or assigning guilt; these are descriptions of the past, and there is plenty of both to be shared. Rather, we want to stress responsibility, which looks to the future.[23]

THE ARGENTINE CRISIS AND THE INTERNATIONAL POLITICAL ECONOMY

The Argentine default of 2001 and the economic crisis surrounding this event should be seen in the context of the global economy and the institutional arrangements that governed it at the turn of the century. In certain institutional respects, this global environment was quite different from that which had existed during the time of the Latin American debt crisis of the 1980s.[24] It is important to understand this changed context prior to examining the relevance of moral principles to the particular case of the Argentine crisis.

First, the IMF had become even more important in the late 1990s as a source of emergency financing than it had been in the 1980s, when the emphasis of IMF lending was on long-term "structural adjustment programs" and highly conditional extensions of credit. The new, more activist and flexible IMF was the result of its own extraordinary efforts, beginning with the Mexican peso crisis in 1995 and continuing on through multiple crises in Asia, Russia, and elsewhere, to intervene in events of financial distress in emerging markets.

Second, during the 1990s, an international bond market for lending to emerging markets, such as Argentina, developed where none had existed during the 1980s, when private lending to emerging markets was confined to a handful of large commercial banks with global experience and connections. In the new, globalized world of the 1990s, with deep pools of highly mobile capital managed by mutual fund and other professional investors, private bondholders by and large became the source of long-term capital for sovereign borrowers, a function that had been filled in the 1980s by a few large commercial banks and multilateral lenders. Clearly, banks were still important financiers, but because they provided short-term loans, banks were more able to manage their loan exposures to Argentina, reducing their lending as the risks of default grew by demanding repayment and not renewing lines of credit. The bond market investors were left holding long-term obligations of the Argentine government, often with maturities in excess of ten years. Hence, other than by selling these bonds at a loss to other investors, the bondholders had little choice but to hold on to their claims as the risk of default grew steadily.

Third, international bonds of sovereign governments in the emerging markets were at the center of eight serious financial crises (in Mexico, Russia, Indonesia, Korea, Thailand, Brazil, Turkey, and Argentina) beginning December 1994, although financial pressures also came from the reductions of cross-border bank lending by commercial banks and reductions in deposits in domestic banks by domestic residents worried about the solvency of the banking system. During most of this time of vastly increased emergency financing of emerging-market borrowers, the IMF was roundly criticized for large bailout packages that appeared to let private creditors off the hook. Although the private sector had to cooperate and bonds were successfully restructured in a number of smaller countries, fears grew that such lending by the IMF encouraged creditor moral hazard. The firm expectation of a large bailout to an important debtor country would, it was feared, make risky lending by private creditors all the more likely, increasing the probability of an eventual bailout.

Finally, the experience of the 1990s led to a broader understanding of the forms of indebtedness that, together or separately, created financial vulnerabilities in the emerging economies. Argentina is a good example of the intricacy of defining what is meant by debt.[25] The classic understanding in the 1980s was that debt was essentially external debt—debt of governments, banks, and private companies sold to foreigners or nonresidents of Argentina. Reality showed that governments can also rely upon other sources of domestic debt financing, however, and, in fact, the dependence of the Argentine government on borrowing from both domestic banks and the domestic capital market grew rapidly as access to international markets became constrained in 2000 and 2001. Maturing external debt and maturing domestic debt do not create quite the same pressures on external reserves and they are governed by different sets of laws. (Maturing foreign debt must be repaid in hard currency, whereas domestic debt is repayable in pesos and is somewhat easier for the Argentine government to renew or "roll over.") Both forms of debt, however—external and domestic—create similar financial vulnerabilities for the government and contribute in similar ways to a crushing debt burden. For example, both forms of debt tend to raise the cost of borrowing for the government, and preempt a share of fiscal spending that could otherwise be used for other purposes, including increased social spending. Argentina's convertibility system, by pegging the Argentine peso to the U.S. dollar in a one-to-one relationship, actually masked the extent to which the rising amount of dollar-denominated debt was becoming a larger and larger proportion of the Argentine economy. (The drastic devaluation of the Argentine peso in 2002 greatly reduced the dollar value of the economy and the relative burden of the debt became much clearer.)

WHAT WENT WRONG IN ARGENTINA?

The Argentine descent into financial crisis was as painful as it was sudden.[26] The post-1999 recession lingered, undermining fiscal revenues. This led to repeated efforts to cut government expenditures, which, in turn, caused growth to slow down even more. The recession made the prospect of further fiscal tightening politically impossible, leading the beleaguered government of Fernando de la Rúa to engage in a series of increasingly desperate economic measures to stave off default and bankruptcy. This period included economic measures starting in early 2001 under the direction of the newly appointed economy minister, Domingo Cavallo. Unable to cut government spending, Cavallo proposed steep tax increases instead. Unable to devalue the currency, he tinkered with the convertibility rules, undermining confidence in the currency and hastening its demise. Desperate to tap into domestic sources of financing when external financing had evaporated, he manipulated the independent Central Bank and borrowed heavily from the domestic banking system. Fearful of running out of cash and unable to borrow abroad, Cavallo pursued debt swaps, which, in exchange for modest amounts of debt relief in the short run, greatly increased the long-run debt burden of the Argentine government.

While Cavallo's arrival at the Finance Ministry in early 2001 and his characteristic energy at first created optimism in the marketplace and renewed capital inflows, the mood soon changed and Argentina found itself virtually shut out of global capital markets. The IMF, often criticized for its rigid and inflexible policies in Latin America, was actually remarkably flexible in the case of Argentina and rushed to provide emergency assistance, eventually lending almost $16 billion to the government. The assistance included a large and controversial financing in August 2001, by which time the government's credibility had been so battered in the market that the chances were heavily weighted against success.[27] The Fund's support could not prevent a rapid erosion of deposits from the Argentine banking sector. This only added more pressure to the government by increasing the risk of a massive collapse of bank lending and placing crushing burdens on Argentine corporations dependent upon such lending.

Thomas J. Trebat

By December 2001, the banking sector was essentially bankrupt and the corporate sector, dependent upon bank lending, was in deep distress. Confidence in the Convertibility Plan fell to zero as the wealthy rushed to move money out of the country at any price. Unemployment peaked at well above 20 percent, with social conditions especially difficult in the rural sectors. Riots led to the death of thirty people and then spread to the capital of Buenos Aires, where there were daily store lootings and attacks on banks. In late December, Cavallo resigned, and shortly thereafter the well-intentioned but hapless President de la Rúa also resigned. Four presidents followed him in rapid succession. One of these, Rodríguez Saá, decreed the end of the Convertibility Plan in January 2002, leading to a strong devaluation of the currency. He also unilaterally suspended payments on the external debt, a move promptly endorsed by the Argentine congress.

In the most common renditions of the complex causes of the crisis, Argentina suffered from four major financial vulnerabilities. First, its rigid adherence to the currency board scheme led to an increasing overvaluation of the Argentine peso, harming the country's ability to compete internationally.[28] Second, the overvalued currency produced growing external imbalances that were increasingly difficult to finance except via external bond issuance by the government.[29] Once the government was no longer able to borrow abroad, the imbalances created strong recessionary pressures. Third, while the fiscal deficits of the government were not enormous, they were large and persistent, and were aggravated by an expensive experiment to privatize the social security system.[30] Fourth, the widespread use of the U.S. dollar in the banking sector produced a currency mismatch as Argentine banks and companies borrowed in dollars to an enormous extent while their revenue bases for the most part remained denominated in Argentine pesos. This made the corporate sector and the banking system extremely vulnerable to an exchange rate crisis.

Five external events played a role in exposing these underlying flaws in the Argentine economy and paved the way for the disaster that followed. First, the Russian default of 1998 increased the cost of borrowing abroad for the government of Argentina through a "contagion" effect by spreading fear among private investors that other large emerging-market borrowers, including Argentina, could also run into difficulties in making debt payments.

Second, with slow growth in the global economy, the prices of Argentina's commodity exports, on which it was highly dependent to generate the foreign currency in which its external debt was denominated, weakened and the terms of trade worsened. Third, the Brazilian devaluation of 1999 affected Argentina's ability to export to that market, which had been one of its most important, and also undermined Argentina's competitiveness relative to that of a large export market such as Brazil in other markets, such as the United States. Following the Brazilian devaluation, new foreign direct investment, for example, tended to be directed to Brazil rather than to Argentina. Fourth, from 1998 to 2001, the U.S. dollar (to which the Argentine peso was tied by the Convertibility Law) underwent a period of strong appreciation, bringing the peso with it and undermining the competitiveness of Argentine exports. Finally, U.S. short-term interest rates rose by almost 2 percent after mid-1999, raising further the costs of borrowing for Argentina and deepening the recession.

Relations between the Argentine government and its creditors (mostly bondholders) were bitter between January 2002, when the country declared a moratorium on debt payments, and September 2003, when it submitted its initial proposal for a settlement. This first proposal was viewed by creditors as punitive and arbitrary. In asking creditors to reduce the country's outstanding debt by 90 percent, Economy Minister Roberto Lavagna set aside the promises made to creditors by a previous generation of Argentine policy-makers. He justified the government's request, which was far in excess of the debt relief requested by Russia in 1998, on the basis of sobering assessments of the country's future ability to repay. Policy-makers couched their position also in moral terms, pointing to the obvious hardships of the poor and the middle classes and the self-evident need to devote more of the nation's fiscal resources to poverty alleviation and, consequently, less to debt servicing. An official Argentine publication summarized the chosen approach: "Given the social reality of Argentina, with high levels of poverty and indigence (50% and 25% of the population, respectively), pursuing a greater fiscal effort through a reduction of public expenditures and not taking care of the internal needs may lead to situations of political instability which may finally affect the economic performance and, therefore, the repayment capacity to foreign creditors. In this regard, a greater fiscal effort through an increase of the tax burden could stifle the economic recovery, which could also end up affecting the repayment capacity of the foreign creditors."[31]

While to a large extent exercising forbearance (few lawsuits were filed by irate bondholders to force faster repayment) and accepting the need for some debt reduction, creditors tended to view the official Argentine position as self-serving in the short term and, ultimately, self-defeating as well for an Argentine economy so reliant on global capital. The Kirchner government, creditors alleged privately, was hiding behind spurious economic assumptions and lashing out against foreign creditors (and foreign-owned banks and companies in Argentina) in order to consolidate its precarious grip on power during a period of great political uncertainty (Néstor Kirchner had polled only 23 percent of the popular vote for president in the April 2003 elections and so assumed office in May 2003 as a virtual unknown). In public presentations, groups representing creditors spoke more diplomatically about the need for "meaningful consultations with bondholders, based upon market precedents, and a more realistic assessment of payment capacity over the medium- and long-run."[32] Loosely translated, in the view of the creditors, the Argentine authorities were willing to convert Argentina into a pariah state for the sake of an agreement that essentially used the international creditors as scapegoats while ignoring their legitimate rights as creditors.

The resolution of the debt crisis did not come until 2005. The final proposal involved payment to creditors amounting to approximately 30 percent of their original claims, with no provision for past-due interest. From the creditors' perspective, the settlement was far harsher than in previous cases of debt defaults in the 1990s, including that of Russia. In other debt reduction agreements dating back to the late 1990s, the average amount of debt reduction was on the order of 35 percent, compared to 70 percent in the case of Argentina. From the government's perspective, the debt accord was a major political accomplishment, allowing forces aligned with President Kirchner to triumph in the important congressional elections of October 2005. Kirchner was able to argue, with considerable basis in fact, that his government had faced down both the IMF and the private bondholders, and held fast to its determination to protect social expenditures that otherwise would have been absorbed by debt-service expenditures. The Argentine economy has been able to stage a relatively rapid recovery: since 2003 economic growth has been averaging almost 8 percent (albeit much of this is merely a recovery from the initial plunge) amid signs that small amounts of foreign capital are once again flowing to Argentina.

APPLYING THE MORAL FRAMEWORK: WRITINGS OF THE ARGENTINE BISHOPS

In their statements issued since the 1980s, Argentine bishops heaped criticism on Argentina's elite, which, in their view, had so failed in its elementary duties to justice as to leave large sectors of the population in deprivation.[33] The critique was even more pronounced in the 1990s as evidence emerged of widespread corruption during the Menem era.[34] The bishops were critical of the economic model as a generator of poverty and unemployment, notwithstanding the stability it had brought to the country. For the most part, however, the Menem government enjoyed ostensibly good relations with the Church hierarchy in Argentina and was received by the pope in Rome on several occasions. Menem benefited from the period of relative prosperity and social stability that followed the introduction of the Convertibility Plan. He also aligned his policies in such areas as reproductive rights with conservative Church thinking.

As the economic prosperity of the early and mid-1990s gave way to recession and signs of social unrest in the late 1990s, the statements of the bishops with respect to the Menem government became more pointed. The bishops called for moral renewal of Argentine society as the descent into chaos gathered momentum and Menem's popularity declined amid disarray in the Peronist party.

The bishops' message emphasized the need for moral renewal at home first and foremost. Writing in early 2000, for example, as the recession deepened and the new government under President de la Rúa settled into office, the bishops commented: "Our crisis is clearly ours as well. We are all, in different degree, responsible for what is happening to us." And "what is happening" in Argentina was "social exclusion, a growing gap between rich and poor, insecurity, corruption, social and family violence, serious

Thomas J. Trebat

deficiencies in the educational system and in public health, the negative consequences of globalization and the tyranny of the markets."

The bishops did point to external aggravating factors beyond the control of the Menem government, or any national government, making particular mention of "the exorbitant interest payments on the so-called external debt" and unfair agriculture subsidies that harm Argentine exports. *"This system of injustice strongly influences Argentine society."*[35] The IMF was a frequent target for its role in advising the Menem government on policy and for imposing its rules on Argentina. In early 2000, the bishops lent their support to a protest march against the Fund led by dissident union leaders. Cardinal Primatesta, the head of the Conferencia Episcopal Argentina, repeatedly criticized the Fund, called for its reform, and added denunciations of the adverse social consequences of the rigid Convertibility Law. As early as mid-2000, Archbishop Karlic was issuing calls for the IMF to reduce Argentina's external debt as well as expressing frequent denunciations of corruption and the lack of adequate poverty strategies. Other prelates made more direct links to the external debt, arguing that while it should be paid, payment should not be at the cost of the hunger of the people.[36] Most of the writings of the bishops did not focus exclusively on problems of external debt, but this is because the Church seemed to accept the need for a drastic restructuring of Argentina's debt as a foregone conclusion, and therefore not worth discussing in detail by setting out the pros and cons. For example, this statement from the bishops in late 2001: "We know that the crisis that we are living has multiple causes, among these especially the very heavy external debt which increases on a daily basis and makes it difficult for us to grow. . . . We have no doubt that a united Argentine people . . . will know how to gain respect among the other nations of the world in order to reach a fair treatment."[37]

At the time in 2001, these statements in favor of a debt restructuring had little if any effect on the policies of the de la Rúa government, which were still firmly in the mold of continuing to service the debt in its entirety through close cooperation with the IMF, increased taxation and fiscal retrenchment, and additional borrowing abroad. In retrospect, the full weight of the bishops' views in favor of debt restructuring (rather than economic adjustment per se) may have fallen more heavily on Argentine governments that succeeded the hapless de la Rúa administration and were confronted with a full-blown economic and social crisis.

The real debt that Argentina owed, the bishops argued, was a social debt to the hundreds of thousands of Argentines in dire circumstances. Repaying this debt had to take precedence over the more narrow objective of balancing the fiscal accounts. It is not enough "that the fiscal accounts be in balance so as to calm the markets nor to make good on debts owed abroad." What is needed is sacrifice by the elites in Argentina in order to benefit the excluded, who struggle to survive on a daily basis. "Has not the time come for grand gestures [by the government] that strengthen our identity as a nation permitting a sustainable economic growth that benefits most those who have the least?"[38]

Criticism became more frequent and more pointed as the de la Rúa government struggled to contain the financial crisis through a series of fiscal cuts. In early 2001, the bishops issued this statement: "Democracy has forgotten its mission. . . . This should have been the moment for the people's reasonable expectations to be realized. How many questions without answers! How many frustrated illusions!"[39] Why, the bishops wondered, were politicians unable to resist the "impositions of the powerful groups both inside and outside the country" who impede the spread of human dignity? They asked, "Who is thinking of the future of Argentina? What is the national project? What can be done to generate hope? The Argentine crisis did not arise from a set of contemporary circumstances; it was the result of a long history of deterioration of social morality which is the backbone of the nation and in danger of becoming paralyzed."[40]

It is difficult to decipher any direct reply by the increasingly paralyzed de la Rúa administration to the criticism of the Church, although the bishops' statements could not but have added to the slide in the president's popularity. One group of religious leaders who met with the embattled president in late 2001, just before the worst of the crisis, relayed that de la Rúa believed that growing unhappiness over the economy was an "exaggeration." One of the religious leaders commented appropriately: "He [de la Rúa] never realized the extent of the problem."[41]

The economic analysis implicit in the bishops' remarks called attention to various factors: theft and corruption by public officials; blind allegiance to economic orthodoxy ("liberalism") through acquiescence to the "tyranny of the market"; tax evasion; lack of respect for the law; loss of meaning in work; abuse of rights through improper use of force; exaggerated defense of economic rights of powerful groups; and the decadence of the educational system. In late 2001, as the government struggled with desperate measures and began closing down the banking system, the bishops became even more direct: "In one word, [our problem in Argentina is] a generalized corruption that undermines the cohesion of the Nation and shames us before the world."[42]

STATEMENTS ON THE EVE OF THE CRISIS

Argentina's recession had dragged on for forty-five months by end of 2001. The messages that followed in quick succession in the depths of this "terminal crisis" in early 2002 were of solidarity and hope while also assessing blame. "No sector of [Argentine] society can say that it is blameless. In particular, those who must examine themselves include the political parties and the labor unions, and also the business groups and the banks, as well as all three branches of government."[43] Significantly, the bishops did not spare themselves: "In a country which professes itself to be Christian in its majority, it is not easy to explain the present crisis without [concluding that there is] a great lack of coherence between the faith [and our preaching of social morality] and life."[44] Almost all of the letters in 2002 echoed these themes as the bishops castigated the political and economic leadership for its role in the degradation of Argentine society and its refusal to mend its ways and make restitution of public funds that had been stolen. The Pope himself endorsed this view of generalized corruption in his own comments on Argentina in early 2002, calling for "a collective examination of conscience regarding the responsibility of each person, the tragic consequences of selfishness, corrupt practices, and the lack of foresight and mismanagement of the affairs of the nation."[45]

Argentina's economic measures of late 2001 and early 2002—the unavoidable devaluation, in particular, and the sequestration of bank funds—did indeed do great damage to the poor. The bishops were a voice for more just burden-sharing by the wealthy and by businesses, including multinationals. The wealthy should pay taxes, politicians should stop wasteful spending, and "those who enjoy privileges which are unjust must know that, while these may be legal, they are also immoral."[46] During this time, the Argentine Church reached out to the Vatican and to other episcopal conferences throughout the world, receiving particular support from the Spanish Church as well as supportive statements from the Pope. In a document widely circulated in Argentina, the Spanish bishops wrote in part about the situation in Argentina: "At the bottom of it all is a generalized lack of justice, of solidarity, and of charity. Many things will have to change in Argentina, but the entire rich world also needs to undergo radical change. People must prevail over economic interests. The right to life must prevail over the right to property. The external debt cannot become a factor of slavery and death."[47]

Under the leadership of Archbishop Karlic, the Argentine Church, after some considerable hesitation and misgivings, agreed to a role of convener and moderator of a broad national dialogue of government and civic organizations that had been called into existence by President Eduardo Duhalde in the middle of 2002. Many of the bishops' subsequent messages referred to their frustrations as the Duhalde government seemed unwilling or unable to act upon the dialogue's recommendations for reform. In "La Nación que queremos," Karlic and his colleagues called out again for an entirely new civic and political culture, one that could return to all the "pleasure of being Argentines."[48]

As the worst of the economic crisis subsided at the end of 2002 and Argentina began to experience a sustained economic recovery, the fiery tone of the bishops' messages diminished, but emphasis on the need for change remained. The presidential campaign of late 2002 picked up on the national mood, one of repudiation of the old leadership and a search for new faces. Kirchner echoed the themes of a priority focus on poverty and unemployment and took pride in his record of austere fiscal management of an oil-rich province during his time as governor. He promised, explicitly and implicitly, to rid Argentina of the corrupting influence of "corporations" that had enjoyed prominence under Menem. He easily turned back Menem's hapless attempts to reenter the presidential race, and won the elections after two rounds of voting.

As the Kirchner administration settled into office in 2003 and presided over a tentative economic recovery, the bishops cautioned against "false optimism" and enduring "myths" that the country was rich and therefore was out of danger.[49] As the economy appeared to gain momentum under Kirchner throughout 2004 and into 2005, the tone of the messages remained very similar. To those who took comfort in the "incipient economic recovery," the bishops warned again that the road to a new Argentina was a long one and that the causes of the Argentine crisis were so deeply rooted that a brief period of economic recovery might only paper them over. The Kirchner government was not pleased to be reminded by the bishops that the greatest immorality of the large social debt is that "it arises in a nation that has the objective conditions to avoid or correct these injuries, but which unfortunately would seem to opt to aggravate even more these inequalities."[50]

These comments and criticism of corruption and economic oppression have been a source of friction between the Church and the Kirchner government, which cultivated a proactive image through its confrontational stance with the creditors. The Church did lend its moral support to the debt agreement sought by the government, though never to the extent that Kirchner might have hoped for by endorsing the government's actual proposals for a large reduction in the debt. Even when the Church did refer to the debt, it seemed also to remind the government that it needed to negotiate in good faith, echoing a frequent complaint from creditors about the government. It expressed concern for certain creditor groups, including Italian retirees who had purchased government bonds.[51]

THE RELEVANCE OF THE CHURCH'S MORAL FRAMEWORK

The Church's 1980s teaching, as adjusted and updated through the Argentine debt crisis of 2001, provides a reasonably comprehensive moral framework for assessing the crisis and its aftermath. Especially as applied in the writings of the Argentine bishops, the framework clearly leads to the conclusion that social justice required a significant reduction on Argentina's indebtedness. This was especially the case once it had become clear that Argentina had made major and painful efforts to pay, reaching the point of great suffering by the poor and the frightening eruption of civil strife and austerity. But, beyond this initial observation, the bishops never endorsed a particular policy solution to the debt problem, nor did they take sides, thus properly keeping at a distance from government affairs. Instead, they argued that those who were "co-responsible" for the fact of Argentina's indebtedness had an obligation to relieve the suffering of the poor through a solution that would restore the country's capacity for self-reliant growth.

From these disparate elements, is it possible to draw links between Catholic social teaching and activism and the outcome of the Argentine crisis? Can it be argued that such teaching and activism has contributed to a change in the norms and principles of debtors and creditors that will affect the way in which future international debt crises will be addressed? On both counts, a reasonable case may be made.

It is worth summarizing the outcome of the Argentine crisis. It was first and foremost a severe human crisis resulting in more than half of the population falling into poverty or extreme poverty. Unemployment soared to levels similar to those of the Great Depression in the United States and to those in Germany in the aftermath of World War II. Banks and corporations failed. Food riots and demonstrations throughout the country resulted in multiple deaths, including twenty in Buenos Aires alone in December 2001. Argentina's decision to suspend payments on its international debt was not, therefore, a willful act by an irresponsible government.

The Argentine government, in making proposals to creditors, was responsive in some ways to the broad secular society campaign in Argentina, of which the Church was a part. It framed its debt proposal, which was considered by creditors quite radical and extreme, in terms of the preeminent need to restore economic growth and to relieve human suffering in Argentina, goals at the core of the Catholic social teaching on debt.

Every major communication from Argentina to its creditors as the debt was being negotiated referred to the paramount need to address the social situation. This norm was often couched in pragmatic terms easily understood by the creditor community. One of the leading Argentine officials put it this way in a speech to creditors: "We are putting together the pieces of a broken country and also of a broken people. Half of Argentines live today at or below the poverty line. We will face up to our duty [to creditors], but not at the expense of further suffering of the Argentine people. We are

Thomas J. Trebat

aiming for economic recovery, but there is absolutely no way Argentina can pay [creditors] beyond its capacity to ensure a sustainable debt profile."[52] The government then went on, as we have seen, to request an unprecedented amount of debt relief for a middle-income country—near 90 percent forgiveness in its initial proposal—though the offer was eventually "sweetened" to a level of debt reduction closer to 70 percent.

The surprising outcome was that a large majority of creditors came to view this offer as fair and reasonable under the circumstances and voted to accept it. Although discussions with creditors dragged on for several years, creditors representing 76 percent of Argentina's outstanding debt accepted the offer. (Holders of the remaining 24 percent elected not to participate in the debt exchange offer and the debt instruments that these creditors held are not being serviced by the government.) In any reckoning, this was a good deal for Argentina, compared to the 25–30 percent debt relief levels common during the debt negotiations of the 1980s, and the average of 35 percent in other debt negotiations in the late 1990s, such as those with Russia and Ecuador. Very few lawsuits were filed by disgruntled "holdout" creditors, and those that were appear to have little chance of succeeding in court because sovereign borrowers enjoy substantial effective protection from litigation.[53]

Experienced international creditors accepted the fundamental logic behind the Argentine proposal and saw the need for significant debt relief. In fact, they saw this well before any final agreement was reached. Market prices for Argentine debt throughout the period of debt renegotiation (from 2002 through 2005) reflected the fact that the market believed the Argentine debt to be worth only 30 cents on the dollar. Most investors, using "mark-to-market" accounting principles to value their portfolios, had marked down the value of their debt well before a final settlement was reached.

Creditors realized Argentina had made reasonable efforts to pay the debt and, even after debt settlement, the country was committing to maintain an austere fiscal policy in order to service its remaining debt. For example, in the immediate aftermath of the debt reduction agreement, Argentina's debt-to-GDP ratio (a common measure of creditworthiness) was still on the order of 90 percent, considered very high by international standards. Moreover, Argentina made a commitment to maintain a large budget surplus (on the order of 3 percent of GDP) for the next several *decades* in order to service its remaining debt burden. This was a significant fiscal undertaking by Argentina in light of the fact that the government fiscal accounts had registered consistent budget deficits (not surpluses) during most of the 1990s.

Just as extraordinary as the debt reduction deal is what has happened in Argentina following the agreement. Since 2003, the Argentine economy has been growing at rates close to 8–9 percent, among the highest in Latin America. It has fully recovered the output that had been lost between 1998 and 2002. Foreign creditors began to extend *new* credits to Argentina even before the ink was dry on the debt reduction agreement, defying the predictions of those in the market who argued the debt renegotiation would inevitably cut Argentina off from global capital markets for generations to come. Poverty and unemployment remain high in Argentina but well below the levels of 2001–2002, and are likely to continue improving given the vigor of the economic recovery. In other words, the debt agreement did allow Argentina a "fresh start" in economic terms and it appears to be taking advantage of it, contributing to the relief of human suffering.

While it would be naive in the extreme to argue that creditors and debtors were consciously acting in conformity with a moral framework on international debt spelled out in the teaching of the Church, the final outcome of the crisis was not inconsistent with that teaching. Compared to the 1980s experience in Latin America, the crisis was resolved in a shorter (though still very long) period of time and allowed Argentina to stage a far faster economic recovery than had been the case in the 1980s, when debt problems led to a lost decade of development. Significantly, the debt crisis in Argentina did not spread to other Latin American countries, unlike the situation in the 1980s, when Mexico's problems spread throughout the hemisphere. At the same time, other Latin American countries, cognizant of the human costs of the crisis in Argentina, did not rush to emulate Argentina by repudiating their own external debt obligations. On the contrary, in countries such as Brazil, the government redoubled efforts to avoid a fiscal crisis that would lead to a suspension of international payments precisely to avoid the human suffering that would inevitably be at the core of any financial crisis. Other countries did not see Argentina as having taken "the easy way out."

Thomas J. Trebat

Finally, it would be a great mistake to see the moral weight of the Church as being lined up against creditors and on the side of the government or the Church acting as an arbiter seeking to assign blame to one side or another. Its teaching was consistent with creditor beliefs in a moral presumption that Argentina should expend efforts to repay the debt, and also with the conclusion of the Argentine government that such efforts had been made and that significant debt reduction was in order and should be granted.

The main lesson of the Church's teaching in the case of Argentina may have been the simple observation that Argentina's ability to adjust to economic adversity will always have strict limits in terms of the incremental and disproportionate burden austerity imposes on the poor. Therefore, creditors must enter into contracts under the expectation that once a reasonable effort to repay has been made, demands for repayment according to strict contractual terms may be legal but not morally defensible. This is a risk that must be properly factored into investment decisions. Similarly, governments and ruling elites in Argentina must be cognizant that theirs is a profoundly unjust society and that priority in matters of debt must be given to human development rather than blind adherence to what the bishops call "the tyranny of the markets."

CONCLUSION

The Argentine debt crisis of 2001–2002 was a traumatic experience for creditors and debtors alike, yet its outcome gives us much to reflect upon in considering the changing norms pertinent to international debts. How much of this change in norms can be traced to Church activism is highly debatable, and some may argue that there is no connection at all. I believe, however, that the way in which this terrible Argentine debt crisis was worked out illustrates large and positive changes in the institutional management of debt crises in Latin America, certainly by comparison to the 1980s.

Civil society, of which the Church is a part, has a clear role to play in demanding that debt service not take precedence over human development once reasonable efforts have been expended to pay the debt. Governments in Latin America must take the demands of civil society into account. Gone are the days when great matters of economic policy are discussed behind closed doors between governments, representatives of multilateral institutions, and small, secretive groups of creditors. Messy as it was, the Argentine debt restructuring was conducted in full public view with both creditor and debtor viewpoints thrashed out in the court of public opinion and on the basis of a shared understanding of Argentina's debt obligations, its payments capacity, and its social conditions.

The most important change in international debt negotiations probably came within the universe of creditors themselves. In one respect, the world has become more used to emerging-market financing crises, and creditors are better able to distinguish a crisis in Argentina from a more general crisis affecting all other borrowers. Creditors are also much better informed than they used to be about economic and financial conditions in emerging-market countries. Moreover, when they have made a mistake in terms of their decision to extend credit, as they and their advisors certainly did in the case of Argentina, the market affords more flexibility to them to take their losses and to move on. Most important, creditors have developed a much better understanding of social and economic conditions in debtor countries, which effectively place limits required by social justice on the capacity of a government to continue making payments on debt obligations past a certain point.

Paradoxically, the final outcome of the Argentine crisis was not to spread the risk of moral hazard more broadly through the global capital markets. On the contrary, interest rates on lending to other emerging-market borrowers have declined to near historic lows since 2002, which means that investors are not fearful of a wave of future defaults along the lines of Argentina. It might be too much to conclude that the markets have learned to take a default by a major borrower in stride, but something like that appears to have happened in Argentina.

Looking to the future, it does not require much of a crystal ball to forecast that other financial crises will erupt in Latin America and elsewhere as foolish credit decisions combine with bad policy choices by emerging-market governments to result in debt-servicing difficulties. The outcome of the Argentine crisis may be showing us that these crises can be handled with a greater degree of pragmatism rooted in shared concerns for social justice

Thomas J. Trebat

than had been possible in the past. For that, the moral framework of the Catholic Church on matters of international debt may deserve some of the credit.

NOTES

[1] World Bank, "Argentina—Crisis and Poverty 2003: A Poverty Assessment," Report 26127-Ar, July 24, 2003, p. 1; available at wblno018.worldbank.org/lac/lacinfoclient.nsf/d29684951174975 c85256735007fef12/3d29a0ed02294a8b85256db10058dbdd/$FILE/ArgentinaPAMainReport.pdf. Note that most of the reduction in poverty after 1990 was probably due to the reduction of inflation rather than to specific social policies. The steady rise in poverty after 1994 occurred as the economy struggled in the aftermath of the financial crisis in Mexico in 1994–95.

[2] World Bank, "Argentina at a Glance," August 12, 2006; available at devdata.worldbank.org/AAG/arg_aag.pdf.

[3] Michael Mussa, *Argentina and the Fund: From Triumph to Tragedy* (Washington, D.C.: Institute for International Economics, 2002), p. 2.

[4] World Bank, "Argentina—Crisis and Poverty 2003," p. 1.

[5] See, e.g., International Monetary Fund, *Report on the Evaluation of the Role of the IMF in Argentina, 1991–2001* (Washington, D.C.: International Monetary Fund, 2004); available at www.imf.org/External/NP/ieo/2004/arg/eng/index.htm; and Michael Cohen and Margarita Gutman, eds., *Argentina in Collapse? The Americas Debate* (New York: The New School, 2002).

[6] Jeffrey Klaiber, *The Church, Dictatorships, and Democracy in Latin America* (New York: Orbis Books, 1998).

[7] Fabio Ladetto, "Ante un Estado desertor, el primer sustituto social es la prensa," *etcétera* (April 2002); available at www.etcetera.com.mx/pag64ne18.asp. The cited article refers to a survey done by the Centro de Estudios para la Nueva Mayoria in Argentina in April 2001. The survey purported to show that the Church was the most favorably viewed institution in Argentina, followed by the press.

[8] One of the earliest publications is Consejo Episcopal Latinoamericano, *La Brecha Entre Ricos y Pobres en América Latina* (Bogotá: CELAM, 1985).

[9] Ibid., pp. 96–99.

[10] Some of the leading members of CELAM included its president in the 1990s, Cardinal Oscar Andres Rodriguez Maradiaga of Tegucigalpa, who was assisted by representatives of the Chilean Church. The publication referred to is the Vatican document entitled "At the Service of the Human Community: Ethical Dimensions of International Debt" (Pontifical Commission, Justitia et Pax, 1986); available at www.jesuit.ie/ijnd/iustitia%20et%20pax.html.

[11] See these 1980s-era publications of the U.S. Conference of Catholic Bishops: "Economic Justice for All" (on the U.S. economy) (Washington, D.C.: USCCB, 1986), and "Relieving Third World Debt" (Washington, D.C.: USCCB, 1989).

[12] USCCB, "Relieving Third World Debt," p. 2.

[13] For background on Catholic social thinking on debt, the following documents are usually cited: Pope John Paul II, "Tertio Millennio Adveniente" (The Vatican, 1994); "Sollicitudo Rei Socialis" (1987); "At the Service of the Human Community: Ethical Dimensions of International Debt" (1986); USCCB, "Relieving Third World Debt" (1989); and "Economic Justice for All" (1986).

[14] USCCB, "Relieving Third World Debt," p. 22.

[15] Ibid., p. 24. "The moral categories go beyond the attitudes that should prevail between debtors and creditors; they examine the justice of the relationship itself as well as the fairness of the mechanisms through which debt is incurred and is to be repaid."

[16] This was a particularly germane point in the 1980s, as various Church leaders addressed the debt issue. They had in mind that the extraordinary rise in U.S. interest rates had resulted in a situation in which countries had already paid much more in debt service than could reasonably have been predicted at the outset of the contract.

[17] USCCB, "Relieving Third World Debt," p. 29.

[18] Ibid., p. 28.

[19] This co-responsibility theme is laid out most explicitly in the basic Vatican document "At the Service of the Human Community."

[20] In contrast to the situation in the 1980s, the case of Argentina in 2001 less overtly involved a role for wealthy countries, except as creditors through the IMF. This was because the possibility

of nonpayment by Argentina did not create the same systemic risk to the global banking system that was posed by the 1980s crises.

21 USCCB, "Relieving Third World Debt," p. 32.

22 This call for reform of the major institutions of the global economy dealing with trade, aid, finance, and investment was a feature of the U.S. bishops' pastoral on the U.S. economy, "Economic Justice for All."

23 Ibid., p. 39.

24 For example, one could usefully compare William Cline, *International Debt Reexamined* (Washington, D.C.: Institute for International Economics, 1995), with the lessons drawn from the crises during the era of bond financing in the more recent work of Nouriel Roubini and Brad Setser, *Bailouts or Bail-Ins? Responding to Financial Crises in Emerging Economies* (Washington, D.C.: Institute for International Economics, 2004).

25 Roubini and Setser, *Bailouts or Bail-Ins?*, p. 14.

26 A useful source for more information would be Guillermo Perry and Luis Serven, *Argentina: What Went Wrong?* (Washington, D.C.: World Bank, 2003).

27 The Fund's flexibility in the case of Argentina was certainly heightened by the political support for Argentina from the leaders of the G-7, particularly President Bush, but also Prime Minister Blair and Chancellor Schröder of Germany. Argentina had cultivated friends in high places and knew how to tap into their support. Michael Mussa, a former senior official with the IMF, was later bitterly critical of the decision to extend financing in summer 2001, considering that by that time "prospects for a favorable outcome were pure fantasy." Mussa, *Argentina and the Fund*, p. 45.

28 Competitiveness was being gradually restored via a painful deflation of prices in the period preceding the crisis in 2001. Much of the overvaluation had occurred in the early 1990s from the lagged effects of inertial inflation after the exchange rate was fixed in 1991.

29 Privatization inflows had masked this vulnerability in the 1990s, but these inflows dissipated after privatization was essentially completed in the late 1990s.

30 The poor fiscal performance is stressed in Mussa, *Argentina and the Fund*, in his analysis of what went wrong in Argentina.

31 Consulate of Argentina in the United Kingdom, *Argentina Economic Overview 2004* (London: Consulate of Argentina, 2004); available at www.consuargensh.com/ArgentinaEconomic Overview200505NO37.pdf.

32 Argentina Bondholders Committee, *Restructuring Guidelines,* December 3, 2003, p. 11; available at www.emta.org/ndevelop/ABC_Final_Restructuring_Guidelines_12-3-03.pdf.

33 Conferencia Episcopal Argentina (hereafter CEA), "Necesidades Extremas y Violencia," May 30, 1989; available at www.cea.org.ar/06-voz/documencea/1989-7Necesidades.htm. In an early document, entitled "Iglesia y Comunidad Nacional" (1981), the bishops argued that all of the ills that affected Argentina were of a moral order, setting out a vision of Argentine society that included corruption in almost all facets of its life.

34 CEA, "Reflexiones sobre la Justicia," April 26, 1997; available at www.cea.org.ar/06-voz/documencea/1997-Justicia.htm. Earlier documents echo this theme of generalized corruption, lack of independence of the judiciary, laws that are not enforced, and growing poverty.

35 Ibid. Emphasis added.

36 See Archbishop Osvaldo Musto, as quoted in "Karlic denunció corrupción política y llamó a luchar contra la pobreza," *El Cronista*, November 7, 2000.

37 Ibid.

38 Ibid.

39 Los Obispos de la República Argentina, "Hoy la Patria requiere algo inédito," May 12, 2001; available at www.aica.org/aica/documentos_files/CEA/Asambleas_Plenarias/81a_Asamblea_Plenaria/Hoy_la_Patria.htm.

40 CEA, "Queremos ser Nacion," August 10, 2001; available at www.cea.org.ar/06-voz/documencea/queremos_ser_nacion.htm.

41 Chris Herlinger, "Churches on Argentina's Fiscal Crisis: 'It's a Mess,'" Religion News Service, January 16, 2002; available at www.pcusa.org/pcnews/oldnews/2002/02023.htm.

42 CEA, "Carta al Pueblo de Dios," November 17, 2001; available at www.cea.org.ar/06-voz/documencea/carta_al_pueblo_de_dios.htm.

43 CEA, "Reconstruir la Patria," January 8, 2002; available at www.cea.org.ar/06-voz/documencea/reconstruir_la_patria.htm.

44 Ibid.

45 As quoted in Agencia Mexicana de Noticias, February 12, 2002.

Thomas J. Trebat

[46] CEA, "Para que Renazca el Pais," March 31, 2002; available at www.cea.org.ar/06-voz/documencea/para__que__renazca__el__pais.htm.

[47] Conferencia Episcopal Española, "Argentina nos duele," January 31, 2002. Much of the diplomatic work was arranged by Bishop Estanislao Karlic of Paraná, the president of the CEA.

[48] Conferencia Episcopal Argentina, "La Nacion que queremos," September 28, 2002.

[49] Comisión Permanente de la Conferencia Episcopal Argentina, "Recrear la voluntad de ser Nación," March 14, 2003; available at www.aica.org/aica/documentos_files/CEA/Comision%20Permanente/2003_03_14_Recrear.htm.

[50] CEA, "Para profundizar la pastoral social," November 11, 2004; available at www.cea.org.ar/06-voz/documencea/2004-ParaProfundizarLaPastoralSocial.htm.

[51] "La Iglesia respaldó al Gobierno en su postura frente a la deuda," Infobae, October 8, 2004.

[52] Remarks by Secretary of Finance Guillermo Nielsen at a meeting of the Emerging Markets Traders Association, December 4, 2003.

[53] For background, see Roubini and Setser, *Bailouts or Bail-Ins?*, p. 291.

Achieving Democracy

*Thomas Pogge**

D emocracy means that political power is authorized and controlled by the people over whom it is exercised, and this in such a way as to give these persons roughly equal political influence. Democracy involves voting—on political issues or on candidates for political offices—in accordance with the general idea of one person, one vote. But genuine democracy involves a lot more besides.

Elections must feature alternatives that give voters a genuine choice. People must have a way of influencing the agenda (political issues and options) or the list of candidates. Voters must be shielded from pressure and retaliation by government officials and private citizens alike; they must, more generally, be safe from extreme economic need and from arbitrary physical violence and psychological duress, any of which might make them excessively dependent on others. Voters must be free to assemble and discuss, and free also to inform themselves, which presupposes freedom of the press and of the other mass media. Political power must be exercised pursuant to standing, public rules that ensure that the consequences of electoral results on political decisions can be assessed and at least roughly predicted by voters. Last but not least, democracy requires certain dispositions and conduct on the part of citizens: a readiness to accept majority decisions and a commitment to exercise their responsibilities as voters by informing themselves about candidates and political issues and by going to the polls.[1]

A democratic regime might take many institutional forms consistent with these core requirements. Such regimes, present or historical, fall short

* This essay is based on a lecture given in honor of my friend Otfried Höffe on the occasion of his honorary doctorate from the Pontifícia Universidade Católica in Porto Allegre, Brazil. For important comments, which I have tried to accommodate in this written version, I thank my respondent Wilson Mendonça as well as Alvaro de Vita, Sônia Filipe, Otfried Höffe, Thomas Kesselring, and Alessandro Pinzani. I also gratefully acknowledge support through a grant from the Research and Writing Initiative of the Program on Global Security and Sustainability of the John D. and Catherine T. MacArthur Foundation.

of being fully democratic in some respects—democracy is a scalar predicate, as political regimes can be more or less democratic in multiple dimensions. A rough and vague distinction can nonetheless be drawn between broadly democratic regimes and the rest, which I will blandly label "authoritarian."

Many countries have become democratic, or more democratic, in recent years. Most of these new democracies seem weak and fragile, and the trend may not last. Still, the phenomenon has been remarkable enough to spawn a burgeoning literature—composed mostly in the rich and well-established democracies—offering political analysis and advice to newly democratic regimes.[2] My essay fits this "transition-to-democracy" genre.

The analysis pays far more attention than is common to the global context within which national democratic regimes succeed or fail, and the advice I offer fledgling democracies consequently has a strong foreign-policy component. In the former respect, my essay is continuous with another body of work that argues that the global order maintained by the rich democracies and their foreign policies is a significant contributor to the lack of democracy elsewhere.[3] I am sympathetic to such work in that I share its goal of global institutional reform toward achieving a more democratic *global* regime.[4] Still, this essay is not focused on the critique or reform of the rich democracies or of the global order they impose. Rather, its focus is on what the political leaders of a fledgling democracy can and should do—*other than* repeating justified yet ineffective demands upon the rich democracies. Though I will, for dramatic effect, use "we" and "us" in reference to such political leaders of a fledgling democracy, I am in fact a German citizen living in Manhattan. If this essay is worth reading nonetheless, it is because of how its analysis and advice differ from the mainstream.

THE STRUCTURE OF THE PROBLEM FACED BY FLEDGLING DEMOCRACIES

Let us imagine ourselves in a typical transition-to-democracy scenario. We are associated with a fledgling democratic government newly installed or restored after a period of undemocratic and repressive rule. We must work to establish the essentials of democratic government, of course, including civil and political rights and the rule of law; but we must also come to terms with the enemies of democracy and in particular with the former authoritarian

Thomas Pogge

rulers and their supporters. The transition-to-democracy literature focuses on these two tasks and, often, on more specific questions about how a fledgling democracy ought to cope with the legacy of an authoritarian past: To what extent should we recognize as valid economic transactions and administrative policies executed under the laws of the authoritarian predecessor regime? To what extent should we expose and punish the crimes of former rulers and their supporters? And what measures should we take to compensate surviving victims of the preceding regime, to recognize their suffering and to restore their dignity?[5]

These questions are about coping with the past, and backward-looking considerations bear on them—for instance, considerations concerning compensatory and retributive justice. And yet, intelligent answers to these questions must also take the future into account. Of the many future-oriented considerations that may come into play, let us concentrate on the most weighty: those that concern the impact of *our* conduct—that of the new democratic government—on the prospects for democracy. These specific considerations may be grouped under three distinct headings.

The first and most obvious set of such considerations concerns the immediate resistance or support generated by particular policies we might pursue. Prominent here are dangers that may emanate from remnants of the authoritarian predecessor regime. These dangers may be negligible when this prior regime is thoroughly destroyed and discredited, as in the cases of Nazi Germany, South Africa, and some of the communist regimes in Eastern Europe. But these dangers have been quite serious in other cases, as when military juntas have turned over power to civilians and returned to their barracks, notably in Latin America and also recently in Nigeria. In such situations, any attempt to expose and punish abuses that officers committed during the period of military rule is fraught with the danger of provoking elements of the military to rebel and even to seize power once again. Yet, on the other hand, we also may face resistance from the victims of the predecessor regime. They may be strongly opposed to leaving prior abuses unpunished, and their opposition, too, may endanger the new democratic order.

A second, somewhat less obvious set of future-oriented considerations concerns the incentive effects produced by our decisions if they are understood as inaugurating or continuing a standing practice. For example, by making no attempt to expose and punish the former authoritarian rulers, we may send a signal to potential predators that any future undemocratic acquisition and exercise of governmental power will run no serious risk of punishment. This signal may encourage, or insufficiently *discourage*, coup attempts and may thereby undermine the stability of our democratic government and future ones. Yet, on the other hand, by displaying a disposition to punish severely such former rulers who have ceded power without an all-out fight, we may encourage future authoritarian rulers to cling desperately to power by any means, including extreme ruthlessness and violence.[6] This second set of considerations is broader and more principled than the first. Attending to the effects of our conduct through the dispositions it displays, these considerations expand our perspective beyond the present democratic period to all other democratic periods into the indefinite future.

The third set of future-oriented considerations expands the perspective once again—in spatial rather than temporal dimensions. When predators assess the risks and rewards of their undemocratic acquisition or exercise of governmental power or weigh the costs and benefits of stepping down, they will be mindful not only of the (possibly quite sparse) evidence about how previous authoritarian rulers in their own country have fared. They are likely also to take account of the fate of authoritarian rulers in other, similarly situated, countries. The way we deal with our former repressive rulers will then also send a signal abroad and will therefore, by influencing the calculations of actual and potential authoritarian rulers there, affect the prospects for democracy in other countries. An example of this recently played out in South Korea, which has been criticized for treating its former military rulers too harshly. The critics protest that such severe treatment will make it harder to get other authoritarian rulers—those in Burma and Cambodia, for example—to step down.

Now one may think that a fledgling democratic government should focus exclusively on entrenching democracy at home and thus should pay no attention to how its decisions affect the prospects for democracy elsewhere. But there are two reasons for paying attention to the third set of future-oriented considerations. First, giving no weight to how our decisions affect the prospects for democracy elsewhere is myopic in that the prospects for democracy in our country are likely to be affected by whether other countries are democratic or not. Thus, the more Latin America is governed democratically, the more stable any one of its democracies is likely to be. Second, exclusive concentration on the aim of entrenching democracy at home is likely to be collectively self-defeating: *Each* fledgling democratic government is likely to be less successful with regard to this aim than it would be if *all* of these democratic governments also gave some weight to the entrenchment of democracy elsewhere.[7]

What bearing do these three sets of considerations have on the prospects for democracy? The distinctions among them may become clearer if we consider a more familiar small-scale context. How should you behave when you are blackmailed for ransom of a child by a kidnapper? The first set of considerations suggests that you should deal with the kidnapper so as to maximize the prospects for the safe return of your child. The second set of considerations suggests that you should also think about the signal that your conduct in this case sends to persons who may be ready to blackmail you similarly in the future: Your willingness to meet extravagant demands for the safe return of your child could make your children favorite kidnap targets. The third set of considerations suggests, in addition, that your conduct in this case may also affect the kidnap risk to which children other than your own are exposed: Your willingness to meet extravagant demands may attract more people to a career in the kidnapping business.

Its easy to see that the futu re-oriented considerations in the second and third sets are broader than those in the first: Actors who optimize locally, at each decision point, may not succeed in optimizing globally, over time. This is so because such actors influence how the world goes not merely through their conduct (which, we assume, is optimal), but also through their disposition to optimize, which, if known, may well encourage harmful or unhelpful conduct by others. Suppose some generals know that, if they seize and hold power by force and then lose it again sometime later, they will be dealt with in whatever way optimizes the prospects for democracy, and suppose they predict that our optimal response to this eventuality would then be to let them go unpunished. Our known disposition toward "local" democratic optimization would then *encourage* such generals to take power undemocratically, or would at least fail to *dis*courage them from doing so. (The same disposition may also encourage them to use their power, while they have it, to change the situation so as to make it less opportune for us to punish them later.) A disposition on our part flexibly to do what is best for democracy in our country may well then not be best for democracy in our country—just as your disposition always flexibly to do what is best for your children's safety may not be best for your children's safety.

Juxtaposing potential kidnappings and potential coups d'état does not merely help clarify questions of strategic rationality. It also highlights the importance of the second and third sets of considerations. That getting your children to stop screaming by giving them a piece of candy will tend to cause them to scream more often in order to receive more candy—this thought is almost too obvious for words. That meeting the demands of kidnappers and hijackers will tend to increase the incidence of kidnappings and hijackings—this point, too, is generally understood. But the thought that reconciliation with, and amnesty for, former authoritarian rulers will tend to encourage the undemocratic acquisition and repressive exercise of political power—this insight is often missed in more journalistic contributions to the transition-to-democracy literature.

While it is clear that we should pay attention to the second and third sets of considerations, it is much less clear how these considerations should affect our policies. The only straightforward case is that where the former authoritarian rulers have clung to power with violence and ruthlessness as long as they could and were thoroughly defeated. In cases of this sort, all considerations point toward severe punishment: The authoritarian rulers were, despite their best efforts, defeated, and thus pose no serious threat to the present democratic order (first set of considerations). They displayed behavior that should be severely discouraged for the future. And they displayed no behavior—such as stepping down gracefully—that we have reason to encourage. In such cases, we should aim at a quite severe punishment—while also spreading the word, perhaps, that this punishment would have been less severe if they had agreed to relinquish power without all the bloodshed.

In less straightforward cases, however, there are no easy answers. It all depends on how one estimates the various incentive effects and probabilities—and on whether and how one discounts the future and discounts transnational externalities. The resulting uncertainty is good news for many politicians who can defend whatever response they like as being driven by a

Thomas Pogge

sincere and sophisticated concern for the prospects of democracy. It is good news also for the pundits in academia and the media, who can go on rehearsing the old arguments without risk of ever being refuted. But it is bad news for the prospects of democracy: The more uncertain it is what a commitment to democracy demands, the less agreement there will be among those who, sincerely or not, profess such a commitment.

REDUCING THE EXPECTED REWARDS OF COUPS D'ÉTAT

My attempt to break new ground takes the just-developed framework of future-oriented considerations beyond issues of coping with the past. Our fledgling democratic government has some power to shape the incentives that in turn will influence conduct on which the future survival and stability of democratic institutions depend. So my general question is: Beyond coping well with the past, what *else* can a fledgling democratic government do to entrench democracy and, in particular, to discourage the undemocratic acquisition and exercise of power in the future?

My response focuses not so much on measures that make a coup d'état more difficult as on measures that render even a successful coup less lucrative. In some respects such measures are analogous to those employed by corporations to discourage hostile takeover bids. But there is an important difference between the two cases. Those who seek to take over a corporation can ordinarily do this only in accordance with its existing charter and bylaws, which they can change only *after* a successful takeover. Those who seek to take over a country, by contrast, can do so by force and, if successful, can then undo many of the measures we may have put in place in order to discourage their takeover.

This significant distinction between the two sorts of takeovers may seem to suggest that there is no interesting parallel at all. But I don't think that this is so. The reason why those who want to take over a corporation must abide by its present rules is that these rules are backed by the coercive apparatus of a more comprehensive social system. If gangsters succeed in seizing control of Microsoft headquarters, Bill Gates can simply call the police and have them evicted. In fact, the police are known to be preauthorized and disposed to do this, which in turn discourages gangsters from making any such attempt in the first place. Measures to deter takeovers must then involve some mechanism that survives a successful takeover and continues to reduce the payoff that the predators reap from their success.

Modeled on my Microsoft example, the simplest way of transferring this deterrence idea to the case of countries is to create some international analogue to the police, which a fledgling democratic regime could preauthorize to intervene in the event that it is overthrown by a predator. Unsurprisingly, leading American political scientists have volunteered the United States for this noble role. They have proposed treaties through which small countries—notably those in the Caribbean—would preauthorize military interventions against themselves in the event that a future government significantly violates democratic principles (Tom Farer) or human rights (Stanley Hoffmann).[8] The point of such treaty preauthorizations would be to facilitate outside interventions in defense of democracy and thereby to deter coup attempts, thus making less frequent the occasions that trigger the preauthorization. Preauthorizing a military intervention against one's own country is then akin to the business world's poison pills and golden parachutes in this respect: Their point is that predators should be less likely to strike as the expected payoff associated with victory is reduced.

The proposals by Farer and Hoffmann are not likely to be widely adopted. The main reason is that many democrats in the developing countries, and in Latin America especially, are suspicious of U.S. foreign policy and U.S. military interventions, which historically have often supported the enemies of democracy rather than its friends. It is unlikely then that fledgling democratic governments would find the United States a sufficiently reliable guarantor of their democratic institutions or would be able to convince their peoples of the wisdom of preauthorizing U.S. military interventions. Still, preauthorized military interventions by the UN or under the auspices of regional bodies like the Organization of American States (OAS) may be a different matter, especially if the preauthorizing government itself had significant influence on specifying the conditions under which the authority to intervene would become effective and on composing the agency that would decide whether these conditions were met.

Thomas Pogge

UNDERMINING THE BORROWING PRIVILEGE OF AUTHORITARIAN PREDATORS

There are other, better ways of affecting the dispositions of foreign states that would without violence reduce the rewards of, and thereby tend to discourage, an undemocratic takeover. One such measure is a constitutional amendment requiring that debts incurred by future unconstitutional governments—by rulers who will acquire or exercise power in violation of our democratic constitution—must not be serviced at public expense. The idea behind this amendment is that successful predators will be able to borrow less, and this at higher interest rates. If it were able to achieve this purpose, the amendment would stabilize our fledgling democratic regime by reducing the payoff associated with a successful coup d'état and thereby weakening the incentives for attempting such a coup in the first place.

Now it is true that predators can, after a successful coup, simply declare the amendment suspended—or the whole constitution, for that matter. However, should they eventually lose power, the successor government can nonetheless refuse repayment of its debts on the grounds that the coup was illegal, that the constitution was never rightfully suspended, and that creditors had fair notice that the people of our country were not assuming responsibility for any debts incurred by their authoritarian rulers.

Could our constitutional amendment enable such a successor government to fend off demands by foreign creditors that it service the debts incurred by its unconstitutional predecessor? To be sure, governments of the rich democracies—with the help of international financial institutions they control—have often supported their banks by bringing severe pressure to bear on fledgling democratic governments to repay the debts of their authoritarian predecessors. But if the constitutional amendment were in place, governments of the rich democracies would find it far more embarrassing to give such support to their banks, which would therefore no longer be able to count on such help from their governments.

Imagine the following scenario. Phase One: The Brazilian people, through their elected representatives, ask foreign banks not to lend money to future unconstitutional rulers of themselves and also constitutionally bind any future government of theirs not to repay such debts. Phase Two: A military junta takes power in Brazil by force, suspends the constitution, and receives large loans from Citibank. Phase Three: Brazil's constitution is restored, and the new democratic government refuses to service the debts to Citibank. Citibank complains to the U.S. government. Would the United States, under such circumstances, exert pressure on the new Brazilian government to assume responsibility for the junta's debt, threatening, for example, to shut Brazil out of the international financial system?

Serious public-relations problems, both at home and abroad, could arise from exerting such pressure, and governments of the rich democracies may therefore find it prudent to refrain. It could not be taken for granted, at least, that they would intercede on behalf of their banks. By creating uncertainty about the outcome in Phase Three, our constitutional amendment would thus increase the risks associated with lending to authoritarian predators in Phase Two. In light of these greater risks, banks in Phase Two would make less money available to our unconstitutional successors, and this on less favorable terms. This foreseeable fact of reduced access to credit, in turn, would weaken the incentives of potential authoritarian predators in Phase One to attempt a coup in the first place. The proposed constitutional amendment thus stabilizes our democratic regime by reducing the expected rewards of overthrowing it.

The key idea of the proposed constitutional amendment is that it should reduce the ability of any future authoritarian governments—but not that of democratic governments—to borrow abroad. Three important problems must be solved in order to achieve these intended asymmetric effects.

THE CRITERIAL PROBLEM

While the loss of constitutionally democratic government is quite obvious in some cases (for example, when there is a military coup), other cases are more doubtful and thus subject to controversies, real or contrived. Such more difficult cases may, for instance, involve allegations that some government has engaged in massive electoral fraud, has unreasonably postponed elections, has placed excessive limits on opposition activities, or has greatly exceeded its constitutional powers in other ways. Such allegations can be presented to the domestic judiciary, of course, for internal resolution. But the opponents of the government may allege that this domestic judiciary has lost its integrity and independence, that deciding judges have been corrupted, intimidated, dismissed, or killed by the government or its supporters. The prospect of such hard cases, in which it is doubtful or controversial whether a particular government does or does not count as legitimate under our constitutional amendment, disturbs its intended asymmetric effects. Banks will be reluctant to lend to *any* government of a country that adopts the proposed amendment because they will worry that repayment may be—reasonably or unreasonably—refused in the future on the ground that the government receiving the loan was not legitimate under the terms of the amendment.

To avoid such ambiguities and doubts, a fledgling democracy should officially, preferably within the text of the amendment itself, empower some external agency to settle such controversies quickly and authoritatively in the manner of a court. This agency should not be another government, or group of governments, as such judgments by governments would often be, and even more often be suspected or accused of being, influenced by self-serving political concerns or by political pressures and incentives.[9] More suitable would be an international panel, composed of reputable, independent jurists living abroad who understand our constitution and political system well enough to judge whether some particular group's acquisition and exercise of political power is or is not constitutionally legitimate.

If several fledgling democracies pass variants of the proposed constitutional amendment, they can initiate the creation of a standing Democracy Panel under the auspices of the United Nations. This panel should have at its disposal sufficient personnel to monitor elections and other pertinent developments in the participating countries in order to be able to decide quickly whether any of them is governed in violation of the constitutional rules it had democratically imposed upon itself. The prospect of quick and authoritative decisions of this kind would strengthen the amendment's deterrent effect on potential authoritarian predators and their potential lenders. Yet the panel's existence would also safeguard the ability of democratic governments to borrow abroad, as each participating country assumes full responsibility for debts incurred by any of its governments in power that has not been declared unconstitutional by the Democracy Panel.

As its name suggests, the Democracy Panel should only monitor countries with broadly democratic constitutions. It should not, for instance, support the entrenchment of authoritarianism by agreeing to monitor a constitutional amendment that forbids governments to repay the loans of future governments that rule in violation of an existing *un*democratic constitution. The Democracy Panel requires then not merely diverse *specific* criteria for the constitutional legitimacy of governments of the various countries it agrees to monitor, but must also have one *general* criterion for deciding whether a country that is, or requests to be, monitored (still) has a *broadly democratic* constitution.

This single general criterion can be formulated by the governments setting up the Democracy Panel. Its application, however, should be left entirely to the jurists on the panel. By assigning to themselves the task of judging one another's democratic credentials, the governments of participating countries would expose themselves to severe political pressures (as when a superpower is eager to have a "friendly" client regime officially recognized as "broadly democratic"), as well as to suspicions and accusations of having been influenced by inappropriate political motives and pressures. Of course, participating governments may find it necessary to modify the general criterion later on, and so should agree from the start on a procedure for revising it. However, they should also agree to a significant time lag between the adoption of a revision and its entering into force. Under no circumstances should a revision be applied retroactively to a case that was pending at the time of its adoption.

There is much to be said about how the general criterion for a broadly democratic constitution should be formulated. I can here only add two points to my opening paragraphs: First, the word "constitution" must be understood as including more than the canonical constitutional text, which may be beautifully democratic and yet widely ignored in practice. The general criterion therefore must be sensitive to whether the written constitution really governs the conduct of all branches of government and how particular constitutional provisions are actually interpreted and applied. The general criterion should guide the Democracy Panel to focus on what basic rules are actually operative in the society under examination. Second, one may ask whether a country's constitution should count as

Thomas Pogge

broadly democratic if essential parts of it are protected from democratic amendment. Here I am inclined to think that the answer should depend on how restrictive the relevant constitutional provisions are. If they merely entrench a broad commitment to democracy (as is the case with the "untouchable" Articles 1 and 20 of the German *Grundgesetz*), then these provisions should not disqualify a constitution from being counted as "broadly democratic."

It is possible for a broadly democratic constitution to be—through a sequence of constitutionally legitimate alterations—subverted into an authoritarian one. If this happens, the Democracy Panel should resign its authority at the point when the constitution in question ceases to be broadly democratic. It should not allow itself to be lured into the service of a (however popular) constitutional authoritarianism. It is also possible, of course, that a constitutionally democratic country that had adopted a version of the proposed amendment later repeals it democratically. In this case, the Democracy Panel should accept that its authorization to judge the constitutional credentials of the country's governments has been withdrawn and should cease its monitoring of the country in question. Finally, the Democracy Panel should also be instructed to allow for the possibility that a regime, although it came to power in violation of a constitution that includes the proposed amendment, may later legitimate itself through a new broadly democratic constitution. If this new constitution has wide popular support, the Democracy Panel should accept it as having superseded the old constitution.

A Democracy Panel of the kind I have sketched would not be expensive to run. Even a single small and poor country could afford to put such a panel together by finding some distinguished international lawyers willing to serve—though it is to be hoped, of course, that additional and unconditional financial support would be offered by the UN, by some more affluent democratic states, and by some governmental and nongovernmental international organizations. If constituted and instructed in accordance with the ideas sketched above, the Democracy Panel would significantly reinforce the intended asymmetrical effects of the proposed constitutional amendment.

THE TIT-FOR-TAT PROBLEM

In countries where democracy is fragile, there is a possibility that authoritarianism will reemerge despite passage of the proposed constitutional amendment. If this were to happen, the new authoritarian government might well find it prudent to refuse to service the debts incurred by its democratic predecessors. Unable to borrow in the name of the whole country anyway, it has little to lose by such a refusal and may also be in special need of preserving the more limited funds at its disposal.

Anticipating that possible authoritarian successors of ours may well refuse to service the debts we incur, foreign banks will be more reluctant to lend to us as well. By adopting the proposed constitutional amendment, our fledgling democratic government is thus liable to undermine its own ability to borrow abroad along with the ability of its potential authoritarian successors. The amendment may therefore render our fledgling democratic government less stable than it would be if we continued the going practice under which a country's democratic and authoritarian governments assume responsibility for each other's debts. In the end, *all* Brazilian governments, authoritarian or democratic, could be hurt by the amendment—contrary, once again, to its intended asymmetric effects.

This difficulty could be neutralized through an International Democratic Loan Guarantee Fund ("Democracy Fund" for short), which temporarily services the debts of countries with broadly democratic constitutions, as recognized by the Democracy Panel, in the event (and *only* in the event) that unconstitutional rulers of such countries refuse to do so. The existence of the Democracy Fund does not alter the fact that authoritarian rulers—no matter how illegal and illegitimate their acquisition and exercise of political power may be domestically—are obligated under international law to service their country's public debts abroad and should be sanctioned if they fail to do so. The sole point of the Democracy Fund is to neutralize precisely the risk that the constitutional amendment under discussion might otherwise add to the ordinary risks of lending money to countries with fledgling democratic governments.

To be fully credible, the Democracy Fund must have the ability to mobilize sufficient funds to service the debts incurred by fledgling democratic

Thomas Pogge

governments in the event of their unconstitutional overthrow. To achieve such full credibility, it is desirable that the Democracy Fund be backed jointly by many democratic societies, including rich and stable ones that have not adopted and see no need to adopt the proposed constitutional amendment. It is true that the enduringly stable democracies will then contribute to an arrangement from which they will probably never profit directly. This financial contribution by these (mostly wealthy) democracies would however be well justified in view of the resulting global gain for democratization, which would be associated with a reduction in wars, civil wars, and human rights problems and hence with a reduced need for the absorption of refugees and other humanitarian initiatives.

Moreover, the financial contributions required to sustain the Democracy Fund might well be quite small. This is so because the more financial backing democratic states give to this fund, the less it may actually have to spend. If the Democracy Fund is fully credible, then fledgling democracies can, by passing the amendment, discourage potential predators without weakening their own position (access to credit). A fully credible Democracy Fund may thus greatly reduce the number of successful coups d'état that might lead to claims against it. And there is another reason why the Democracy Fund may in the end prove quite cheap to run: The fund should be entitled to reclaim, once democracy returns, any money it expends on servicing the debts of a temporarily authoritarian country. This is important because the existence of the Democracy Fund should not create a moral hazard by giving democratic governments an incentive to orchestrate coups against themselves in order to ease their country's debt burden at the expense of other democratic states.

The Democracy Fund can thus safeguard the desired asymmetric incentive structure: The ability of any authoritarian government to borrow is diminished by the prospect that it will be displaced by a democratic successor forbidden to repay its debts; but the ability of any democratic government to borrow is not diminished by the risk that it will be displaced by an authoritarian successor.

When affluent democracies back the Democracy Fund, they do good by strengthening the credibility of this fund and hence the creditworthiness of fledgling democratic governments. They also do good by signaling their democratic loyalties to banks that might lend to authoritarian predators, thereby discouraging such loans and reinforcing the intended effect of our constitutional amendment. Affluent democracies could do even better in this latter respect—quite apart from whether or not they back the Democracy Fund—by publicly promising not to bring pressure to bear in behalf of any of their banks that choose to lend to our future authoritarian rulers. While pursuing the constitutional amendment, our fledgling democratic government should then also approach the governments of the rich democracies with the request that they publicly promise to respect our democratically promulgated amendment and publicly warn their banks that they will not consider our country liable for debts incurred by its future unconstitutional rulers.

THE ESTABLISHMENT PROBLEM

It is not likely that the governments of the most powerful states would readily agree to back the Democracy Fund, to respect our constitutional amendment, and to warn their banks. It is more likely, in fact, that some of these governments would even bring pressure to bear on us not to proceed with the amendment. In doing so, they may urge that it is important for the stability of the international financial system that lenders be able to rely on governments to repay the debts of their predecessors, irrespective of what they believe (or pretend to believe) about these predecessors' legitimacy.

On the level of argument, we can respond to such pressure by pointing out that our constitutional amendment will have no negative effects on the stability of the international financial system and on our own ability to borrow if the rich democracies help sustain the full credibility of the Democracy Fund. Even if this response fails to win their backing for the Democracy Fund, it highlights the nice point that it is *only on account of their refusal* that our amendment engenders instability. This point reduces the pressure rich democracies can bring to bear against our plan without risking losses in the arena of world public opinion.

The foreseeable refusal of various rich democracies to support our amendment and the Democracy Fund does not show the idea to be impractical. The capital facility needed for the Democracy Fund can be financed through contributions by democratic developing countries, by the more progressive developed democracies, by international organizations, and by contributions from banks and multinational corporations. Moreover, risks could be greatly reduced through reinsurance and through securitization (whereby private investors assume some of the risk in exchange for a fixed premium).

Obviously, the entire plan, Democracy Panel and Democracy Fund included, has a better chance of succeeding if it is pursued jointly by several democratic developing countries. If such cooperation turns out to be infeasible, it makes sense nonetheless for a single such country to pass the amendment, provided its present democratic government can cope with the expected reduction in its ability to borrow.[10] This unilateral step makes sense because it would build moral momentum. It would highlight inequities in the existing global economic order, where poor populations are held responsible for debts incurred by their thoroughly illegitimate rulers and are thus often forced, after having suffered an extended ordeal of brutal oppression, to pay—with interest—for the weapons that were used against them. It would highlight the ways in which this international practice contributes to the frequency of *un*democratic government in the developing countries and demonstrate that people in these countries are seeking to change that practice. A single developing country could get the ball rolling, might induce other developing countries to follow its example, might get a Democracy Panel organized, and might finally build sufficient support for the Democracy Fund.[11]

SUMMING UP

Let me briefly relate this discussion back to the three sets of future-oriented considerations distinguished in the first section. It is natural for a fledgling democratic government to be primarily concerned with its own survival, stability, and influence. Reasoning in terms of this first set of considerations alone, we may well find that we have no compelling reason to spend scarce political capital on an attempt to undermine the international borrowing privilege. Getting the constitutional amendment passed is likely to require considerable political effort that might instead be expended on other goals. And even if such effort were to succeed, the benefit of our amendment (discouraging potential authoritarian predators by reducing their expected access to foreign loans they could use for their own enrichment and the entrenchment of their rule) may be balanced by its drawback (reducing our own access to credit—the "tit-for-tat problem").

The case in favor of the amendment initiative becomes much stronger, however, once we bring in the second and third sets of considerations, thus broadening our concern beyond the prospects of *this* fledgling democratic government to the prospects of democratic institutions in the long run and in the developing world at large. Governments of the developing countries have, for the most part, been corrupt, authoritarian, and often brutal. In the wealthy countries, this problem is seen as the responsibility of the people in the developing world, often attributed to their lacking the courage to resist oppression or the cultural sophistication to distinguish between the might of their rulers and their right to rule. In truth, however, the *developed* countries are the chief upholders of the might-is-right principle. It is they who insist that the mere fact that someone holds effective power over us—regardless of how he came to power, of how he exercises power, and of the extent to which he is opposed by the people he rules—gives him the right to incur legally binding international obligations on our behalf.

Their imposition of this principle creates a strong and continuous headwind against democracy in the developing countries. By focusing attention on this principle and its pernicious effects, and by seeking the support of other countries and their citizens toward its repeal, we have a good chance to achieve a great and lasting advance for democracy in the developing world. Expending the political capital of a fledgling democratic government on this project may not be the individually optimal strategy for each, but it is very likely to be the collectively optimal strategy for all, especially if full weight is also given to the concern to secure democracy for future generations. To make enduring progress toward democracy, the democrats in the developing world must look beyond our diverse spatially and temporally limited stability problems and unite in the attack on the root causes of our vulnerability to oppressive government. To facilitate such unity, we should set an example here and now by working to pass the proposed constitutional amendment.

Thomas Pogge

UNDERMINING THE RESOURCE PRIVILEGE OF AUTHORITARIAN PREDATORS

There is another peaceful way of affecting the dispositions of other states that would reduce the rewards of, and thereby tend to deter, undemocratic takeovers. This is a constitutional amendment in which our country declares that only its constitutionally democratic governments may effect legally valid transfers of ownership rights in public property, and forbids any of its governments to recognize ownership rights in property acquired from a preceding government that lacked such constitutional legitimacy. Now, of course, once they have seized power, authoritarian rulers can hand over public property to anyone they like. But recipients of such property are, through the amendment, put on notice that their ownership rights will be contested once democracy returns. This will tend to reduce the revenue authoritarian rulers can raise through sales of public property, thus making it harder for them to enrich themselves and to entrench their rule. And this in turn will reduce the attractions of a coup attempt, thus tending to enhance the stability of our fledgling democratic regime.

In attempting to explain and support this proposal, let me first point out that the sale of public property really is an important causal contributor to the incidence of undemocratic government. It has been well known among economists for quite some time that there is a significant *negative* correlation between a developing country's resource endowment and its rate of economic growth. Offhand, this is surprising. One would think that being well endowed with natural resources is good for a country's economic growth prospects, putting at its disposal a stream of revenues that can be used for productivity-enhancing investments. It turns out, however, that the availability of such a revenue stream also has the effect of attracting predators, so that resource-rich countries are more likely to be victimized by coup attempts, civil wars, and authoritarian governments, all of which tend to reduce economic growth. The fact that the de facto rulers of resource-rich developing countries can sell these resources, or use them as loan collateral, provides strong incentives to seek power in such a country, by whatever means. And, since the officials of such countries have resources to sell and money to spend, it is also more lucrative to corrupt them than their resource-poor peers. For these reasons, ample resources become an obstacle to growth, because they foster coups, civil wars, oppression, and corruption.

The empirical connection I have just asserted has been documented in detail by two Yale economists, Ricky Lam and Leonard Wantchekon. The empirical part of their paper specifically supports the hypothesis that the causal connection between resource wealth and poor economic growth—the so-called Dutch Disease[12]—is mediated through reduced chances for democracy. The authors' cross-country regression analysis shows that "a one percentage increase in the size of the natural resource sector [relative to GDP] generates a decrease by half a percentage point in the probability of survival of democratic regimes. . . . In order to improve economic performance, one has to limit . . . elite discretion over the process of rent distribution."[13] The purpose of the second proposed amendment is precisely to restrict "elite discretion over the process of rent distribution"—at least insofar as such elites lack democratic legitimation.

Could this further proposal possibly work? The second proposed amendment might well have a salutary effect by reducing the price an authoritarian government could fetch for immovable domestic public property, such as government-owned land or buildings. In these cases there is a real danger that a successor government, recognizing its constitutional obligation, will deprive buyers of their possessions on the grounds that they had been acquired through what they should have known were invalid transactions. But how could the amendment succeed with regard to the much more important case of movable goods, such as natural resources, which can easily be exported?[14] Is there any chance that the second proposed amendment would induce foreign governments and legal systems not to recognize ownership rights conferred by any future authoritarian government?

At first blush, this does not seem likely. The rich democracies may not like a plan that diminishes the opportunities of their banks to make profitable loans to authoritarian governments of developing countries; but this change is for them no more than a minor irritant. The prospect of not being able to acquire ownership rights in natural resources controlled by such authoritarian governments is, by contrast, catastrophic. The economies of the rich democracies are heavily dependent on importing such resources and would be severely hurt if they could import only from democratically governed countries. Just imagine what would happen if the affluent countries had to meet their crude oil import needs through purchases solely from democratically governed countries! The price of crude oil would be much higher and more volatile, sharply reducing prosperity and economic growth in the developed world.

To make the problem more vivid, let me once again embed it in a concrete example. Suppose the current democratic government of Nigeria passes the second proposed constitutional amendment. A few years later, some generals take power once again (Nigeria has been ruled by unelected military officers for twenty-eight of the last thirty-four years). Would the governments and courts of the United States, Great Britain, and the Netherlands conclude that Shell can then no longer acquire ownership rights in crude oil through contracts with, and payments to, the new military rulers? And would these governments and courts allow a subsequent democratic government of Nigeria to sue Shell for the value of any Nigerian crude oil Shell "bought" from the military strongmen?

I confess that the answer to these questions is no. The second proposed amendment would not work this sort of miracle. And yet, it should be passed nonetheless. It should be passed, first and foremost, because it clarifies the moral situation. We live within a global economic order that is structured in accordance with the interests of the affluent high-consumption countries and coercively imposed by them.

An important feature of this order—highlighted by the second proposed amendment—is the international resource privilege: the privilege of any person or group exercising effective power within a country to confer internationally valid legal ownership rights in its natural resources. This general privilege is of great benefit to authoritarian rulers and a strong incentive to any predators aspiring to this role. More important for its persistence, however, is the fact that this privilege is also very much in the interest of the rich consumer societies: It guarantees them a reliable and steady supply of resources, because they can acquire internationally valid legal ownership rights in such resources from anyone who happens to exercise effective power in a foreign country—without regard to how this ruler acquired or exercises power, without regard to how he can be expected to spend the sales revenues, and without regard to how strongly his subjects may be opposed to him or to his sales. And this privilege also greatly reduces the price of such resources—because no supplier is excluded (for example, for lack of demo-cratic legitimation), and also because authoritarian rulers, produced and entrenched by the international resource and borrowing privileges, tend to maximize sales in the short term in order to serve their own personal inter-ests, whereas democratic supplier governments serving the needs of a coun-try's present and future people would be more inclined to budget its resources for maximum long-term benefit.[15]

The second proposed constitutional amendment would focus attention on these issues and could thus help change the attitudes of citizens in the more affluent countries toward the plight of the poorer populations. The now preva-lent attitude of condescending pity for peoples somehow unable to get their act together, allowing themselves to be ruled by autocrats who ruin their economies, may give way to a realization that the rich democracies have a causal and moral responsibility for the great difficulty poorer countries have in estab-lishing and maintaining stable democratic regimes. As more persons in the affluent societies recognize their involvement and responsibility, they may change their behavior as consumers, reducing their use of products that incor-porate resources purchased from authoritarian governments. Such shifts will not have much of an economic effect—natural resources are, for the most part, quite fungible. But they will have a political effect, making it increasingly diffi-cult for the governments of the rich democracies to collude with authoritarian rulers by enforcing ownership rights acquired from them and thereby recog-nizing these rulers' legal power to confer internationally valid legal ownership rights in their country's property.

The previous paragraph suggests why I have not chosen a narrower title for this essay, such as "Achieving Democracy in the Developing World." There is a serious democracy deficit also in the developed countries, whose citizens have not approved, and for the most part do not even understand, very important foreign policies and international practices that are conduct-ed and upheld in their name. To be sure, many of these citizens may find it convenient to be ignorant and aloof in this way and may endorse in a gener-al way the proposition that their government should conduct whatever for-eign policy is best for them. But democracy requires more than such gener-al endorsement. Democracy involves the fulfillment not only of important

Thomas Pogge

rights, but also of important responsibilities of citizens. To the extent that citizens abandon their responsibility to control the power that is exercised in their name, their country is less than fully democratic.

Most citizens of the developed countries are abandoning this responsibility insofar as they choose to understand very little about how the vast quantities of imported resources they consume are acquired and about the impact that the terms of such acquisitions have in the countries where these resources originate. A challenge to the international resource privilege would make these issues harder to avoid and thus would produce a gain for democracy in the developed world. And people in the developing countries would surely suffer less harm if people in the developed world paid more attention to their political responsibilities regarding foreign affairs: Even if the latter will be too selfish to agree to modify the international resource privilege, they will at least better understand how they are causally connected to poverty and oppression in the developing countries. They will better understand that they and their countries face here not merely opportunities for occasional charitable contributions, but a weighty duty to mitigate the severe harms to which their economic practices and policies are substantially contributing.

CONCLUSION

The currently popular topic of democratic transition covers some vexed issues that are extremely difficult to resolve in a general way. But it also covers some less complicated issues with respect to which considerable real progress could be made. Those who really care about democracy and economic progress in the developing countries might do well to focus, for now, on these less complicated issues and, in particular, on the formulation of measures that would reduce the economic payoffs from, and thus incentives toward, authoritarian rule. It is clear, I believe, that measures of the kind I have described could be devised, though doing so in full detail would surely require careful attention to more complexities than I could cope with here. The greatest obstacles we face are not intellectual but political, as authoritarian rulers and the developed consumer societies have a very powerful common interest in blocking reforms that would enhance the prospects for democracy in the developing countries—and throughout the world.

1 To complement this brief account, let me mention some important works on large-scale modern democracy: Charles Beitz, *Political Equality* (Princeton, NJ: Princeton University Press, 1989); Norberto Bobbio, *The Future of Democracy* (Minneapolis: University of Minnesota Press, 1984); Thomas Christiano, *The Rule of the Many: Fundamental Issues in Democratic Theory* (Boulder, CO: Westview Press, 1996); David Copp et al., eds., *The Idea of Democracy* (Cambridge: Cambridge University Press, 1993); Robert Dahl, *A Preface to Democratic Theory* (Chicago: University of Chicago Press, 1956); Robert Dahl, *Democracy and Its Critics* (New Haven, CT: Yale University Press, 1989); Jon Elster and Rune Slagstad, eds., *Constitutionalism and Democracy* (Cambridge, MA: Cambridge University Press, 1988); Jon Elster, ed., *Deliberative Democracy* (Cambridge, MA: Cambridge University Press, 1998); Lani Guinier, *The Tyranny of the Majority* (New York: The Free Press, 1994); Amy Gutmann and Dennis Thompson, *Democracy and Disagreement* (Cambridge: Harvard University Press, 1996); Jürgen Habermas, *Between Facts and Norms* (Cambridge: MIT Press, 1996); David Held, *Models of Democracy* (Stanford, CA: Stanford University Press, 1990); Claude Lefort, *Democracy and Political Theory* (Minneapolis: University of Minnesota Press, 1988); Bernard Manin, *Principles of Representative Government* (Cambridge: Cambridge University Press, 1997); John Rawls, *Political Liberalism* (New York: Columbia University Press, 1996 [1993]); Nancy Rosenblum, ed., *Obligations of Citizenship* (Princeton, NJ: Princeton University Press, 2000); Joseph Schumpeter, *Capitalism, Socialism, and Democracy* (New York: Harper, 1984 [1943]).

2 This literature is vast and still growing very rapidly. Here and in note 5, I can list only a few representative samples: Bruce Ackerman, *The Future of Liberal Revolution* (New Haven, CT: Yale University Press, 1992); Larry Diamond, *Developing Democracy: Toward Consolidation* (Baltimore: Johns Hopkins University Press, 1999); John H. Herz, ed., *From Dictatorship to Democracy* (Boulder, CO: Westview Press, 1982); Samuel Huntington, *The Third Wave: Democratization in the Late Twentieth Century* (Norman: University of Oklahoma Press, 1991); Juan J. Linz and Alfred Stepan, *Problems of Democratic Transition and Consolidation: Southern Europe, South America, and Post-Communist Europe* (Baltimore: Johns Hopkins University Press, 1996).

3 Some representative examples are Immanuel Wallerstein, *The Capitalist World-Economy* (Cambridge: Cambridge University Press, 1979), *The Politics of the World-Economy* (New York: Cambridge University Press, 1984), *After Liberalism* (New York: New Press, 1995), and *The Essential Wallerstein* (New York: New Press, 2000); Richard Falk, *The End of World Order* (New York: Holmes & Meier, 1983); Roberto Unger, *Democracy Realized: The Progressive Alternative* (London: Verso, 1998).

4 Regarding this goal, see Otfried Höffe, *Demokratie im Zeitalter der Globalisierung* (Munich: Beck Verlag, 1999).

5 Important instances of such work include David A. Crocker, "Reckoning with Past Wrongs: A Normative Framework," *Ethics & International Affairs* 13 (1999), pp. 43–64; Pablo de Greiff, "Trial and Punishment, Pardon and Oblivion: On Two Inadequate Policies for the Treatment of Former Human Rights Abusers," *Philosophy and Social Criticism* 12 (1996), pp. 93–111; Priscilla B. Hayner, *Unspeakable Truths: Confronting State Terror and Atrocity* (New York: Routledge, 2001); Carla Hesse and Robert Post, eds., *Human Rights in Political Transitions: Gettysburg to Bosnia* (New York: Zone Books, 1999); Neil J. Kritz, ed., *Transitional Justice: How Emerging Democracies Reckon with Former Regimes*, 3 vols. (Washington, D.C.: U.S. Institute of Peace Press, 1995); David Little, "A Different Kind of Justice: Dealing with Human Rights Violations in Transitional Societies," *Ethics & International Affairs* 13 (1999), pp. 65–80; Jaime Malamud-Goti, *Game Without End: State Terror and the Politics of Justice* (Norman: University of Oklahoma Press, 1996); Martha Minow, *Between Vengeance and Forgiveness* (Boston: Beacon Press, 1998); Carlos Nino, *Radical Evil on Trial* (New Haven, CT: Yale University Press, 1996); Robert Rotberg and Dennis Thompson, eds., *Truth v. Justice* (Princeton, NJ: Princeton University Press, 2000); Naomi Roht-Arriaza, *Impunity and Human Rights in International Law and Practice* (New York: Oxford University Press, 1995); Ruti G. Teitel, *Transitional Justice* (New York: Oxford University Press, 2000); Lawrence Weschler, *A Miracle, a Universe: Settling Accounts with Torturers* (New York: Pantheon, 1990).

6 See Derek Parfit, *Reasons and Persons* (Oxford: Oxford University Press, 1984), sec. 2.

7 Ibid., sec. 36.

8 Tom J. Farer, "The United States as Guarantor of Democracy in the Caribbean Basin: Is There a Legal Way?" *Human Rights Quarterly* 10 (1988) pp. 12, 157–76; Tom J. Farer, "A

Thomas Pogge

Paradigm of Legitimate Intervention," in Lori Fisler Damrosch, ed., *Enforcing Restraint: Collective Intervention in Internal Conflicts* (New York: Council on Foreign Relations Press, 1993), pp. 316–47; Stanley Hoffmann, "Delusions of World Order," *New York Review of Books* 39, no. 7 (1992), pp. 37–43; Stanley Hoffmann, *The Ethics and Politics of Humanitarian Intervention* (Notre Dame, IN: University of Notre Dame Press, 1996).

[9] When a democratically legitimate government has been unconstitutionally replaced by an authoritarian junta, for example, some governments may not want to judge the change unconstitutional because they view the new government as "friendlier" and perhaps even had a hand in bringing it to power. Other governments may come under pressure from more powerful states to refrain from such a judgment—pressure they find it hard to resist when doing so would adversely affect their own interests.

[10] One way to cope would be for this government to offer future resource exports as collateral for its debts. Potential authoritarian successors could then renege on these debts only by halting such resource exports altogether.

[11] As evidence that something like this can happen, consider the 1997 Convention on Combating Bribery of Foreign Officials in International Business Transactions, which ended a longstanding practice under which most developed states (though not the United States after 1977) permitted their companies to bribe foreign officials and even to deduct such bribes from their taxes. Public pressure, generated and amplified by Transparency International, played a vital role in building momentum for this convention, which thus sets a hopeful precedent. Still, one should not overlook the fact that while the suppression of bribery may well be in the collective self-interests of the developed states and their corporations, the Democracy Panel and the Democracy Fund are not.

[12] This name alludes to a period in Dutch history that began with the discovery of huge natural gas reserves in 1959 and, by the 1970s, produced revenues and import savings of about $5 to $6 billion annually. Despite this windfall (enhanced by the "oil-shock" increases in energy prices), the Dutch economy suffered stagnation, high unemployment, and finally recession—doing considerably worse than its peers throughout the 1970s and early 1980s.

[13] Ricky Lam and Leonard Wantchekon, "Dictatorships as a Political Dutch Disease" (Working Paper, Yale University, January 19, 1999), pp. 35–36. In a later paper, Wantchekon presents data to show that "a one percent increase in resource dependence as measured by the ratio of primary exports to GDP leads to nearly 8 percent increase in the probability of authoritarianism." Wantchekon, "Why Do Resource Dependent Countries Have Authoritarian Governments?" (Working Paper, Yale University, December 12, 1999), p. 2, available at www.yale.edu/ leitner/pdf/1999-11.pdf. For earlier work on the Dutch Disease, see Jeffrey D. Sachs and Andrew M. Warner, "Natural Resource Abundance and Economic Growth" (Development Discussion Paper No. 517a, October 1995), available at www.hiid.harvard.edu/pub/pdfs/517.pdf.

[14] The value of immovable public property abroad is rarely significant, and I will therefore ignore such property, which, in any case, poses problems very similar to those posed by movable goods.

[15] The developed countries also enjoy more lucrative business opportunities as a third dubious benefit: Authoritarian rulers, made more frequent by the international resource privilege, are more likely to send the proceeds from resource sales right back to the affluent countries, to pay for high-margin weaponry and military advisers, as well as for advanced luxury products, real estate, and financial investments.

The Due Diligence Model: A New Approach to the Problem of Odious Debts

*Jonathan Shafter**

Odious debt is sovereign debt incurred by a government lacking popular consent, utilized for no legitimate public purpose. This specific subset of sovereign debt is separate from such issues as unsustainable debts incurred by democratic or quasi-democratic developing countries, or debts incurred by nondemocratic regimes for legitimate public ends. This essay is concerned with the narrow problem of money borrowed by dictators from foreign creditors that is then either spent on illegitimate ends, such as repressing the country's population, or simply looted and deposited into the private offshore bank accounts of the ruling class. Many legal scholars advocate that international law grants successor regimes permission to repudiate inherited debts meeting the odious debt standard. Whether international law theoretically does or does not provide for such a remedy, however, the fact remains that for practical purposes successor governments to illegitimate regimes do not invoke the odious debt doctrine, out of fear that doing so would deprive them of necessary access to global credit markets.

Odious debt is a moral issue, as it is manifestly unfair to demand that a population repay what are basically the personal debts of its former captors—loans that were in many cases used to actually fund the machinery of public repression. But beyond purely ethical considerations, there are significant prudential reasons for the international community to reform the treatment of odious debts. Successor governments to fallen dictatorial regimes are often placed in the position of rebuilding a shattered nation with scarce resources. This scarcity is severely compounded when the meager

* I would like to thank Lee Buchheit, Michael Kremer, Seema Jayachandran, and Ko-Yung Tung for their assistance with this work.

resources of a successor government are diverted toward servicing the odious debts of the prior regime rather than invested in constructing a secure
and sustainable platform for national development. This is a problem of economic development, but it is also a problem of national security. Failed
states are increasingly recognized as posing significant threats to the security
of the global community through such vectors as destabilizing broad neighboring regions, hosting potentially hostile nonstate actors, and providing
breeding grounds for infectious diseases outside the reach of coordinated
medical intervention. It is in the security interest of the global community
to forestall state failure where possible and to facilitate the rebuilding of
failed states in an expedient manner. A properly designed policy on odious
debts can help to prevent state failure by limiting the spoils available to a
potential autocrat from looting the state—thus hopefully discouraging
some would-be state destabilizers at the margin—and it can also free
resources for the use of postauthoritarian governments. These additional
resources might in some cases make the difference between sustainable
democratic redevelopment or a relapse into chaotic autocratic state failure.

Most supporters of reforms in the area of odious debt believe that such
debt should be challenged in courts and other judicial-style fora. While this
would likely be preferable to the status quo, there are several reasons why
another type of reform model would yield superior results. The determination of whether a certain regime does or does not enjoy popular consent for
its actions is at least as much a political issue as a legal one, and thus the judiciary may be an inappropriate venue for implementing an odious debt
policy. Second, it is critical to secure as much *ex ante* certainty for potential
creditors to sovereign governments as possible; that is, creditors should be
highly confident in the legal enforceability of their rights before loans are
made. The importance of global capital flows to developing countries in today's globalized financial environment is significant, and any policy that
curtailed legitimate lending to sovereigns due to unnecessary *ex ante* uncertainty might cause more harm than good.

As an alternative to the traditional reform program, which will be referred to as the Classical Model, this essay proposes a Due Diligence Model
for the resolution of odious debts.[1] The Due Diligence Model requires that
a country be officially declared "odious debt–prone" in order for debts to

Jonathan Shafter

potentially fall within the scope of invalidity, and, crucially, only debts incurred after the declaration would be eligible.[2] This safeguard, and the anticipated rarity with which countries would be placed on such a list, ensures that the vast bulk of sovereign lending to developing countries would be securely outside the scope of any potential interference. Under the Due Diligence Model, lenders to countries declared odious debt–prone would be required to cite the specific legitimate ends that the funds are intended for and the due diligence monitoring plan that the lender intends to implement to ensure that the funds go toward these stated uses. A loan would only be invalidated if the funds were diverted toward illegitimate ends and the lender failed to make a good faith effort to comply with its own pre-approved due diligence plan. This policy structure is a promising way not only to achieve most of the objectives of odious debt reform in a manner which should be largely acceptable to creditor countries, global financial intermediaries, and sovereign debt investors.

REASONS TO RETHINK THE STATUS QUO

Can it truly be fair to demand responsibility of a population for debts that were incurred not only against its will but were in many cases used to fund the mechanisms of its prior torment? Debt incurred by a governing regime for personal benefit or nefarious purpose should be considered the private debt of the illegitimate regime and the country's citizens should not be held responsible for its repayment.[3] Individuals do not have to repay money that others fraudulently borrow in their names, in the same way that a corporation is not liable for contracts that the chief executive officer enters into without the authority to bind the firm. Basic logic and justice demand that a corresponding rule exist for sovereign borrowing. While this moral argument is a strong and sufficient case for reform on its own, there are additional rationales for a new policy approach toward odious debts that are directly rooted in the national interests of the developed world powers.

The Economic Rationale for Reform

A precondition to the proper functioning of financial markets is a stable body of legal rules governing the full investment cycle from initial due diligence through liquidation. Without a known and transparent playing field of legal governance, the risk premium for making any investment is too high to qualify as anything but speculative gambling.

In the aftermath of the 2003 invasion of Iraq, there were widespread calls across the political spectrum to eliminate what commentators openly declared Iraq's "odious debts."[4] For example, House Resolution 2482, introduced but not passed by the 108th Congress, with twenty-eight co-sponsors from both the Republican and Democratic parties, called for the cancellation of loans made to Iraq by the multinational financial organizations. The bill argued for the necessity of canceling debts incurred by dictators not only on grounds that such debts impede a successful rebuilding of post-authoritarian states, but also because those debts were never legitimate inheritances of the new government due to the doctrine of odious debts.

House Resolution 2482 should serve as a warning call to the international financial community that the status quo of traditional sovereign lending law could be radically reformed by legislative action with possible retroactive impact. While the resolution failed to pass, its existence with nontrivial bipartisan support should alert lenders that the prospect of future legislative reforms in this area are far from negligible. It is therefore in the interest of the international financial community to embrace the issue head-on and work to develop a fair body of prospective rules governing sovereign lending that address the issues raised by odious debt and cause minimal disruption of beneficial lending to developing nations. Purely prospective rules will not solve the problem of existing debts, but they will establish a stable framework to assure present investors in new loans that there is not a contingent danger to their capital in the form of future retroactive legislative actions.

Financial intermediaries and investors should consider that eventual odious debt reform is sufficiently likely and that any small loss of profits from a slightly curtailed scope of lending activities would be more than offset by the decreased risk that future reforms with possible retroactive effect could place a broader swath of investments made today in jeopardy. By way of analogy, in the past several years, increasing numbers of companies in the energy industry have recognized the economic merits of coming to a regulatory solution to the problem of carbon emissions sooner rather than later. The energy sector is highly capital-intensive and projects can have multi-decade timelines. These firms realize that eventual carbon emission regulation is a sufficiently likely scenario and that it is better for them if these rules are established now, when they can be incorporated into prospective planning. The benefits from delaying any regulation are outweighed by the potentially catastrophic financial impact if tomorrow's regulations eviscerate the value of large investments made today. Forward-looking capital market participants should take a similar attitude toward odious debt reforms.

The National Security Rationale for Reform
National security is rarely cited as a motivating factor behind campaigns to reform existing policies on odious debts. Yet changes in Western strategic doctrine in the post–Cold War era offer an opportunity for traditional civil society advocates of odious debt reform to forge an alliance with the national security community. This shift in doctrine concerns a renewed focus on failed states as a source of national security threats to the developed world.

In truth, the concept of a linkage between state failure and national security did not suddenly materialize on September 11, 2001; failed states were identified by the Clinton administration as a significant threat to U.S. interests.[5] Domestic opposition to U.S. military casualties stemming from failed state interventions, however, and a lack of bipartisan support for what was viewed in some quarters as "global social work" rather than defense policy, limited the consistent application of failed state doctrine as a core pillar of U.S. national security policy. But following September 11, 2001, the threats failed states pose to national security have been widely recognized and well documented. Indeed, the dominant security concern of the West with Iraq today is how state failure can be forestalled given the catastrophic waves of regional destabilization that event would trigger.

This strategic concern with the causes and consequences of state failure has several connections to odious debt. First, the ability of autocrats to loot the proceeds of foreign borrowing provides an incentive to seize power in the first place.[6] If we are able to design new institutions that dissuade creditors from making such loans, we can reduce the incentives for potential autocrats to destabilize fragile regimes.

Second, by limiting the enforceability of odious debts in postauthoritarian environments, we can bolster the chances that emerging representative governments will sustain the path toward stable governance. For example, a Congressional Budget Office study released in January 2004 noted that servicing a reasonable estimate of outstanding Iraqi debt would "leave no funds in the Iraqi budget for capital investment and produce substantial shortfalls in the government's ability to meet its day-to-day operating expenses."[7] This is hardly a fiscal position conducive to rebuilding a conflict-torn country and establishing the popular credibility of a new government as an effective provider of basic state services. As the rebuilding of failed states has come to absorb a tremendous proportion of available Western defense resources, severely straining the strategic flexibility of the military, proposals that would assist in the rapid reconstruction of failed states are likely to gain a receptive ear in the national security community.

FROM THEORY TO PRACTICE

This section outlines a new policy approach to the problem of odious debts. Whether there is already a right for debtor countries to repudiate odious debts under an existing doctrine founded in customary international law or established principles of common law is not discussed. Rather, the focus is on what an optimal doctrine of odious debts ought to look like were it brought into force by a positive act. Accordingly, while this proposal envisions reforms with solely prospective application to debts incurred subsequent to enactment of the new policy, the present-day rights and obligations of creditors and debtors regarding preexisting debts are in no way impacted. This prospective focus is guided by several factors. First, as a matter of justice, rules with retrospective application to situations in which parties acted within what they believed was a settled legal framework should only be enacted in the most severe circumstances. Second, as a practical matter, it will be far easier to gain "buy in" from key governments and interest groups, such as the financial community, with a solely prospective proposal. By separating the issue of debts made prior to and following the enactment of reforms, the chances of reaching a solution to the latter is dramatically increased without much impact on the chances for resolving the former.

Principles of Design

This proposal will charge an international institution, either already in existence or created de novo, with implementation of the new odious debt doctrine. This institution will have two primary responsibilities: first, declaring *ex ante* which countries are odious debt–prone, and second, regulating new loans to those states.

There are three general principles that should guide our selection or design of that institution. First, care must be exercised to develop arrangements that strike an appropriate balance between realizing the benefits of a more logical approach toward the resolution of odious debts and the corresponding potential for a chilling impact on legitimate sovereign borrowing. Extreme diligence must be devoted to ensuring that the new incentive structure does not discourage beneficial capital flows to the developing world. Any new odious debt policy will be sharply circumscribed in the frequency of its application. Global capital flows to the developing world, on the other hand, can be a force for the alleviation of poverty faced by billions of men and women. In light of this imbalance, new policies must pass a test that any impairments of beneficial capital flows to the developing world are minimal to nonexistent.

Second, new arrangements should be informed by a practical view toward their implementation by global financial institutions. This is in part a corollary of the first guiding principle, as arrangements that place unworkable implementation burdens on financial institutions will raise the costs of sovereign lending beyond a point where even wholly legitimate loans can earn a sufficient rate of return. It is also realistic to say that the chances for a new policy toward odious debts to make the leap from theory paper to implementation are much greater if the opposition of powerful interest groups, such as the financial services industry, is not needlessly provoked. The primary interests of lenders are in clear *ex ante* rules of the road and the potential costs of compliance. If lenders can be assured that a new policy both makes clear what they must do to ensure that their loans are granted legitimate status and demonstrates that the costs of that process are not so burdensome as to unreasonably impact the return on capital earned in sovereign lending, then resistance to the reforms should be relatively muted.

The third major principle to consider is the matter of bias. Recall that declaring a debt odious requires that the borrower regime lack public consent for its actions and that the loans be utilized for nonpublic purposes. No matter how well the conditions necessary to satisfy these categories are defined, as with any other matter of law, application of these rules to specific situations will always call for some degree of discretion—and with discretion comes the possibility of bias.

One possible vector of bias is creditor-debtor bias at the level of the institution charged with overseeing this policy.[8] No legal rule is so precise that the biases of the implementing institution—be it a judicial or political forum—are not highly relevant. In this case, political ideology, external geostrategic and economic relationships, or lobbying by affected interest groups could affect an institutional bias in favor of either creditors or debtors. To mitigate these risks, the institution could be empowered to invalidate sovereign loans only if the borrowing regime had been declared odious debt–prone prior to the loan's issuance. This will substantially increase *ex ante* certainty for lenders.

Another possible vector of bias is regime bias. This leads from the rather cynical yet factual observation that questionable regimes often have many more friends while in power than after they have been deposed. This is simply the fact of a world ultimately governed by realpolitik.[9] While some ability for the major powers to exert a level of protection for certain regimes on the basis of economic or geopolitical interest may be an inevitable if distasteful cost of building sufficient support to enact policy reforms, one should aim to design a system that at least mitigates the most egregious abuses of this discretion. Similarly, our institution should establish checks and balances to prevent this tool from being invoked against disfavored nations for purely political reasons.

Critique of the Classical Model

Whether or not there presently exists a right to repudiate the enforcement of odious debt under international law is a subject well debated by other

Jonathan Shafter

scholars. If such a right does exist, then it takes the form described, for example, by Jeff King in a recent essay.[10] The legal structure described by King is referred to in this essay as the Classical Model. Under King's formulation, odious debts are debts contracted with an absence of consent, an absence of benefit, and subjective creditor awareness of the above two conditions. It is presumed that claims under the Classical Model would be pursued in some form of judicial venue.

There is a serious, if ultimately unpersuasive, argument that the Classical Model states what the law is. But serious problems with the Classical Model approach make it difficult to accept that it is what the law ought to be. First, the Classical Model contemplates that judicial institutions would be empowered to make the determination that a population did not consent to the debt transaction in question. In cases where the basis for this claim is that the debtor regime lacked sufficient institutional capacity to ensure that the proceeds of loans entered into by elected officials were not excessively squandered via corruption, a judicial forum might be able to evaluate the appropriate evidence and rule accordingly. In cases, however, where the claim rests upon allegations that the debtor regime's structure of government was insufficiently democratic to form a basis for popular consent to government policies, then the capacity of a judicial forum is far more questionable. There are simply no legal definitions of democracy with sufficient clarity for a judicial forum to consistently make predictable and solidly grounded rulings.

Consider some of the difficulties posed by contemporary political structures: Iran holds popular elections, but candidates for office are strictly screened by unelected religious authorities who circumscribe the scope of the elected officials' powers. The United States holds elections, but the authority of elected officials is limited by lifetime-appointed judges whose decisions in some areas can only be overridden by a process (constitutional amendment) so difficult and rare as to render it almost impossible. Certainly one of these models seems more democratic than the other, but explaining why evades categorical, rule-based legal classification. One is reminded of the words of Justice Potter Stewart, who in a Supreme Court decision on pornography famously declared of the movie in question, "I shall not today attempt further to define the kinds of material I understand to be embraced within that shorthand description [of pornography]; and perhaps I could never succeed in intelligibly doing so. But I know it when I see it, and the motion picture involved in this case is not that."[11] Unfortunately, the "I know it when I see it" standard of judicial review is hardly the ideal basis for a system with sufficient *ex ante* clarity to prevent excessive interference with legitimate sovereign lending.

King defines four types of regimes—democratic, quasi-democratic, quasi-dictatorial, and dictatorial. Where the debtor is dictatorial or quasi-dictatorial, we may presume that a given loan is not beneficial to the population. A quasi-dictatorial regime is a government that operates primarily without the consent of the population, but which may have a strictly limited franchise or highly limited forms of public representation. A quasi-democratic regime is defined as a government that is generally representative and accountable under regular elections, but which may have a poorly informed electorate, monopolistic party system, limited franchise, or substantially unrepresented minorities. With due respect to King, who at least tries to tackle head-on a question that most proponents of the Classical Model evade, these classifications remain too broad for clear application to the manifold political-institutional structures of the world's nations.

King is certainly right to interpose the categories of quasi-democratic and quasi-dictatorial between a simple binary classification of democracy and dictatorship. While a regime wholly unaccountable to elections is de facto lacking in public consent, elections alone without other aspects of institutional support for popular accountability are an insufficient sole proxy for public consent. But the form and legitimacy of every state's political institutions is so rooted in a nation's unique social, historical, economic, and religious path that it may be impossible to develop clear, predictable rules with universal applicability.

It is well possible that thinkers with more legal ingenuity than myself are capable of developing clear and precise rules to sort national governments into these categories. Yet, until someone does so, I must conclude that—as Stewart said of the effort to define pornography—defining democracy and dictatorship with adequate legal clarity may be "trying to define what may be indefinable."[12] Some might argue that judicial forums have long been charged with the task of applying vague and general rules to specific situations, but this doesn't quite work in the context of international

Jonathan Shafter

adjudication, where there is insufficient customary practice or other sources of authoritative reference to guide courts in their determination on the matter.

This indeterminacy would leave lenders floundering as to which of their loans are at risk of subsequent odious classification. In the absence of clarity, lenders will pursue one of two options: either they will withdraw from all lending that might possibly fall within the classification of odious debt, with a very wide margin of error, or they will substantially increase interest rates on sovereign lending to compensate for the risk of uncertainty. Either path will result in the significant curtailment of legitimate capital flows to developing nations. Given the importance of those capital flows for global economic development, the cure for odious debt might be more painful than the disease. In light of an anticipated tightening of sovereign credit, one would also expect an absence of widespread support for implementing the odious debt agenda among the developing countries of the world.

Finally, under the Classical Model, lenders must have subjective awareness that their loans lack either consent or benefit. King understands this definition to encompass actual knowledge, willfully shutting one's eyes to the obvious, and willfully and recklessly failing to make such inquiries as an honest and reasonable person would make.[13] This standard is too lenient on determining whether a creditor has awareness that a loan will not benefit the debtor nation's population. Where a creditor has awareness that a regime is odious debt–prone, it should be required of the creditor to perform a higher level of due diligence. It is simply too easy to disguise fraud with sufficient camouflage to evade a willful and reckless standard of due diligence.

THE DUE DILIGENCE MODEL OF ODIOUS DEBT RESOLUTION

In this section, the Due Diligence Model is advanced as an alternative policy approach that hopefully rectifies many of the shortcomings in the Classical Model. The basic contours of the Due Diligence Model are as follows: An international organization will have the power to declare that specified regimes are prone to odious debt. If, and only if, a regime has been so designated in advance, creditors to that government must employ reasonable best practices of due diligence to ensure that the proceeds of subsequent lending will be utilized for prespecified public purposes.

Determining Proneness to Odious Debt

This model proposes that an international organization should be enlisted or designed to declare *ex ante* that a specific government is odious debt–prone—which is to say that the targeted government is either unwilling or unable to provide for a reasonable modicum of public consent to its policies and where the likelihood that levels of sovereign borrowing material to the nation's economy will be used for illegitimate purposes crosses an unacceptable threshold. While the organization would be required to justify its decision on the basis of international law, it is envisioned that diplomatic political appointees from member states to the organization will make this decision.

This decision-making structure resolves several issues with the Classical Model. While the organization would justify its decision according to international legal standards, this model recognizes that the decision to declare a nation odious debt–prone will be, in part, a political decision. It is highly unlikely that any odious debt proposal without this safeguard would ever make the transition to reality. There are nations whose credentials on grounds of popular consent are tenuous at best, but where their economic or geopolitical importance is so massive that any proposal threatening capital flows or diplomatic relations with them as a matter of automatic application without political safeguards would be a nonstarter. While this level of discretionary application is not ideal from the perspective of a pure legal construct, in this imperfect world an actually implemented system alleviating the suffering of the citizenry in most odious debt–prone nations is superior to a theoretically perfect system never put into place due to insurmountable political resistance. This system also resolves a key flaw with the Classical Model, the indeterminacy of trying to classify governments as democratic or dictatorial by strictly formal legal logic. In such a condition of formal legal indeterminacy, a political organization is far better positioned to make legitimate decisions than a judicial forum.

The *ex ante* structure of the Due Diligence Model also minimizes the impact of the policy on legitimate sovereign lending. Only loans made to countries that were specifically targeted by the implementing organization prior to the loan's issuance would be at risk for possible invalidation. Since designating a nation as odious debt–prone would be a rare event, reserved for the most egregious violators of legitimacy standards, the vast bulk of sovereign lending would be unaffected by the policy and, accordingly, lenders will require no additional risk premium for sovereign loans to nondesignated regimes.

There is a question of whether lenders might demand an additional risk premium for loans to nondesignated regimes if they feared that subsequent designation would trigger a liquidity crisis in the debtor country. The policy should therefore permit the refinancing of predesignation loans as a legitimate transaction for odious debt–prone governments.[14] Also, the risk premium for loans to nondesignated regimes should be lower under this proposal than under the current status quo, as today there exists some possibility that a court might find that the classical doctrine of odious debts exists under international law, whereas the due diligence proposal makes clear that loans to nondesignated regimes are entirely safe from the odious debt standard.

Reasonable Best Practices of Due Diligence
Under the Due Diligence Model, the designation of a government as odious debt–prone does not bar lenders from extending credit to it. Rather, lenders are placed on notice that, in order to guarantee that their loans will be enforceable in the event of regime change, they must utilize reasonable best practices of due diligence to ensure that the borrowed funds will only be utilized for prespecified, legitimate purposes.[15] Due diligence refers to the structures utilized by the lender for ongoing monitoring over the life of the loan to ensure that the loan proceeds are being used for their stated purposes. It is not enough to simply perform due diligence at the time the loan is originated; rather, it is necessary that structures of continuous monitoring are put in place to limit opportunities for funds to be diverted from legitimate purposes via corruption or intentional fraud.

How would lenders comply with such a standard? The term "best practices" makes this a ratcheting standard that evolves over time as innovative techniques of auditing technologies and deal structuring are developed. But this requirement is modified by a secondary rule of reasonableness. Factors that would weigh upon whether a given plan of due diligence is reasonable in a specific situation should include the cost of compliance relative to the importance of the public purpose underlying the loan, the degree of corruption in the debtor government, and the potential harm that the debtor could cause through illicit diversion of the funds (for example, a government engaged in a war of aggression not supported by its citizens could purchase additional weapons). Mechanisms of implementation might include the employment of certified outside auditors, escrow accounts, offshore special-purpose vehicles, or numerous other deal-structuring technologies to lower the risk of illicit funds diversion.

To ensure that lenders have sufficient *ex ante* certainty that their loans comply with the requisite level of due diligence for the circumstances, the international organization implementing the agreement should establish a mechanism to issue "no action" letters. No action letters are a device utilized by administrative agencies of the U.S. government to reconcile the broad language of many American regulatory statutes and rules with the need for *ex ante* certainty in specific situations. For example, the U.S. Securities and Exchange Commission describes a no action letter as "[a letter] in which an authorized staff official indicates that the staff will not recommend any enforcement action to the Commission if the proposed transaction described in the incoming correspondence is consummated."[16] In this system, the implementing organization would establish a system whereby prospective creditors could submit a detailed analysis of their loan proposal, including the intended uses by the debtor government and the due diligence structures to be put into place to monitor the fund flows. If both the use of funds and the due diligence plan are approved, the enforceability of the loan in a regime change situation would be assured so long as the creditor has sufficient evidence that it made a good faith effort to comply with its preapproved due diligence structuring.[17]

There are several advantages of the due diligence standard over the legal standard embedded in the Classical Model. First, *ex ante* certainty for lenders is increased by the preapproval process for due diligence plans, and an emphasis on monitoring good faith compliance with that plan, rather than, as the Classical Model calls for, trying to ascertain whether a lender

Jonathan Shafter

had subjective knowledge that their funds were being put to illegitimate purposes. Were the Classical Model brought into force, it is likely that most creditors would cease any lending to odious debt–prone regimes, or they would demand exorbitant rates of interest to compensate them for their risk. The Due Diligence Model, however, establishes a secure channel for creditors to make legitimate loans to odious debt–prone regimes, for even the worst of regimes may from time to time consider the public interest. So long as creditors make good faith efforts at compliance with their pre-approved due diligence plans, they are not penalized for outcomes that lie outside of their control. It is true that this places the potential cost of fraudulent evasion of due diligence structures upon the populations of odious debt–prone regimes rather than creditors, but this is a necessary allocation of burdens to keep lines of credit open to odious debt–prone regimes seeking loans for authorized public purposes.

The problem of the fungibility of funds exists and is a difficult issue. For example, even if loan proceeds are used solely for prespecified legitimate purposes, this may nevertheless free up general state revenues for illegitimate use. Still, the Due Diligence Model would at least improve upon the status quo. Currently, a given government has the capacity to spend its full fiscal resources, composed of internal fiscal resources and available borrowing capacity, on illegitimate purposes. Under this proposal, access to credit would be conditioned on at least some proportion of the government's full fiscal resources going toward legitimate public spending. Thus, the total available fiscal resources that can be devoted to illegitimate ends are reduced. Consider the case of an odious debt–prone government with internal fiscal resources of $100 all devoted toward legitimate purposes, which in the absence of debt reforms would borrow $200 for illegitimate purposes. That government might be able to borrow $200 for approved legitimate purposes, but because money is fungible, this would free the $100 of internal resources previously allocated to legitimate spending for the illegitimate purposes. Still, on a net basis, there is $100 less of illegitimate spending, leaving the population in an improved position. Furthermore, as a practical matter, the supervising organization could require covenants holding the borrower regime to aggregate fiscal expenditure guidelines (for example, no more than a certain percent of the total budget may be applied toward defense) as a requirement for giving approval to any lending. In reality, there are many variables that impact the determination of the risks from fungibility in specific situations, and it makes sense to leave these decisions to be made on a case-by-case basis, which the no action procedure would allow. Of course, in some cases the fungibility problem might be judged too difficult to overcome, and no no action letter would be issued.

Second, the Due Diligence Model will be more effective than the Classical Model in situations where the debtor government is highly corrupt. The "willful and reckless failure to make inquiries" requirement of subjective knowledge for creditors under the Classical Model establishes incentives for lenders to make only the most glancing inquiries into the actual usage of their funds. The trivial level of due diligence required to meet the willful and reckless standard would almost certainly fail to check anything more than the most brazen cases of corruption, while lenders would be discouraged from going much deeper with their inquiries for fear that they might actually acquire the subjective knowledge that would imperil their lending relationship. Alternatively, the Due Diligence Model will require lenders to take reasonable best practice safeguards proportionate to the known corruption level of the debtor government. This may even have positive spill-over effects for the debtor nation. Because the implementing organization may deem that certain debtor governments are so corrupt that any reasonable deal structuring to safeguard the borrowed funds is extremely onerous (an expense that will presumably be factored into the rates charged by the lender), the debtor government may have some incentive to improve its institutions of governance to access lower-cost credit.

Venues for Implementation
There is a range of possible ways that an institution could be established to assess the odious debt–prone nature of regimes, from unilateral implementation to a system inclusive of all the world's countries. From the standpoint of effectiveness, there are two key dimensions to consider: critical mass and legitimacy. Critical mass refers to the aggregate quantity of credit controlled by the country or countries that implement this proposal. Universal adoption of the proposal is not necessary to achieve much of the anticipated benefits from the policy. Consider a world in which countries

controlling half the world's credit supply adopted this proposal and half did not. Odious debt–prone regimes would still have full access to credit from the nonparticipating nations of the world. Nonparticipant countries would know, however, that should the odious debt–prone regime collapse, the successor government in that country would have full access to the credit markets of participant countries if it repudiated its predecessor's illegitimate debts. Since access to credit markets is a primary reason why successor regimes do not repudiate odious debts, if the participant countries control a sufficient percentage of the world's credit supply that the successor government could safely meet its financing needs from participant nation creditors, it is most likely that even nonparticipant nations would sharply restrict the supply of potentially odious credit to odious debt–prone regimes.[18]

While it is possible that one entity, such as the United States or the European Union, might have the critical mass to implement this proposal unilaterally, to maximize global perceptions of legitimacy a multilateral implementation may be preferable. One possible venue for implementation is the United Nations. The UN has the advantage of preeminent global legitimacy and a preexisting institutional architecture. The Security Council currently has the authority to impose trade sanctions, and one can envision the Security Council also being the body that declares regimes odious debt–prone and supervises compliance, assisted by a dedicated bureaucratic staff. It is the UN's universal inclusiveness, however, that raises questions over its suitability as an implementing venue. This is again a consequence of the legal indeterminacy in adjudicating whether a government falls into the category of being odious debt–prone. So long as there is enough indeterminacy that this decision calls for some subjective value judgment, a coordinated odious debt policy is only possible among nations with sufficiently similar worldviews and interests. Gaining such a consensus at the level of the UN, even in the Security Council, could be problematic. Not all of the permanent or rotating Security Council members place equal priority on the goal of democracy promotion. That said, in some important historical cases, such as apartheid-era South Africa or Tudjman-era Croatia, it might well have been possible to gain necessary consensus for action at the Security Council level, so the UN should not be viewed as a wholly impossible implementation venue.[19]

A more practical alternative to the UN might be implementation among the advanced industrial democracies that comprise the G-7 or the OECD (although the implementation need not occur through these bodies themselves). These countries encompass a sufficient quantity of the world's credit pool that the aims of a coordinated odious debt policy would be realized. In addition, while the interests and worldviews of the member countries are clearly not identical, there remains enough of a shared fundamental outlook that implementing an odious debt policy would be more feasible at this level than at the level of the UN. There are precedents for the advanced industrial democracies to coordinate external policies on financial matters without universal inclusiveness of all the world's governments. For example, the OECD Convention on Combating Bribery of Foreign Public Officials in International Business Transactions makes it a crime for citizens of convention signatories to offer, promise, or give a bribe to a foreign public official in order to obtain or retain international business deals.

The actual structure of the organization should be designed with an eye toward minimizing the problem of regime bias. Negative regime bias, whereby some governments might falsely target a country as odious debt–prone to advance an unrelated diplomatic agenda, would be mitigated through the necessity of gaining some form of supermajority approval from the member countries in order to place a debtor government on the odious debt–prone list. No doubt this would allow certain participant countries leverage to shield their favored strategic allies. As a partial mitigation against this risk of positive regime bias there should be a parallel policy of disclosure along the lines of the Extractive Industries Transparency Initiative (EITI)—a movement to increase the transparency of transactions between governments and extractive industries. The EITI calls for "Regular publication of all material oil, gas and mining payments by companies to governments ('payments') and all material revenues received by governments from oil, gas and mining companies ('revenues') to a wide audience in a publicly accessible, comprehensive and comprehensible manner."[20] Similarly, financial institutions of participant countries could be required to

Jonathan Shafter

disclose the quantity and nature of their sovereign lending to a publicly accessible repository. Furthermore, it could be required that financial institutions disclose in their financial reports whether they have any subjective knowledge that the proceeds of their lending are being used for illegitimate purposes. Merely shining light on the financial relationships between lenders and sovereign governments might be sufficient to mitigate some of the most extreme situations where positive regime bias protects the debtor government from more formal monitoring.

CONCLUSION

This essay advances a Due Diligence Model of dealing with the problem of odious debts that achieves most of the goals one would seek to accomplish in this area, but does so in a conservative manner that won't impact the vast bulk of global capital flows to the developing world, prove politically infeasible, or unreasonably curtail the legitimate borrowings of even autocratic regimes. The model is structured so that its use will be rare. Curtailing the most abusive cases of odious sovereign borrowing would be a significant achievement and is achievable through a policy that is moderate enough to win broad support for implementation. A more sweeping, universal policy model would likely face much greater obstacles to move from academic discussion to policy adoption.

Much work remains to be done in translating the Due Diligence Model into the basis for actual policy. First, this essay does not discuss differences among the several types of sovereign lending. Sovereign lending can be bilateral (government to government), multilateral (that is, World Bank), or private sector. The basic model presented in this essay assumes that all types of debt should be treated in the same manner, but this is obviously an assumption that demands further analysis. Second, much work will be necessary to translate the concept of due diligence into real world deal-structuring and auditing guidelines. Finally, advances in financial technology from privatization to credit default swaps raise the question of whether the concept of odious debt must be extended to other types of financial securities and derivatives to be relevant in the twenty-first century.

Odious debt arises as a topic of public debate on occasions when some particularly egregious example of a dictator's borrowing and the consequences of servicing that debt for a successor government are revealed. In the past several years, there was a dramatic upsurge in interest on the topic of odious debts in response to the collapse of Saddam Hussein's regime. It was one of the fortuitous and rare instances where both the Right and Left came together to argue that Saddam's odious debts should not be bequeathed to the newly emerging Iraqi government. Yet, even with all of this attention, while Saddam's debts were mitigated through several rounds of global diplomatic arm-twisting, the broader doctrine of odious debts gained little real traction. One reason for this is that once a dictator has fallen and the impact of his borrowing on the reconstruction of his country is revealed, it is largely too late to help that specific case. For very good reasons, the norm against retroactive application of legal rules, such as changing terms for creditors after loans have been disbursed, is quite strong.

The first question many advocates of odious debt reform face is often, to whom would this apply right now? While there are certain governments today who might be candidates for odious debt–prone designation, it is also the case that the fiscal position of many developing nations is highly correlated to commodity prices, and with those prices as high as they are today the dependence of many nations on external financing is cyclically low. Yet it is exactly because odious debt is not being incurred on a major scale today that it is the perfect time to put in place prospective mechanisms to forestall the otherwise almost certain tragic consequences of the next turn of the cycle.

NOTES

[1] Two important contributions in this literature are Thomas Pogge, "Achieving Democracy," this volume, pp. 249–73; and Ashfaq Khalfan, Jeff King, and Bryan Thomas, "Advancing the Odious Debt Doctrine" (Quebec: Centre for International Sustainable Development Law, 2003). See also Anna Gelpern, "What Iraq and Argentina Might Learn From Each Other," *Chicago Journal of International Law* 6, no. 1 (2005), p. 391; Kevin Anderson, "International Law and State Succession: A Solution to the Iraqi Debt Crisis?" *Utah Law Review* 2 (2005), p. 401; and Anupam Chander, "Odious Securitization," special issue, *Emory Law Journal* 53 (2004), p. 923.

[2] See Seema Jayachandran and Michael Kremer, "Odious Debt," *American Economic Review*, March 2006.

[3] See Lee C. Buccheit, G. Mitu Gulati, and Robert B. Thompson, "The Odious Debts of an Odious Regime: Piercing the Governmental Veil," *Duke Law Journal* (forthcoming).

Jonathan Shafter

4 Admittedly without extensive empirical investigation, it is unlikely that there are many other policy initiatives for which Joseph Stiglitz and Oxfam on one side, and the Cato Institute and Heritage Foundation on the other, would unite in advocating. See Joseph Stiglitz, "Odious Rulers, Odious Debts," *Atlantic Monthly* 292, no. 4 (November 2003), pp. 39–45; Patricia Adams, "Iraq's Odious Debts," Policy Analysis 526, Cato Institute, Washington, D.C., September 28, 2004; Nile Gardner and Marc Miles, "Forgive the Iraqi Debt," Executive Memorandum 871, Heritage Foundation, Washington, D.C., April 30, 2003; and Oxfam, "A Fresh Start for Iraq: The Case for Debt Relief," Oxfam Briefing Paper 48, Oxfam International, Washington, D.C., May 2003.

5 White House, "A National Security Strategy for a New Century" (December 1999), p. 2, available at clinton4.nara.gov/media/pdf/nssr-1299.pdf.

6 See Jayachandran and Kremer, "Odious Debt."

7 Congressional Budget Office, "Paying for Iraq's Reconstruction," CBO Paper, prepared for the Senate Budget Committee and the House Budget Committee, January 2004, p. 13.

8 See Jayachandran and Kremer, "Odious Debt."

9 One need only observe the fact that no matter what was thought of the merits of the Iraqi war, Saddam Hussein's regime had many more international friends prior to his fall than afterward. The same can be said for nearly any fallen authoritarian regime.

10 Jeff King, "The Doctrine of Odious Debt under International Law: Definition, Evidence and Issues Concerning Application," in Ashfaq Khalfan and Jeff King, eds., *Odious Debt Doctrine in International Law and Policy* (New York: Cambridge University Press, forthcoming).

11 Jacobellis v. Ohio, 378 U.S. 184 (1964).

12 Ibid.

13 King, "The Doctrine of Odious Debt under International Law."

14 See Jayachandran and Kremer, "Odious Debt."

15 In the case of a bond debt rather than bank credit, this monitoring role would be assigned to a servicer.

16 *Procedures Utilized by the Division of Corporation Finance for Rendering Informal Advice*, Securities Act Release No. 6253, 21 S.E.C. Docket 320 n. 2 (October 28, 1980).

17 It is true that determining whether a lender complied with its due diligence plan is to a limited degree an *ex post* decision, which raises the previously discussed issue of a potential institutional bias against creditors or debtors. Since, however, the scope of the institution's *ex post* inquiry will be limited to the empirical question of whether a creditor adhered to its set plan of due diligence rather than the more open-ended and subjective Classical Model questions of whether loans were made with proper public consent and for legitimate public purposes, the potential that creditor-debtor biases will significantly affect outcomes in this system is acceptably low.

18 One recent problem for advocates of responsible sovereign lending has been the emergence of lending nations with very different interests and worldviews from the traditional sources of developing world capital. For example, the president of the World Bank recently complained that Chinese banks were flouting social and environmental principles in their developing country lending activities. While China has full rights to make loans as it sees fit, other nations equally have the right to decide if a successor's repudiation of those loans is valid and thus should not be punished by curtailing access to fresh capital. Odious debt reform could give nations who believe in the importance of certain lending standards some leverage against perceived "rogue lenders" and alleviate pressure to engage in a regulatory race to the bottom since a critical mass of nations following such a policy would lower the *ex ante* risk-adjusted returns to nonparticipating creditors. That said, in cases where rogue lenders are driven more by geopolitical than economic incentives, it is unclear how much actual impact this would have.

19 See Jayachandran and Kremer, "Odious Debt."

20 Extractive Industries Transparency Initiative, "EITI Principles and Criteria," available at eitransparency.myaiweb15.com/principlesandcriteria.htm.

Reviving Troubled Economies

Jack Boorman

T here would be few dissenters from the general proposition that we should try to deal justly with debt. We have all watched in horror the collapse that has taken place in Argentina and the enormous cost paid by so many people in that country—as well as by the creditors of Argentina—from the massive financial and economic dislocation and disruption. I do not believe that what has occurred was inevitable.

Unfortunately, some who address this issue of dealing with unmanageable debt situations have offered advice that, while emotionally appealing, is not operationally helpful. I will describe and justify the rationale and design of the proposal put forward by the International Monetary Fund for a Sovereign Debt Restructuring Mechanism (SDRM). Its major goal is to help reduce the unacceptably large costs associated with disorderly defaults by sovereign governments whose debt burdens have become unsustainable. The SDRM aims to get the countries' debts to sustainable positions and deal with the broader needs of the countries through the full array of aid and other mechanisms that are available—and, indeed, to enlarge and enhance these initiatives. I will also explain my misgivings about some of the other proposals, including the ones coming from the NGO community.

THE NEED FOR A FORMAL MECHANISM

The dislocation and disorder that occurs when governments default is often the result of reluctance on the part of the countries' authorities to confront the underlying policy problems or to approach the countries' creditors for relief when their debts have become unsustainable. In too many cases, the authorities gamble for redemption through ill-devised policy measures rather than face the uncertainty of approaching the countries' private-sector creditors for the needed relief. Argentina in the summer and fall of 2001 is all too dramatic an example of this phenomenon.

And why are these countries hesitant to approach creditors? One reason for this is reputation: No government official likes to admit the true nature of his or her country's debt problem. Indeed, these officials are often the same people who were partly responsible for the policies that led to the accumulation of that debt. Ministers are also concerned about undermining their countries' future access to capital markets. But, importantly, it is also because at present there is no mechanism to assure that countries that approach their creditors will be able to reach a negotiated settlement with them to restructure the countries' debts in a way that is consistent with their capacity to pay it. Moreover, they have no assurance that the process of negotiating with creditors will be orderly, predictable, and transparent.

In order to address these problems, a proposal was developed in the IMF that has come to be known as the Sovereign Debt Restructuring Mechanism. Five principles guided its development. First, the mechanism should only be used to restructure debt that is determined to be unsustainable. It should neither increase the likelihood of restructuring nor encourage defaults. It must not unduly inhibit the capacity of markets to provide appropriate financing to indebted countries in the future by undermining the presumption of the validity of contracts.

Second, any interference with contractual relations should be limited to those measures that are necessary for resolving the collective action problems that can complicate the process of reaching agreement on a restructuring. The danger is that individual creditors will decline to participate in a voluntary restructuring in the hope of recovering payment on the original contractual terms, even though creditors, as a group, would be better served by agreeing to such a restructuring. This problem increases the likelihood of defaults and the large economic and social dislocations that usually follow.

Third, the framework should promote greater transparency in the restructuring process, and encourage early and active creditor participation in it. It should not increase the role of the Fund in this regard.

Fourth, the integrity of the mechanism's decision-making process should be safeguarded by an efficient and impartial dispute-resolution process.

Finally, the SDRM should not expand the Fund's legal powers.

Jack Boorman

THE SOVEREIGN DEBT RESTRUCTURING MECHANISM

Guided by these principles, the Fund's SDRM proposal was designed with five major features. First, the sovereign debtor would, if needed, have protection from disruptive legal action by creditors during negotiations. This could be provided, in appropriate circumstances, through a stay on litigation, preventing creditors from seeking court decisions for repayment while negotiations are under way. The possible automaticity and the triggers for such possible stays have been widely discussed in the debate on the SDRM. Some favor, similar to the process of domestic bankruptcy, an automatic stay at the time the SDRM is activated. Others see this as both unnecessary and possibly counterproductive in certain cases where it would be preferable to continue to service some of the outstanding debt, such as that held by domestic banks.

Second, the creditors would be provided with assurance that debtors will negotiate in good faith and will pursue policies—which will most likely be designed in conjunction with seeking financial support from the IMF—that help to protect the value of creditor claims, to limit the dislocation in the economy, and to limit the likelihood of contagion to other countries. The Fund's policy on lending into arrears is key in this regard.

Third, creditors would be permitted to protect and prioritize fresh private lending during the restructuring process in order to facilitate ongoing economic activity through the continued provision of, inter alia, trade credit (something akin to Chapter 11 debtor-in-possession financing).

Fourth, a supermajority of creditors could vote to accept new terms under a restructuring agreement. If new terms were adopted, minority creditors would be prevented from blocking such agreements or enforcing the terms of the original debt contracts.

Fifth, a dispute-resolution forum would be established to verify the claims of different parties to the negotiation. This forum would assure the integrity of the voting process, and adjudicate disputes that might arise.

A RESPONSE TO THE CRITICS

Some have faulted the proposal because "only private creditors would have to reduce their claims."[1] This is not correct. It is true that the proposal assumes continuance of the preferred creditor status of the IMF and some other multilateral organizations, but bilateral official creditors would be expected to provide relief on their claims on the country. It was always foreseen in the proposal that bilateral official creditors would share the burden, and the Paris Club has been actively examining the implications of this.

A second point that critics make is that the "SDRM would not return poor, indebted countries to viability/sustainability."[2] I believe there is some confusion here: the SDRM is not aimed at the poorest countries. It may be relevant to a few of them that have large amounts of debt outstanding to private creditors (such as Nigeria), but for the low-income countries, generally, there is the Highly Indebted Poor Countries Initiative—criticism of it notwithstanding.

There are also those in the NGO community who fault the proposal for not including a process through which countries can be discharged of their obligation to repay what they call "odious" debt. While I have no illusions about the existence of odious debt, focusing on it shifts attention away from the real issue: how to deal with the total stock of unpayable debt. The international community has shied away from mechanisms built on concepts such as odious debt and has concentrated on the broader issue. There are various reasons for that. On the political side, some governments, I suspect, may not want to recognize or defend the consequences of lending decisions they have taken in the past and, moreover, may want to protect their future ability to pursue geopolitical ends through international lending. The seriousness of this obstacle is evident from the way in which the initial calls for invoking the concept of odious debt for loans made to Iraq during Saddam Hussein's regime have quickly subsided. On the economic side, dealing with debt in this way could introduce a new source of risk that could seriously affect the workings of the secondary market, where investors exchange government securities among themselves, and hence the ability of sovereigns to mobilize new money. If purchasers in the secondary market had to assure themselves of the integrity of the process through which the claim was originally created, that market would cease to operate.

In addition, there are many questions to be asked about the practicality of the NGO approach with regard to odious debt. Who decides which debt falls into this category? What are the values or criteria to be applied in deciding who ought to bear the costs of dealing with odious debt? For example, if the odious debt deals were cut between one government and another, who should decide, and by what criteria, what balance should be struck between the wronged citizens of the debtor country and the taxpayers of the creditor country who would absorb the cost of the debt relief?

The SDRM has a specific purpose: to help deal with the problems of market-access countries whose debt has become unsustainable, and to establish a system for more orderly and coordinated negotiation between the country and its creditors for debt relief in such circumstances. Interestingly, neither private creditors, who presumably would have to give less relief if odious debt were set aside, nor the emerging market countries themselves have voiced support for this proposal to write off odious debt.

Questions and challenges have also been raised about the role of the IMF under the SDRM. One relates to the appropriate procedure through which the SDRM is to be institutionalized. The IMF has proposed that it be created through an amendment to its articles of agreement rather than through a new international treaty. The rationale is straightforward: Helping countries to manage their debt problems and the economic and certain institutional aspects of their interface with international capital markets falls squarely under the IMF's mandate. The SDRM fits within the boundaries of that mandate.

Moreover, creating a new international treaty would likely be a much more complicated and uncertain undertaking. The articles of agreement have been amended before and it is therefore a process familiar to the organization's members. An amendment can take effect immediately when three-fifths of the members having 85 percent of the voting power have voted for it—as opposed to an international treaty, which would require unanimous vote and ratification by domestic parliaments. Amending the IMF's articles of agreement would also provide the framework with greater stability. Withdrawing from a freestanding treaty may have little cost to the withdrawing country. Withdrawing from the Fund, however, deprives the country of the benefits of membership provided for under the articles of agreement.

The amendment would create no new legal powers for the Fund itself. The integrity of the process would be ensured through the Sovereign Debt Dispute Resolution Forum—and this forum would be independent of the Fund.

Apparently most controversial in the eyes of some NGOs and other critics of the proposal is that the Fund would continue to play a role in assessing the sustainability of the country's external position, including its debt. Some criticize this on the grounds that it puts the Fund in the position of dictating the terms of any settlement between the country and its creditors. Others claim that it is incompatible with the role of the Fund as a creditor itself, and, indeed, a preferred one.

However, the Fund has traditionally been treated as a preferred creditor by debtor countries and by other creditors, such as private banks, capital markets, and bilateral official creditors. It is widely accepted that, as the institution providing financing to a country in times of crisis and when other sources of credit have often disappeared, it is appropriate for the Fund to have preferred status. The reason for this is that crisis financing would likely not be forthcoming without that protection. This means that when debt relief is sought, the other creditors must provide a greater share of the needed relief than would be the case if the IMF comparably reduced its own claims. It seems odd that this preferred status of the Fund is accepted as appropriate by most private and official creditors affected by it, while NGOs (which are not so affected) have been opposed to it.

The Fund has also been criticized for its role in policy formulation and, thus, judgments regarding debt sustainability. Ann Pettifor, for example, claims that the Fund "would play a preemptive role in shaping the outcome of the debt crisis resolution negotiations by setting the country's level of debt sustainability.... In addition, the Fund will continue to play a substantial role in shaping the debtor's economic policies. . . . the IMF disempowers the debtor, all other creditors, and civil society" (this volume, p. 324). This supposed role of the Fund would certainly surprise anyone who has negotiated a Fund arrangement with a member country. Negotiations are inevitably difficult. They involve extensive discussions, lots of give-and-take, and many concessions from all sides before an agreement is finally reached. The Fund does not ride in with the parameters defining sustainability chipped in stone. There is also no single set of macroeconomic policies dictated by a country's particular condition, even in a crisis situation. There are temporal trade-offs regarding the extent and speed of adjustment, and trade-offs concerning those who need to make the necessary adjustments and sacrifices.

This brings in an important related point rightly emphasized by NGOs: the call for civil society to have a role in the discussions leading to a debt relief plan. The issue, however, is not whether civil society should participate, but through what fora and mechanisms its participation should be organized. In turn, this relates to how policies and debt sustainability are determined. The government budget is the key instrument of policy in this regard, since it is the basis on which debt service capacity will be determined. And, contrary to the views of some in the NGO community, the country's budget is not dictated by the IMF. Increasingly, the countries with which the IMF has arrangements are democracies in which the budget comes out of a process of consultation between the government and the national parliament that determines the overall framework of the budget, spending priorities, judgments about taxing capacity, and all the other aspects of the final budget presentation. The Fund is part of that process through its discussions with the government. Civil society should certainly be part of that process as well, through representations to the government, participation in parliamentary debate, the giving of testimony, lobbying, and all other means traditional to the specific culture of each country. Effective participation and transparency for civil society are thus required in the domestic system. If these are assured, the process of establishing the trade-offs that ultimately help to determine debt sustainability holds the promise of being fair and effective.

THE PROSPECT OF THE SDRM

If the world is going to deal justly with debt, it needs to prevent debt crises from occurring in the first place—and many of the initiatives in the Fund and elsewhere are aimed precisely at that objective. Stronger economic and financial policies combined with improving the environment for private-sector decision-making in ways that facilitate the assessment and management of risk offer the best prospect for allowing countries to reap the potential gains from globalization, while minimizing the likelihood, and potential severity, of crises. Robust assessments of the strength and soundness of banking systems and a country's financial system more generally; encouragement of the adoption of internationally recognized standards and codes and of best practices in numerous areas of economic policy-making and institution building; and better surveillance or monitoring of country policies by the authorities themselves, as well as by the IMF, are all part of these efforts. Nevertheless, crises will occur, and we need to find a way that allows for dealing with them at an early stage in order to alleviate the enormous costs they involve for the citizens of the debtor country and its creditors. I believe the SDRM holds that promise.

The SDRM proposal has been formulated in rather specific terms in a statement from the managing director to the Fund's governing body, the International Monetary and Financing Committee, and has evolved as a result of the most ambitious consultative process that the Fund has ever engaged in, including the official sector, bankruptcy practitioners, the international legal community, NGOs, and many others. These consultations have led to many important modifications in the proposal. They have also contributed to a greater understanding of the legal and institutional complexities involved in debt restructuring. Even if the SDRM is never implemented, which would be regrettable, it has advanced the debate concerning debt restructuring in important ways. It has given new impetus to the push in the official community that began in the mid-1990s with the Rey Report to encourage the use of collective action clauses (CACs) in sovereign debt issues. Similarly, there is now widespread agreement—at least in principle—on the desirability of agreeing on a voluntary code of good conduct. Although it would not solve collective action problems, such a code would, among other things, foster greater transparency, provide guidance to debtors and creditors regarding procedures for contact and negotiations, and help to provide greater predictability to the restructuring process under any legal framework. Such a code could be made applicable to a broad set of circumstances, ranging from periods of relative tranquility to periods of acute stress, and could constitute an established set of best practices. In that way, it would enhance the proposals for strengthening arrangements for debt restructuring, which have the more limited scope and purpose of facilitating the resolution of financial crises.

These discussions are already generating change in the financial markets. For example, Mexico, South Africa, and Korea, among other emerging-market countries, have recently included collective action clauses in sovereign bond issues. A system with reasonably comprehensive and robust CACs and a well-defined code of conduct with broad support among debtors and their creditors will be an improvement on the system that currently exists. Nevertheless, I believe the role of these initiatives should be complementary to the SDRM.

They are not sufficiently powerful by themselves to provide what is needed to deal with the more complex and potentially damaging crises that may occur. The past few months have seen a number of news articles speculating on the future of the SDRM. Some have hinted—in my view, prematurely—at its death. However, it took many years to enact bankruptcy legislation in the United States and I believe more work and more thinking is called for—and that is what has been requested by the International Monetary and Financing Committee.

NOTES

[1] Ann Pettifor and Kunibert Raffer, "Report of the IMF's conference on the Sovereign Debt Restructuring Mechanism, 22nd January, 2003, IMF Headquarters, Washington, D.C." (Jubilee Research at the New Economics Foundation, January 23, 2003), available at www.jubileeresearch.org/latest/sdr220103.htm.

[2] Ibid.

The Constructive Role of Private Creditors

Arturo C. Porzecanski

During the 1990s and earlier this decade, policy-makers in Washington and other capitals of countries in the Group of 7 (G-7) promoted the idea that the functioning of the world's financial markets had to be improved by making it easier for insolvent governments, especially in emerging markets, to obtain debt relief from their bondholders and bankers.

Most savvy investors, financial intermediaries, and emerging-market government officials were at a loss to understand why the G-7 and the International Monetary Fund (IMF) believed the international financial system would function better if there were specific mechanisms to facilitate sovereign bankruptcies.

The main reason corporations chartered in the United States that cannot pay their creditors subject themselves to wrenching reorganizations before entering into—or once under—Chapter 11 of the U.S. bankruptcy code is because the alternative is their outright liquidation under the code's Chapter 7. Sovereign governments, in contrast, do not operate under the threat of liquidation, and despite the strong rights that bondholders have on paper under New York, English, and other law, practical experience indicates that the enforcement of claims against sovereign governments is exceedingly difficult. Whereas delinquent corporations can be hauled, de jure and de facto, before a bankruptcy court and forced to change management, restructure operations, dispose of assets, or even liquidate to pay off claims, governments are not subjected to any of that. Chapter 9 of the U.S. bankruptcy code is similarly unhelpful as a model for how to restructure the liabilities of bankrupt governments, since it does not apply to sovereign entities, such as U.S. states and counties, which under the U.S. Constitution are ensured to remain free of federal government interference.[1]

Consequently, those in the business of issuing, underwriting, or investing in sovereign bonds are generally of the view that, if anything, international reforms should focus on making contracts easier to enforce and on facilitating the constructive involvement of bondholders and other private-sector creditors in debt-restructuring negotiations.[2] Yet the G-7 has not called for any actions or penalties against irresponsible governments, such as the attachment of their official international reserves when they are on deposit with central banks like the U.S. Federal Reserve or with the Bank for International Settlements (BIS), the central banks' central bank. At present, for example, the investors who have filed suits and won judgments against Argentina in New York and other jurisdictions, because of the default that took place at the end of 2001, cannot get their hands on the billions of dollars that the government of that country has sheltered in those G-7 institutions. The G-7 initiatives did not contemplate any incentives—let alone principles or procedures—for ensuring that governments will become more accountable for their financial obligations.[3] The intent of the initiatives was wholly one-sided: to expedite the granting of debt relief on the part of bondholders and other private-sector creditors.

THE RECORD SPEAKS

Although various proposals for resolving debt crises were advanced, they all supposed that the lack of collective action among private-sector lenders and investors is the main obstacle to the smooth functioning of the international financial system.[4] Yet there is little if any empirical support for this assumption. On the contrary, private creditors have been much more progressive, flexible, and quick in dealing with sovereign insolvency situations than have been official lenders. In fact, private lenders have provided a good example for how official bilateral and multilateral lenders might themselves deal more fairly and effectively with sovereign insolvency situations.

The absence of innovative mechanisms has not impeded several landmark workouts of sovereign indebtedness. The governments of Ecuador, Moldova, Pakistan, Russia, and Ukraine, for example, have all been able to restructure their bonded debt in recent years—and have done so in record time. Substantial debt-service relief and even sizable debt forgiveness have been obtained through the use of exchange offers, often accompanied by bondholder exit consents that encourage the participation of as many investors as possible in take-it-or-leave-it settlements. Rather than amending bond covenants, the exchange offers typically entail the debtor government presenting its private creditors with a menu of voluntary options, such as accepting new bonds for a fraction (for example, 60 percent) of the principal owed but paying a market interest rate, or new bonds for the original principal but paying a concessional interest rate. Experience has demonstrated that neither the threat of litigation nor actual cases of successful litigation have obstructed these debt restructurings, which have involved large, institutional as well as small, retail investors throughout the world.[5]

A recent case involved the government of Uruguay, which in early 2003 asked investors to consider a debt-restructuring request, and more than 90 percent of them agreed, enabling the operation to be consummated in a matter of several weeks. The Uruguayan authorities previously spent many months debating the nature of the restructuring with the IMF. The Fund wanted Uruguay to default on its obligations to bondholders just like Argentina had done, with the intention of obtaining massive debt forgiveness from private creditors, but the Uruguayan authorities refused to go down this potentially ruinous path. The government there wanted to pursue, instead, a market-friendly debt exchange with the sole purpose of stretching out the maturities falling due in 2003 and the next several years, while respecting the original amounts owed and continuing to make the requisite interest payments. It was only after the Uruguayan authorities sought and obtained support from the U.S. Treasury and the Federal Reserve that the IMF staff backed down and agreed to support a voluntary debt exchange.[6]

Once an understanding between the IMF and Uruguay was reached, matters moved rather quickly. Informal discussions with private creditors were held in March, 2003, a concrete proposal was put forth in April, investor replies were received in May, and by June Uruguay's bonded debt had been successfully restructured. This was accomplished despite the fact that the investor base was scattered around the globe: the operation involved everyone from retail investors in Argentina and Japan to institutional investors in the United States and Europe, all of whom were bound by contracts written in several jurisdictions, each with its own currency and distinct legal features.

The cases of Bolivia, Nicaragua, Ecuador, and Argentina, with which this author had some involvement, bring home the difference between how private and official creditors have treated—and have been treated by—governments in serious financial trouble. The cases of these developing countries offer an interesting variety because they span the range of income categories identified by the World Bank and other multilateral agencies: low income (Nicaragua), middle income (Bolivia and Ecuador), and upper income (Argentina).

Bolivia

In 1988, following many years of debt-servicing difficulties, the government of Bolivia retired most of its commercial bank debt through a buyback, with creditors writing down nearly 90 percent of what the government owed them. In 1992, under the aegis of the Brady Plan, the remaining private creditors were given the option to accept a cash buyback incorporating an 84 percent discount; a short-term bond with a similar degree of forgiveness convertible on maturity into local assets at a premium; or else a thirty-year, collateralized bond bearing no interest. And a year later, in 1993, the government offered yet another debt buyback, funded by grants from the World Bank's International Development Association (IDA) and various donor governments, whereby virtually all remaining commercial creditors tendered their debts and accepted a loss of 84 percent of the principal. As a result, Bolivia's government debt to private creditors, which had exceeded $1 billion in 1980, accounting for half of its external obligations, dropped to less than $75 million by the mid-1990s, equivalent to not even 2 percent of its external obligations. Private creditors had accepted huge upfront losses—but at least they were no longer responsible for Bolivia's remaining debt woes.

In contrast, Bolivia became eligible for debt relief from official bilateral and multilateral creditors under the original Heavily Indebted Poor Countries (HIPC) Initiative in September 1998, a full decade after private creditors began to forgive their share of the country's debt. Bolivia obtained less than $30 million in official debt forgiveness in 1998. This amount was later increased to almost $90 million per year in 1999–2001, and subsequently, having qualified under the Enhanced HIPC Initiative, to an annual average of about $160 million during 2002–2004—or the equivalent of around 1.5 percent of annual GDP. However, despite this steady debt relief, and largely because of growing budgetary deficits as a result of rising government spending, Bolivia's public-sector debt increased from the equivalent of 60 percent of GDP in 2001 to 71 percent of GDP (some $6.7 billion) in 2005. It has dropped since then because of substantially higher oil-related revenues—and not because of official debt relief on the installment plan. The country's external debt-service payments, which averaged 4.3 percent of GDP per year during 2003–2005, are expected to average 2.6 percent of GDP during 2006–2008 after relief under HIPC and the Multilateral Debt Relief Initiative (MDRI), which came to supplement the HIPC Initiative in 2005.[7]

Nicaragua

In 1995, in a buyback of commercial bank debt funded by grants from the IDA and various donor governments, most private creditors forgave 92 percent of the $1.1 billion that the government of Nicaragua owed them. Foreign commercial banks had accounted for more than 15 percent of the government's external debt, but after this immediate debt forgiveness they came to represent a mere 3 percent of the total. Earlier that year, official bilateral creditors in the Paris Club had agreed to cancel up to 67 percent of eligible debts under Naples terms, but the multilateral agencies provided no debt relief—except for the Central American Bank for Economic Integration, which agreed to reschedule the payment of its loans. The government's external debt consequently dropped from nearly $12 billion in 1994—by far the highest debt burden among developing countries, equivalent to more than nine times the country's GDP—to $6 billion by 1996, a still excessive 375 percent of GDP.[8]

Nicaragua never received debt relief under the original HIPC Initiative, but it reached the completion point under the Enhanced HIPC Initiative in January 2004. The government's external debt is presently being reduced from over $7 billion to about $3 billion (representing a high but tolerable 65 percent of GDP) thanks to debt forgiveness by bilateral and multilateral lenders. And yet, its external debt-service payments, which averaged 2 percent of GDP per year during 2003–2005, are expected to remain at that level during 2006–2008 despite HIPC and MDRI-related relief.[9] Nicaragua is also having trouble obtaining all of its HIPC relief because twenty-three of its official creditors—more than double the average of other HIPC countries—do not belong to the Paris Club. Among those, China, Iran, Libya, and Taiwan have refused to grant debt relief, and Libya even resorted to litigation, demanding full payment.[10]

Ecuador

In 1995, following many years of debt servicing difficulties, the government of Ecuador asked private creditors to grant either principal or interest forgiveness as part of a comprehensive Brady Plan restructuring of nearly $8 billion in commercial debt, and to write off a portion of past-due interest. In response, 60 percent of the creditors agreed to thirty-year discount bonds with a 45 percent "haircut," or reduction, on the principal owed, while the rest acquiesced to thirty-year bonds with highly concessional coupons delivering an equivalent amount of relief on the basis of net present value (NPV).[11] As an immediate result, Ecuador's public external debt was reduced by $1.8 billion, or 17 percent of the total.

When Ecuador experienced acute fiscal difficulties again in 1999, the IMF made it clear to the government that it would not get any help from the official community unless it stopped paying its private creditors and obtained debt forgiveness—again. Ecuador thus had the dubious honor of becoming the first country to default on its Brady bonds, and also one of the first (at least in post–World War II history) to default on Eurobonds. In mid-2000, the government proposed a complex debt relief operation whereby the various bonds in default were subjected to haircuts ranging from 19 percent on Brady Par bonds to 47 percent on the Eurobond maturing that year, before being exchanged for a mix of new Eurobonds (maturing in 2012 and 2030) and some upfront cash to help cover arrears. The deal as accepted resulted in a 40 percent reduction in the face value of Ecuador's debt, and in cash-flow savings of about $1.5 billion over the first five years. In the wake of the relief, obligations to bilateral and multilateral creditors came to account for 60 percent of the government's remaining external indebtedness.

In sharp contrast, official bilateral and multilateral lenders have never agreed to any debt reduction for Ecuador. The country appealed for debt relief to the Paris Club time and again—in four instances during the 1980s, as well as in 1992, 1994, 2000, and 2003—and while it was deemed to be insolvent enough to deserve write-offs from private creditors in 1995 and

Arturo C. Porzecanski

2000, it was considered insufficiently needy to deserve write-offs from official creditors even once. At the beginning of the 1990s, the Paris Club was owed about $2 billion, or one-fifth of Ecuador's public-sector external debt, but it agreed merely to reschedule payments falling due in the short run according to Houston terms—namely, with some reduction in interest payments. The last rescheduling by official bilateral creditors, in mid-2003, involved stretching out a mere $81 million falling due in the year through March 31, 2004.[12] The multilateral agencies, for their part, have neither rescheduled nor reduced any of the country's debt, and they have provided little or no net financing to Ecuador. In fact, from 2001 to 2004, amortization payments by Ecuador's government to official bilateral and multilateral creditors actually exceeded disbursements received from those same creditors.[13]

Argentina

The largest and potentially most complex default the world has known was declared by the government of Argentina in December 2001. A punishing, unilateral restructuring offer was presented to bond investors three years later, in January 2005, which was accepted under duress by 76 percent of total bondholders. The government thus obtained principal forgiveness estimated at 56 percent of affected debt, managing to inflict NPV losses of around 75 percent. Eligible for the massive bond exchange were 152 different securities amounting to a total of $82 billion, including a relatively small amount of past-due interest accrued through the end of 2001—because the government refused to recognize interest arrears after that point. Eleven new securities were offered to participating investors, ranging from par bonds that were not subject to a haircut on nominal principal but paid just a token amount of interest and had a final maturity of thirty-five years, to discount bonds with a principal reduction of 66 percent and better terms otherwise, designed to mete out approximately equal NPV losses.[14]

Argentina's insistence on such massive debt relief is without precedent in its own checkered financial history, and also in comparison with the debt relief obtained in the past by other upper-middle-income countries, such as Chile, Mexico, South Africa, and Turkey. It can only be compared with the large-scale relief obtained by much poorer countries such as Bolivia or Nicaragua, as detailed above, or by other HIPCs. Adding insult to injury,

Argentina's fiscal performance and international reserves—and most economic and social indicators—have since fully recovered from their low point in 2001–2002.[15] The government has remained current in its obligations to the multilateral lending agencies, even though they have greatly diminished their disbursements to the country. It has also prepaid all of its debt to the IMF: a whopping $10 billion payment made at the end of 2005, following principal payments of about $13 billion made earlier. And while Argentina has been in default to the bilateral agencies represented by the Paris Club—as of the end of 2006, for more than $6 billion, including interest arrears—all that the government is reportedly expecting is an eventual rescheduling under so-called classic terms.[16]

Arguably, Argentina's bondholders could have fared much better if official bilateral and multilateral creditors, led by the United States and other G-7 governments, had stood up to this rogue sovereign debtor and had insisted on fair treatment for private creditors. Instead, they essentially sided with Argentina, or at best turned a blind eye to its aggressive designs, thereby encouraging the authorities in Buenos Aires to make mincemeat out of its bondholders. First, the BIS allowed itself to be used as a safe harbor for Argentina's hard-currency assets, which, while on deposit there, cannot be attached by bondholders who obtain court judgments against the government. Second, the multilateral lending agencies were actually supportive of Argentina via a series of new loans granted by the IMF, the World Bank, and the Inter-American Development Bank, especially during 2003 and the first half of 2004. This was so despite the fact that the IMF has had a policy of lending to a government in default only when it is pursuing "appropriate policies" *and* when it is making "a good faith effort to reach a collaborative agreement with its creditors."[17]

Argentina also won an important gesture of political support in the form of amicus curiae briefs filed by the U.S. government and the Federal Reserve in U.S. courts in January 2004. The Argentine government succeeded in persuading U.S. authorities that the international payments system was at risk from the potential application of a legal clause (*pari passu*) which had been used by creditors against the governments of Peru and Nicaragua.[18] And then, while Argentina was crafting its request for debt forgiveness (during 2004), the IMF declined to insist upon overwhelming acceptance of

Arturo C. Porzecanski

whatever debt restructuring proposal the country would put forth to its creditors. Doing so would not have been unusual for the Fund, and it would have put pressure on Buenos Aires to come up with a less punishing proposal—or to have added some last minute "sweeteners" to maximize bondholder acceptance.[19]

THE G-7'S UNDERLYING RATIONALE

What then is the rationale of the G-7 and the IMF in devoting so much time and effort to facilitating future workouts of sovereign debt to private creditors? Apparently, G-7 and IMF officials were trying to ameliorate the undesirable consequences of their 1990s practice of bailing out certain troubled sovereign debtors with multibillion-dollar rescue packages. Stung by criticism of these bailouts, and worried about having encouraged too many countries with looming debt crises to come knocking at their door pleading for last-minute help, the G-7 governments wanted to open up an alternative for themselves—a fast track to default, debt forgiveness (at least by private lenders), and financial resurrection. Thus, when in the future an overindebted government that is not strategically important approaches the G-7 for emergency financial help, it would no longer be able to claim that it had to obtain billions of dollars because the alternative was a hopelessly disruptive, delayed, and uncertain default with potential spillover effects around the globe. With some kind of sovereign bankruptcy procedure in place, the G-7 would feel freer to tell that government to seek debt forgiveness from its private creditors, instead, on the belief that a relatively painless and quick debt restructuring would follow.

From late 2001 until early 2003, the IMF staff worked feverishly on a proposed Sovereign Debt Restructuring Mechanism (SDRM) that, in the event, did not gain the necessary political support among a number of governments, including the United States. Its earlier versions envisioned a powerful role for the IMF that would have allowed it to make decisions limiting creditors' rights. In the face of universal criticism from private-sector lenders and investors, the IMF's role was later toned down to the equivalent of the sole expert witness, by passing judgment on how much debt any government could reasonably be expected to service. In this capacity, the IMF and its G-7 shareholders on its executive board would have a procedural advantage that would allow them to protect their claims and influence the amount of debt relief granted by private creditors.

The planned SDRM was not accompanied, however, by a proposal to address what has really undermined the functioning of the international financial system in recent years: the multibillion-dollar G-7 and IMF rescue packages that have been cobbled together for strategically important countries since 1995. Thanks to the string of bailouts involving countries from Mexico to South Korea, and from Brazil to Turkey, the possibility that a country may get a huge package of financial support with which to meet its debt obligations became one of the key elements in the assessment of sovereign creditworthiness. Many credit ratings, analyst recommendations, and investment decisions have come to be based on assumptions about whether a foreign government is viewed with favor by the White House, Downing Street, or another G-7 government. The situation is akin to picking stocks or bonds for a portfolio not on the basis of whether a weak company will manage to turn itself around, but rather on whether it will be nursed back to health via an infusion of large-scale government support. How could the U.S. financial markets possibly function well if state intervention, as in the case of the Chrysler bailout of 1979–80, had become commonplace?

A counterproposal put forward by the U.S. Treasury and endorsed by many investors and financial intermediaries became the preferred alternative. It represented a contractual rather than statutory approach to sovereign bankruptcy situations, involving the introduction of new clauses into bond contracts to facilitate the debt restructuring process. The main idea was that every bond contract should designate a bondholder representative to act as an interlocutor with the sovereign debtor; require the sovereign to provide more key financial information to its bondholders; allow for a supermajority of bondholders to amend payment terms, then often requiring unanimity of consent; and include enforcement provisions that concentrate the power to initiate litigation in a single jurisdiction.[20] These new clauses have since become widely known as collective action clauses (CACs), and while several already existed in bonds issued under English law, most new and outstanding bonds of emerging-market sovereigns are issued in other jurisdictions, such as New York and Frankfurt, where such clauses have not been customary.

Most emerging-market issuers and investors were initially reluctant to introduce CACs in new bond contracts for fear of signaling that they contemplate or countenance an eventual default. Besides, even if such clauses were to be introduced voluntarily in all new debt issues, the stock of outstanding bonds would still be governed by preexisting legal arrangements, so that their practical effect is marginal for years to come. Under strong pressure from the U.S. Treasury, however, the governments of Mexico and Brazil were persuaded in early 2003 to issue new bonds with CACs, and they were successfully placed with institutional investors at no measurable extra cost. Governments such as South Africa's and South Korea's followed suit, although each sovereign bond issued carried its own particular clauses that do not incorporate all of the language recommended by official and private-sector groups. Consequently, a uniform market standard in CACs did not immediately develop.

While wider inclusion of CACs into sovereign bond contracts has probably done no harm, it is doubtful that even their widespread application will make a visible difference to the workings of international finance. Of much greater significance would be a G-7 decision to scale back the massive official support to errant debtor nations. If the IMF were to go back to providing seed money for economic and policy turnarounds on a rules-based, objective basis, this alone would encourage governments and their creditors to consider much more seriously the implications of falling into the abyss of default—regardless of whether improved sovereign bankruptcy mechanisms are instituted. Moreover, it is patently unfair that some governments should be lavished with official aid and others should be starved, when the IMF is supposed to be a cooperative to which its member governments should be able to turn for fairly automatic—albeit limited—help.

In addition, the very notion of a quick and painless debt restructuring is problematic both on an ethical and practical level. Ethically there should not be, I believe, such a thing as a fast track to default, debt forgiveness, and financial resurrection. The smoother the road to sovereign bankruptcy, the more likely it is that governments will exhibit lack of fiscal discipline and "reform fatigue," squandering the proceeds of borrowed hard currency, in the knowledge that, if worse comes to worst, they can obtain a financial pardon. In practice, it is impossible to obtain massive debt forgiveness via quick and painless debt restructurings. The recent tragedy in Argentina, for example, would not have been avoided if the SDRM or the CACs had been in place in 2001. Because a substantial proportion of the Argentine government's debt obligations was held by local banks, pension funds, and insurance companies, any announcement of a payments standstill with the intention to seek meaningful debt forgiveness would surely have triggered a stampede of bank depositors and a collapse of the pension and insurance industries. This would have led to a run on the central bank's official reserves, precipitating a devastating currency devaluation and thus the same economic implosion, political fallout, and popular discontent that was witnessed in late 2001 and early 2002.

CONCLUSION

In sum, one of the clearest lessons from the past couple of decades of sovereign financial crises is that institutional and retail bondholders, as well as commercial and investment bankers in the United States, Canada, Europe, and Japan, have developed a commendable track record in dealing with sovereign debt problems. They have helped to resolve innovatively, expeditiously, and generously the multiple cases of sovereign overindebtedness in which they have been involved in various parts of the world—despite, or possibly because of, the absence of a supranational bankruptcy regime for sovereign debt. The official development community, in contrast, cannot make a similar claim: time and again, the bilateral and multilateral lending agencies have dragged their feet in accepting loan losses and granting debt forgiveness—whether to overindebted middle-income nations or to the poorest countries in the world. More often than not, they have been—and remain—part of the sovereign indebtedness problem, rather than part of its constructive alleviation.

NOTES

[1] Chapter 9 applies to nonsovereign entities such as municipalities, school districts, and publicly owned utilities. For a discussion of why Chapter 9 provides little guidance in the case of sovereigns, see Michelle J. White, "Sovereigns in Distress: Do They Need Bankruptcy?" *Brookings Papers on Economic Activity* 1 (2002), pp. 287–319.

Arturo C. Porzecanski

[2] See, e.g., Institute of International Finance, "Principles for Stable Capital Flows and Fair Debt Restructuring in Emerging Markets" (Washington, D.C.: Institute of International Finance, March 31, 2005), available at www.iif.com/emp/principles/.

[3] Nor, of course, have they even mentioned the idea of subjecting troubled debtor governments to outside intervention of the type that New York City, for example, had to accept when it could not pay its bills in the early 1970s.

[4] According to the then first deputy managing director of the IMF, a new approach to sovereign debt restructuring was needed because "in the current environment, it *may* be particularly difficult to secure high participation from creditors as a group, as individual creditors *may* consider that their best interests would be served by trying to free ride . . . . These difficulties *may* be amplified by the prevalence of complex financial instruments . . . which in some cases *may* provide investors with incentives to hold out . . . rather than participating in a restructuring." See Anne O. Krueger, *A New Approach to Sovereign Debt Restructuring* (Washington, D.C.: International Monetary Fund, April 2002), p. 8 (emphasis added).

[5] For useful background information on sovereign debt defaults and restructurings, see World Bank, *Global Development Finance 2006: The Development Potential of Surging Capital Flows*, vol. 1 (Washington, D.C.: World Bank, 2006), pp. 43–104.

[6] See the TV interview with President Jorge Batlle of Uruguay, "El Default Significaba el Quiebre Institucional de Uruguay," July 4, 2003, available at www.presidencia.gub.uy/noticias/archivo/2003/julio/2003070404.htm. This version of events had previously been revealed by Vice President Luis Hierro of Uruguay, but had been denied by the IMF's spokesman; see IMF, "Transcript of a Press Briefing by Thomas C. Dawson," June 26, 2003, available at www.imf.org/external/np/tr/2003/tr030626.htm.

[7] See IDA and IMF, "Heavily Indebted Poor Countries Initiative (HIPC) and Multilateral Debt Relief Initiative (MDRI): Status of Implementation," Washington, D.C., September 7, 2006, p. 66, available at siteresources.worldbank.org/DEVCOMMINT/Documentation/21046514/DC2006-0016(E)-HIPC.pdf.

[8] See World Bank, *Global Development Finance* (Washington, D.C.: World Bank 2001), table 1.

[9] See IMF and IDA, "Heavily Indebted Poor Countries Initiative (HIPC) and Multilateral Debt Relief Initiative (MDRI)," p. 67.

[10] See ibid., p. 25.

[11] Other shorter maturity bonds were also issued, for example, to cover a portion of past-due interest, and Ecuador paid a small amount of arrears in cash.

[12] See various Paris Club press releases relating to Ecuador available at www.clubdeparis.org/search_form?SearchableText=Ecuador.

[13] See IMF, "Ecuador: First Review under the Stand-by Arrangement and Requests for Modifications and Waiver of Nonobservance and Applicability of Performance Criteria," IMF Country Report No. 03/248, August 2003, available at www.imf.org/external/pubs/ft/scr/2003/cr03248.pdf; and IMF, "Ecuador: 2005 Article IV Consultation," IMF Country Report No. 06/98, March 2006, available at www.imf.org/external/pubs/ft/scr/2006/cr0698.pdf.

[14] See IMF, "Cross-Country Experience with Restructuring of Sovereign Debt and Restoring Debt Sustainability," August 29, 2006, pp. 12, 14, and 48–49, available at www.imf.org/external/np/pp/eng/2006/082906.pdf.

[15] See IMF, "IMF Executive Board Concludes 2006 Article IV Consultation with Argentina," Public Information Notice No. 06/93, August 9, 2006, available at www.imf.org/external/np/sec/pn/2006/pn0693.htm.

[16] In early 2007, Argentina reportedly offered the leading Paris Club governments to pay all outstanding principal and past-due interest over a relatively short period of ten years. See Clarín, "Club de París: la oferta argentina es pagar la deuda en 10 años y sin quita," January 14, 2007, available at www.clarin.com/diario/2007/01/14/elpais/p-01801.htm.

[17] See IMF, "IMF Board Discusses the Good-Faith Criterion under the Fund Policy on Lending into Arrears to Private Creditors," Public Information Notice No. 02/107, September 24, 2002, available at www.imf.org/external/np/sec/pn/2002/pn02107.htm.

[18] The U.S. government and the Federal Reserve also filed amicus briefs for Argentina in April 2006, in support of a U.S. court decision to vacate an order of attachment against certain funds belonging to the Central Bank of Argentina held at the Federal Reserve Bank of New York, which was then on appeal.

[19] See Arturo C. Porzecanski, "From Rogue Creditors to Rogue Debtors: Implications of Argentina's Default," *Chicago Journal of International Law* 6, no. 1 (2005), pp. 327–31.

[20] See Group of Ten, "Report of the G-10 Working Group on Contractual Clauses," September 26, 2002, available at www.bis.org/publ/gten08.pdf.

Resolving International Debt Crises Fairly

Ann Pettifor

I f global economic justice is to be achieved, debt crises must be assessed within the broader context of the international financial system. This system, which has been largely imposed by a small group of powerful financial agents in the Organisation for Economic Co-operation and Development countries, has led to instability and recurrent financial crises that have severely harmed the interests of poor countries and their people. Responsibility for bearing the costs of debt crises and other negative effects of the prevailing international financial system should therefore be assumed by those who have contributed to bringing them about. At present, however, the burden of economic "adjustments" during debt crises has fallen disproportionately on poor debtor nations, and debates regarding debt management have been dominated by individual, corporate, and official creditors. This essay presents the case for institutional reforms that can better protect the human rights of citizens of sovereign debtor nations during debt crises.

RESPONSIBILITY, IMPARTIALITY, AND ACCOUNTABILITY

Several principles should guide the design of institutional arrangements that can deal justly with debt. The first is that there should be recognition that it takes two parties to make a loan, and that each of these two parties can be reckless, irresponsible, and delinquent in its actions. Insofar as either party to a loan acts in this way, it ought to shoulder part of the burden of the crises that often ensue. Losses from bad loans and bad debts should not, therefore, fall solely on the debtor. The second principle, based on a fundamental principle of the rule of law, is that no one ought to be judge in their own court. Any courts that are developed to resolve debt crises must be fair and impartial with respect to the parties to the loans in question. The third principle is the principle of accountability. Sovereign debt crises are public, not private, crises involving the use of taxpayer funds. If the resolution of these crises is to be achieved within a framework of justice, and if democratic scrutiny of public funds is to be strengthened, then it will be vital for the process to be open, transparent, and accountable to citizens and taxpayers.

Unlike proposals recently put forth by the International Monetary Fund (IMF) and by private creditors, the Jubilee Framework for resolving sovereign debt crises expresses these three principles. The framework is based on the proposal originally developed by the Austrian economist Kunibert Raffer and is modeled on Chapter 9 of the U.S. legal code, which regulates the bankruptcy of municipal and governmental organizations.[1] The particular attraction of the Chapter 9 model is its applicability to governmental institutions and its protection of taxpayer and employee interests in the resolution of municipal and other governmental debt crises.

The Jubilee Framework envisions an independent court that would be representative of all creditors and the debtor nation, and would treat their interests on equal par. The framework rejects a role for the IMF that would discriminate against other creditors by protecting its own claims, and is highly critical of a process in which the Fund would have strong agenda-setting powers. However, it recognizes that the IMF will play an important financing role by providing working capital in loans to the debtor country while negotiations proceed, and that the repayment of these loans will take priority over other loans. It also suggests that the UN should oversee debt sustainability analyses but, in the absence of available resources, recognizes that the UN could only play a marginal role in the process. In this respect, the Jubilee Framework differs from the proposals of other civil society organizations, such as Erlassjahr in Germany[2] and the African Forum & Network on Debt & Development,[3] which reject a role for the IMF and instead see the UN as the main arbiter in negotiations. However, such differences are not fundamental, as most civil society organizations agree on the need for an independent, fair, and transparent process of arbitration.

INTERNATIONAL ECONOMIC JUSTICE

The first objective of any sovereign debt crisis resolution process should be the achievement of international economic justice with respect to the designers of the international financial system—the G-7, its members' representatives in the Bretton Woods institutions, the Bank for International Settlements, and the central bankers of the economically powerful countries—and its victims, the people in the indebted countries. The Bank for International Settlements has acknowledged that the liberalization of financial systems, led and promoted by the central bankers and finance ministers of the G-7 countries, has

> Over the past few decades . . . arguably also increased the scope for pronounced financial cycles. In turn, these cycles can contribute to the amplification of cycles in the macroeconomy, and in the past have all too often ended in costly banking system crises. While both industrialised and emerging market economies have been affected, the damage caused by financial instability has been particularly serious for emerging market countries.
>
> At the root of these cycles typically lies a wave of optimism . . . [which] contributes to the underestimation of risk, overextension of credit . . . . Eventually, . . . the imbalances built up in the boom need to be unwound, sometimes causing significant disruption to both the financial system and the real economy.[4]

Such admission of fault and responsibility should provide a backdrop to any consideration of how losses arising from the "significant disruption to the financial system" should be shared between industrialized and emerging market countries. Current international practice places the burden of major economic adjustments for losses on the debtor. What is often not taken into account, however, is that the real burden for such adjustments falls not on the actual borrowers—who are often corrupt presidents, finance ministers, and central bankers of debtor governments—but on the taxpayers of current and future generations, including poor people who experience the costs quite acutely. In the absence of a resolution of the Argentine debt crisis, for example, since the default of 2001, the population living below the poverty line has risen to 50 percent. Of these poor people, 33 percent are indigent, forming the most underprivileged sector of Argentine society. Moreover, a system that allocates the costs of repayment of debt to those that did not incur them engenders further misestimating of risk, leading to further bad borrowing and bad lending.

Neither the IMF's proposal for a sovereign debt restructuring mechanism nor the private-sector alternative reflects any recognition of the role that creditors have played as designers and primary beneficiaries of a financial system that precipitates crises by encouraging reckless lending and borrowing.

Both multilateral and private lenders represent the process of dealing with debt as an act of mercy, rather than as a process for restoring stability and economic efficiency on the one hand, and, on the other, as a struggle to mitigate injustices in the current global financial order. As a result, their proposals serve to maintain the status quo.

The IMF's Sovereign Debt Restructuring Mechanism (SDRM), for example, is not equipped to deal justly with debt because its design does not assure a balanced process in which each interested side is represented on an equal par.[5] It violates the principle of the rule of law—allowing a major creditor to be judge in its own cause. The mechanism would be overseen by the Fund's own executive board, which is dominated by the official creditors of the powerful G-7. The Fund's proposal would ensure that Fund staff and the executive board would play a preemptive role in shaping the outcome of the debt crisis resolution negotiations by setting the country's level of debt sustainability, on the basis of which will be determined the necessary debt reduction. In addition, the Fund will continue to play a substantial role in shaping the debtor's economic policies, by providing technical assistance and advising on fiscal, monetary, and legal policies during the period over which the country is being granted relief. As a result, the IMF will effectively draft the composition plan for restructuring debts and financing their repayment that should rightly be presented, as in domestic bankruptcy law, by the debtor in order to provide the basis for fair and effective negotiations.

By determining the composition plan, the IMF disempowers the debtor, all other creditors, and civil society. The IMF could, and very likely will, set the debt sustainability to a level that does not place its own claims economically at risk, even if they were legally exempt from debt cancellation, in case the debtor transferred all its available resources to the repayment of private-sector debts.[6] Indeed, it was even suggested at an IMF conference that took place in Washington, D.C., on January 22, 2003, that if debtors were to agree to solutions that were considered "too generous" by the staff of the Fund, the IMF would penalize the debtor—for example, by withholding funds—thus blocking the solution agreed to by both parties. Above all, this would allow the Fund to play the role of a judge in its own cause—the defense of its own claims. While the Fund might argue that its preferred creditor status enables it to provide crisis financing, much of the outstanding IMF debts do not represent crisis financing but development financing. This is because the IMF has long overstretched its fire-fighting role in international finance and has increasingly engaged in micromanaging economies. The case of Argentina is a striking example of this—the country's debts have been accrued as a result of sustained lending and failed structural adjustment programs over the course of more than fifty years.

By enshrining the SDRM in its articles of agreement, the Fund would go further. First, it would change the present situation where the IMF and the World Bank together engage in poor country debt management. Second, if the IMF were to enshrine the executive board's authority to define the behavior of the debtor as a breach of its obligations under the articles of agreement and to determine sanctions against the member country, it would put debtor countries in a situation of coerced choice—since the costs of exiting the Fund are very large. Third, the amendment to the articles of agreement would legally entrench the IMF's present status of preferred creditor.

The approach preferred by private creditors, that of collective action clauses (CACs), would pit powerful creditors against a weakened debtor in behind-the-scenes negotiations. There may be circumstances in which the debtor is powerful enough to engage forcefully with creditors. Past experience of poor country debtors, however, shows that they lack the resources to hire the legal staff necessary to ensure equality and justice in the negotiations. The imbalance in the relationship between creditor and debtor can only be corrected by a proper legal framework in which both are protected. It is the statutory framework (in this case Chapter 11 of the U.S. legal code) that provides incentives for private creditors to negotiate with the management of defaulting companies like Enron. It is the lack of a comparable framework that leaves them unwilling to do so with Argentina.

A further objective for any framework of debt negotiation should be to reduce and punish the incidence of corruption, fraud, and criminality associated with international lending and borrowing. The only way in which this can be achieved, and indeed is achieved in Western economies like that of the United States, is through mechanisms that ensure public scrutiny of public officials. It is the existence of regulatory authorities, transparent reporting, and the threat of punishment that discourages corruption in financial centers like London, New York, and Zurich.

We have been pleased to note that the IMF's latest draft of its SDRM proposal calls for much greater transparency in the sovereign debt restructuring process.[7] Unfortunately, one major weakness in the IMF's Sovereign Debt Dispute Resolution Forum remains.[8] Although the IMF has consulted the UN Commission on International Trade Law to ensure its independence, the IMF nevertheless denies the Sovereign Debt Dispute Resolution Forum powers to challenge the decisions of the Fund, such as its assessments of the amount of debt reduction that will be needed to resolve a particular debt crisis.

EFFICIENCY, STABILITY, DEVELOPMENT

The second objective of any insolvency framework should be economic efficiency, stability, and development. The main rationale for bankruptcy law is that releasing bankrupt economic agents from debt bondage will encourage them to contribute productively to the economy once again.

There is ample evidence to suggest that the economic policies effectively imposed by foreign creditors over the past thirty years, particularly through the IMF, have failed to return countries to sustainability, or to encourage economic growth.[9] Using their influence in the IMF, the G-7 countries have effectively been imposing economic policies on indebted countries in Latin America and Africa since 1982, and over that period economic growth in those continents has been lower than during the period between 1945 and 1980, with a consistent decline in GDP in some cases.[10] On the whole, and perhaps logically from the point of view of the creditors who dominate the executive board, IMF policies have been designed to extract and transfer assets from debtors to creditors. One of the most likely and predictable outcomes of the SDRM is that countries would not be returned to sustainability. Just as under the failed Brady Plan of the 1980s, under the SDRM only private creditors would have to reduce their claims. As the IMF's proposal stands, public creditors like the Fund, the World Bank, and all the regional development banks would have their debts excluded from debt restructuring negotiations. There have been some suggestions in informal talks during meetings and conferences that the Paris Club of sovereign creditors would be included within the SDRM but an official intention to do so has not been confirmed. This would be ineffective and unjust because it fails to ensure that the debtor's crisis is addressed comprehensively and limits

Ann Pettifor

the accountability of official creditors like the IMF and World Bank. Indeed, even relatively generous debt reductions by the private sector might be insufficient to return debtor nations to sustainability. With respect to unsecured creditors, the IMF's proposal asserts that they would receive a combination of "cash and new securities."[11] If this cash is provided in the form of an IMF loan—because the overindebted country has no hard currency—the principal debt will increase. Furthermore, the debt will rise, because the IMF gives out harder loans, that is, loans that normally have to be repaid over a relatively short period at interest rates that may not be concessional.

Any framework for debt restructuring will involve the assessment of the assets of the sovereign. The institution that provides these assessments must include transparent and inclusive procedures that involve the citizens of the debtor nation. It will also be necessary to develop reasonably precise principles for determining levels of debt sustainability that are consistent with the protection of human rights. We believe that UN agencies such as the United Nations Development Programme and UNICEF are best placed to advise the court on the resources that will be required to ensure that the human rights of the people of the debtor nation are well protected. Indeed, much of the work currently being undertaken by the UN to measure the costs of achieving the Millennium Development Goals could contribute to assessments of a debtor's sustainability.

The Jubilee Framework calls for an ad-hoc, independent debt crisis resolution body, with transparent procedures, representing the interests of both the creditors and the citizens of the debtor country, with an independent judge ruling on the final composition plan. This body can be modeled on the arbitration panels used by the International Chamber of Commerce for the resolution of disputes between corporates and sovereigns. Specifically, all civil society frameworks call for a forum made up of an equal number of representatives from the creditor and the debtor side, who in turn would appoint a third or a fifth person to act as chair, or judge, of the panel. Such ad-hoc panels could begin work now—and would be particularly effective in cases like that of Argentina. With time they would build up a body of practice and law, which could later provide the basis for an international statutory agreement.

BRINGING THE PROPOSAL TO REALITY

The only process needed for the resolution of a debt crisis and the establishment of an ad-hoc panel is political will, on the part of both the debtor and G-7 official creditors (who will in turn require the support of private creditors). In doing so, the G-7 creditors will have to overcome the strong incentive of private creditors to resist any proposals for restructuring debts that limit their current control over the process. At the same time the process must respect the rights of creditors by giving them an equal voice in negotiations with the debtor and by not discriminating among them in a way that benefits some creditors and disadvantages others.

A UN resolution may be required to secure the cooperation of UN staff who would provide the independent oversight of the framework and develop principles for determining sustainability levels. Were the G-7 to implement an ad-hoc, independent, and transparent process, it would then be able to mobilize the active participation of the IMF for the provision of working capital, known in the U.S. legal code as debtor-in-possession finance. The IMF would thus have its original mandate restored—to provide financial support in crises, and to correct, rather than precipitate, imbalances, thereby fostering stability and growth in the international economy.

A review of the history of bankruptcy law in the United States reveals that it was only when rich debtors needed protection from their creditors after the major external economic shocks of the late eighteenth century that a body of law began to evolve that respected the rights of the debtor as well as the interests of the creditor.[12] So long as rich countries are protected from their creditors through, for example, the power to print the currency in which they repay their debts, so long will they be reluctant to develop a just framework for resolving international debt crises. Indeed, it may be that a rich country needs to encounter a major debt crisis before we can expect a new framework to evolve and justice to be achieved in international financial relations. This is regrettable since just, economically efficient, and effective frameworks for resolving debt crises are both feasible and available.

Ann Pettifor

NOTES

1   Kunibert Raffer, "Applying Chapter 9 Insolvency to International Debts: An Economically Efficient Solution with a Human Face," *World Development* 18, no. 2 (1990), pp. 301–13. See also Professor Raffer's Web site, mailbox.univie.ac.at/~rafferk5/art.html.

2   Erlassjahr, "A Fair and Transparent Arbitration Process for Indebted Southern Countries," available at www.erlassjahr.de/15_publikationen/15_dokumente/englisch/ftap_englisch_rz.pdf.

3   AFRODAD, "AFRODAD's Call for a Fair and Transparent Arbitration Court for Debt," available at www.afrodad.org/HTML/Examination%20of%20FTA.htm.

4   Bank for International Settlements, "71st Annual Report: 1 April 2000–31 March 2001," p. 123, available at www.bis.org/publ/ar2001e.pdf.

5   International Monetary Fund, "The Design of the Sovereign Debt Restructuring Mechanism—Further Considerations," November 2002, available at www.imf.org/external/np/pdr/sdrm/2002/112702.pdf.

6   Ibid., paras. 84, 85, p. 25.

7   Ibid., paras. 14, 273, and 291, pp. 6–8, 70, and 74.

8   Ibid., paras. 28, 230–63, pp. 11–12, 57–67.

9   For evidence of the impact of these policies on economic growth in emerging markets, see Ann Pettifor, ed., *Real World Economic Outlook,* vol. 1 (London: Palgrave, 2003).

10 See Mark Weisbrot, Robert Naiman, and Joyce Kim, "The Emperor Has No Growth: Declining Economic Growth Rates in the Era of Globalization" (Center for Economic and Policy Research Briefing Paper, May 2001), available at www.cepr.net/globalization/The_Emperor_Has_No_Growth.htm.

11 International Monetary Fund, "The Design of the Sovereign Debt Restructuring Mechanism," n. 17, pp. 35–36.

12 See Bruce H. Mann, *Republic of Debtors: Bankruptcy in the Age of American Independence* (Cambridge, MA: Harvard University Press, 2003).

Contributors

hristian Barry is Lecturer in Philosophy
d Research Fellow in the Centre for
pplied Philosophy and Public Ethics at
stralian National University. He holds a
.D. in Philosophy from Columbia Univer-
y. He has served as a contributing author
three of the United Nations Development
ogramme's *Human Development Reports,*
d was formerly editor of the journal *Ethics*
International Affairs. He has published
dely on the topic of international eco-
mic justice, most recently a book (co-
thored with Sanjay G. Reddy), entitled
ternational Trade and Labor Standards: A
oposal for Linkage (forthcoming, Colum-
a University Press).

ck Boorman is former Counselor and
rector of the Policy Development and
view Department of the International
onetary Fund. Before that, he held posi-
ns in the European and Asian depart-
ents of the IMF, including a posting as
sident Representative of the IMF in
donesia. He also served as a Financial
onomist at the Federal Deposit Insurance
rporation. He holds a Ph.D. from the
niversity of Southern California, and has
ught both there and at the University of
aryland.

exander W. Cappelen is Professor of Eco-
mics at the Norwegian School of Eco-
mics and Business Administration and
ad of the Centre for Ethics and Econom-
. His research interests are distributive
stice, experimental economics, and corpo-
te governance. He has published exten-
vely in international journals, including

the *American Economic Review, Journal of*
Public Economics, Economics and Philosophy,
and *Social Choice and Welfare.*

Elizabeth A. Donnelly is a Ph.D. candidate
in Government at Harvard University. She
has served as a Maryknoll Lay Missioner in
Lima, Peru, and on the staffs of the Presidential Commission on World Hunger and
the ecumenical lobbying group Bread for
the World. Her writings on the ethics of debt
relief and the coalition of churches and nongovernmental organizations working on the
issue include "Proclaiming Jubilee: The
Debt and Structural Adjustment Network,"
in Sanjeev Khagram, James V. Riker, and
Kathryn Sikkink, eds., *Restructuring World*
Politics: Transnational Social Movements,
Networks, and Norms (2002); a 1999 case
study for the Brookings Institution's Global
Public Policy Project; and the discussion
summary of the Catholic Church–sponsored
Conference on the Ethical Dimensions of
International Debt, held at Seton Hall Uni-
versity in October 1998.

Axel Gosseries is Permanent Research Fellow of the Belgian Fund for Scientific
Research and is based at the Chaire Hoover
in Economic and Social Ethics, University of
Louvain. He holds LL.M. from the University
of London and Ph.D. in philosophy from the
University of Louvain. He is the author of
Penser la justice entre les générations (2004)
and of about twenty-five articles in edited
volumes and academic journals such as
Oxford Handbook of Practical Ethics, Eco-
nomics & Philosophy, Loyola of Los Angeles
Law Review, Revue de métaphysique et

morale, New York University Environmental Law Journal, Canadian Journal of Philosophy, and *Stanford Encyclopedia of Philosophy.*

Barry Herman is Visiting Senior Fellow at the Graduate Program in International Affairs of The New School in New York, where he teaches in the Socioeconomic Development concentration. He is also a member of the Board of Directors of Global Integrity, a nongovernmental research organization based in Washington that works with independent scholars and investigative reporters on assessing governance and corruption in developed and developing countries. He completed almost thirty years in the United Nations Secretariat in 2005, during the last two years of which he was Senior Advisor in the Financing for Development Office in the Department of Economic and Social Affairs. Before joining the UN Secretariat in 1976, he taught development and international economics. He holds a Ph.D. from the University of Michigan and an MBA from the University of Chicago. He has edited three books and published essays and chapters in books on North-South financial issues and global negotiations on development.

Rune Jansen Hagen is Researcher at the Institute for Research in Economics and Business Administration in Bergen, Norway. His research interests are in the fields of development economics, international economics, and political economy. He has published essays on foreign aid in the *Journal of Development Economics* and the *Review of Development Economics*. He is presently heading the project "Responsibility for Sovereign Debt: Theory and Empirical Investigations," financed by the Research Council of Norway.

Ann Pettifor helped design and lead t international Jubilee 2000 campaign. No as director of Advocacy International, s advises governments and internatio organizations. She is the author of *The Co ing First World Debt Crisis* (2006) and t editor of "*Real* World Economic Outloc (2003), a report on the global economy ch lenging the economics of the IMF's ann "World Economic Outlook." Among l other publications are "Debt, the M Potent Form of Slavery" (1995); "Kicking t Habit" (1998), on a lasting solution to d crises; "It Takes Two to Tango" (2001), on t Argentina crisis; and "Chapter 9/11?" (200 on the need for a sovereign insolven framework.

In early 2005, **Arturo C. Porzecan** brought to an end three decades of work an international economist on Wall Stre where he rose to become chief economist f emerging markets at several financial ins tutions, the latest one of which was t European banking group ABN AMRO. l has since devoted himself to teaching a research in international economics a international finance, and is affiliated fu time with American University as a prof sor of international finance, and part-tir with Columbia University as an adjun professor of international affairs. I majored in economics at Whittier Colle and then earned M.A. and Ph.D. degrees economics at the University of Pittsburgh

Having received his Ph.D. in philosop from Harvard, **Thomas Pogge** has publish widely on Kant and in moral and politic philosophy, including various books (Rawls and global justice. He is Professor Political Science at Columbia Universit Professorial Fellow at the Centre for Appli Philosophy and Public Ethics at Australi